THE PHILOSOPHICAL STAGE

The Philosophical Stage

DRAMA AND DIALECTIC
IN CLASSICAL ATHENS

JOSHUA BILLINGS

PRINCETON UNIVERSITY PRESS
PRINCETON & OXFORD

Copyright © 2021 by Princeton University Press

Princeton University Press is committed to the protection of copyright and the intellectual property our authors entrust to us. Copyright promotes the progress and integrity of knowledge. Thank you for supporting free speech and the global exchange of ideas by purchasing an authorized edition of this book. If you wish to reproduce or distribute any part of it in any form, please obtain permission.

Requests for permission to reproduce material from this work should be sent to permissions@press.princeton.edu

Published by Princeton University Press
41 William Street, Princeton, New Jersey 08540
99 Banbury Road, Oxford OX2 6JX

press.princeton.edu

All Rights Reserved
First paperback printing, 2024
Paperback ISBN 9780691225074
Cloth ISBN 9780691205182
ISBN (e-book) 9780691211114

Library of Congress Control Number: 2021935564

British Library Cataloging-in-Publication Data is available

Editorial: Rob Tempio and Matt Rohal
Production Editorial: Nathan Carr
Jacket / Cover Design: Karl Spurzem
Production: Erin Suydam
Publicity: Alyssa Sanford and Amy Stewart
Copyeditor: Harry Haskell

Jacket / Cover image: Piero di Cosimo (1462–1521), *The Myth of Prometheus*, ca. 1515, oil on panel, 64 cm. × 116 cm. / Musée des Beaux-Arts, Strasbourg

This book has been composed in Arno

Es ist der Gegenstand der philosophischen Kritik zu erweisen, daß die Funktion der Kunstform eben dies ist: historische Sachgehalte, wie sie jedem bedeutenden Werk zugrunde liegen, zu philosophischen Wahrheitsgehalten zu machen. Diese Umbildung der Sachgehalte zum Wahrheitsgehalt macht den Verfall der Wirkung in dem von Jahrzehnt zu Jahrzehnt das Ansprechende der früheren Reize sich mindert, zum Grund einer Neugeburt, in welcher alle ephemere Schönheit vollends dahinfällt und das Werk als Ruine sich behauptet. (Walter Benjamin, *Ursprung des deutschen Trauerspiel* in *Gesammelte Schriften* I.1, 358)

It is the object of philosophical critique to show that the function of artistic form is just this: to make historical matter-contents, such as lie at the basis of every important work, into philosophical truth-contents. This transformation of matter-contents into truth-content makes the lessening of effect, in which from decade to decade the attractiveness of earlier charms diminishes, into the basis of a new birth, in which all ephemeral beauty wholly falls away and the work asserts itself as a ruin.

CONTENTS

Acknowledgments ix
Note on the Text xi

Introduction: Tragedy in the Philosophical Age of the Greeks   1

1   Catalogs and Culture   23
    Cataloguing the Human   27
    Palamedes: The Catalog and Invention   36
    Prometheus between Divine and Human   50
    The Gifts of the God: Euripides' Suppliants   64
    Polar Anthropology: Antigone   72
    Fictions of Divinity: The Sisyphus Fragment   84

2   Intrigue and Ontology   91
    Deception and Dikē   93
    Apatē *and Ontology*   101
    The Ethics of Intrigue: Sophocles' Electra   108
    On Not Being Female: Aristophanes' Women at the Thesmophoria   120
    Language and Necessity: Sophocles' Philoctetes *(I)*   131
    Deception, Myth, and Truth: Sophocles' Philoctetes *(II)*   141
    Trust and Community: Iphigenia at Aulis   151

3   *Agōn* and Authority   159
    Debating Wisdom   165
    Suspicions of the Sophos: Antiope *(I)*   170
    Praise of Sophia: Antiope *(II)*   178

Old and New Learning: Frogs *(I)*	186
Sophia *and Salvation:* Frogs *(II)*	196
Reasoning Divinity: Bacchae *(I)*	203
"What Is the Wise?": Bacchae *(II)*	213
Conclusion: The Stages of Early Greek Thought	223

Works Cited 239

Index 265

ACKNOWLEDGMENTS

THIS BOOK WAS BEGUN in a moment of personal sorrow and completed at a time of collective grief, anger, and fear. Reading and teaching ancient Greek tragedy, as ever, has been my way of addressing myself to loss, upheaval, and possibility. Today, this feels more inadequate and more vital than ever. What hope I have comes from the students I have been lucky to learn from in universities and prisons. Their passion, determination, and commitment to justice is inspiring, and in this dark period, they offer reasons to imagine a better future.

This project has been shaped and enriched by too many people to name, and leaves me with many debts. The first, and greatest, is collective, to my colleagues and students in the Princeton Classics Department, who have supported this project's development since its very first presentation as a job talk. Their warmth and generosity through the past five years have smoothed the many bumps and turns on the path to completion, while their insights and provocations have contributed immeasurably to the result.

I am profoundly grateful to the colleagues who have read and commented on versions of the project from its inception. Victoria Wohl generously read the entire manuscript in draft, and while I was unable to do justice to the profundity of her comments, they provided an ideal for the book to aspire to. Felix Budelmann has seen this project through too many iterations to count, and his readings of successive proposals and drafts substantially sharpened the result. Christopher Moore has been a regular collaborator on fifth-century intellectual history; his readings and our conversations brought clarity and insight to my understanding of the philosophical context. Kristin Gjesdal pushed me to think about the wider conversation between philosophy and drama. This project has developed in continuous discussion with Constanze Güthenke and Hindy Najman in Oxford and Princeton, and their friendship has been a constant source of inspiration and warmth. Peter Agócs, Andrew Ford, André Laks, Pauline LeVen, Glenn Most, Melissa Mueller, Sarah Nooter, Mark Payne, Jim Porter, Mario Telò, and Anna Uhlig read and commented on pieces of the project, and their reactions have improved the book in ways large and small. I am grateful to Jonas Grethlein, Athena Kirk, and David Williams for sharing work in progress, from which I learned a great deal. Malina Buturovic and Paul Eberwine, at different stages, cast their careful eyes over the entire manuscript, and improved it both in style and substance. Finally, Harry Haskell prepared the manuscript for typesetting with acuity.

Fellowships at the Center for Hellenic Studies, the Institute for Advanced Study, and the Fondation Hardt launched me into the project in ideal conditions, and the Magie Fund at Princeton supported work toward its completion. It has again been a pleasure to work with Rob Tempio and Matt Rohal at Princeton University Press.

The pleasure of thanking those who have made this book possible is diminished only by the sadness that two of the people who most shaped it can no longer receive my gratitude. Albert Henrichs was an advisor, mentor, and friend, and we had many formative conversations about what eventually would become this book. I regret profoundly that he will not see it. Even more, this project has been shadowed by the loss of my father, Andy Billings, who died just as I began work five years ago. I miss him every day, and my writing has been marked continually by his absence. This book is dedicated to his memory.

NOTE ON THE TEXT

CITATIONS OF CLASSICAL TEXTS follow standard numeration procedures and, where possible, are based on the current Oxford Classical Text (OCT). In some cases, I have preferred different readings from the editors of standard editions, and where these divergences are material to my argument, I explain them in notes. Where numeration is ambiguous, I include the editor's name for clarity.

Citations of tragic fragments and testimonia are based on the text and numeration in *Tragicorum Graecorum Fragmenta*, ed. Bruno Snell et al., 5 vols. (Göttingen: Vandenhoeck & Ruprecht, 1971–2004) [*TrGF*]. F for fragment, T for testimonium. Sources for fragments are only cited where relevant to the discussion.

Citations of comic fragments are based on the text and numeration in *Poetae Comici Graecae*, ed. Rudolf Kassel and Colin Austin (Berlin: de Gruyter, 1983–).

Citations of early Greek philosophy are based on the text and numeration in *Die Fragmente der Vorsokratiker*, 6th ed., ed. Hermann Diels and Walther Kranz, 3 vols. (Zürich: Weidmann, 1951) [DK]; DK citations are followed by citations in the Loeb *Early Greek Philosophy*, ed. André Laks and Glenn W. Most, 9 vols. (Cambridge, MA: Harvard University Press, 2016) [LM].

All dates, unless otherwise noted, are BCE.

All translations are my own, and aim for transparency.

THE PHILOSOPHICAL STAGE

INTRODUCTION

Tragedy in the Philosophical Age of the Greeks

"WISE IS Sophocles, wiser Euripides, of all men Socrates is wisest" (σοφὸς Σοφοκλῆς, σοφώτερος δ' Εὐριπίδης, ἀνδρῶν δὲ πάντων Σωκράτης σοφώτατος). According to one report, this is the reply of the Delphic oracle to a question concerning the wisdom of Socrates.[1] Though almost certainly apocryphal, the oracle's identification of the three men as distinguished—and competing—in wisdom is not wholly implausible. As the leading tragedians of the time, Sophocles and Euripides were among the most prominent public intellectual figures in Athens, celebrated throughout the Greek-speaking world for their dramas. Socrates, though probably not yet so widely known, must have had a significant reputation for such an oracular consultation to be undertaken. The response indicates that poets and philosophers could be thought to possess the same quality of wisdom (*sophia*). This may not be intuitive today: poetic skill appears different in kind from philosophical intelligence, and a comparison of the two would seem to lack any criterion for judgment.

Poetic and philosophical thinkers were felt to be much closer in the fifth century BCE. The strong differentiation of poetry from philosophy with which we are familiar largely postdates the notional date of the oracle (around 420), and has little purchase for understanding this period. The late fifth century in Athens witnessed a productive and often competitive interaction of poetic and

---

1. The anecdote is reported in the scholia to Aristophanes, *Clouds* 144 and to Plato, *Apology* 21a. Chaerephon's question and the oracular response are reported in Plato, *Apology* 20e–21a and Xenophon, *Apology* 14 in slightly different forms, neither of them mentioning the tragedians.

philosophical thinking and writing, which would have made a comparison of Socrates and the tragedians possible and even natural. All three figures were looked to as intellectual authorities, able to help Athenians fulfill the Delphic injunction to know themselves. The oracular response, though probably not historical fact, speaks to the historical situation of the late fifth century.

This book is an attempt to reanimate the intimate and multiform relation of philosophical and poetic thought that obtained before philosophy defined itself in contradistinction to other discourses.[2] It suggests that drama can be recognized as significantly philosophical, and read alongside the canonical texts of early Greek philosophical writing. Drama's awareness of developments in philosophical thought has already been the subject of much research. A selection of the evidence is collected in the appendix, "Philosophy and Philosophers in Greek Comedy and Tragedy," to the recent edition of *Early Greek Philosophy* by André Laks and Glenn Most, which gathers allusions and references in Attic drama, organizing them by philosophical topic and philosopher.[3] The collection (and substantial previous research it draws on) demonstrates that drama frequently integrates developments in philosophical thought, and that this integration is significant and widespread. My contention here is stronger: that dramatic texts are *themselves* developments in philosophical thought, and should be recognized as part of the canon of early Greek philosophical writing. By attending to the thinking of drama, we recover important dimensions of fifth-century intellectual culture, and bring into view a wider, more dynamic, and more vibrant philosophical field.

The idea that Greek drama is importantly philosophical is famously in evidence in Aristophanes' *Frogs*, in which Euripides touts himself for introducing Athens to new ways of thinking. Plato's *Symposium* suggests a different, but just as intimate relation between drama and philosophy, portraying in the dialogue's final pages Socrates deep in conversation with Agathon and Aristophanes, tragedian and comedian, respectively. The ancient scholarly tradition frequently emphasizes Euripides' reputation as the "philosopher of the stage,"

---

2. On philosophy's demarcation from other discourses, see Andrea Wilson Nightingale, *Genres in Dialogue: Plato and the Construct of Philosophy* (Cambridge: Cambridge University Press, 1995); Edward Schiappa, *The Beginnings of Rhetorical Theory in Classical Greece* (New Haven: Yale University Press, 1999); Håkan Tell, *Plato's Counterfeit Sophists* (Washington, DC: Center for Hellenic Studies, 2011).

3. André Laks and Glenn W. Most, "Appendix: Philosophy and Philosophers in Greek Comedy and Tragedy," in *Early Greek Philosophy*, Vol. IX: *The Sophists*, Part 2 (Cambridge, MA: Harvard University Press, 2016), 256–365.

and the widely circulated *Life of Euripides* connects him biographically to Anaxagoras, Protagoras, Prodicus, and Socrates.⁴ There is much less ancient discussion of the philosophical interests of Aeschylus, whose death in 458 puts him well before the heyday of philosophy in Athens, or of Sophocles, who, though he lived until 406, would have been well into adulthood by the time that Anaxagoras famously brought philosophy to Athens (probably around 455). Modern scholars have recognized ways that both dramatists are in dialogue with contemporary philosophical thought—and this study extends these arguments—but the conventional story of fifth-century thought sees Euripides' philosophical interests as distinctive within tragic tradition.⁵

Among modern variations on this story, none has been so influential as Nietzsche's in *The Birth of Tragedy*. Although the outlines of Nietzsche's discussion of the association of Euripides and Socrates were familiar and even cliché at the time, his telling of tragedy's decline under the influence of rationalism gave the familiar story a polemical spin.⁶ It importantly cemented a modern idea—though one with ancient precedents in Plato—of tragedy as the genre of the unreason, and of Greek culture as a whole as fascinated by the irrational.⁷ Socratic philosophy appeared to Nietzsche as an alien imposition

---

4. T 1.IA.2 *TrGF*; further reports are T 35–48 *TrGF*, adding (on very thin traditions) Archelaus and Heraclitus. Descriptions of Euripides as the "philosopher of the stage" (σκηνικὸς φιλόσοφος) are collected in T 166–69 *TrGF*, and seem to be familiar by the imperial period.

5. This may be changing for Aeschylus; full-length studies of his relation to early Greek thought are Wolfgang Rösler, *Reflexe vorsokratischen Denkens bei Aischylos* (Meisenheim am Glan: Hain, 1970); Richard Seaford, *Cosmology and the Polis: The Social Construction of Space and Time in the Tragedies of Aeschylus* (Cambridge: Cambridge University Press, 2012); Nuria Scapin, *The Flower of Suffering: Theology, Justice, and the Cosmos in Aeschylus' "Oresteia" and Presocratic Thought* (Berlin: de Gruyter, 2020). There is much less written on Sophocles and philosophical thought: Meggan Jennell Arp, "Pre-Socratic Thought in Sophoclean Tragedy" (Ph.D. diss., University of Pennsylvania, 2006). See further the essays in Douglas Cairns, ed., *Tragedy and Archaic Greek Thought* (Swansea: Classical Press of Wales, 2013). I cite more targeted studies as they arise.

6. The background to Nietzsche's account is discussed in Ernst Behler, "A. W. Schlegel and the Nineteenth-Century *Damnatio* of Euripides," *Greek, Roman, and Byzantine Studies* 27 (1986): 335–67; Albert Henrichs, "The Last of the Detractors: Friedrich Nietzsche's Condemnation of Euripides," *Greek, Roman, and Byzantine Studies* 27 (1986): 369–97.

7. For Plato's view of tragedy as antirational, see Stephen Halliwell, *The Aesthetics of Mimesis: Ancient Texts and Modern Problems* (Princeton: Princeton University Press, 2002), 98–117. Classic on the irrational is E. R. Dodds, *The Greeks and the Irrational* (Berkeley: University of California Press, 1951).

on tragedy and Greek culture in general, which brought about tragedy's "suicide," the end of the truly productive age of philosophical thought, and a catastrophic cultural shift that persisted to his own day.[8]

The historical narrative of this study is quite distinct from Nietzsche's, suggesting that Greek drama was, for all of its history that we can trace, profoundly philosophical.[9] Yet Nietzsche's account of the "rational" qualities of (Euripidean) tragedy is valuable for pointing to the way that Attic tragedy was significantly engaged in its own philosophical project, involving consideration of the way that intellectual novelty bears on traditional stories. To Nietzsche, this appeared a wholly destructive project, which led Euripides to reject the unreason that had conditioned Aeschylean and Sophoclean tragedy. I will propose, by contrast, to understand all the canonical dramatists as thoroughly engaged with philosophical thought. Nietzsche, though, points to a crucial—and too often neglected—facet of drama's place in the wider intellectual culture: its self-consciousness concerning its own relation to the emerging discourse of philosophy. Drama is not just thinking philosophically, but thinking about philosophical thinking.

Reversing the title of one of Nietzsche's early lecture courses, I investigate here "tragedy (and comedy) in the philosophical age of the Greeks." Posing the relationship of drama and philosophy in this manner, in terms of a historical period rather than discrete interactions, brings into focus a wider and more dynamic field than has typically been considered relevant. The late fifth century brought with it a profusion of novel questions and ideas, as well as an expansion of the range of professional profiles and discursive forms. These developments are often associated with those we call "sophists," but their origins and significance were much broader. They reach back at least as far as the decisive Greek victory over the Persians at Plataea in 479, and had much to do with the increasing wealth and prominence of Athens as a cultural center. Individuals who came to Athens from outside (among them Anaxagoras and, slightly later, the canonical sophists) took part in an atmosphere of thought,

---

8. The narrative of tragedy's "suicide" is concentrated in *Birth of Tragedy* §11–14: Friedrich Wilhelm Nietzsche, *The Birth of Tragedy and Other Writings*, trans. Ronald Speirs (Cambridge: Cambridge University Press, 1999), esp. 54–71.

9. The young Nietzsche has great sympathy with early Greek philosophy—or really, early Greek philosophers, including Socrates, whom he sees as exemplifying "archetypes of philosophical thought:" Friedrich Nietzsche, *Philosophy in the Tragic Age of the Greeks*, trans. Marianne Cowan (Chicago: Regnery, 1962), 31.

exchange, and debate sometimes described as an "Attic Enlightenment."[10] This enlightenment encompassed not just conventional philosophical figures like the sophists and the circle of Socrates, but historians, musicians, rhetoricians, doctors, and politicians, to indicate only a few of the important exponents of late fifth-century intellectual culture. Though there may have been incipient divisions between these areas of inquiry, they were all significantly predisciplinary, without strictly defined methods or discursive forms.[11] Fifth-century modes of writing and thinking were substantially open and engaged with one another, while, at the same time, they sought to establish their own claims to authority. Late fifth-century culture as a whole can be described as "sophistic"—not in the sense of being influenced predominantly by the sophists but, rather, as being preoccupied with questions of wisdom, *sophia*. For this culture, the nature and location of intellectual authority are central concerns, continually subject to negotiation and debate.

Drama, my readings will suggest, stakes its claim within this wider cultural negotiation of authority. It shows a consciousness of new modes of thinking, and addresses them with its own distinctive perspective and approach. Drama's relation to other discourses can be cooperative or antagonistic, but it is more than a mere receptacle or reflection. Rather, I argue that drama takes part in philosophical discussions as directly and forcefully as the texts we designate as "philosophy." It presents philosophical questions and ideas in ways that differ from and sometimes conflict with other discourses. Ultimately, it asserts the importance of its own perspective, and of its position within the discursive landscape of the fifth century. This would have been unsurprising to a contemporary audience: mythological poetry was at the center of Greek learning and erudition, and drama a vital and massively popular form. As much as any discourse, it had a claim to be at the center of fifth-century intellectual culture, broadly understood. By contrast, the texts that we identify as philosophical appear to have been relatively marginal, and to lack the authority that they would gain after the institution of philosophy as a discipline. This is reflected

---

10. The term "Enlightenment" seems to gain wide currency through the standard work of nineteenth-century history of philosophy: Eduard Zeller, *Die Philosophie der Griechen in ihrer geschichtlichen Entwicklung*, 2nd ed. (Tübingen: Fues, 1856), 1, 793–98. Volume III of Guthrie's *History of Greek Philosophy* (1969), encompassing Socrates and the sophists, is entitled *The Fifth-Century Enlightenment*, though the term has not been in wide use since.

11. Edward Schiappa describes early rhetoric as predisciplinary: Edward Schiappa, "'Rhêtorikê': What's in a Name? Toward a Revised History of Early Greek Rhetorical Theory," *Quarterly Journal of Speech* 78 (1992): 1–15.

in the transmission of material: the extant texts of tragedy and comedy, though a shadow of what was staged and performed in antiquity, represent an extraordinary wealth and diversity of material—orders of magnitude greater than what survives of early Greek philosophical writing. If we want to understand the intellectual history of the fifth century, we have no better source than drama.

———

Philosophical thought before the discipline of philosophy had no normative discursive form. What we call "early Greek philosophy" could be written (or, probably just as frequently, performed) in prose or poetry of various meters; could take the form of argument, narration, or enactment; could be spoken in the first, second, or third person; and could employ contemporary or mythological figures (or none at all). It could, moreover, take in a wide range of concerns: relatively familiar are natural science, cosmology, ontology, epistemology, and ethics, but more surprising may be biology, zoology, theology, literary criticism, anthropology, grammar, and medicine. Whether it makes sense to classify such a heterogeneous field of material—which I have drawn only from authors and works included in the Laks-Most *Early Greek Philosophy* edition—as "philosophy" at all, and what the consequences of such a classification are, are questions I cannot enter into here.[12] At the very least, we should be wary of assuming continuity in the practice of what we now call philosophy either synchronically, at any given time in early Greek culture, or diachronically, from philosophy's beginnings through its establishment as a discipline to the present day. In 400 BCE, what constituted a philosophical text or claim (much less an authoritative one) was a significantly open question.

Even the vocabulary of description is difficult: Christopher Moore has recently argued that the term "philosopher" is likely first used as a derisive appellation (roughly, "sage-wannabe"), directed against the Pythagoreans, and is appropriated by those pursuing related activities in response.[13] To be called a "philosopher" for much of the fifth century was probably not a very flattering

---

12. A profound consideration of these issues is in André Laks, *The Concept of Presocratic Philosophy: Its Origin, Development, and Significance*, trans. Glenn Most (Princeton: Princeton University Press, 2018), 35–52.

13. Christopher Moore, *Calling Philosophers Names: On the Origin of a Discipline* (Princeton: Princeton University Press, 2020).

designation, and, though the word comes to acquire a more neutral valence, it does not name anything like a discipline until the end of the century, or more probably, the beginning of the following. What language the canonical early Greek philosophers used for their writing and thinking is largely lost to us, making it difficult or impossible to classify such a heterogeneous group of figures and works.[14] It is therefore tempting—and probably preferable, from a strictly historical standpoint—to do away with "philosophy" and its cognates for the predisciplinary context, except in the very limited circumstances when we can be confident of its use and meaning. But beyond the practical difficulty of there not being an obviously more adequate English term to describe such practice ("thought" and "thinker" seem the closest, though they are frustratingly vague), the word "philosophy" has a totemic value that is worth holding on to, if only for the purposes of appropriating it. In what follows, I use the term "philosophy" narrowly to describe the discipline, while using the adjective "philosophical" to characterize a much wider range of predisciplinary thinking and writing. The boundaries of philosophy in this predisciplinary phase cannot be clearly fixed, and scholars have drawn them primarily based on contributions to what are taken, retrospectively, to be philosophical discussions. This study insists that drama contributes to these same discussions and thus has significant philosophical importance; it uses the terminology of philosophy in the service of redefining it.

The claim that drama is itself philosophical would be a weak one if it only amounted to the idea that drama deals with issues of conceptual substance and import. This could be said of most early Greek poetry, which is often ethical and occasionally metaphysical in its concerns (and is certainly an important background for early Greek philosophical writing). "Philosophical" has to describe something about the kind of exploration, and not just the subject matter—about method, the way that an investigation is structured. Yet philosophical method, like the form of philosophical writing, is exceptionally fluid in the fifth century and earlier. Though there may be an emergent understanding of method, it would have to be quite a capacious one, able to encompass a range of different modes of thinking and writing. I propose here that dramatic staging can be understood as one of these philosophical modes, and that the persistence of certain scenic forms demonstrates a commitment—though not

---

14. The *Phaedo* refers to "inquiry into nature" (96a: περὶ φύσεως ἱστορία) as a name for some fifth-century inquiries, and it seems to be current in the later fifth century, but the scope and origin of the term are obscure: Laks, *The Concept of Presocratic Philosophy*, 2–4.

necessarily a conscious one—to structured investigation of conceptual questions. Particular types of scenes are used recurrently across dramatic works and dramatists to explore philosophical issues, and can thus be understood as guided by a kind of method. These scenic forms, moreover, are not limited to drama, but have important contemporary presence in other discourses, where they often do related work. These continuities of form across works and discourses can be recognized as philosophical structures for inquiry, which have a role in soliciting and shaping thought. They constitute a kind of scenic grammar through which fifth-century intellectual culture investigates philosophical questions within and across discourses.

At the core of my approach is the idea that form shapes thinking. Though at some level this is uncontroversial, I intend to press its consequences here with the argument that scenic form in drama constitutes a kind of philosophical method. The scenic forms I identify are not bare containers, forms that could be filled with anything, but are rather constituted by a nexus of a discursive structure (catalogs, prologues, debates) with a particular topic (human culture, deception, wisdom). This sense of form is defined by emergence rather than stability, and seeks to capture the way that certain scene types recur in different contexts and shapes, while retaining a basic similarity. The dramatic forms I discuss are found across works and authors, enabling them to be read as a structured conversation. Though the forms are developed differently in each drama, and can extend beyond the bounds of a single scene, they are importantly unified in the way that they pose and investigate a central question or problem. It is because of this linkage of topic and form that they can be read as guided by an implicit method. The argument of each chapter involves, first, identifying the form and describing its use across dramas, and then elaborating the philosophical inquiry that the form pursues.

Enactment is essential to drama's method of investigating philosophical topics. Dramatic thinking takes place not just through assertions and counter-assertions, but through staging situations and characters across time. The philosophical work of this thinking has to be understood as a process, in which questions recur and answers are reshaped in response to events. Such a staging of the process of thought is familiar from Platonic dialogue, in which form and setting shape the way we understand the utterances of the characters, and thus, the philosophical work of the whole. Drama, in the same way, presents positions, ideas, and possibilities in the words of its characters, but refracts these through character, story, setting, and development. As I discuss below, I see this processual character as a distinctive aspect of (especially later) fifth-century philosophical writing in general. Drama, philosophical dialogue, and a host of other, related philosophical forms all stage thinking as a process, and attention to this staging illuminates not only the way that drama thinks through enactment, but the way that philosophical writing can as well.

———

This study proposes a new way of understanding Greek drama as philosophical. There are, broadly speaking, two ways the relation of ancient drama and philosophy has been discussed in the past: the first, which emerges around 1800 in the thought of German Idealism and has been pursued more or less continuously since, reads Greek tragedy for its contribution to modern philosophical questions.[15] From Schelling's reading of *Oedipus the King* to Martha Nussbaum's *Fragility of Goodness*, philosophers have found in Greek tragedy a vital perspective on the philosophical issues with which they are grappling, and elaborated readings that seek to actualize those perspectives for their own time. This is a profoundly important approach, which has enriched both literary and philosophical study, but it tends to do greater justice to the philosophical issues at stake for a modern reader than for an ancient audience. My interest here, by contrast, is on how ancient tragedy (and comedy) addresses the philosophical questions of its own time. I attempt to develop a historicized mode of reading drama philosophically, which takes account of the form and substance of philosophical and dramatic thought in classical Athens.

The other, more historically oriented method of understanding the relation of Attic drama and contemporary philosophical thought has been to seek out lines of influence or allusion. This is a valuable project, which has shown that

---

15. I trace the emergence of modern philosophical readings of Greek tragedy in Joshua Billings, *Genealogy of the Tragic: Greek Tragedy and German Philosophy* (Princeton: Princeton University Press, 2014). See further (among important recent contributions) Terry Eagleton, *Sweet Violence: The Idea of the Tragic* (Oxford: Blackwell, 2003); Vassilis Lambropoulos, *The Tragic Idea* (London: Duckworth, 2006); Pierre Judet de la Combe, *Les tragédies grecques sont-elles tragiques? Théâtre et théorie* (Montrouge: Bayard, 2010); Miriam Leonard, *Tragic Modernities* (Cambridge, MA: Harvard University Press, 2015); Joshua Billings and Miriam Leonard, eds., *Tragedy and the Idea of Modernity* (Oxford: Oxford University Press, 2015). Approaches to the relation of modern drama and philosophy, often taking classical texts as a starting point, are pursued in modern language and theater studies: Freddie Rokem, *Philosophers and Thespians: Thinking Performance* (Stanford: Stanford University Press, 2009); Martin Puchner, *The Drama of Ideas: Platonic Provocations in Theater and Philosophy* (Oxford: Oxford University Press, 2014).

there are important historical and interpretive gains in recognizing drama's philosophical interests.[16] There are, to be sure, still gaps in our knowledge, but these gaps—at least the ones that the extant evidence allows us to fill in—are increasingly small ones. At the same time, the interpretation of philosophical allusions in Attic drama, working with a relatively small corpus of material, has grown substantially in complexity, forcing new contributions to be dialectically (and usually polemically) related to what has gone before. There is surely more to say about dramatic allusions to philosophical thought, but the terrain of this approach has broadly been mapped; there has, however, been relatively little effort to interrogate its method.

The primary argument of this study is its method. It fills no gaps, but seeks rather to open one. It does not contest an established story, but tells it in a different way. There is very little raw material here that would be novel or unexpected to a reader interested in the relationship of drama and fifth-century intellectual culture, but I believe that the configuration of material and the way of investigating it tell a substantially new story of this relation, and indeed, of Greek intellectual history and the origins of philosophy. The method is oriented by the aim of reading drama as intellectual history, rather than as a source for the history of philosophy or, conversely, reading the history of philosophy as a source for drama. This entails a different approach to the philosophical nature of drama than has been employed by previous studies.

There are two main tenets of this study's method. The first is synchrony, treatment of the primary material of each chapter as coincident in time, and therefore, independent. I understand the late fifth century as a constellation of sources, whose most important relations are conceptual rather than chronological.[17] I elicit theoretical connections between the texts studied—notional

---

16. Important recent contributions on connections between Greek drama and philosophy are D. J. Conacher, *Euripides and the Sophists: Some Dramatic Treatments of Philosophical Ideas* (London: Duckworth, 1998); Franziska Egli, *Euripides im Kontext zeitgenössischer intellektueller Strömungen: Analyse der Funktion philosophischer Themen in den Tragödien und Fragmenten* (Munich: Saur, 2003); Matthew Wright, *Euripides' Escape Tragedies: A Study of "Helen," "Andromeda," and "Iphigenia among the Taurians"* (Oxford: Oxford University Press, 2005); Ashley Clements, *Aristophanes' "Thesmophoriazusae": Philosophizing Theatre and the Politics of Perception in Late Fifth-Century Athens* (Cambridge: Cambridge University Press, 2014). Seaford, *Cosmology and the Polis* is more complex methodologically.

17. The figure of the constellation is borrowed, loosely, from Walter Benjamin's *Origin of the German Trauerspiel* and from the work of Dieter Henrich on German Idealism: Walter Benjamin, *Origin of the German Trauerspiel*, trans. Howard Eiland (Cambridge, MA: Harvard

lines between different points in space—that render an image of the thinking surrounding a given topic. This does not preclude tracing the background to each chapter's primary material (which is often necessary to make sense of the philosophical concerns in historical perspective), or noting development where it is plain in the sources, but the weight of the argument is never on diachronic connections or allusions, but rather on the synchronic constellation of thinking. The organization of material is governed by a conceptual logic developed in each chapter, which occasionally results in anachrony. Still, I want to insist that this is a historical project: most of the dramatic texts studied are dated to between 425 and 405 BCE (though there are, especially in the first chapter, some earlier sources), and our evidence for philosophical thought is largely nonspecific and homogeneous across this period. There must have been more local intellectual developments, but these are effectively lost to us. Treating this period as broadly unified in its conceptual concerns allows these concerns to emerge more fully than would an analytic approach that tries, on scanty evidence, to trace development. We gain a more holistic picture, which does greater justice to the richness of the period's thinking. The book thus proposes an intellectual history without chronology.

The synchronic approach has two primary consequences: negatively, it entails the avoidance of arguments concerning influence or dependence, which have been the primary methods for investigating the relation of drama and philosophy. Arguments for direct dependence, I believe, are only rarely able to withstand critical examination, both because of the inherent difficulty of demonstrating one source's similarity to another and because of our lacunose evidence for fifth-century intellectual culture. The state of our knowledge means that it is nearly impossible ever to be sure that a similarity is a facet of direct (as opposed to indirect or more diffuse) influence, and often makes establishing relative chronology—and thereby the directionality of influence—difficult. Such direct influence is therefore a very uncertain basis for constructing the relation of drama and philosophy, and inevitably, the more ambitious the argument, the more speculative and open to doubt. A synchronic mode of investigation, on the contrary, because it does not make claims of dependence, is able to make robust and securely founded historical arguments.

The arguments enabled by a synchronic method are, moreover, more consequential than those constructed around dependence. This constitutes a

---

University Press, 2019), 10–11; Dieter Henrich, *Konstellationen: Probleme und Debatten am Ursprung der idealistischen Philosophie (1789–1795)* (Stuttgart: Klett-Cotta, 1991).

positive consequence of a synchronic investigation, and is best demonstrated by the study as a whole. But to anticipate these results: synchronic investigation allows for a consideration of parallels between different areas of culture that recognizes distinctive concerns and modes of investigation, while also being open to their connection. Rather than defining the concerns of philosophy in the terms of drama or vice versa, synchronic consideration allows for each area to emerge as independent, while still related by common questions or problems. Drama, I argue, is most philosophical not when it reflects existing philosophical doctrines, but when it assumes philosophical questions as its own, investigating them in ways that are distinctive to dramatic form. While a diachronic method presumes that philosophy is the primary discourse and drama the receptive one (or, in very rare instances, the reverse), a synchronic method assumes that drama thinks in parallel with philosophy, and seeks to show the significance of this thinking.

The other major tenet of this study's method is dialectic, a term I use in a broad sense to describe juxtaposition of different views on a subject (without the teleology implicit in the post-Hegelian or Marxian senses of the term). Kant's dismissive description of ancient dialectic as a "logic of illusion" actually captures my use of the term well, provided one understands "illusion" in a more generous fashion than Kant: dialectic is a process of accounting for potential realities or outlooks.[18] Dialectic postulates an image of reality, and enacts the conditions and consequences of such an understanding over the course of a narrative. When Aristotle claims that drama is akin to philosophy in that it stages "what kinds of things might happen" (οἷα ἂν γένοιτο) and thereby gives insight into "the universal" (1451b: τὰ καθόλου), I understand him to be drawing attention to such dialectic. It is the process of thinking through a viewpoint, following an idea as it is realized in action and thought.

I read dramatic texts as enacting the process of thinking, a process that is ongoing and open-ended, and which inevitably brings alternatives into implicit or explicit conflict. The dialectical approach adopted here is distinct from two tendencies that are prevalent in philosophical and literary readings of drama, respectively. Where my approach differs from most philosophical readings of drama is that I do not believe that drama issues in discrete positions on philosophical topics, but rather, that it makes a plurality of viewpoints available without hierarchy or conclusion. I do not take drama as having a

---

18. *Critique of Pure Reason* A61/B85–86: Immanuel Kant, *Critique of Pure Reason*, trans. Paul Guyer and Allen W. Wood (Cambridge: Cambridge University Press, 1998), 198–99.

doctrine or message that is deciphered over the course of a work, but rather, as presenting multiple possibilities for meaning that are available directly to an audience member or reader. As I discuss in the next section, I believe on historical grounds that a dialectical method is the best way of approaching fifth-century philosophical writing, and this is even more true of literature. Drama, because of its dialogic form, conduces to the presentation of thinking without conclusion, and readings should recognize this open-endedness.

As a literary intervention, this may appear an unobjectionable, if not banal, claim. Studies of Greek drama today consistently find it to problematize dominant discourses or render its themes ambiguous, and my study is certainly shaped by these tendencies. I take it as a hermeneutic principle that drama's multiple voices make it impossible to isolate one as authoritative, or to extract a unified "message" from a work. But the dialectical method pursued here differs also from the modes of dialectical critique that animate approaches to tragic ambiguity, whether inflected historically or formally.[19] Though I am interested in forms in history, I do not engage in immanent critique, which would entail reading the formal dialectic of a work in terms of its social world and ideology.[20] This is not because of any hostility to dialectical critique in its consequential, Marxian forms, but because I adopt here an approach to the literary object different from the one that is presupposed by critical aesthetics.

The primary difference lies in an understanding of form. Immanent critique, though its aims are historical and political, rests on a conception of the literary object as the bounded space within which dialectic takes place. In this sense, it has a strong conception of form similar to the ahistorical, "formalist" approaches that it often opposes. Both take the singular work as the elementary unit of analysis, and the critical task lies in understanding the way that different formal elements within the work are resolved or held in suspension by the whole (and then, in the Marxian version, elucidating the ideology of this form). My approach understands form in a somewhat weaker sense: I am not interested in the

---

19. On the possibilities of immanent critique for the interpretation of Greek tragedy, see Victoria Wohl, *Euripides and the Politics of Form* (Princeton: Princeton University Press, 2015), esp. 3–8. Wohl argues, drawing on Adorno and Jameson, that a meaningfully political reading in the Marxian tradition has to be a formal one.

20. I understand immanent critique here along Jamesonian lines (though this is not, to be sure, the only version of dialectical reading): Fredric Jameson, *Marxism and Form: Twentieth-Century Dialectical Theories of Literature* (Princeton: Princeton University Press, 1971), esp. 306–416; Fredric Jameson, *The Political Unconscious: Narrative as a Socially Symbolic Act* (Ithaca: Cornell University Press, 1981), esp. 17–102.

form of a single work, but in forms across works, scenic types and possibilities that are realized in different dramatic contexts.[21] This reflects a conception of the Greek dramatists as craftsmen more than artists, who frequently worked by repurposing, combining, and borrowing elements from their own and others' works in order to produce as many as four new plays in the course of a year. Because our post-Romantic notion of artistic creation entails a strong sense of authorship and of intentional form, we tend, I believe, to focus too much on the unit of the work in our studies of Greek literature, and too little on connections across works and discourses (and, for the same reason, often ignore relevant fragmentary material). My approach assumes that dialectic across works is just as important as dialectic within a work. A weaker sense of form thus enables a stronger understanding of drama within the totality of Greek culture.

The primary questions for early Greek intellectual culture, this study will argue, concern authority: who is able to speak about major questions of human existence, and what are the sources of this ability?[22] This is a binding thread between figures conventionally termed "Presocratics" and those conventionally termed "sophists" and "Socratics." For all these thinkers, whose inquiries were conducted before philosophy had established a relatively unified method of investigation, prior to any questions of content were questions of form: what medium to write in, what kinds of evidence or demonstration to employ, how to construct speech so as to be persuasive. These questions reach well beyond those thinkers we conventionally describe as "philosophical"; they are preoccupations of what we can glean of early Greek prose in general.[23] As Maria

---

21. My approach to form draws inspiration from that of Caroline Levine, who employs a relatively weak sense of form to connect forms in literature to the social world: Caroline Levine, *Forms: Whole, Rhythm, Hierarchy, Network* (Princeton: Princeton University Press, 2015). Anna Uhlig has recently offered an important study in form across genres in classical Greece: Anna Uhlig, *Theatrical Reenactment in Pindar and Aeschylus* (Cambridge: Cambridge University Press, 2019).

22. I understand authority, following Bruce Lincoln, primarily as an effect, which is produced by the conjunction of speaker, speech, and situation within culturally established parameters: Bruce Lincoln, *Authority: Construction and Corrosion* (Chicago: University of Chicago Press, 1994), 10–11. That is, authority is primarily a matter of whose voice counts within a society.

23. For notions of authority in early Greek prose, see Rosalind Thomas, *Herodotus in Context: Ethnography, Science and the Art of Persuasion* (Cambridge: Cambridge University Press, 2002), esp. 249–69.

Michela Sassi has shown, the emergent discourse of philosophical writing had to grapple with the challenge of establishing itself in relation to the existing authorities of Greek intellectual culture, claiming a space for its own forms of thought as authoritative.[24] In consequence, early Greek philosophical thought, to a degree largely alien to the development of philosophy as a discipline, is concerned with the speaker rather than the speech.

The most distinctive aspect of the late fifth-century context for intellectual culture was its proliferation of authorities: the public intellectual sphere came to include not just the traditional authorities who combined political, religious, and often poetic roles, but those who defined their contribution in novel ways—by the ability to argue both sides of a question, to give an account of the origins of the Persian War, to write a persuasive speech for the assembly or a defense for the law courts, to explain the connection of music and character, to conduct an inquiry into the validity of conventional beliefs. All of these might have been facets of the authority of earlier thinkers, but the later fifth century saw intellectuals increasingly differentiating themselves into distinct social roles. The public intellectual sphere of Greece, which had always been highly agonistic, increasingly became a space for contestation between forms of authority. Poet did not only strive with poet, but with politician, historian, and philosopher.

Democratic Athens was an important stage for this contestation of authority. Particularly in the latter half of the fifth century, the city's wealth, power, and relative openness to outsiders made it an intellectual center that attracted thinkers from across the Greek world. Athens' democratic constitution, which involved the entire male citizenry in regular deliberation and adjudication, fueled an interest in skills of analysis, debate, and persuasion, and a demand for those who could demonstrate or teach these skills. The importance of contestation in public life is hardly unique to Athens, which was not the only Greek democracy or intellectual center of the period, but our evidence for other cities is simply too scanty to permit us to draw any secure comparisons.[25] We know that in Athens important intellectuals performed and circulated their writings for entertainment and education, and found ready audiences and pupils. Relations between philosophical and political contexts must have

---

24. Maria Michela Sassi, *The Beginnings of Philosophy in Greece* (Princeton: Princeton University Press, 2018).

25. On intellectual culture and debate outside of Athens, see Eric W. Robinson, "The Sophists and Democracy beyond Athens," *Rhetorica* 25 (2007): 109–22.

been multidirectional: developments in philosophical and rhetorical training influenced the ways that citizens expressed themselves in political situations, and the demands of public expression shaped the ways that intellectuals wrote, thought, and taught. Similarly, drama both offered its audience models of speech and took on contemporary modes of argumentation, in a relationship of reciprocity with political and philosophical debate.

Late fifth-century philosophical thought is characterized above all by the relative absence of authoritative statements, a tendency to see all conceptual positions as open to question and debate. While earlier Greek philosophical writing had tended to construct its own authority in more or less monologic fashion, usually invoking modes of divine sanction, the late fifth century sees an explosion of different forms for thinking, many of them characterized by multiple voices, mythical figures and settings, and conceptual experimentation. While earlier Greek philosophers tended to create relatively few, unified works expounding their views, the thinkers of the later fifth century seem not to have held (or at least not to have expounded) doctrines in the same way. More characteristic were discursive forms that were, in one way or another, dialectical, that assumed a position and sought to defend it, encompassed different voices, or interrogated the views of another. This dialectical character may appear an aberration in the history of philosophy as we now understand it, but it would hardly have seemed exceptional at the time, since it placed philosophical writing in close proximity to other modes of contemporary expression.

Two discursive modes are particularly distinctive to late fifth-century philosophical thought: antilogy, the assumption of opposing viewpoints, and prosopopoeia, speaking through the voice of another. A number of texts testify to the importance of antilogical writing: Antiphon's *Tetralogies* and the *Dissoi Logoi* are extant examples of a mode that included writings by Thrasymachus and some of Protagoras' most important works, known as the *Antilogies* or *Overthrowing Arguments*.[26] The idea that an argument exists for both sides of a question is associated with Protagoras by later sources, as is the claim to be able to make the weaker argument the stronger, parodied in Aristophanes'

---

26. Two books of *Antilogies* are attested for Protagoras: Diogenes Laertius 9.55 (A1 DK/D1 LM). This is probably the same as his *Overthrowing Arguments* (Καταβάλλοντες), mentioned in Sextus Empiricus, *Against the Mathematicians* 7.60 (B1 DK/D3 LM) and alluded to in Plato, *Sophist* 232d–e (B8 DK/D2 LM). Thrasymachus' similarly titled *Overpowerings* (Ὑπερβάλλοντες: B7 DK/D5 LM) is probably antilogistic as well.

Clouds.²⁷ The importance of antilogy probably has to do in part with the growth of rhetorical training, which would have sought to enable students to speak on both sides of a question as preparation for forensic and deliberative contexts. The philosophical dialogue as it is known from Plato and Xenophon (whose works represent only the tip of the iceberg of the Socratic dialogues that circulated contemporaneously), though not formally structured by antilogy, likewise manifests the centrality of dialectical modes to late fifth-century philosophical thought. The widespread adoption of antilogical and dialectical forms testifies to the provisional nature of much argumentation in the sophistic era.

The philosophical dialogue involves, almost by definition, prosopopoeia, the other characteristic mode of late fifth-century thought. Much philosophical writing involves the taking on of character, which can be mythological (Gorgias' *Defense of Palamedes*) or real (the Socratic dialogue). Even a work like Gorgias' *Helen*, which does not impersonate a defined figure, is assuming a kind of role by taking on the defense of Helen; the same goes for the opposing speakers in Antiphon's *Tetralogies*. Antilogical forms are often combined with mythological or allegorical prosopopoeia, as in Antisthenes' paired speeches of Ajax and Odysseus or Prodicus' *Choice of Heracles* (which Xenophon recounts in a Socratic dialogue, still another layer of prosopopoeia). Indeed, the two modes broadly entail one another: to argue opposing sides of a question requires voices to do it in, and thinking through characters inevitably involves the assumption of different viewpoints. Together, antilogy and prosopopoeia (and other modes, to be sure) contribute to making the philosophical discourse of the late fifth century notably open-ended. To think philosophically was not (or not only) to argue a position, but to explore possible views on a subject.

Antilogy and prosopopoeia, are, of course, characteristic of drama. Dramatic thinking is enacted in characters and situations that inevitably present difference or disagreement. Drama thus constantly negotiates authority among the viewpoints presented, and no single figure, with the possible exception of the parabatic chorus of comedy (which addresses the audience in the persona of the author), has a claim to speak for the piece as a whole. Dramatic

---

27. Diogenes Laertius 9.51 reports that Protagoras was the first to claim that there are opposed arguments for any question (A1 DK/D26 LM; compare A20 DK/B27 LM). The claim to make the weaker argument the stronger is attested by Stephanus of Byzantium quoting Eudoxus (A21 DK/D28 LM), but this may simply be a projection of Aristophanes' *Clouds*.

discourse is thus quite closely analogous to much of the discourse of fifth-century philosophy, and the thinking of both can be understood dialectically, as a staging of possibilities.[28] Not all fifth-century philosophical writing exhibits this tendency to nonauthoritative presentation, but where it does, we can often recognize the proximity to drama. The most salient difference between dramatic and nondramatic forms of thought lies not in their formal possibilities but in their occasion: drama was performed at a few public festivals, while the occasions of philosophical thought seem to have been quite varied, including both written and oral transmission, in public and private contexts. This categorical difference in occasion, however, should not obscure substantial similarities in the ways that dramatic and philosophical thought explore topics of shared concern. Whether or not there is a genetic connection between the discourses—a question I leave open—philosophical writing in the late fifth century shares the dialectical mode of drama, thinking through characters, situations, and opposing positions.

This recognition constitutes grounds for reformulating the thesis of Marcel Detienne in his crucial study *The Masters of Truth in Archaic Greece*. Detienne argues that over the course of the fifth century, the concept of truth (*alētheia*) became secularized and politicized.[29] This brings with it a shift from an archaic "logic of ambiguity" that sees truth as a property of speech and a speaker (and is thus always potentially deceptive) to the classical "logic of contradiction" that understands truth as a property of statements (and is thus open to debate). Though Detienne's language is at times troublingly beholden to a teleological opposition of *muthos* and *logos*, I believe the shift he points to is real—provided one understands the poles of his discussion not as absolute possibilities, but as regimes of intellectual authority.[30] "Mythical" and "rational" would name ways of understanding what it is that makes a statement true—its proceeding from an authoritative source, or its emerging from a

---

28. An alternative account of the philosophical dialogue's generic affiliations is found in Leslie Kurke, *Aesopic Conversations: Popular Tradition, Cultural Dialogue, and the Invention of Greek Prose* (Princeton: Princeton University Press, 2011), 241–64.

29. The shift in concepts of truth is traced in Marcel Detienne, *The Masters of Truth in Archaic Greece*, trans. Janet Lloyd (New York: Zone Books, 1996), esp. 89–106.

30. The classic statement of the transition from myth to reason is Wilhelm Nestle, *Vom Mythos zum Logos: Die Selbstfaltung des griechischen Denkens von Homer bis auf die Sophistik und Sokrates* (Stuttgart: Kröner, 1940). Much philosophical thought of the second half of the twentieth century offered a critique of this opposition: see Martin Jay, *Reason after Its Eclipse: On Late Critical Theory* (Madison: University of Wisconsin Press, 2016).

persuasive argument.[31] The fifth century becomes increasingly self-conscious concerning the sources of truth, and comes to see intellectual authority as something that can be demonstrated, questioned, and debated.[32] Detienne describes the emergent form of speech as "dialogue," and though he only glancingly discusses drama, his argument has implications for understanding dramatic as well as philosophical dialogue.[33] Most significant, it suggests that drama and philosophy alike are governed by the same shifting regimes of truth and manifest, in their dialogic form, a developing relation to intellectual authority.

Central to all the dramatic scenes of thought discussed in this study, I argue, is a negotiation of authority. This negotiation can be more or less direct, but it has the philosophical function of subjecting implicit or explicit claims to dialectical examination. My approach, then, explores not just the making of philosophical claims in drama, but the working out of these claims through the construction of a work as a whole. There is a necessary connection between scenic thinking and questions of authority: any philosophical claim made in drama is necessarily refracted through the speaker and situation, and examining this claim involves an examination of the speaker's authority in making it. All of drama's utterances have to be understood as provisional or hypothetical, subject to interrogation over the course of the work. The dialectical approach of this study entails such attention to authority, since considering different positions or viewpoints within a play inevitably means considering the characters who hold them. Before philosophical authority was defined in disciplinary terms, its source was never a given, but always subject to negotiation and contestation. Drama confronts this issue directly by staging authority as a continual question.

The centrality of questions of authority to intellectual culture goes along with a persistent theological concern. To negotiate authority, in the fifth century at least, was inevitably to consider the role of the gods as authorities themselves or as guarantors for human authority. Each of the following

---

31. A different view of the "rational" quality of Greek thought is found in G.E.R. Lloyd, *The Revolutions of Wisdom: Studies in the Claims and Practice of Ancient Greek Science* (Berkeley: University of California Press, 1987), esp. 1–49.

32. Maria Michaela Sassi has importantly emphasized that the shift in authority is not absolute, and most fifth-century thought (including Detienne's favored example of Parmenides) in fact witnesses a "cohabitation" of different forms of authority: Sassi, *The Beginnings of Philosophy in Greece*, 170.

33. Detienne, *Masters of Truth*, 105–6.

chapters thus traces a theological dimension to its inquiry. A teleological viewpoint would see this theological dimension as residual, a way that drama has not yet left behind the thinking of *muthos* for *logos*, but I argue, to the contrary, that the relevant concerns are essentially theological, that the role of the gods in human culture, knowledge, and cognition is a central preoccupation of philosophical thought. One dimension of this preoccupation is obvious enough when one surveys the major thinkers and controversies of the later fifth century—atheism, agnosticism, and unconventional views of divinity are all attested, even if our evidence makes it difficult to work out just what these amounted to in practice—but I find theological questions and anxieties operative in drama well beyond issues of human belief or normative practice (though these are addressed directly in chapter 3). More fundamental, I argue, are attempts to figure the relation of divinity to human existence—as a source of culture, of knowledge, of intellectual authority. Each of the chapters addresses one dimension of this relation, while, collectively, they demonstrate the way that philosophical and theological concerns are inextricable for fifth-century intellectual culture as a whole.

Throughout the book, I discuss comedy (and possibly satyr play, depending on the status of the Sisyphus fragment) in relation to forms that develop primarily in tragedy. This is possible because of comedy's marked and self-conscious positioning of itself in relation to other discourses, its openness to the contemporary world, which makes a strong contrast to tragedy's apparent closure.[34] Old Comedy frequently picks up and elaborates ideas, plot elements, and scenic forms from tragedy and philosophical writing, as well as bringing major figures of contemporary intellectual life on stage. My readings will suggest, though, that its mode of openness is primarily receptive, and that, in comparison to tragedy, Old Comedy does somewhat less productive philosophical work on the scenic forms and questions it engages. Its relation to philosophical thought takes place primarily through parody and critique, and while these tactics often illuminate important dimensions of the ideas and

---

34. The contrast between the genres is discussed in Oliver Taplin, "Fifth-Century Tragedy and Comedy: A Synkrisis," *Journal of Hellenic Studies* 106 (1986): 163–74. For comedy's openness to other genres see Charles Platter, *Aristophanes and the Carnival of Genres* (Baltimore: Johns Hopkins University Press, 2007); Emmanuela Bakola, Lucia Prauscello, and Mario Telò, eds., *Greek Comedy and the Discourse of Genres* (Cambridge: Cambridge University Press, 2013). Tragedy's (more covert and subtle) receptiveness to comedy is treated in Craig Jendza, *Paracomedy: Appropriations of Comedy in Greek Tragedy* (Oxford: Oxford University Press, 2020).

forms they address, I do not find the same degree of independent philosophical work that I do in tragedy. This may be due simply to the limits of the method employed here, and a different approach might better bring out comedy's philosophical contribution. For the present purposes, though, we find in Aristophanic comedy a deep engagement with the questions raised by tragedy and philosophy, and a penetrating response.

While the three parts of the study can be read independently, they can also be understood to chart, in exemplary form, the changing notions of intellectual authority that Detienne points to, from the monologic form of the catalog discussed in the first chapter through the second chapter's dialogic but imbalanced intrigue scene to the balanced debates of the third. The catalog, though formally premised on the speaker's authority to give a complete (in some sense) account, through its dramatic form becomes open to question and doubt, as the utterances of the catalog come into implicit or explicit conflict with the speaker's situation and other statements. The next form, the intrigue scene, begins with a hierarchy of power between an instructor and pupil, but this hierarchy, as the plays go on, comes to reflect doubts concerning the authority of the instructor, or even breaks down entirely. Finally, the debate form is premised on a relatively balanced confrontation between two figures, and uses their confrontation to explore consequential and opposed notions of intellectual authority. Over the course of the three forms, we see, in exemplary fashion, a democratizing of authority, as monologue gives way to dialogue and debate.

Whether this accurately charts a historical development over the course of the fifth century is hard to say, but the chapters do proceed in a roughly chronological order, and each of the forms discussed is associated with one of the three canonical tragedians. The form of the cultural catalog is notably Aeschylean, and is used to survey the inventions or capacities that make human beings civilized. The form extends well beyond Aeschylus (of whose catalogs we only have a few fragments), but some of its central instances in Sophocles and Euripides are notably Aeschylean. The next form discussed, the intrigue prologue, shows parallels to philosophical scenes of instruction such as those in the poems of Parmenides and Empedocles, and treats issues related to their inquiries into reality, knowledge, and the evidence of the senses. The intrigue prologue, in the particular form I discuss, is associated with later Sophocles (though related forms are found in Euripides), who uses it, as Aristophanes does as well, to explore the ethics and politics of deception in the tense years surrounding the oligarchic coup of 411. The final form, debate, is recognized as a broadly Euripidean specialty, and I identify an important subform that stages questions of intellectual authority through confronting opposed claims to wisdom (*sophia*). These debates take place against a philosophical background that, as discussed above, frequently thinks by opposing speakers and speeches, and the dramatic form of the contest, witnessed also in the Aristophanic *agōn* of Euripides and Aeschylus, should be understood as continuous with a wider inquiry into the meaning and location of wisdom.

The three parts of the study unfold in a roughly logical and historical development, though (in accordance with the synchronic method discussed above) none of my central claims relies on accepting such a development, or the associations I propose between forms and dramatists. The developments are, though, helpful in providing a heuristic scaffolding for understanding the disparate material of the study as a whole. Other configurations of the material are surely possible, and the constellations traced here are not in any sense complete or exhaustive. I begin to suggest some possible extensions of the study's approach in the Conclusion, and hope others will critique and refine my methods. This work takes part in a much wider attempt, already well underway, to understand the history of early Greek thought without disciplinary divisions or teleological assumptions. Drama is only one part of this project, and my approach here is ultimately more an experiment than a conclusion. There is much more to be done. The history of philosophical thought before philosophy substantially remains to be written.

1
Catalogs and Culture

IN PLATO's *Phaedrus*, Socrates tells a story about invention:

> Ἤκουσα τοίνυν περὶ Ναύκρατιν τῆς Αἰγύπτου γενέσθαι τῶν ἐκεῖ παλαιῶν τινα θεῶν, οὗ καὶ τὸ ὄρνεον ἱερὸν ὃ δὴ καλοῦσιν Ἶβιν· αὐτῷ δὲ ὄνομα τῷ δαίμονι εἶναι Θεύθ. τοῦτον δὴ πρῶτον ἀριθμόν τε καὶ λογισμὸν εὑρεῖν καὶ γεωμετρίαν καὶ ἀστρονομίαν, ἔτι δὲ πεττείας τε καὶ κυβείας, καὶ δὴ καὶ γράμματα. βασιλέως δ' αὖ τότε ὄντος Αἰγύπτου ὅλης Θαμοῦ περὶ τὴν μεγάλην πόλιν τοῦ ἄνω τόπου ἣν οἱ Ἕλληνες Αἰγυπτίας Θήβας καλοῦσι, καὶ τὸν θεὸν Ἄμμωνα, παρὰ τοῦτον ἐλθὼν ὁ Θεὺθ τὰς τέχνας ἐπέδειξεν, καὶ ἔφη δεῖν διαδοθῆναι τοῖς ἄλλοις Αἰγυπτίοις· ὁ δὲ ἤρετο ἥντινα ἑκάστη ἔχοι ὠφελίαν, διεξιόντος δέ, ὅτι καλῶς ἢ μὴ καλῶς δοκοῖ λέγειν, τὸ μὲν ἔψεγεν, τὸ δ' ἐπῄνει. (274c–d)

> Well then, I heard that at Naucratis in Egypt there was one of the ancient gods of the place, whose sacred bird is the one they call Ibis. The name of the divinity himself was Theuth. And he was the first to invent number and calculation, and geometry and astronomy, and also draughts and dice, and best of all, letters. At that time Thamus was the king of all Egypt surrounding the great city of the upper part, which the Greeks call Egyptian Thebes, and the god they call Ammon. Theuth came to him and displayed his skills, and he said they should be given to the other Egyptians. And Thamus asked him what benefit each of them had, and when Theuth explained, as he seemed to speak well or badly, some Thamus blamed and some he praised.

What follows is the famous critique of writing, in which Thamus rejects the technology of letters on the grounds that it will serve merely as an "elixir of reminding" (275a: ὑπομνήσεως φάρμακον) rather than of memory, making humans "apparently wise" (275b: δοξόσοφοι) rather than truly so.¹ The myth is likely a Platonic invention, but Socrates emphasizes the antiquity of the events it describes: it is a story (ἀκοή, literally, "thing heard") of "those earlier" (τῶν προτέρων), and concerns "one of the ancient gods" (274c: παλαιῶν τινα θεῶν) of Egypt, a civilization thought to be much older than the Greeks.² Despite this exotic background, the content of the story nevertheless evokes familiar Greek myths of invention, which seem to have gained a particular salience in the later fifth century, as part of a widespread interest in human skills or crafts.³ Moreover, the context of the telling points directly to the myth's application to the contemporary practice of rhetoric, a theme from the beginning of the dialogue.⁴ Locating the myth among the Egyptian gods has the effect of placing its events outside of historical time, even as the thrust of the telling points to its timeliness as a comment on writing and rhetoric in the sophistic era.

---

1. The literature on the critique of writing is massive. Formative for modern accounts is Jacques Derrida, "Plato's Pharmacy," in *Dissemination*, trans. Barbara Johnson (Chicago: University of Chicago Press, 1981), 61–171. Places to begin are Ronna Burger, *Plato's "Phaedrus": A Defense of a Philosophic Art of Writing* (Tuscaloosa: University of Alabama Press, 1980); G.R.F. Ferrari, *Listening to the Cicadas: A Study of Plato's "Phaedrus"* (Cambridge: Cambridge University Press, 1987), 204–32; Christopher Moore, "The Myth of Theuth in the 'Phaedrus,'" in *Plato and Myth: Studies on the Use and Status of Platonic Myths*, ed. Catherine Collobert, Pierre Destrée, and Francisco J. Gonzalez (Leiden: Brill, 2012), 279–303; Daniel S. Werner, *Myth and Philosophy in Plato's "Phaedrus"* (Cambridge: Cambridge University Press, 2012), 181–235. For my purposes, the significance of the myth lies not in Socrates' or Plato's critique of writing specifically, but in its view of invention and human culture.

2. On the idea of Egypt, see Erik Iversen, *The Myth of Egypt and Its Hieroglyphs in European Tradition* (Princeton: Princeton University Press, 1993), 42–43; Luc Brisson, "L'Égypte de Platon," *Études philosophiques* 2/3 (1987): 153–168; and the essays in Ian Rutherford, ed., *Greco-Egyptian Interactions: Literature, Translation, and Culture, 500 BC–AD 300* (Oxford: Oxford University Press, 2016).

3. The importance of *technai* for thought about human culture is emphasized by Christian Meier, "Ein antikes Äquivalent des Fortschrittsgedankens: das 'Könnens-Bewusstsein' des 5. Jahrhunderts v. Chr.," *Historische Zeitschrift* 226 (1978): 265–316; Christian Utzinger, *Periphrades Aner: Untersuchungen zum ersten Stasimon der Sophokleischen "Antigone" und zu den antiken Kulturentstehungstheorien* (Göttingen: Vandenhoeck & Ruprecht, 2003), 97–99.

4. On the role of the myth in the *Phaedrus* as a whole, see (in addition to the citations above) Marina McCoy, *Plato on the Rhetoric of Philosophers and Sophists* (Cambridge: Cambridge University Press, 2007), 167–96; Harvey Yunis, "Dialectic and the Purpose of Rhetoric in Plato's 'Phaedrus,'" *Proceedings of the Boston Area Colloquium in Ancient Philosophy* 24 (2009): 229–59; Robin Reames, *Seeming and Being in Plato's Rhetorical Theory* (Chicago: University of Chicago Press, 2018), 47–76.

Though Socrates is most of all interested in the invention of writing and its consequences, the myth suggests a much wider view of human culture. The inventions that Socrates attributes to Theuth constitute a minor catalog, organized from the substantial ("he invented numbers and calculation") to the relatively trivial ("and also draughts and dice"), and capped by the most important, "and best of all [καὶ δὴ καί], letters." Theuth's innovations relate broadly to numeracy: with the crucial exception of letters, all the items mentioned can be understood as developments of the invention of number.[5] As this chapter will show, the inventions of Theuth were widely attributed to the Greek hero Palamedes, and would probably have been recognizable as such.[6] In transferring these inventions from a Greek hero to an Egyptian god, the myth places the sources of culture at a deep remove, and leaves open the question of how the Greeks gained these inventions (not to mention how writing was introduced in Egypt after its initial rejection). Thamus' response to the inventions of Theuth suggests a general skepticism of innovation: accepting some but not others, he addresses Theuth as *technikōtatos* (274e: "most skillful," or even "most inventive"), which turns out to be a rather equivocal distinction, as Thamus goes on to reject Theuth's prized *technē*.[7] Inventiveness, it appears, is not a good in itself, but must be judged by the uses to which it is put. On the whole, the myth suggests a pessimism concerning invention, a concern that advances in human technology could prove setbacks in human culture as a whole.[8]

---

5. There may be a relation between the myth and Pythagoreanism: Pythagoras is reputed to have said that "number is the wisest of all things" (πάντων σοφώτατον ὁ ἀριθμός; C2 DK/D25 LM). See Phillip Sidney Horky, *Plato and Pythagoreanism* (Oxford: Oxford University Press, 2013), 204–6.

6. The most distinctive Palamedan benefactions (number, draughts and dice, and letters) are all present in the *Phaedrus* myth, and the only unparalleled element is geometry. Plato refers to Palamedes' discovery of number (and thereby of calculation) at *Republic* 522d. It is often thought that the primary model for the inventor Theuth is Prometheus (relying primarily on the *Prometheus Bound*): for example, in C. J. Rowe, ed., *Plato: "Phaedrus"* (Oxford: Aris & Phillips, 1986), 208–9. The tradition of Prometheus as inventor, though, is a minority one, while the inclusion of draughts and dice clearly suggests Palamedes as the primary model.

7. Nightingale argues that the *Phaedrus* passage represents a veiled criticism of Palamedes: Nightingale, *Genres in Dialogue*, 149–54. More likely, I think, is the reverse: given the persistent identification of Socrates with Palamedes among the Socratics (Plato, *Apology* 41b; Xenophon, *Apology* 26; *Memorabilia* 4.2.33), the displacement of these inventions to an Egyptian god is better read as sparing Palamedes the ignominy of the invention of writing.

8. On Plato's critique of invention, see Horky, *Plato and Pythagoreanism*, 210–22.

Socrates' skepticism concerning inventors and inventions is extreme but not unique. The *Phaedrus* myth emerges from a wider discourse concerning the sources of culture, which attributes lists of inventions or capacities to discrete individuals, divine or human, or to culture generally. These lists frequently express a sense of doubt or pessimism concerning the apparent advances of human culture, doubts which tend to center on the authority of the inventor, and specifically, the relation between human abilities and divine power. The myth's suggestion that mortals are better off without certain inventions speaks to tensions within a wider effort to grasp human cultural achievement and locate humanity in relation to the gods. This chapter will trace these tensions in Attic drama, where they concentrate around the form of the "cultural catalog," a listing of inventions, gifts, or capacities that provides an image of culture as a whole, and reflects on the sources of authority and power in human existence. So much was evident already in Socrates' myth, which, despite its relatively simple list of inventions, set out a series of hierarchies—among the gods and between gods and humans—that determined the role of invention as an ambiguous mediation between mortals and divinity.

A central preoccupation of all the catalogs is the place of humans in the hierarchy of existence—subjected to gods on one hand, but ascendant over (nonhuman) animals on the other.[9] The most salient conceptual differences arise from different ways of figuring relations of power—of the gods over humans, and of humans over animals. Humans' mastery of their environment appears in the dramatic catalogs as one of the essential achievements of culture, and often as a mark of ascent from an initial, animal-like phase of existence.[10] At the same time, all the catalogs retain an acute consciousness of

---

9. For ease of reading, I will refer to nonhuman animals simply as "animals" in the rest of the chapter, though recognizing the anthropocentrism of such usage (which the Greek texts by and large seem to share).

10. The idea of an early, bestial phase of culture is known as the "doctrine of primeval brutishness." On its sources, see Michael J. O'Brien, "Xenophanes, Aeschylus, and the Doctrine of Primeval Brutishness," *Classical Quarterly* 35 (1985): 264–77; J. H. Lesher, "Xenophanes on Inquiry and Discovery: An Alternative to the 'Hymn to Progress' Reading of Fr. 18," *Ancient Philosophy* 11 (1991): 229–48; Alexander Tulin, "Xenophanes Fr. 18 D.-K. and the Origins of the Idea of Progress," *Hermes* 121 (1993): 129–38. In attempting to date the doctrine, much hangs on the interpretation of Xenophanes B18 DK/D53 LM, and on the attribution of Aeschylus F 181a (discussed below). The earliest evidence for an idea of differentiation of human from animal life outside of these fragments appears to be Archelaus A4 DK/D2 LM (thought to be ca. 450), though there is a possibility that something similar figured earlier in Anaxagoras: Gábor Betegh, "Socrate et Archélaos dans les 'Nuées': Philosophie naturelle et éthique," in *Comédie et philosophie: Socrate et les "Présocratiques" dans les "Nuées" d'Aristophane*, ed. André Laks and Rosella

divine power, which can be viewed either negatively, as a limitation on human capacity, or positively, as the source of human achievement. The catalogs do not take categories of "human," "animal," and "divine" for granted, but construct them out of observed and imagined processes. This construction yields an aporetic picture to careful reading, which throws into question the authority of the speakers and the content of their catalogs. I understand this tendency of the catalogs to undermine their own claims as revealing an anxiety, present in Socrates' myth as well, concerning the sources of culture: whether it is an achievement of humans or the gods, and what its ultimate value is. This is an element of a much broader questioning of divinity and the role of the gods in human affairs that will be explored, in different ways, throughout the study, and is, I will argue, the major motivation behind the catalog's attempt to fix the human place in the cosmos.

The chapter will follow different forms of the cultural catalog from the relatively simple (and probably historically prior) speeches of Palamedes and Prometheus to the more dramatically complex catalogs of Theseus in Euripides' *Suppliants* and the first stasimon of the *Antigone*. In all these texts, I will argue, the cultural catalog seeks to grasp the essential elements of human culture and understand the relationship to divinity. Yet instead of yielding a clear picture of human and divine agency, the rhetoric and staging of the catalogs have a tendency to complicate the theological issues they raise. Finally, I turn for comparison to the "Sisyphus fragment" attributed to Critias, which shows an extreme form of such theological questioning, and also illustrates a major formal difference between the cultural catalog and developmental narratives of human civilization, which seem to have circulated around the same time. The cultural catalog emerges as a form that is at once distinctive in the intellectual work it does and informed by the most urgent questions of fifth-century intellectual culture.

Cataloguing the Human

A literary catalog is more and less than the items it contains. More, in the sense that the power of the whole is greater than the cumulative power of its items; less, in that each item is relatively indifferent to the whole. Catalogs outside of

---

Saetta Cottone (Paris: Rue d'Ulm, 2013), 87–106; Gábor Betegh, "Archelaus on Cosmogony and the Origins of Social Institutions," *Oxford Studies in Ancient Philosophy* 51 (2016): 1–40. Betegh argues that Archelaus' originality lies in combining a cosmogony (a standard feature of earlier philosophical writing) with an account of culture.

literature (shopping lists, attendance rosters, indices) are basically functional: they record information efficiently, with minimal connection between items— even when, as often, the selection and organization of items are rhetorically or ideologically motivated. In Greek culture as in our own, such functional catalogs were widespread and familiar.[11] They have often been connected to the origins of writing, and many of the earliest written documents we possess are lists of various kinds.[12] Literary catalogs, though they may transmit information (the ships that sailed to Troy, the children of Iapetus), have a more complicated relation to function.[13] They generally do not advance narrative, and often act to interrupt plot. Moreover, the specific information they transmit is usually of limited importance to the work as a whole. The significance of a literary catalog lies, I suggest, in the way it establishes a relation between a speaker or text and an audience or reader.

This relation is most importantly a relation of authority. Literary catalogs propose completeness, and thereby claim authority for the speaker. The listener may or may not assent to this claim, may doubt the accuracy of the catalog or the knowledge of the speaker, but the pretense to authority is crucial to understanding the operations of literary catalogs. Catalogs are a widespread feature of oral epic across cultures, frequently employed by the Homeric and Hesiodic bards, and have an important role in establishing the ability of their speakers to tell of long-past and divine occurrences.[14] Epic catalogs, by and

---

11. On catalogs in Greek culture generally, see Athena Kirk, *The Tally of Text: Catalogs and Inventories in Ancient Greece* (forthcoming).

12. Essential on early lists and writing is Jack Goody, *The Domestication of the Savage Mind* (Cambridge: Cambridge University Press, 1977), 77–111. Goody's argument that lists are products of a literate society seems to be undermined by the Greek example, but the historical and anthropological evidence is nevertheless valuable. A more nuanced view is in Richard Gordon, "'What's in a List?' Listing in Greek and Graeco-Roman Malign Magical Texts," in *The World of Ancient Magic: Papers from the First International Samson Eitrem Seminar at the Norwegian Institute at Athens, 4–8 May 1997*, ed. David R. Jordan, Hugo Montgomery, and Einar Thomassen (Bergen: Norwegian Institute at Athens, 1999), 239–77.

13. On the relation of literary and pragmatic lists generally, see Robert Belknap, "The Literary List: A Survey of Its Uses and Deployments," *Literary Imagination* 2 (2000): 35–54. One should not, though, press the distinction between literary and pragmatic lists too far: as Kirk, *Tally of the Text* convincingly shows, both types of list have similar relations to the items catalogued (though their functions may be substantially different).

14. Catalogs are often thought to be connected to the origins of epic poetry generally, and there is a voluminous literature on epic catalogs. On Homer, major references are: Benjamin Sammons, *The Art and Rhetoric of the Homeric Catalogue* (Oxford: Oxford University Press,

large, claim completeness: they purport to list the entirety of a collective, and the bard's authority is premised on comprehensive knowledge and a virtuosic abililty to perform it, often guaranteed by the Muses.[15]

In contrast to these exhaustive catalogs, there is another catalogic impulse in which the items listed do not constitute the entirety of the collective, but rather present an exemplary subset. This chapter will focus on such exemplary catalogs. Solon's *Elegy to the Muses* offers an early and important example. In the course of describing the ways that humans delude themselves, the speaker lists a series of professions, introduced by a statement of the variety of human pursuits:

σπεύδει δ' ἄλλοθεν ἄλλος· ὁ μὲν κατὰ πόντον ἀλᾶται
    ἐν νηυσὶν χρῄζων οἴκαδε κέρδος ἄγειν
ἰχθυόεντ' ἀνέμοισι φορεόμενος ἀργαλέοισιν,
    φειδωλὴν ψυχῆς οὐδεμίαν θέμενος·
ἄλλος γῆν τέμνων πολυδένδρεον εἰς ἐνιαυτὸν
    λατρεύει, τοῖσιν καμπύλ' ἄροτρα μέλει·
ἄλλος Ἀθηναίης τε καὶ Ἡφαίστου πολυτέχνεω
    ἔργα δαεὶς χειροῖν ξυλλέγεται βίοτον,
ἄλλος Ὀλυμπιάδων Μουσέων πάρα δῶρα διδαχθείς,
    ἱμερτῆς σοφίης μέτρον ἐπιστάμενος· (13 West 43–52)

Everyone strives differently. One wanders across the fishy sea in ships seeking to bring profit home, borne by harsh winds, undertaking no sparing of

---

2010); Christos Tsagalis, "The Dynamic Hypertext: Lists and Catalogues in the Homeric Epics," *Trends in Classics* 2 (2010): 323–347; Pietro Pucci, "Between Narrative and Catalogue: Life and Death of the Poem," *Métis* 11 (1996): 5–24; Elizabeth Minchin, "The Performance of Lists and Catalogues in the Homeric Epics," in *Voice into Text: Orality and Literacy in Ancient Greece*, ed. Ian Worthington (Leiden: Brill, 1996), 3–20; William G. Thalmann, *Conventions of Form and Thought in Early Greek Epic Poetry* (Baltimore: Johns Hopkins University Press, 1984); Mark W. Edwards, "The Structure of Homeric Catalogues," *Transactions of the American Philological Association* 110 (1980): 81–105. The literature on catalogs in Hesiod is less extensive (and much of the literature on the Hesiodic *Catalog of Women* does not address the form of the catalog explicitly): Marcel Humar, "Catalogues and Ring Compositions in Hesiod's 'Theogony,'" *Hermes* 144 (2016): 384–400; Christopher A. Faraone, "The Poetics of the Catalogue in the Hesiodic 'Theogony,'" *Transactions of the American Philological Association* 143 (2013): 293–323; Christos Tsagalis, "Poetry and Poetics in the Hesiodic Corpus," in *Brill's Companion to Hesiod*, ed. Franco Montanari, Antonios Rengakos, and Christos Tsagalis (Leiden: Brill, 2009), 131–77.

15. Kirk, *Tally of the Text*, ch. 1 discusses the way that catalogs paradoxically present their contents as uncountable.

his life. Another, to whom the curved plow is a care, works for hire, cutting the much-wooded land throughout the year. Another, who has learned the works of Athena and many-skilled Hephaestus, makes his living with his two hands; another [makes his living] having been taught the gifts of the Olympian Muses and knowing the measure of lovely skill.

It is not entirely clear what this is a catalog of, but it goes on to list diviners and doctors as other professions subject to uncertainty, for whom "there is no end at hand" (58: οὐδὲν ἔπεστι τέλος). Though the professions listed contribute something important to the poem, they are presented, in effect, *exempli gratia* and could, within the logic of the catalog, be exchanged for others that would illustrate the same conclusion.[16] Such catalogs, though claiming a kind of completeness, thus differ substantially from the exhaustive catalogs of epic—and even more from the functional catalogs of everyday life. The authority of Solon's catalog is based not on comprehensive knowledge of particulars, but on the speaker's insight into universal qualities of human culture.[17]

Catalogs in drama differ from both the exhaustive catalogs of the inspired bard and the exemplary catalogs of the wise speaker. Drama has no authoritative voice, so its catalogs are always importantly refracted through character and situation, and involve listeners, on stage and off, in a complex judgment. The dramatic speaker's claim to authority constitutes an assertion that the rest of the play may or may not bear out, and is thus inherently insecure. This is particularly evident in comedy, which frequently employs lists to humorous

---

16. For interpretation of the Solonic list, see Maria Noussia Fantuzzi, *Solon the Athenian: The Poetic Fragments* (Leiden: Brill, 2010), 175–77; Christopher A. Faraone, *The Stanzaic Architecture of Early Greek Elegy* (Oxford: Oxford University Press, 2008), 35–40. The immediately previous topic is the way that humans are deluded by hopes, which introduces a three-item catalog of such delusions. The catalog of professions seems to be loosely connected to the last of these, the poor man who hopes to be wealthy, and the first groups mentioned (sailors, farmers, artisans, and poets) appear illustrative of the ways that humans secure a livelihood. This focus lessens, though, with the relatively lengthy descriptions of prophets and healers, which do not mention earning a livelihood explicitly, and emphasize the uncertainty of the outcomes of their professions. The links between items seem to be associative, and the whole is probably best understood, along the lines I suggest concerning the cultural catalog, as a form of anthropology, which offers an encompassing view of human activity organized by Solon's ethical outlook.

17. Solon's generalizing perspective is thus akin to the Shield of *Iliad* 18, which similarly presents its contents as exemplary of a totalizing view of human life. On the contrast between the Homeric Shield and catalog, see Umberto Eco, *The Infinity of Lists*, trans. Alastair McEwen (New York: Rizzoli, 2009), 9–18.

effect, juxtaposing the authority of the act of list making with the triviality of the items listed.[18] Indeed, dramatic catalogs may inevitably elicit challenges, implicit or explicit, to the authority they claim (as was evident in Theuth's catalog, which was immediately undermined by Thamus' judgments of his inventions). Consider the way that Aeschylus employs catalogs in *Persians*: the work begins with the chorus chanting anapests, the bulk of which are given over to a list of Persian commanders (16–58) infused with a sense of power and pride. Over the course of the play, two further, partially overlapping catalogs of names track the utter destruction visited on the Persian army, first in a messenger speech listing the dead from the battle of Salamis (302–29), and then in an exchange between the chorus and Xerxes, in which the chorus inquires about commanders individually, and is told that they have all perished.[19] Aeschylus' employment of the catalog over the course of the work encapsulates the way that the Persians go from a proud, conquering army to a defeated, lamenting force. Catalogs in drama claim a monologic authority, but such authority is not necessarily (or even frequently) upheld by the rest of the play.

Aeschylus' works are full of catalogs, mostly of people and places: beyond those of the *Persians*, important ones are the locations of Clytemnestra's beacon relay in the *Agamemnon*, the gods to whom the Pythia prays in the *Eumenides*, and the names and descriptions of the Seven against Thebes.[20] Such catalogs of proper names occur, too, in the works of Sophocles and Euripides, though with somewhat lesser frequency, and often have an epic flavor.[21] But

---

18. Comic list making is discussed in Kirk, *Tally of the Text*, ch. 5; M. S. Silk, *Aristophanes and the Definition of Comedy* (Oxford: Oxford University Press, 2002), 126–35; Elias S. Spyropoulos, *L'accumulation verbale chez Aristophane: Recherches sur le style d'Aristophane* (Thessaloniki: Aristotelian University, 1974).

19. The lists of *Persians* have attracted a good deal of attention: A. F. Garvie, ed., *"Persae"* (Oxford: Oxford University Press, 2009), 161; Susanne Saïd, "Tragedy and Reversal: The Example of the 'Persians,'" in *Oxford Readings in Classical Studies: Aeschylus*, ed. Michael Lloyd (Oxford: Oxford University Press, 2007 [originally 1988]), 81–83; Mary Ebbott, "The List of the War Dead in Aeschylus' 'Persians,'" *Harvard Studies in Classical Philology* 100 (2000): 83–96; Simon Goldhill, "Battle Narrative and Politics in Aeschylus' 'Persae,'" *Journal of Hellenic Studies* 108 (1988): 192.

20. On Aeschylean lists in general, see Thomas G. Rosenmeyer, *The Art of Aeschylus* (Berkeley: University of California Press, 1982), 109–17.

21. Euripidean catalogs frequently call up poetic predecessors: lists of the Seven against Thebes in *Phoenician Women* (119–92, 1104–40) and *Suppliants* (860–908) draw heavily on Aeschylus' *Seven* (and, in the first case, the Homeric *teichoskopia* as well), and the catalogs of

there is another Aeschylean catalogic impulse, more akin to the Solonic example, of catalogs focused on inventions, benefactions, or achievements that characterize human culture as a whole. These Aeschylean catalogs, which form the prehistory to the inventions of Theuth, are the focus of this chapter. The most famous examples are the "Great Speech" of Prometheus in the *Prometheus Bound* attributed to Aeschylus and the first stasimon of Sophocles' *Antigone*, both of which celebrate the skills of human beings and their mastery over the natural world. They take the form of a listing of various inventions or capacities that human beings possess, whether divinely given (as in the *Prometheus*) or developed by mortals (in the *Antigone*). These lists—and others like them—are quite similar in the items mentioned, and seem to draw from a shared repertoire. Commonalities of form and content argue for a consideration of such catalogs together, as a coherent body of thought, which I call the "cultural catalog."

The prevailing assumption about these catalogs is that they draw their content from contemporary philosophical discourse associated with the sophists and other thinkers of the mid-to-late fifth century. Two distinct but overlapping traditions are thought to contribute: the investigation of the origins and development of human culture, and an interest in inventors and inventions. Both inquiries, though not unique to the classical period, seem to develop into preoccupations for late fifth-century intellectual culture, in close connection with concerns of *nomos* ("law" or "custom") and *phusis* ("nature"), and the historical and encyclopedic impulses of intellectuals like Hippias.[22] As I will

---

commanders and ships (192–205, 242–93) in the parodos of the *Iphigenia at Aulis* are strongly Homeric. The authenticity of all but the *Suppliants* passage has been doubted: on the *Phoenician Women*, see Donald J. Mastronarde, ed., *Euripides: "Phoenissae"* (Cambridge: Cambridge University Press, 1994), 168–73, 456–59. On the *Iphigenia at Aulis*: Christopher Collard and James Morwood, eds., *Euripides: "Iphigenia at Aulis"* (Liverpool: Liverpool University Press, 2017), 293–95. Assuming the authenticity of at least some of these, Euripides would be using catalogs in a highly self-conscious way to signal proximity and distance from his predecessors: Anna A. Lamari, "Aeschylus' 'Seven against Thebes' vs. Euripides' 'Phoenissae': Male vs. Female Power," *Wiener Studien* 120 (2007): 5–24; Isabelle Torrance, *Metapoetry in Euripides* (Oxford: Oxford University Press, 2013), 94–129.

22. On *nomos* and *phusis*, see Felix Heinimann, *Nomos und Physis: Herkunft und Bedeutung einer Antithese im griechischen Denken des 5. Jahrhunderts* (Basel: Reinhardt, 1965); W.K.C. Guthrie, *The Sophists* (Cambridge: Cambridge University Press, 1971), 55–84; G. B. Kerferd, *The Sophistic Movement* (Cambridge: Cambridge University Press, 1981), 111–30; Richard Bett, "Nature and Norms," in *The Cambridge Companion to the Sophists*, ed. Joshua Billings and Christopher Moore (Cambridge: Cambridge University Press, forthcoming). On Hippias' catalogs

argue, however, the cultural catalog in drama, though drawing on some of the same impulses, is importantly distinct from both these strands, and constitutes a parallel discourse. To be sure, the dramatic discourse shares in a widespread sense that humanity in the present is profoundly shaped by its history—this is a major binding thread to fifth-century thought broadly—but the cultural catalog affords a distinctive mode of inquiry into human culture and its historical existence.[23]

The fifth century's developmental perspective on human culture is attested by a heterogeneous range of texts, which point to a broadly shared but significantly dispersed inquiry, with no clear origin. Important sources include the Sisyphus fragment attributed to Critias (to which this chapter will turn in closing), the Hippocratic *On Ancient Medicine*, the Prometheus myth of Plato's *Protagoras*, and reconstructions of Democritean anthropology.[24] By virtue of its direct transmission in the Hippocratic corpus, *On Ancient Medicine*, widely dated to the late fifth or early fourth century, represents the most reliable evidence for what such an inquiry may have entailed.[25] It describes a teleology of discovery, in which medicine arose in response to necessity (ἀνάγκη) and continues to develop toward a state of perfection. From the simple observation that human beings and animals require different foods to thrive, there developed a method for the improvement of human diets by attention to individual needs, which constitutes the basis of medicine. The author confidently asserts that by medicine "many excellent discoveries have been

---

generally, see Paul Christesen, "Imagining Olympia: Hippias of Elis and the First Olympian Victor List," in *A Tall Order: Writing the Social History of the Ancient World*, ed. Jean-Jacques Aubert and Zsuzsanna Várhelyi (Munich: Saur, 2005), 322–24. Hippias' *Synagoge* appears to have been a large collection of quotations organized thematically, and was a major source for ancient doxography: Andreas Patzer, *Der Sophist Hippias als Philosophiehistoriker* (Freiburg: K. Alber, 1986); Jaap Mansfeld, "Aristotle, Plato, and the Preplatonic Doxography and Chronology," in *Studies in the Historiography of Greek Philosophy* (Assen: Van Gorcum, 1990), 22–83; Jean-François Balaudé, "Hippias le Passeur," in *La costruzione del discorso filosofico nell'età dei Presocratici*, ed. Maria Michela Sassi (Pisa: Edizioni della Normale, 2006), 287–304.

23. On form as a kind of "affordance," see Levine, *Forms*, 6–11.

24. Major discussions of cultural development are Woldemar Uxkull-Gyllenband, *Griechische Kultur-Entstehungslehren* (Berlin: Simion, 1924); Thomas Cole, *Democritus and the Sources of Greek Anthropology* (Cleveland: Western Reserve University Press, 1967); O'Brien, "Doctrine of Primeval Brutishness"; Deborah Levine Gera, *Ancient Greek Ideas on Speech, Language, and Civilization* (Oxford: Oxford University Press, 2003); Utzinger, *Periphrades Aner*.

25. On the intellectual context of the work and its dating, see Mark J. Schiefsky, ed., *Hippocrates: "On Ancient Medicine"* (Leiden: Brill, 2005), 46–64.

discovered over a long time and the remainder will be discovered" (2.1: τὰ εὑρημένα πολλά τε καὶ καλῶς ἔχοντα εὕρηται ἐν πολλῷ χρόνῳ, καὶ τὰ λοιπὰ εὑρεθήσεται). The text reflects a widespread interest in human *technai*, and places these skills into a historical narrative that envisions a gradual, and continuing, development. The developmental logic of the text is exceptionally clear, and suggests a wider background of conceiving the processual nature of human culture.[26]

The interest in invention, by contrast, addresses the origins, rather than the development, of human *technai*. Archaic Greek literature often points to a "first inventor" (*prōtos heuretēs*) of objects or practices, and from the fifth century onward this could take on a more organized, catalogic form, ascribing a series of inventions to their inventors.[27] Though such catalogs seem to come into their own in the Hellenistic period, they have earlier roots, for which our best evidence is a few ethnographic texts by Critias dating to the late fifth century. A fragment of Critias' elegiac poetry (B 2 DK/2 West) consists of a series of ascriptions to different regions of practices and objects more or less directly connected to the symposium: the game of *kottabos* comes from Sicily, the most comfortable chair from Thessaly, and so on. The listing, which seems rather miscellaneous, demonstrates the poet's learning and cosmopolitanism, and calls attention to the diverse origins of many things that would have been taken for granted.[28] Such catalogs of inventions and their sources suggest a view of culture as a composite of heterogeneous practices. This is a very different tendency from that of the developmental narratives discussed above: rather than presenting culture as governed by laws of necessity leading logically from past to present, invention narratives trace present culture backwards and suggest

---

26. The closest parallel to *Ancient Medicine*'s developmental logic is found in (disputed) reconstructions of Democritus: Schiefsky, *Hippocrates: "On Ancient Medicine,"* 157–60.

27. The interest in first inventors is surveyed in Martin Kremmer, *De catalogis heurematum* (Leipzig, 1890); Adolf Kleingünther, πρῶτος εὑρετής: *Untersuchungen zur Geschichte einer Fragestellung* (Leipzig: Dieterich, 1933); Klaus Thraede, "Das Lob des Erfinders: Bemerkungen zur Analyse der Heuremata-Kataloge," *Rheinisches Museum* 105 (1962): 158–86; Leonid Zhmud, *The Origin of the History of Science in Classical Antiquity*, trans. Alexander Chernoglazov (Berlin: de Gruyter, 2006).

28. Critias' ethnographic texts are discussed in Alessandro Iannucci, *La parola e l'azione: I frammenti simposiali di Crizia* (Bologna: Nautilus, 2002), 79–107; Frances Pownall, "Critias' Commemoration of Athens," *Mouseion* 8 (2008): 333–54. The conjunction of the developmental perspective of the Sisyphus fragment with the more ethnographic texts on invention could suggest that a general perspective on human culture was a central preoccupation for Critias.

its contingency. Invention narratives thus have a tendency to denaturalize their objects, pointing to the local and specific origins of familiar practices and technologies.

The primary intellectual contribution of the cultural catalog in drama has most often been described in terms of an account of human development (the German word is often used: *Kulturentstehungslehre* or *-theorie*) or a "concept of progress"—which, though importantly different, are often assimilated in scholarship.[29] Most of the texts discussed in this chapter, for example, are included under the rubric "The Progress of Civilization" in the Dramatic Appendix to the Laks-Most *Early Greek Philosophy*.[30] I argue, however, that catalogs of culture function most importantly not to elaborate a historical or quasihistorical account of the origins and development of human society—to say nothing of a theory of progress. Rather, I suggest that the central intellectual function of the cultural catalog is to outline an anthropology, an account of the distinctiveness of human life, the extent of human capacities, and the conditions of human autonomy.[31] The core idea is not diachronic—progress or development—but synchronic, the differentiation of humans from animals, on one hand, and from divinity, on the other. An important and overlooked index of this synchronic tendency is that, unlike the developmental accounts mentioned above, none of the catalogs describe intermediate stages between precivilized and developed culture, offering instead an exemplary listing of the inventions or capacities that distinguish human beings from other forms of life. Even when progressive or developmental in framing, these catalogs exhibit the tendency of all lists to dissolve sequence into accumulation, to spatialize the thinking they incorporate. The cultural catalog considers what makes human beings who they are, rather than how they got that way.

---

29. Major sources on the concept of progress are Eric A. Havelock, *The Liberal Temper in Greek Politics* (New Haven: Yale University Press, 1957); Ludwig Edelstein, *The Idea of Progress in Classical Antiquity* (Baltimore: Johns Hopkins University Press, 1967); E. R. Dodds, "The Ancient Concept of Progress," in *The Ancient Concept of Progress and Other Essays on Greek Literature and Belief* (Oxford: Clarendon Press, 1973), 1–25; Meier, "Ein antikes Äquivalent des Fortschrittsgedankens."

30. André Laks and Glenn W. Most, *Early Greek Philosophy* (Cambridge, MA: Harvard University Press, 2016), 9, 328–45.

31. I use the term "anthropology" in a narrower sense than does Hose, who draws on the Kantian idea of anthropology as general knowledge of humans and their motivations: Martin Hose, *Euripides als Anthropologe* (Munich: Bayerische Akademie der Wissenschaften, 2009).

Recognizing these texts as catalogs implies a complex relation to the works in which they appear. A literary catalog necessarily stands out, to some degree, from its context. Literary catalogs generally have the effect of arresting plot, though they have various internal means of suggesting narrative (as the cultural catalog often does).[32] They can be more or less ordered (including temporally, to give an effect of narrative) and more or less coherent, but necessarily have a degree of structural closure in relation to the rest of a text.[33] The structural closure of catalogs has important consequences for criticism, which must grapple with their rhetorical density. Doing this rhetoric justice entails giving somewhat less weight than most close reading would to the specific terms of the catalog (which are relatively interchangeable) than to modes of presentation, connection, and organization. What emerges from such reading is an understanding of the way the catalog configures authority between speaker, speech, audiences (internal and external), and situation. This configuration can change over the course of a given work, with important consequences for understanding the catalog's philosophical significance. Though the catalog is itself a static, relatively enclosed form, its thinking within a work is dynamic, and reflects on the speaker's other utterances and actions as a kind of hypothesis. This creates the possibility of a dialectic in which the authoritative speech of the catalog is challenged and alternative anthropologies posited. For the sake of concision, I will limit myself to considering the challenges of the speaker's own utterances, but the inquiry could be extended to the entirety of a play's anthropological discourse. Understanding the poetics of the catalog in drama entails attention to the way its thinking is open to the rest of the work and to its audience.

Palamedes: The Catalog and Invention

The most basic form of the cultural catalog is a simple listing of gifts or inventions attributed to a single individual, like the inventions of Theuth. The fifth century sees a range of examples of such catalogs centering on the figures of Palamedes and Prometheus, which enumerate broadly similar items. Such

---

32. The relation of catalogs to narrative is a guiding concern in Sammons, *The Art and Rhetoric of the Homeric Catalogue*. His readings convincingly demonstrate the ways that narrative is often implicit in Homeric catalogs.

33. The various possibilities of the catalog form are well enumerated in Sabine Mainberger, *Die Kunst des Aufzählens: Elemente zu einer Poetik des Enumerativen* (Berlin: de Gruyter, 2003), 6–13.

dramatic listings are clearly related to the archaic interest in *prōtoi heuretai* and to catalogs of inventions attested from later in the century, but they actually do something quite different: not trace discrete inventions backwards to their inventors—a genealogical impulse—but explain the entirety of society as the work of a single inventor—an anthropological impulse, which lays the weight much more on the present than on the past. While invention narratives present an analytic view of the present as made of discrete pasts, the cultural catalog suggests a synthetic view, presenting culture as the totalizing work of a single figure. Another, more speculative, context for the dramatic catalogs may be ritual practice, which often incorporates lists of deeds of a single figure (aretalogies), important persons or events, or even, apparently, abstract concepts.[34] Though the evidence is somewhat later, the Isis aretalogies are quite similar in form to fifth-century benefaction catalogs: they involve extensive lists, written in the first person, of the deeds of the god, with almost no connection between them ("I did this . . . I did this . . .").[35] The benefaction catalogs of Palamedes and Prometheus can have an incantatory quality, which may be heard against a ritual background.[36] Their content, at any rate, clearly establishes their speakers as powerful (and, in Prometheus' case, divine) figures, who have made human existence what it is.

The similarities between Palamedes and Prometheus within their respective dramas are significant: both are understood as benefactors of human society, who play an important (and often foundational) role in the development of culture; both are nevertheless objects of hatred and ultimately punishment—Palamedes is framed by Odysseus for treason, while Prometheus is punished by Zeus for his gift of fire to humans—and this dynamic of generosity and suffering gives dramatic tension to the stagings. Like Theuth, they are figures

---

34. For aretalogies, see Michael Lipka, "Aretalogical Poetry: A Forgotten Genre of Greek Literature," *Philologus* 162 (2018): 208–31. Foundation catalogs: Renaud Gagné, "What Is the Pride of Halicarnassus?" *Classical Antiquity* 25 (2006): 1–33. Lists of abstract concepts: M. L. West, "The Orphics of Olbia," *Zeitschrift für Papyrologie und Epigraphik* 45 (1982): 17–29.

35. On the Isis aretalogies, see Paraskevi Martzavou, "Isis Aretalogies, Initiations, and Emotions: The Isis Aretalogies as a Source for the Study of Emotions," in *Unveiling Emotions: Sources and Methods for the Study of Emotions in the Greek World*, ed. Angelos Chaniotis (Stuttgart: Steiner, 2012), 267–91. I am grateful to Angelos Chaniotis for pointing out this intriguing parallel. On possible fifth-century roots, see Albert Henrichs, "The Sophists and Hellenistic Religion: Prodicus as the Spiritual Father of the Isis Aretalogies," *Harvard Studies in Classical Philology* 88 (1984): 139–58.

36. On lists in magical contexts, see Gordon, "'What's in a List?,'" esp. 247–50.

of formidable intellect, whose benefactions nevertheless expose them to suspicion and hatred. Palamedes' and Prometheus' catalogs have to be understood at least in part as quasiforensic defenses, attempts to convince listeners onstage and off- of their essential innocence by pointing to the good things they have brought humans. As a rhetorical display, the catalogs evidently appealed broadly, becoming set-pieces in stagings of the Palamedes story by all three canonical tragedians, and in at least two stagings of the Prometheus story.

The earliest evidence for the cultural catalog in drama is found in texts attributed to Aeschylus, and we have traces of Aeschylean catalogs spoken by Palamedes and Prometheus.[37] The proximity of the two figures is suggested by the way that their catalogs are quoted in Stobaeus, introduced by the heading "from the Prometheus of Aeschylus":

ἦν δ' οὐδὲν αὐτοῖς οὔτε χείματος τέκμαρ
οὔτ' ἀνθεμώδους ἦρος, οὔτε καρπίμου
θέρους βέβαιον· ἀλλ' ἄτερ γνώμης τὸ πᾶν
ἔπραττον, ἔς τε δὴ σφιν ἀντολὰς ἐγὼ
ἄστρων ἔδειξα τάς τε δυσκρίτους ὁδούς,
ἀριθμὸν εὑρών, ἔξοχον σοφισμάτων. [≈ *Prometheus Bound* 454–59]

ἔπειτα πάσης Ἑλλάδος καὶ ξυμμάχων
βίον διῴκησ' ὄντα πρὶν πεφυρμένον
θηρσίν θ' ὅμοιον· πρῶτα μὲν τὸν πάνσοφον
ἀριθμὸν εὕρηκ' ἔξοχον σοφισμάτων. [= F 181a] (Stobaeus, 1.Proem.)

There was not for them any secure indicator of winter, nor of flowering spring, nor of fruitful summer. But they did all things without thought until I showed them the risings and courses of the stars, hard to discern, inventing number, outstanding among contrivances.

Then I organized the life of all Hellas and its allies, which earlier was confused like that of beasts. First, I invented all-wise number, outstanding among contrivances.

Given the nearly verbatim repetition in its final line, the second passage can obviously not be the continuation of the first, and must come from a different

---

37. I describe the *Prometheus Bound* as "attributed to Aeschylus" or "Aeschylean," though I share the conviction of most Anglo-American scholars that it is a text of the later fifth century. I do, though, think its catalog is significantly Aeschylean, as I discuss below.

work. Since the invention of number is consistently attributed to Palamedes in later texts, along with the organization of the Greek forces, the second quotation seems certain to come from a speech of Palamedes. Because of the Aeschylean context, it is broadly, though not universally, accepted that the source is Aeschylus' *Palamedes*.[38] The suspicion is bolstered by scholia to the *Prometheus* passage—though to which lines precisely is unclear—that report that Aeschylus "attributed the invention of these things (or this invention) to Palamedes also," and Palamedes, one scholiast reasons, must have learned them from Prometheus (!).[39] Stobaeus would have assimilated the two into a single quotation, recognizing that the two passages come from parallel catalog speeches.

The *Palamedes* passage is evidently the continuation of a narrative and the beginning of a list, describing how Palamedes organized human life. The verb for this organization, διοικέω (literally, "to domesticate thoroughly"), is common for the administration and ruling of cities and households alike, and here suggests top-down ordering and regimentation in the specific context of the Greek expedition. Palamedes' actions, he implies, mark a transition from collective disorder to civilization, and he would presumably have gone on to enumerate the other inventions that made this possible. Like many narratives of humanity emerging from a state of "primeval brutishness," Palamedes describes a transition from "animal" to "human" social orders (using the verb φύρω, "confuse," which recurs in the *Prometheus Bound* and *Suppliants* catalogs to describe the same unenlightened state).[40] The distinction between human

---

38. Doubts about attributing the passage to Aeschylus are raised by O'Brien, "Doctrine of Primeval Brutishness," 271–72; Utzinger, *Periphrades Aner*, 183–85. The grounds for doubts are primarily that the theory of cultural development suggested by the fragment is only attested after Aeschylus' lifetime. This is circular: there is no reason to believe that such ideas could not have circulated decades earlier (and the evidence for the *Prometheus* dramas suggests that Aeschylus may well have attributed a similar organization of human life to Prometheus). The *Prometheus* scholia and F 182 (discussed below) make clear that Aeschylus' *Palamedes* included a catalog, so even if the attribution of this passage is doubted, evidence for the Aeschylean catalog is secure.

39. The scholia to *Prometheus Bound* 457/458a/459b preserve this identification, with different lemmata indicating variously that the shared invention(s) would be astronomy or numbers (with letters possibly included in the plural).

40. φύρω is used also at *Prometheus Bound* 450; Euripides, *Suppliants* 202. The recurrence of the verb in these cultural catalogs may suggest an even closer intertextual relation between them. It has often led all three to be traced to a single, philosophical, source; just as likely is that the dramatic texts are primarily influenced by and responding to one another.

and nonhuman animal life was a recurrent topic in early Greek thought, whether or not connected to a moment of differentiation.[41] The Aeschylean fragment implies a narrative of separation, but it does not dwell on the particulars of the transition (unlike, say, the *Prometheus* passage quoted with it in Stobaeus), and moves quickly on to the enumeration of particular inventions.

Palamedes' most significant contributions to the ordering of life seem to be connected to the invention of number (which, since Greek numerals were alphabetical, almost inevitably implies some form of literacy).[42] In the context of the Trojan War expedition, numeracy would have helped the Greeks survive a famine at Aulis by enabling an equitable distribution of food.[43] Another fragment attributed to Aeschylus' *Palamedes* suggests that regulation of the diet of the soldiers was a significant part of his legacy, connected to a broader organization of the army into ranks (which similarly presumes numeracy):

καὶ ταξιάρχας †καὶ στρατάρχας καὶ ἑκατοντάρχας†
ἔταξα, σῖτον δ' εἰδέναι διώρισα,
ἄριστα, δεῖπνα δόρπα θ' αἱρεῖσθαι τρίτα. (F 182)

And I appointed taxiarchs and army commanders and hundred-commanders, and I distinguished meals for them to know, to take breakfasts, dinners, and suppers third.

---

41. Greek ideas of the distinction between humans and animals are discussed in John Heath, *The Talking Greeks: Speech, Animals, and the Other in Homer, Aeschylus, and Plato* (Cambridge: Cambridge University Press, 2005); Catherine Osborne, *Dumb Beasts and Dead Philosophers: Humanity and the Humane in Ancient Philosophy and Literature* (Oxford: Clarendon Press, 2007), esp. 24–40. Important texts are Anaxagoras B21b DK/D81 LM, Archelaus A4 DK/D2 LM, Democritus B154 DK/D203 LM.

42. On the interrelation of numeracy and literacy, see Reviel Netz, "Counter Culture: Towards a History of Greek Numeracy," *History of Science* 40 (2002): 325–29; Greg Woolf, "Ancient Illiteracy?" *Bulletin of the Institute of Classical Studies* 58 (2015): 31–42.

43. According to a scholion to Euripides, *Orestes* 432, Palamedes distributed food in Aulis by teaching the Greeks Phoenician characters. The precise mechanism is not entirely clear, but most likely seems to be that Palamedes introduced letters for purposes of numeracy. This would have expedited distribution among a large number of soldiers (which would presume also the use of weights, measures, and some forms of arithmetic, inventions that Palamedes regularly claims in other catalogs). We have no way of knowing if the invention of writing played a role in Aeschylus' *Palamedes*, though the regulation of meals suggests a likely context, and the parallel with *Prometheus Bound* 460–61 (claiming the invention of writing) is suggestive.

The paratactic connections ("I did this . . . and I did this . . .") suggest that this passage comes from a catalog of Palamedes' benefactions, which would have ranged from mental entities like number to concrete organizational innovations like creating hierarchies and establishing fixed meal-times for the Greek forces. Though there was certainly more to the catalog, the recurrence of the idea of ordering in the two passages (first generally, "the life of Hellas," and then particularly, by appointing commanders and dividing meal-times) suggests that the play's catalog saw numerical organization as the heart of Palamedes' benefactions. Since this would presumably have involved the making of lists, the catalogic impulse might even inhere in the mythological outlines of the figure of Palamedes. It is important to note that there is no evidence for Palamedes' benefactions initiating a stepwise developmental process; rather, he appears to be the source of a simple transformation from savagery to civilization, enabled most of all by the new technology of numeracy.

The most likely context for such a catalog would have been in Palamedes' defense of himself against accusations of treachery lodged against him: by pointing to the many good things he had done for the Greeks, he would have sought to show that he should be held above suspicion.[44] Though it does not convince its internal audience of Greek soldiers, the speech as it occurred in Aeschylus must have been quite memorable: catalogs of Palamedes' benefactions become a recurring feature of Palamedes dramas, and we have numerous fragments attributed to Sophocles and Euripides. These catalogs can be delivered by Palamedes himself or by another on his behalf, and could occur in the trial itself or after Palamedes' death, as a way of driving home to the Greeks the injustice of their condemnation. Though the tragedies are transmitted indirectly and in very partial form, there is enough preserved to suggest the persistence of the catalog as a set-piece, and its likely place in the dramas.[45]

---

44. On the reconstruction of Aeschylus' *Palamedes*, see Alan H. Sommerstein, "The Prologue of Aeschylus' 'Palamedes,'" *Rheinisches Museum* 143 (2000): 118–27; Alan H. Sommerstein, ed., *Aeschylus: Fragments* (Cambridge, MA: Harvard University Press, 2009), 182–89.

45. Reconstructions of the three versions are found in Ruth Scodel, *The Trojan Trilogy of Euripides* (Göttingen: Vandenhoeck & Ruprecht, 1980), 43–61; Raffaella Falcetto, ed., *Il "Palamede" di Euripide: Edizione e commento dei frammenti* (Alessandria: Edizioni dell'Orso, 2002), 17–29; Alan H. Sommerstein and Thomas H. Talboy, eds., *Sophocles: Selected Fragmentary Plays*, Volume II (Oxford: Aris & Phillips, 2011), 110–73. On the central issue of letters, see Paola Ceccarelli, *Ancient Greek Letter Writing: A Cultural History (600 BC–150 BC)* (Oxford: Oxford University Press, 2013), 79–85.

Together, these fragments of Palamedean catalogs demonstrate the persistence of the form, and the appeal of its way of conceiving human culture.

Sophocles may have written as many as three plays on the subject of Palamedes' trial and its aftermath, which, though not a trilogy, seem to have presented successive phases of the story.[46] Two catalog fragments survive, neither spoken by Palamedes (a fragment of a possible third might be). This is interesting in itself, as Sophocles seems not to have given Palamedes the chance to defend himself. Instead, in the trial scene, it is likely that Odysseus pretended to come to the defense of Palamedes, and in the process enumerated a catalog notable for its anemic quality:[47]

οὐ λιμὸν οὗτος τῶνδ' ἔπαυσε, σὺν θεῷ
εἰπεῖν, χρόνου τε διατριβὰς σοφωτάτας
ἐφηῦρε φλοίσβου μετὰ κόπον καθημένοις,
πεσσοὺς κύβους τε, τερπνὸν ἀργίας ἄκος; (F 479)

Did this man not stop the famine from these [soldiers] here, to speak by the grace of god, and did he not discover the wisest pastimes for those sitting after the toil of the waves, draughts and dice, a pleasing cure for boredom?

The idea of a feigned defense fits with the less impressive list of benefactions invoked here, which extends beyond the famine—a sore point for Odysseus, since he had failed in his efforts to relieve the Greeks' hunger—only to the invention of draughts and dice, "the wisest pastimes" in a very restricted sense.[48] Draughts and dice were two of the inventions most frequently attributed to Palamedes, and a single line from one of the *Nauplius* plays mentions "both five-sided draughts and tossings of dice" (F 429: καὶ πεσσὰ πεντέγραμμα

---

46. Sommerstein proposes that Sophocles wrote a *Palamedes* (staging the trial and execution), *Nauplius Katapleōn* (the arrival of Palamedes' father in Troy and his treatment by the Greek army), and *Nauplius Pyrkaeus* (Nauplius' revenge of setting false beacons to wreck the Greek ships on their way home from Troy): Alan H. Sommerstein, "Sophocles' Palamedes and Nauplius Plays: No Trilogy Here," in *The Tangled Ways of Zeus and Other Studies in and around Greek Tragedy* (Oxford: Oxford University Press, 2010), 250–58.

47. Servius, *Commentary on Vergil's "Aeneid"* on 2.81 reports the feigned defense, and the story recounted there is usually thought to be based on Sophocles' play.

48. Kurke shows that the game of draughts is often understood to mirror the activity of the city: Leslie Kurke, *Coins, Bodies, Games, and Gold: The Politics of Meaning in Archaic Greece* (Princeton: Princeton University Press, 1999), 254–75. This would make Palamedes' invention of the game a potent symbol of his cultural importance as an orderer of life.

καὶ κύβων βολαί). Odysseus' rhetorical question uses the recollection of these inventions as a form of defense against the charge that Palamedes could betray the Greeks—but as we know, this defense, omitting the more transformative benefactions of other catalogs, was intended to fail.

The other Sophoclean catalog excerpt is much more extensive—so much so that recovering any principle of organization has proven difficult, and has led to various rearrangements of the lines.[49] Despite the jumble of the text, it is evident that the speech consisted of an extended list of Palamedes' accomplishments with little connection beyond simple conjunctions, introduced by repetition of the verb εὑρίσκω ("find" or "discover") and its compounds. Quoted by one Achilles Tatius in the *Introduction to Aratus*[50] as the words of Nauplius (though in which play is unclear), the lines recall a Palamedes whose inventions, though military in origin, contribute to the greater understanding of the natural world:

> οὗτος δ' ἐφηῦρε τεῖχος Ἀργείων στρατῷ,
> σταθμῶν, ἀριθμῶν καὶ μέτρων εὑρήματα
> τάξεις τε ταύτας οὐράνιά τε σήματα.
> κἀκεῖν' ἔτευξε πρῶτος, ἐξ ἑνὸς δέκα
> κἀκ τῶν δέκ' αὖθις ηὗρε πεντηκοντάδας
> καὶ χιλιοστῦς, καὶ στρατοῦ φρυκτωρίαν
> ἔδειξε κἀνέφηνεν οὐ δεδειγμένα.
> ἐφηῦρε δ' ἄστρων μέτρα καὶ περιστροφάς,
> ὕπνου φυλάξι πιστὰ σημαντήρια
> νεῶν τε ποιμαντῆρσιν ἐνθαλασσίοις
> ἄρκτου στροφάς τε καὶ κυνὸς ψυχρὰν δύσιν. (F 432; Achilles Tatius,
>   *Introduction to Aratus* 1)

This man devised the wall for the army of the Argives and the inventions of weights, numbers, and measures, and these formations, and the heavenly signs. And he was the first to do this, discovered how to count from one to ten and from ten in turn to fifty and then to a thousand. He showed the army's beacons, and revealed things that were earlier hidden. And he

---

49. I print the transmitted text without reorganization, though I adopt emendations to make obelized passages in *TrGF* legible.

50. This Achilles Tatius appears to be a second- or third-century (CE) author, to whom is attributed a περὶ σφαίρας from which the *Introduction* seems to have been fashioned; it is probably not the Achilles Tatius of the novel *Leucippe and Clitophon*.

discovered the measures and revolutions of the stars, signs for the watch during sleep, and, for seagoing shepherds of ships, the turnings of the Bear, and the cold setting of the Dog.

The most distinctive quality of the catalog is its concern with celestial events, which evidently recommended it to a commentator on Aratus. The invention of astronomy (which probably figured in Aeschylus' catalog as well) is given a prominent place, and appears as primarily military in nature, helpful for the night watch and navigation. Some familiar elements recur: the marshaling of the army and invention of number (which could easily extend to weights and measures), while beacons and night watching are associated with Palamedes in texts discussed below.[51] Within the context of the play, the list of benefactions appears full of portentous echoes of other plot elements: weighing and measuring reflect on the discovery of gold stashed under Palamedes' tent, while fire-beacons and navigation look forward to Nauplius' revenge. Sophocles evidently seized on the irony of Palamedes inventing the technologies that would be used to convict and then to avenge him.

The decisive advances associated with Palamedes by Sophocles group around processes of organization (weights, numbers, measures, battle formations) and signification (heavenly signs, fire signals, star movements). The former, which is more or less inevitable in representations of Palamedes, makes him into a figure of top-down division and classification much like that found in Aeschylus.[52] The latter may be a kind of expansion of the importance of writing, but suggests an idea of Palamedes as one who rendered inscrutable events and patterns comprehensible, and gave sense and regularity to what appeared chaotic. His claim to have benefited the Greeks rests on his helping them to understand the complexities of the world around them. Though framed by the military context, the cultural advances described in the catalog suggest an image of human beings acquiring intellectual mastery over their world.

For Euripides' Palamedes, culture seems to be more a product of recording and securing knowledge. This is the image presented by a fragment on the invention of letters:

---

51. Beacons are mentioned in the catalogs of Gorgias' *Defense of Palamedes* and Alcidamas' *Odysseus against the Treachery of Palamedes*, and in Euripides F 589.

52. The gift of measures, weights, and numbers is attributed to Ἰσότης (Equality) by Jocasta in Euripides' *Phoenissae* (541–42), in a speech that reflects similar anthropological speculation: Franziska Egli, *Euripides im Kontext*, 198–203.

τὰ τῆς γε λήθης φάρμακ' ὀρθώσας μόνος,
ἄφωνα φωνήεντα, συλλαβὰς τιθεὶς
ἐξηῦρον ἀνθρώποισι γράμματ' εἰδέναι,
ὥστ' οὐ παρόντα ποντίας ὑπὲρ πλακὸς
τἀκεῖ κατ' οἴκους πάντ' ἐπίστασθαι καλῶς,
παισίν τ' ἀποθνήσκοντα χρημάτων μέτρον
γράψαντα λείπειν, τὸν λαβόντα δ' εἰδέναι.
ἃ δ' εἰς ἔριν πίπτουσιν ἀνθρώποις κακὰ
δέλτος διαιρεῖ, κοὐκ ἐᾷ ψευδῆ λέγειν. (F 578)

I alone set up remedies for forgetfulness, speaking without speech, creating syllables, I invented letters for men to know, so that a man absent across the plain of the ocean could know well all the matters back there in his house, and a dying man could leave for his children a written measure of his wealth, and the one receiving it could know. And the evils that befall men in quarreling, a tablet dissolves, and does not allow anyone to speak lies.

No doubt there was more to the catalog, but writing appears to be Palamedes' prize invention, and is valued for the certainty it provides in human affairs.[53] Palamedes suggests that writing serves as an "elixir of forgetfulness" (λήθης φάρμακον, which may have influenced Plato's "elixir of memory") by preserving and transmitting knowledge across temporal and spatial distance.[54] Euripides seems to have afforded writing a central role both in the catalog and in the play as a whole, bringing out the irony that Palamedes is implicated by a forged letter, and making script an integral part of the intrigue.[55] As in Sophocles' catalog, the inventions call up central plot elements: Nauplius will hear of his

---

53. Another possible catalog fragment is F 589, which mentions the use of bells for night watches.

54. The contrary uses of *pharmakon* as, respectively, "elixir *against* [forgetfulness]" (in Euripides) and "elixir *for* [memory]" neatly illustrates Derrida's central observation concerning the polar quality of *pharmakon*. There is a similar ambiguity present in Critias' description of γράμματα (letters) as ἀλεξίλογα, "defending *logos*" or "defending against *logos*" (B 2 DK/2 West): Gabriele Burzacchini, "Remarques sur quelques fragments élégiaques de Critias," in *La muse au long couteau: Critias, de la création littéraire au terrorisme d'état*, ed. Jean Yvonneau (Bordeaux: Ausonius, 2018), 50–55.

55. The importance of script in Euripides' *Palamedes* is discussed in Torrance, *Metapoetry in Euripides*, 142–44. However, I see no reason to believe that Euripides was the first dramatist to attribute the invention of writing to Palamedes (and strong reason to believe this figured in Aeschylus at least).

son's execution from across the sea, a measure of wealth will be implicated in Palamedes' conviction, and most of all, the writing that is supposed to dissolve strife will in fact lead to further injustice as a forged letter implicates Palamedes. The catalog presents a kind of *mise en abîme* of the story as a whole, and shows Palamedes unwittingly creating the conditions for his own downfall.

In contrast to Sophocles' catalog, which emphasized the military context of Palamedes' inventions, the benefits envisioned by Euripides' protagonist are almost entirely severed from their martial uses. The importance of writing is described primarily in terms of social relations, and within contexts of exchange. Euripides' Palamedes suggests an idea of culture as constituted by a network of interpersonal and economic interactions, which writing helps to regulate. The uses of writing mentioned—transmitting information across wide distances, ensuring generational continuity, and arbitrating disputes—all presume a relatively centralized form of society, and a level of mobility and commercial activity that seems out of place in the Bronze Age. Such anachronism is common in tragedy, but it suggests that the play presented Palamedes' inventions as enabling a highly centralized, commercial, and even imperial society—one not so different from Euripides' own.

The persistence of the Palamedean catalog as a dramatic set-piece after Aeschylus is in itself notable, as nothing in the mythological outline demands it. It speaks, certainly, to the aesthetic appeal of the catalog form, and to the particularities of Palamedes' situation, which make the catalog a locus for questions of truth and authority surrounding the figure. But equally important is the intellectual work of the catalog in imagining the technologies that make civilization what it is. Though each invention is registered individually, their cumulative power is relatively independent of the items mentioned, and collectively offers a vision of human technological achievement. The vision differs from author to author, and the lacunose evidence makes it hard to draw secure conclusions, but some suggestive accents are already apparent: Aeschylus' Palamedes claims the transition from savage to civilized society to be a consequence of his invention of number and the regularization it enables; Sophocles' is more of an interpreter, who makes obscure signs comprehensible and organizes chaotic social forms; Euripides', finally, is a clever entrepreneur, who uses the technology of writing to secure social relations and commerce. Each implies a vision of culture and the skills and technologies that allow it to flourish.

Concurrently with these tragic texts, prose writers were grappling with the very same questions, and using the figure of Palamedes to explore them.⁵⁶ Though it is rarely discussed as a theory of culture, Gorgias' *Defense of Palamedes* can be understood to articulate a kind of anthropology in its catalog of Palamedes' inventions. The address, written in the voice of Palamedes, introduces the catalog in a series of arguments from probability that seek to show that, even if he could have betrayed the Greeks, he would not have chosen to do so. As evidence for this likelihood, Palamedes offers his past benefactions, seeking to show that he is "not only unerring, but even more, a great benefactor of you and of the Greeks and of all humans" (B11a DK/D25 LM 30: οὐ μόνον ἀναμάρτητος ἀλλὰ καὶ μέγας εὐεργέτης ὑμῶν καὶ τῶν Ἑλλήνων καὶ τῶν ἁπάντων ἀνθρώπων). As such, Palamedes implies, he should be held above suspicion:

> τίς γὰρ ἂν ἐποίησε τὸν ἀνθρώπειον βίον πόριμον ἐξ ἀπόρου καὶ κεκοσμημένον ἐξ ἀκόσμου, τάξεις τε πολεμικὰς εὑρὼν μέγιστον εἰς πλεονεκτήματα, νόμους τε γραπτοὺς φύλακας τοῦ δικαίου, γράμματά τε μνήμης ὄργανον, μέτρα τε καὶ σταθμὰ συναλλαγῶν εὐπόρους διαλλαγάς, ἀριθμόν τε χρημάτων φύλακα, πυρσούς τε κρατίστους καὶ ταχίστους ἀγγέλους, πεσσούς τε σχολῆς ἄλυπον διατριβήν; (B11a DK/D25 LM 30)

> For who could have made human life resourceful from resourceless, and ordered from disordered, discovering military formations, the most important thing for success; written laws, the guardians of justice; letters, the instrument of memory; measures and weights, the resourceful exchanges of commercial dealings; number, guardian of wealth; fire beacons, the strongest and swiftest messengers; and draughts, the harmless pastime of leisure?

The catalog is carefully constructed to move from most general and substantial (making human life resourceful) to the most particular and least significant (inventing draughts), with each invention receiving brief comment. Though the military setting is noticeable, the dominant context for Palamedes' inventions now looks to be the home front: laws, letters, and measures are described for their benefit to a collective that sounds much more like a fifth-century *polis* than Palamedes' Trojan expedition. There is nevertheless a great deal of

56. In addition to Gorgias' *Defense* discussed here, there is also a prosecution speech of Odysseus attributed to Alcidamas, which now appears possibly to have been written substantially later: Neil O'Sullivan, "The Authenticity of [Alcidamas'] 'Odysseus': Two New Linguistic Considerations," *Classical Quarterly* 58 (2008): 638–47. Since this adds relatively little to the catalog discourse and is controversial in date, I leave it aside.

overlap with the other catalogs: ordering human life, military formations, letters, measures, weights, numbers, fire beacons, and draughts are all attested in either Aeschylus or Sophocles, leaving only written laws as anomalous. While it is possible that written laws were included in a previous catalog, the hysteron-proteron by which they precede letters here is particularly striking. The invocation of written laws seems out of place in the Homeric world, but would have been highly significant in the *polis* context.[57] At the same time, however, the irony of the situation—Palamedes' condemnation by a piece of false writing—also brings up the potential of writing to act as an inflexible and dangerously unanswerable mode of communication. On the whole, though, Gorgias' catalog presents a Palamedes confident in his own importance, and in the advances he has brought to society.

All the catalogs, whether or not explicitly claiming to have organized humanity in general, suggest an image of Palamedes as a formative figure for human culture. Yet none of the catalog fragments preserved describe the transformation brought about by Palamedes in any detail or as a meaningful sequential development. What we find instead is reference to a binary transition from a state of animal confusion and disorder to one of recognizably human order and social organization. The emphasis is moreover squarely on this developed state, not on the precultural "primeval brutishness" or the process of transition. The inventions of Palamedes present ideas of culture (whether in the Homeric age or the Athenian present) as a product of human invention and ingenuity. This was not the only possible viewpoint: in archaic and classical texts, it is at least as often the gods who have granted humans their cultural achievements. Indeed, Palamedes' claim to be the sole source of such achievements could well have appeared arrogant and even blasphemous.

Palamedes was a valuable figure to think with and the catalog a valuable form for thought because they could be used to reflect on the extent and limits of human cultural achievement. Though Palamedes' catalogs are quite (self-)celebratory of invention, the plays as a whole must have offered a much darker picture of human culture. The irony of Palamedes' accusation on the basis of forged writing would have been unmistakable, and his trial before the military

---

57. Athens, among other states, prided itself on its written and publicly accessible laws, so Palamedes would be associating himself with a powerful aspect of *polis* ideology; see Euripides, *Suppliants* 433–37. The problematic character of written laws is brought out by Deborah Tarn Steiner, *The Tyrant's Writ: Myths and Images of Writing in Ancient Greece* (Princeton: Princeton University Press, 1994), 229–32.

that he himself had organized may also have portrayed his cleverness in a more doubtful light. This reflects, I suggest, an ambivalence toward technology and intellectual accomplishment in general, which was already obvious in the myth of Theuth. Men who know too much often come to bad ends in Greek mythology, if one thinks of Orpheus, Daedalus, Oedipus, or, of course, Prometheus.[58] Fifth-century Athens was evidently conflicted about some of its most visible intellectuals. It seems that in the 430s a decree against impiety was established and used to prosecute Anaxagoras.[59] Similar stories circulated in addition about Protagoras and Prodicus, though these may be retrojections of the trial and condemnation of Socrates.[60] Despite its ideology of *parrhēsia*, Athens was not always a welcoming environment for new ideas, and part of the dramatic appeal of the Palamedes story must have lain in the way it focalized tensions surrounding contemporary intellectuals (a topic to which I will return in chapter 3). The dramas as a whole would have presented a significantly more aporetic view of invention than Palamedes himself does, juxtaposing the triumphant anthropology of their catalogs with a more pessimistic view of culture suggested by his condemnation. However far-reaching Palamedes' claims were, they would have brought to bear a fundamental irony of the catalog form in drama: that its totalizing viewpoint inevitably solicits doubts

---

58. A partial exception to the distrust of the excessively knowledgeable prophets, who are often suspected for their knowledge, even as they are vindicated in the end. On the "sin of knowledge" from antiquity onward, see Theodore Ziolkowski, *The Sin of Knowledge: Ancient Themes and Modern Variations* (Princeton: Princeton University Press, 2000).

59. For the decree of Diopeithes (the authenticity of which is controversial), see Alexander Rubel, *Stadt in Angst: Religion und Politik in Athen während des Peloponnesischen Krieges* (Darmstadt: Wissenschaftliche Buchgesellschaft, 2000), 85–95. Diogenes Laertius 2.12–14 is the most extensive treatment of Anaxagoras' condemnation, reporting two different stories of the trial, both for impiety (with one story adding Medism). There are myriad difficulties in assessing the evidence for the trial and establishing a chronology; Jaap Mansfeld, "The Chronology of Anaxagoras' Athenian Period and the Date of His Trial. Part II: The Plot against Pericles and His Associates," *Mnemosyne* 33 (1980): 17–95; Leonard Woodbury, "Anaxagoras and Athens," *Phoenix* 35 (1981): 295–315. On the musician Diagoras of Melos, who was prosecuted for impiety in the 410s, see Marek Winiarczyk, *Diagoras of Melos: A Contribution to the History of Ancient Atheism* (Berlin: de Gruyter, 2016).

60. Reports of the prosecution of Protagoras circulated already in the fourth century (Aristotle, F 67 Rose and Timon of Phlius A12 DK) and so seem much more plausible than those concerning Prodicus, for which the earliest extant evidence is in the Byzantine Suda. A skeptical view on the evidence (not widely accepted) is expressed by K. J. Dover, "The Freedom of the Intellectual in Greek Soceity," *Talanta* 7 (1975): 24–54.

and challenges. Palamedes' catalogs offer a vision of how human culture is constituted—and also, implicitly, how it breaks down.

Prometheus between Divine and Human

The catalog discourse surrounding Palamedes' inventions was evidently well known and widespread. Though most of the surviving texts are fragmentary, their collective weight shows that Palamedes was often presented as a defining figure for varied realms of human culture. In turning to catalogs of Promethean inventions, the tradition looks quite different: although Prometheus' "Great Speech" in the *Prometheus Bound* includes the most substantial extant enumeration of an individual's benefactions, the play's image of Prometheus as inventor has little currency beyond the work.[61] All our evidence suggests that Prometheus' importance remained primarily connected to the gift of fire—a gift not even mentioned in the *Prometheus Bound* catalog. In the *Prometheus Bound* and beyond, to be sure, there is a sense that fire enables a wide range of activities not directly connected to it, but no other classical Greek text attributes anything like the panoply of inventions to Prometheus that the *Prometheus Bound* does. Moreover, these inventions take the form and much of the substance we have seen in catalogs of Palamedes' inventions. As catalogers of cultural innovation, Palamedes and Prometheus seem to be practically interchangeable in the Aeschylean tradition (as Stobaeus' quotation and the scholia discussed above recognize): Palamedean inventions are attributed to Prometheus, and Prometheus' foundational role for human culture appears to be transferred to Palamedes. While one cannot draw any firm conclusions about the priority of one or the other catalog, the similarities between them make it important to consider the two together, as interdependent inquiries into human culture. Whether or not Aeschylus wrote the *Prometheus Bound*, its cultural catalog is, in an important sense, Aeschylean.

If Prometheus was not already a mythological inventor in the archaic tradition, he was certainly one of the figures responsible for crucial aspects of human existence. In Hesiod's *Theogony* and *Works and Days*, the reasons for Prometheus' gift and the precise benefits of fire are left obscure, but they must be substantial enough to cause the anger of Zeus and his retaliation against the human race. The consequences of the gift of fire in the *Prometheus Bound*,

---

61. For possible Near Eastern roots of the image of Prometheus as inventor, see Stephanie West, "Prometheus Orientalized," *Museum Helveticum* 51 (1994): 129–49.

likewise, are difficult to discern precisely, but are understood in relation to human *technai*, the arts or skills that have allowed civilization to flourish. Fire, it seems, enables the development of the skills and technologies through which civilization takes on a recognizably human form. The narrative of human development implied is thus quite different from Hesiod, even if both point to Prometheus' theft of fire as a crucial watershed: in Hesiod, Prometheus' gift is a somewhat equivocal one, since it brings about the loss of the happy state of early humans. In the *Prometheus Bound*, by contrast, the gifts of Prometheus seem to be entirely beneficial to the human race (though, as the play emphasizes, they redound to the extreme detriment of Prometheus himself). Hesiod's epics narrate how humanity fell from an initial life of ease and abundance; Aeschylus' drama describes the way that humans have risen from an early state of need and confusion.[62] In enumerating his gifts to humanity, Prometheus emphasizes not only his own generosity, but the extent of human intellectual powers and cultural achievements.

One important piece of evidence for the Promethean catalog has largely been neglected. A quotation found in Plutarch suggests that another Aeschylean Prometheus drama similarly included a catalog of benefactions. Explaining that humans are superior to animals in their reasoning abilities, Plutarch puns on the name Prometheus, "forethinker," in recalling the Titan's subjugation of animals:

> ἵππων ὄνων τ' ὀχεῖα καὶ ταύρων γένος
> δοὺς ἀντίδουλα καὶ πόνων ἐκδέκτορα. (F 189a; Plutarch, *On Chance* 98c)
>
> ... giving the males of horses and asses and the offspring of bulls as slaves [literally: as taking-the-place-of-slaves] and relievers from labors.

Lacking the full sentence, it is hard to say anything about the speech from which the text comes, but the language is consistent with a place in a larger catalog of benefactions such as we find in the *Prometheus Bound*. There, the domestication of animals for work is one of the first elements of the catalog, described after the teaching of astronomy and the invention of number and letters:

---

62. On the relation between the *Prometheus Bound* and Hesiod, see Friedrich Solmsen, *Hesiod and Aeschylus* (Ithaca: Cornell University Press, 1949), 124–77; Mark Griffith, ed., *Aeschylus: "Prometheus Bound"* (Cambridge: Cambridge University Press, 1983), 1–10; Zoe Stamatopoulou, *Hesiod and Classical Greek Poetry: Reception and Transformation in the Fifth Century BCE* (Cambridge: Cambridge University Press, 2017), 127–59.

κἄζευξα πρῶτος ἐν ζυγοῖσι κνώδαλα
ζεύγλαισι δουλεύοντα σώμασίν θ' ὅπως
θνητοῖς μεγίστων διάδοχοι μοχθημάτων
γένοινθ', ὑφ' ἅρμα τ' ἤγαγον φιληνίους
ἵππους, ἄγαλμα τῆς ὑπερπλούτου χλιδῆς. (462–66)

And I first yoked wild beasts in yokes, enslaved to yoke-loops and their bodies, so that they would be successors for mortals of the greatest toils, and I led horses accepting the rein before carts, ornament of most wealthy luxury.

I will return to the speech as a whole below, but for now the important thing is to see the similarity between this text and the other *Prometheus* fragment. The claim is effectively the same, and uses the same word roots: Prometheus has made animals slaves to humans in order to take on their labors.[63] Prometheus' benefactions to humans include, in both texts, the idea that he established their power over animals. This suggests that the catalog of the *Prometheus Bound* was closely connected to another Promethean catalog, either delivered in the same trilogy or in a different one.[64] On the basis of these parallels and the context in Plutarch, it is safe to assume that this lost Aeschylean catalog would likewise have attributed to Prometheus the basic abilities that define human existence and culture.

---

63. The different formations of the same ideas are interesting as well: ἀντίδουλα is only attested here and in *Libation Bearers* (135, Electra describing her lot as like a slave), while δουλεύοντα is much more familiar language. ἐκδέκτορα is a *hapax* in classical Greek, from the same root as διάδοχοι. The *Prometheus Bound*'s language is in both cases simpler, but close enough that the two are likely to be related.

64. Numerous similarities between the *Prometheus Bound* and fragments of other Aeschylean Prometheus dramas have led scholars to argue against a coproduction of the two and for the dependence of one on the other (since watching two such similarly constructed dramas in succession would be exceptionally tedious), most likely the extant *Bound* on a lost *Unbound*: Eckard Lefèvre, *Studien zu den Quellen und zum Verständnis des "Prometheus Desmotes"* (Göttingen: Vandenhoeck & Ruprecht, 2003); Florence Yoon, "Against a Prometheia: Rethinking the Connected Trilogy," *Transactions of the American Philological Association* 146 (2016): 257–80. Though nothing in my larger point rests on it, I find these arguments compelling: such a scenario would explain the evident similarities between the *Prometheus* dramas (which have usually been taken to argue, wrongly, for their performance together), the formal differences between the *Bound* and the rest of the Aeschylean corpus, and its assimilation into Aeschylus' works. The *Prometheus Bound* would be Aeschylean in quite a strong sense, relying for its basic form and much of its content on an Aeschylean original.

The catalog of the *Prometheus Bound*, though centering on the Titan's gifts, outlines an image of culture as the product of human intellectual capacities. Prometheus grants not only discrete skills and inventions to humans (as Palamedes does), but the basic thinking abilities that set them apart from animals. Speaking to the chorus of Oceanids, he begins his enumeration with a general statement of the cultural enlightenment he has brought:

> βροτοῖς δὲ πήματα
> ἀκούσαθ', ὥς σφας νηπίους ὄντας τὸ πρὶν
> ἔννους ἔθηκα καὶ φρενῶν ἐπηβόλους. (442–44)

Hear the ills of mortals, how, though they had previously been fools, I made them capable of thought and possessed of wits.

The gift of thought to benighted human beings forms the starting point and effective *sine qua non* for Prometheus' further benefactions. The association of Prometheus with human reason seems to have been widespread in the fifth century, and is visible as well in a fragment of the comic poet Plato, "*promēthia* is for men the mind" (F 145: προμηθία γάρ ἐστιν ἀνθρώποις ὁ νοῦς).[65] Similarly, the Prometheus myth in Plato's *Protagoras* suggests that Prometheus' gift of fire was coupled with the gift of a kind of wisdom: "He [Prometheus] steals from Hephaestus and Athena technical wisdom together with fire—for without fire it [technical wisdom] could not be acquired or become useful—and thus gives it to man" (321d: κλέπτει Ἡφαίστου καὶ Ἀθηνᾶς τὴν ἔντεχνον σοφίαν σὺν πυρί—ἀμήχανον γὰρ ἦν ἄνευ πυρὸς αὐτὴν κτητήν τῳ ἢ χρησίμην γενέσθαι—καὶ οὕτω δὴ δωρεῖται ἀνθρώπῳ). Plato's Protagoras interprets or allegorizes Prometheus' gift of fire as a gift of the skill that will allow humans basic forms of existence and culture.[66] The emphasis, in keeping with Protagoras' intellectual focus, is on the wisdom brought by Prometheus rather than the fire itself. The *Prometheus Bound* effectively elides the distinction between fire and intellection; early in the play, Prometheus describes fire as "teacher of all skill for mortals and great resource" (110–11: διδάσκαλος τέχνης / πάσης βροτοῖς . . . καὶ μέγας πόρος) and he goes on to claim that

---

65. The citation comes, intriguingly, from the play *Sophists*, though we know practically nothing about the plot: Serena Pirrotta, *Plato Comicus: Die fragmentarischen Komödien* (Berlin: Verlag Antike, 2009), 88–90.

66. The gift of "technical wisdom" is referred to in the next sentence as σοφία περὶ τὸν βίον, "wisdom concerning life." There is probably an echo here of Hesiod's Zeus hiding the βίος of men (*Works and Days* 42).

"from it they will learn many skills" (254: ἀφ' οὗ γε πολλὰς ἐκμαθήσονται τέχνας). The close association between fire and human *technai* is not found in Hesiod, but seems to have been widespread in the fifth century.[67] The *Prometheus Bound*'s account, though positing fire as the root of human culture, nevertheless is primarily interested in the culture that emerges from fire—and not in fire itself.

The catalog of the *Prometheus Bound* offers a distinctive image of human culture, which emphasizes the situation of humans between animal and divine life. As discussed famously by Jean-Pierre Vernant, a concern with differentiating forms of life is central to the Hesiodic Prometheus narratives, and the drama substantially carries this questioning forward.[68] Promethean knowledge is a mediating knowledge, which enables humans to exist between the spheres of brute, animal life and the numinous forces of divinity. This mediating function places Prometheus, though a god, in a much closer relationship with human beings than his Hesiodic counterpart. He appears, especially as the catalog goes on, as a quasihuman inventor figure more than a remote divine benefactor.

Prometheus paints an exceptionally bleak picture of the mental and physical lives of humans before his interventions:

οἳ πρῶτα μὲν βλέποντες ἔβλεπον μάτην,
κλύοντες οὐκ ἤκουον, ἀλλ' ὀνειράτων
ἀλίγκιοι μορφαῖσι τὸν μακρὸν βίον
ἔφυρον εἰκῇ πάντα, κοὔτε πλινθυφεῖς
δόμους προσείλους ἦσαν, οὐ ξυλουργίαν,
κατώρυχες δ' ἔναιον ὥστ' ἀήσυροι
μύρμηκες ἄντρων ἐν μυχοῖς ἀνηλίοις. (447–53)

---

67. There may be parallels between early philosophical writing and the role of fire in the *Prometheus*: Georgia L. Irby-Massie, "'Prometheus Bound' and Contemporary Trends in Greek Natural Philosophy," *Greek, Roman, and Byzantine Studies* 48 (2008): 133–57; Patrick Glauthier, "Playing the Volcano: 'Prometheus Bound' and Fifth-Century Volcanic Theory," *Classical Philology* 113 (2018): 255–78. Fire figures prominently in reconstructions of Democritean anthropology as well: Cole, *Democritus and the Sources of Greek Anthropology*, 30–32.

68. Jean-Pierre Vernant, "At Man's Table: Hesiod's Foundation Myth of Sacrifice," in *The Cuisine of Sacrifice among the Greeks*, ed. Marcel Detienne and Jean-Pierre Vernant, trans. Paula Wissing (Chicago: University of Chicago Press, 1989), 21–86; Jean-Pierre Vernant, "The Myth of Prometheus in Hesiod," in *Myth and Society in Ancient Greece*, trans. Janet Lloyd (New York: Zone Books, 1990), 183–201.

At first, though seeing, they saw in vain, and though hearing, they did not hear, but like shapes of dreams they jumbled all things at random through their long life, nor did they know brick houses against the sun or woodworking, but they dwelled underground like light ants in the sunless depths of caves.

Aspects of this image can be paralleled in contemporary accounts of early culture, but the picture on the whole is strikingly negative. Prometheus describes early human livelihood as completely lacking in basic intellectual capacities.[69] Early humans appear unrecognizable: Prometheus likens them to "shapes of dreams" and "light ants." The comparison of human to animal life is familiar from the Aeschylean *Palamedes*, while the *Homeric Hymn to Hephaestus* similarly places early life in caves: until Hephaestus taught them "works" (5: ἔργα), "they lived in mountain caves like beasts" (4: ἄντροις ναιετάασκον ἐν οὔρεσιν ἠύτε θῆρες). The *Protagoras* myth, too, had suggested that humans were created below earth (320d). In the *Prometheus Bound*, the form of the idea emphasizes not the moral depravity of early humans, as in some accounts, but their complete lack of any intelligence, which makes them effectively sub- or prehuman.

Prometheus' first gifts are aimed at remedying the chaos of early existence by giving a kind of regularity to human life. He describes teaching a basic understanding of the year's cycle (presumably allowing humans to grow crops effectively), and then introducing numbers and letters:

> ἀντολὰς ἐγὼ
> ἄστρων ἔδειξα τάς τε δυσκρίτους δύσεις.
> καὶ μὴν ἀριθμόν, ἔξοχον σοφισμάτων,
> ἐξηῦρον αὐτοῖς, γραμμάτων τε συνθέσεις,
> μνήμην ἁπάντων, μουσομήτορ' ἐργάνην. (457–61)

> I showed them the risings of stars and their hard-to-discern settings. And number, outstanding among contrivances, I discovered for them, and combinations of letters, memory of all things, instrument that is mother of the Muses.

The step from recognizing astronomical patterns to creating numbers and letters may seem like a large one, but all effect means of setting humans into time:

---

69. Heraclitus B1 DK/D1 LM uses a similar trope, that humans fail to understand what is heard, and exist in a sleeplike oblivion even while awake.

numbers allow for recordings of time passing, and writing serves as a form of memory (the "mother of the Muses" is Mnemosyne). Writing appears as a defense against forgetfulness, an anchor to something that persists amid the passage of time—and so a kind of corollary to the recognition of seasonal change. The same association of astronomy, numbers, and letters is evident among Palamedes' inventions. These first teachings of Prometheus remedy early humans' animal confusion by introducing capacities and technologies that enable them to establish basic forms of culture.

The enumeration of Prometheus' benefactions can seem rather haphazard, and beyond these initial teachings, which seem to be the most fundamental, it is hard to see a systematic progression, except in the rather casual sense that one often suggests the next.[70] This casualness indicates that the catalog is less concerned to offer a diachronic narrative of human culture (in which the progression from one stage to the next is at issue) than a synchronic panorama of human capacities (in which the specific sequencing is unimportant). In contrast, the Prometheus myth of the *Protagoras* is clearly divided into different stages of creation, with each gift to humans remedying a specific deficit of the previous state. It is significant that in the drama, after the initial stages of Prometheus' description of his benefactions there are no temporal markers, such as we would expect in a sequential narrative. Prometheus describes humans' early state with a series of imperfect verbs and the temporal marker ἔστε ("until") before shifting into the aorist to describe his own benefactions. After this point there are no relative markers of time, but only an accumulation of aorist verbs linked by simple conjunctions. Prometheus goes on to describe the yoking of animals, which relieves humans of the burden of working the fields (462–65), the taming of horses (465–66), and then the invention of ships (467–68) before a brief interruption by the chorus. The apparently odd member of this trio, ships, are described by the periphrasis "sea-wandering, flax-winged carts of sailors" (θαλασσόπλαγκτα ... λινόπτερ' ... ναυτίλων ὀχήματα), invoking both birds and cart-animals as comparisons. The first stage of Prometheus' benefactions can thus be understood as a differentiation of human from animal life, enabled by techniques of mastery—first of time, then of their physical environment.

---

70. Discussions of the range of Prometheus' benefactions are found in Seth Benardete, "The Crimes and Arts of Prometheus," *Rheinisches Museum* 107 (1964): 126–39; Desmond Conacher, "Prometheus as Founder of the Arts," *Greek, Roman, and Byzantine Studies* 18 (1977): 189–206.

It has been observed that this picture is importantly lacking in certain respects—there is no mention of political or social organization, as there is in the Prometheus myth of the *Protagoras*—but the truly striking fact about it is how much *more* it describes than any other account of Prometheus' gifts.[71] The range of benefactions claimed has no parallel in other classical tellings of the Prometheus myth and can only be compared to that of Palamedes. At the same time, the lack of a broader social perspective (which was implicit in the Palamedean catalogs and emphatically present in the *Protagoras* myth) presents Prometheus' anthropology as quasi-utopian, a fantasy of human flourishing in the absence of political hierarchy, and with stable relations to gods and animals.[72] This is consistent with the bottom-up quality of Prometheus' benefactions. He claims that he was the first to develop these *technai*—not that he gave something preexistent—and so we gain an image of him as actually modeling or teaching skills to humans. Accordingly, the most frequent verbs in the speech are compounds of εὑρίσκω ("discover") and δείκνυμι ("show"), rather than verbs of giving or implanting. This suggests a far less hierarchical relation than that presumed in other Prometheus narratives, which focus on the gift of fire: though a Titan, Prometheus acts like a human culture hero. The contrast to the play's image of Zeus, portrayed as a remote, abusive tyrant, is plain: Prometheus appears as a figure of anarchic resistance to divine power, while the human world he claims to have furnished presents an image of peaceful existence within the order of the universe.

The next section of Prometheus' speech departs from inventions and techniques of mastery to skills involving higher knowledge. If the first series had established humans in relation to the apparent, physical world, the second portrays them learning to live amid unseen, mysterious forces connected to divinity. Responding to the chorus comparing him to "a bad doctor, one who has fallen sick" (473–74: κακὸς δ' ἰατρὸς ὥς τις ἐς νόσον / πεσών), Prometheus describes how he showed the arts of medicine to humans:

τὸ μὲν μέγιστον, εἴ τις ἐς νόσον πέσοι,
οὐκ ἦν ἀλέξημ' οὐδέν, οὔτε βρώσιμον
οὐ χριστὸν οὐδὲ πιστόν, ἀλλὰ φαρμάκων
χρείᾳ κατεσκέλλοντο, πρίν γ' ἐγὼ σφισιν

---

71. Conacher, "Prometheus as Founder of the Arts," 195; Stephen White, "Io's World: Intimations of Theodicy in 'Prometheus Bound,'" *Journal of Hellenic Studies* 121 (2001): 113–15.

72. I am grateful to Victoria Wohl for suggesting this point.

ἔδειξα κράσεις ἠπίων ἀκεσμάτων,
αἷς τὰς ἁπάσας ἐξαμύνονται νόσους. (478–83)

The greatest was, if someone fell into disease, there was no remedy, neither to be eaten, nor rubbed on, nor drunk, but they withered away in need of medicines, that is, until I showed them the mixings of soothing remedies, by which they ward off all diseases.

Again, there are no markers of sequence; medicine is described as "the greatest" (of his inventions), but there is no clear sense of its connection, temporal or logical, to the others mentioned. The claim that "they ward off all diseases" may seem hyperbolic, but the exaggeration is balanced against Prometheus' own need of remedies (which the chorus has just brought up), and his description of early humans' lack of medical arts. The esteem granted to medicine is not anomalous: Solon's *Elegy to the Muses* mentions medicine last in its list of human professions (13 West 57–60), and the first stasimon of the *Antigone*, considered below, places healing remedies last among the concrete examples of man's skills. In *On Ancient Medicine,* moreover, the existence of medical techniques serves as an index of the distance between human and animal forms of life, and plays a major role in a story of progress from an initial state of *aporia*.[73] In the context of the *Prometheus Bound*'s exploration of the relation of humanity and the gods, the development of medicine demonstrates a way that humans have taken on capacities conventionally associated with divinity.

Of all his benefactions, the one Prometheus enumerates in the greatest depth, by some measure, is divination (μαντική, a capacity described also in Solon's *Elegy*, 13 West 53–55). This is clearly appropriate to the play's emphasis on his own prophetic gifts, and corresponds to the mediating character of Promethean knowledge. He says that he "systematized many ways of divination" (484: τρόπους τε πολλοὺς μαντικῆς ἐστοίχισα), using the verb στοιχίζω, literally, "set into a line," an act of regularization rather than whole-cloth invention. The five methods of interpretation Prometheus lists move from relatively everyday occurrences to the highly charged context of sacrifice: making forecasts from dreams, understanding significant utterances and meaningful meetings on journeys, interpreting bird-flight, and then two related to sacrifice,

---

73. *On Ancient Medicine* 3. See Jacques Jouanna, *Hippocrates* (Baltimore: Johns Hopkins University Press, 1999), 232–43; Schiefsky, *Hippocrates: "On Ancient Medicine,"* 36–43; Francis Dunn, "'On Ancient Medicine' and Its Intellectual Context," in *Hippocrates in Context*, ed. Philip J. van der Eijk (Leiden: Brill, 2005), 49–67.

reading burnt entrails and grasping "fiery signs" (498: φλογωπὰ σήματα) in the smoke of offerings. These last two constitute the only explicit mention of fire or sacrifice—two signal Hesiodic elements—in the entire speech, though Prometheus does not claim to have given or originated either. The language of these benefactions is particularly interesting: he "placed mortals on the way" (498: ὥδωσα θνητούς) and "opened their eyes" (499: ἐξωμμάτωσα), physical verbs transferred to mental processes, which attribute to Prometheus the role simply of pointing out what is already existent. Prometheus is not shy of making claims for his own importance in this speech, but he places himself here in the role of intermediary, who shows humans how best to understand what they are already somehow conscious of, teaching them to see when they look and listen when they hear.[74]

At first glance, Prometheus' final item appears a rather different form of benefaction from the knowledge-based arts of medicine and divination: he has discovered (503: ἐξευρεῖν) precious metals, "things helpful to men hidden below the earth" (501: κεκρυμμέν' ἀνθρώποισιν ὠφελήματα). This could imply the use of fire, since any of these metals would require the art of metallurgy in order to become useful.[75] Yet Prometheus only claims the discovery of metals themselves, leaving unspoken the way they become beneficial. We can perhaps make sense of the discovery by understanding it as another form of knowledge of the unseen, which relies, like medicine and divination, on Prometheus' divine insight. Even more than the *technai* mentioned, the discovery of metals beneath the earth would have seemed miraculous, since it responded to no existing human need or propensity.[76] On this reading, the discovery of metals represents the furthest extension of Promethean knowledge. It is the pinnacle of humans' ability to gain control over the unseen.

Prometheus concludes his catalog with a triumphant play on his own name, invoking its etymological sense of "forethought" (or, more broadly, careful

---

74. For divination as "surplus knowledge," see Peter T. Struck, *Divination and Human Nature: A Cognitive History of Intuition in Classical Antiquity* (Princeton: Princeton University Press, 2016).

75. Benardete, "The Crimes and Arts of Prometheus," 130; Griffith, *"Prometheus Bound,"* 176.

76. There is an intriguing parallel to the discovery of metals in a Sophoclean catalog quoted above: "he revealed things that were not apparent" (F 432 7: κἀνέφηνεν οὐ δεδειγμένα). There is also a likelihood that mining was included in Democritean anthropology: Cole, *Democritus and the Sources of Greek Anthropology*, 35–40.

reflection):[77] "In brief, learn all things together: all arts for mortals are from Prometheus/forethought" (505–6: βραχεῖ δὲ μύθῳ πάντα συλλήβδην μάθε· / πᾶσαι τέχναι βροτοῖσιν ἐκ Προμηθέως). This statement, which could again seem hyperbolic, points to the totalizing nature of the speech: the items listed are merely *exempli gratia* and do not exhaust the full range of Prometheus' benefactions. This is, as I have argued, characteristic of catalogic discourse: the individual items are relatively indifferent to the whole (which is not to deny that the elements chosen are interesting and important). Without enumerating each art or skill possessed by mortals, Prometheus claims the whole lot as his own, arrogating an exceptional authority. Just as interesting, though, is the way that the catalog frames this authority. As Prometheus emphasizes, his teaching of these skills is of no avail in his present plight:

τοιαῦτα μηχανήματ' ἐξευρὼν τάλας
βροτοῖσιν αὐτὸς οὐκ ἔχω σόφισμ' ὅτῳ
τῆς νῦν παρούσης πημονῆς ἀπαλλαγῶ. (469–71)

Though having discovered such contrivances for mortals, I myself, wretched, have no stratagem by which I might end my present suffering.

The same duality is present in Palamedes' catalogs: despite the authority assumed by the listing of inventions, he, like Prometheus, is trapped in a situation from which he cannot escape. Prometheus' catalog both asserts his power and points to its limits.[78]

The equivocal presentation of Prometheus as a figure of authority corresponds to the play's presentation of human culture as a whole, and the anthropology of the catalog must be read in light of the play's other images of human beings. Though the catalog presents quite a positive, and even triumphal, view of human intellect and achievement, other aspects of the play's anthropology suggest a darker perspective, which emphasizes human ignorance and vulnerability in relation to the gods. A wider reading of the play's presentation of humanity qualifies or undermines the utopian existence sketched in the catalog, by pointing to the many ways that humans remain subject to a malign divinity. In his first dialogue with the chorus, Prometheus describes how he

---

77. On the meaning of *promētheia*, see Christopher Moore, "Promētheia ('Forethought') until Plato," *American Journal of Philology* 136 (2015): 381–420.

78. Stronger (I believe untenable) views of the limits of Prometheus' authority are found in White, "Io's World"; Richard Rader, "The Radical Theology of 'Prometheus Bound'; or, On Prometheus' God Problem," *Ramus* 42 (2013): 162–82.

saved human beings from destruction by Zeus, an element of the story with no Hesiodic precedent, which is likely drawn from the Cyclical *Titanomachy*.[79] Prometheus recounts how, after ascending the seat of power among the gods, Zeus gave no consideration to human beings, but "having wiped out the race entirely, intended to beget a new one" (232–33: ἀιστώσας γένος / τὸ πᾶν ἔχρῃζεν ἄλλο φιτῦσαι νέον). The details of both Zeus' plan and Prometheus' resistance are quite vague, and we never understand why Zeus should have wanted to destroy humanity or Prometheus to save it (or how he did so). Prometheus recalls how, alone among the gods, he opposed the plan and "released mortals from going to Hades utterly destroyed" (235–36: ἐξελυσάμην βροτοὺς / τὸ μὴ διαρραισθέντας εἰς Ἅιδου μολεῖν). This act, he claims, is the reason for his punishment, tracing his suffering to an action even more heroic and dangerous than the theft of fire. Prometheus thus establishes himself from the beginning of the play as much more than Hesiod's beneficent trickster. Yet in pointing to the way that he saved human beings from destruction, Prometheus also emphasizes their vulnerability, living or dying by the whims of the gods.

Prometheus' salvation of humanity is only the beginning of his beneficence. While Prometheus presents himself in the catalog as increasing human intellectual capacity, he also describes a decrease in knowledge, paradoxically, as one of his gifts:

ΧΟ. μή πού τι προύβης τῶνδε καὶ περαιτέρω;
ΠΡ. θνητούς γ' ἔπαυσα μὴ προδέρκεσθαι μόρον.
ΧΟ. τὸ ποῖον εὑρὼν τῆσδε φάρμακον νόσου;
ΠΡ. τυφλὰς ἐν αὐτοῖς ἐλπίδας κατῴκισα.
ΧΟ. μέγ' ὠφέλημα τοῦτ' ἐδωρήσω βροτοῖς. (247–51)

Chorus. Did you not perhaps in fact in any way go beyond these things? *Prometheus.* Yes, I stopped mortals from foreseeing their doom. *Ch.* Finding what kind of drug for this disease? *P.* I lodged blind expectations in them. *Ch.* A great benefit this was you gave to mortals.

Ignorance of one's own death appears to be a "great benefit," effected by Prometheus' removal of foresight and implanting of blind *elpis* ("expectation" or "hope") in humans. *Elpis* functions as a "drug" (*pharmakon*) for the "disease"

---

79. Prometheus' salvation of humans may be related to a flood story, a tradition that is paralleled in Near Eastern mythologies, and was circulating in the fifth century (attested by the fragments of Epicharmus' *Prometheus and Pyrrha*): West, "Prometheus Orientalized," 132–39.

of foreknowledge, which seems to afflict humans before Prometheus' intervention.[80] The mention of *elpis* in this context cannot but recall Hesiod's *Works and Days*, in which the jar opened by Pandora releases "baneful evils" into the world, while *elpis* is the only thing that remains inside (94–99). Interpretation of this passage is exceptionally vexed, but it is at least clear that, since the theft of fire is the reason for Zeus to create Pandora, Prometheus is somehow responsible for the role of *elpis* in human life.[81] The *Prometheus Bound* makes this connection explicit, filling in some of the gaps in Hesiod's narrative to suggest that *elpis* is given to humans as an escape from foreknowledge of death, making their mortal state bearable by blinding them to it. Prometheus in the catalog presents his benefactions as gifts of knowledge, but here his greatest gift appears to be ignorance.

It is only after having described saving humans and removing their knowledge of their own death that Prometheus comes to the gift of fire, almost as an afterthought. He continues:

πρ. πρὸς τοῖσδε μέντοι πῦρ ἐγώ σφιν ὤπασα.
χο. καὶ νῦν φλογωπὸν πῦρ ἔχουσ' ἐφήμεροι;
πρ. ἀφ' οὗ γε πολλὰς ἐκμαθήσονται τέχνας. (252–54)

Prometheus. In addition to these things I also gave them fire. *Chorus.* So now the creatures of a day have blazing fire? P. Indeed, from which they will learn many skills.

Having substituted blindness for foreseeing, Prometheus gives humans the gift of fire, which might be understood as a kind of compensation. The two elements, blind expectations and fire, suggest a submerged causality, such as they had, more directly, in Hesiod (where the opening of the jar containing hope is an extended consequence of the theft of fire): hope helps humans to bear their own mortality, while fire allows them to acquire skills to rise

---

80. The myth of Plato's *Gorgias* (523d–e) likewise depicts Prometheus removing humans' foreknowledge of death, in this case so that they would be judged in the afterlife without being able to prepare a case on their behalf—an act that the myth describes as a loss for humans (though an advance in cosmic justice). I discuss the myth briefly in the Conclusion, but in the present context it is interesting that Plato presents Prometheus as an ally of Zeus rather than a competitor (as he does in the *Protagoras*, discussed in this chapter, and the civilizational myth of *Statesman* 274b–d).

81. On Hesiod's *elpis* as itself ambiguous, see Lilah-Grace Fraser, "A Woman of Consequence: Pandora in Hesiod's 'Works and Days,'" *Cambridge Classical Journal* 57 (2011): 21–24.

above it.[82] While the loss of foresight cuts humans off from divinity, the gift of fire elevates them above animals. The sequencing of the exchange is significant: fire appears as a positive benefaction after two negative ones (saving from destruction and removing foreknowledge), together presenting an image of human culture defined as much by lack as by resourcefulness.

The play's depiction of human culture is further fleshed out in Prometheus' long exchange with Io, the young woman who is seduced by Zeus, turned into a cow by Hera, and then tormented unceasingly by a gadfly as she wanders across the known world. Io, the only mortal to appear in the play—though in animal form—is a prime example of human subjection to divine whim, and the play's depiction of her confusion and agony could hardly be more pathetic. As victims of the Olympian gods, Prometheus and Io have a natural kinship, but the scene tends to emphasize their differences, which center on Prometheus' knowledge of the future and Io's desperate ignorance. When asked to reveal the extent of Io's future wanderings, Prometheus is initially reluctant, claiming that "not to know is better for you than to know these things" (624: τὸ μὴ μαθεῖν σοι κρεῖσσον ἢ μαθεῖν τάδε). Despite his reluctance, he goes on to describe, in minute detail, Io's future wanderings, a "stormy sea of baneful misery" (746: δυσχείμερόν γε πέλαγος ἀτηρᾶς δύης) so grievous that she contemplates suicide. Knowledge of the future appears hard for humans to bear, a reminder that Io's ignorance is itself a Promethean benefaction. Yet whereas Prometheus' earlier exchanges had focused on his gifts to humans as compensation for the shortcomings of human nature, Io's suffering at the hands of gods appears impossible to alleviate. Subjection to a cruel divinity renders humanity, despite all its intellect and skills, little better than the animal into which she has been transformed.

Though the *Prometheus Bound* includes the fewest mortals of any extant Greek drama, it is profoundly concerned with humanity. There is much more to say about the way the *Prometheus Bound* reflects, directly and indirectly, on human culture, but it is clear enough that the anthropology of the work as a whole is not identical with that of the cultural catalog. While the catalog celebrates the capacities that raise human beings above animal life, much of the rest of the play emphasizes their ignorance and powerlessness in relation to the gods. The utopian image of the catalog is juxtaposed with a bleak vision of the subjection of humanity. Both, though, have real claims to truth: humans

---

82. See the discussion in Suzanne Saïd, *Sophiste et tyran: ou Le problème du "Prométhée enchaîné"* (Paris: Klincksieck, 1985), 122–30.

possess all the skills Prometheus mentions, and yet they remain profoundly ignorant and vulnerable. I understand this tension as a way that the play posits different anthropologies and mediates between them, without offering a single, unified vision. Prometheus' triumphal view in the catalog is counterposed both with his own suffering and with the vulnerability of humans generally, and this juxtaposition suggests divergent anthropologies: humans are both the endlessly resourceful creatures of the catalog and the vulnerable, ignorant beings in desperate need of protection glimpsed in the rest of the play. Prometheus' role in human existence focalizes both viewpoints, and the different relationships to divinity they entail. As a figure mediating between humans and gods, Prometheus becomes the figure for the ambiguity of the play's anthropology.

The Gifts of the God: Euripides' *Suppliants*

In content, Theseus' speech of thanksgiving in Euripides' *Suppliants* represents the closest parallel to Prometheus' catalog. Because the speech describes humans as receiving benefactions from the gods, it is often left aside in discussions of the idea of progress, but its affinities with the *Prometheus Bound*, the *Antigone*, and the Palamedes fragments show it to be part of the same interest in the constituents of human culture. Like them, it takes the form of a catalog of benefactions, which it attributes to an unspecified "one of the gods." Speaking to the Argive king Adrastus, who has come to beg for Athenian assistance in recovering and burying the dead from the recent Theban war, Theseus offers a circuitous response, in which he outlines an optimistic view of divinity's role in human affairs:

> ἄλλοισι δὴ 'πόνησ' ἁμιλληθεὶς λόγῳ
> τοιῷδ'· ἔλεξε γάρ τις ὡς τὰ χείρονα
> πλείω βροτοῖσίν ἐστι τῶν ἀμεινόνων.
> ἐγὼ δὲ τούτοις ἀντίαν γνώμην ἔχω,
> πλείω τὰ χρηστὰ τῶν κακῶν εἶναι βροτοῖς.
> εἰ μὴ γὰρ ἦν τόδ', οὐκ ἂν ἦμεν ἐν φάει. (195–200)

With other men I labored contending with this kind of speech: for someone said that for mortals there are more of worse than of better things. But I hold the opposite opinion to these, that there are more good than bad things for mortals. For if this were not so, we would not be in the light of day.

The connection to Adrastus' preceding appeal is quite loose, and the speech has often been considered an irrelevant rhetorical display.[83] I will suggest, however, that it has an important role in establishing Theseus' intellectual and political authority, which much of the play reflects back on. Theseus clearly marks the opinions he is describing as part of a familiar debate ("this kind of speech"), as to whether humans have more of bad or of good things in life. An idea of dialectic, and the possibility of alternative views, is thus embedded in the speech's presentation. What follows, though, is not a logical demonstration of the point, but a broader answer to what Theseus takes to be Adrastus' perspective, and indeed, to a substantial strain of Greek pessimism. He responds in particular to Adrastus' failure to heed an oracular utterance in deciding to go to war, which Theseus characterized as "turning away from the divine" (159: τὸ θεῖον . . . ἀπεστράφης). In contrast to Adrastus' heedlessness, Theseus emphasizes the beneficence of divinity, and drives home the folly of disobedience to the gods. Human beings, his account suggests, must accept their subordinate position in the cosmos if they are to enjoy the good things of existence. Adrastus—and the dead he begs for help recovering—would appear to be an example of the opposite relation to divinity, and Theseus will initially reject the plea for assistance, before changing his mind after an appeal by his mother.

Theseus articulates a vision of human nature and existence informed by anthropological speculation, but which differs substantially in its accent from other dramatic examples.[84] He enumerates benefits conferred by "one of the gods" in a short catalog of benefactions:

> αἰνῶ δ' ὅς ἡμῖν βίοτον ἐκ πεφυρμένου
> καὶ θηριώδους θεῶν διεσταθμήσατο,
> πρῶτον μὲν ἐνθεὶς σύνεσιν, εἶτα δ' ἄγγελον
> γλῶσσαν λόγων δούς, ὥστε γιγνώσκειν ὄπα,
> τροφήν τε καρποῦ τῇ τροφῇ τ' ἀπ' οὐρανοῦ
> σταγόνας ὑδρηλὰς ὥς τά τ' ἐκ γαίας τρέφῃ
> ἄρδῃ τε νηδύν· (201–7)

> I praise the one of the gods who separated our living from the confused and bestial, first implanting reason, then giving the tongue, messenger of words, so that we understand voice, and the nourishment of fruit for nourishment

---

83. D. J. Conacher, "Rhetoric and Relevance in Euripidean Drama," *American Journal of Philology* 102 (1981): 3–25.

84. On potential intertexts for Theseus' speech, see Egli, *Euripides im Kontext*, 203–7.

and the watery drops from the sky to nourish things from the earth and quench our belly's thirst.

Theseus presents this catalog as a reasoned praise of divinity, based on an account of divine benevolence in granting the means of survival.[85] The god is not named, adding to the sense that the statement is based more on deduction than on an existent myth. The parallels with the first elements of Prometheus' catalog are notable: the raising of humans above confused (using the same verb, φύρω) animal life, the giving of reason and the means of subsistence. But Theseus' perspective is notably top-down, describing divinely granted aspects of existence that allow for human flourishing, rather than the human techniques enumerated by Palamedes and Prometheus. There is little celebration of human abilities; rather, the guiding idea of the speech is gratitude for the beneficial constituents of a teleologically ordered universe. This strand of teleology links Theseus' theology to ideas associated with Socrates, who likewise seems to have postulated that human existence was created by the gods for the best.[86] Theseus' speech offers what is probably our earliest document of this turn toward natural theology, and should be recognized as a serious contribution to thinking about divinity.

The specific items Theseus mentions—intellect, followed by language and nourishment—contribute to an image of distinctive human endowments. The priority of intellect is familiar from Prometheus' account, and here suggests a uniquely human capacity of reason, which raises early humans above their animal state. The word σύνεσις seems to be a favorite of Euripides, and may have a high-flown, neologistic sound.[87] The next item, speech, likewise could

---

85. αἰνέω is not conventionally used for religious praise, but for approval of human activity. There is another Euripidean use of a god at *Ion* 1609, but there too it expresses a reasoned judgment of divine action.

86. On teleology in early Greek thought, see David Sedley, *Creationism and Its Critics in Antiquity* (Berkeley: University of California Press, 2007), esp. 78–92. The crucial comparison, which shares much with Theseus' speech (an argument from design, mentioning reason, speech, and divination as proof of divine care for humans), is Socrates' discussion with Xenophon, *Memorabilia* 1.4. Though Sedley is dismissive of the parallel with *Suppliants*, I think there is good reason to see both Socrates and Euripides as taking part in a wider questioning of the relationship of humans to divinity. Christian Wildberg brings out a different (though probably compatible) coincidence between Socrates' views and religious conceptions found in Euripides: *Hyperesie und Epiphanie: Versuch über die Bedeutung der Götter in den Dramen des Euripides* (Munich: Beck, 2002), 91–112.

87. Euripides is the only tragedian to use the word σύνεσις, and his fondness for it is parodied in *Frogs* 893: Christopher Collard, ed., *Euripides: "Supplices"* (Groningen: Bouma, 1975), 162–63.

be thought a uniquely human capacity.⁸⁸ Intellect and speech constitute the crucial aspects of the division of human from animal life. The catalog then changes focus to the natural environment, with the third item Theseus lists being in some ways the strangest, since nourishment (τροφή, the root repeated three times) and water could hardly be considered distinctly human needs.⁸⁹ Food and drink, moreover, are simple gifts and not capacities like intellect or speech, and imply a wider role for the god than the granting of abilities or technologies: the gods have constituted the environment in a way that conduces to human survival and flourishing. Given the Eleusinian setting of the play, these items no doubt suggest agriculture (a gift found early in Prometheus' catalog as well), but the emphasis is on the divinely created conditions rather than human learning or ability.

The next items mentioned continue the focus on the environment, describing the ways that humans can overcome its harshness:

πρὸς δὲ τοῖσι χείματος
προβλήματ' αἰθόν <τ'> ἐξαμύνασθαι θεοῦ,
πόντου τε ναυστολήμαθ' ὡς διαλλαγὰς
ἔχοιμεν ἀλλήλοισιν ὧν πένοιτο γῆ.
ἃ δ' ἔστ' ἄσημα κοὐ σαφῶς γιγνώσκομεν,
ἐς πῦρ βλέποντες καὶ κατὰ σπλάγχνων πτυχὰς
μάντεις προσημαίνουσιν οἰωνῶν τ' ἄπο. (207–13)

And in addition to these, defense against the winter and means of warding off the heat of the god, and sailing on the sea, so that we have exchanges with others for things the land lacks. And the things that are unseen and we do not know clearly, prophets foretell by looking into fire and at folds of entrails and from [the flight of] birds.

The connections between items in Theseus' speech are more associative than they are logical or developmental. The first items, defenses against cold and heat, presumably refer to shelter and clothing, and follow naturally as responses to the agricultural and climatic conditions mentioned just before. They return Theseus to specifically human capacities and skills, which are seen as means of compensation for shortcomings in their environment. Similarly,

---

88. A fragment of Democritus (B154 DK/D203 LM) suggests that human song imitates animal song, and speech figures in reconstructions of Democritean anthropology: Cole, *Democritus and the Sources of Greek Anthropology*, 33–35.

89. Collard, "*Supplices*," 163–64.

ships are presented as a means of making up the deficiencies of one's surroundings by enabling trade with far-off places. Finally, divination is likewise introduced as the compensation for human inability, as a response to "things that are unseen and we do not know clearly." The theme of divination, with which the catalog ends, appears as the final, and perhaps the consummate, way in which divinity guides human beings, and returns Theseus to the immediate context of Adrastus' failure to heed the oracular utterance. The idea of a divinity compensating benevolently for human lack is familiar also from the myth of Plato's *Protagoras*, but Theseus' statement is distinctive among the dramatic catalogs. There is little emphasis on the learned or invented quality of these skills, as we find in Prometheus' catalog (which likewise includes shelter, ships, and divination in a prominent role). Though human capacities, they are granted as a gift from the god. If Prometheus had been portrayed as a quasihuman inventor and human culture as the enlightened result of his interventions, Theseus' god appears as a mysterious, numinous benefactor granting basic means of subsistence to needy human beings.

As in Prometheus' catalog, the idea of development is present but unemphatic: after the initial stages (πρῶτον μὲν ... εἶτα δ'), there is no clear sequence described; the only further connector, πρὸς δὲ τοῖσι, suggests simple addition rather than temporal progression. The "progress" of the speech, then, is more binary than developmental: after granting σύνεσις, the god's benefactions come in a cascade, the cumulative effect of which is to bring about the differentiation of human from animal life.[90] There are no intermediate stages, in contrast to the Prometheus myth of the *Protagoras*, the Sisyphus fragment, and reconstructions of Democritus. This has consequences for what we understand the speech to be doing: not describing early human development, but setting out the basic constituents of human civilization.[91] As such, the items mentioned are not exhaustive, and point to a much wider body of gifts:

---

90. Mendelsohn persuasively connects the differentiation of humans from animals to a deeper anxiety of the play concerning gender and the boundaries of civilized life: Daniel Mendelsohn, *Gender and the City in Euripides' Political Plays* (Oxford: Oxford University Press, 2002), 155.

91. See Ann Michelini, "The Maze of the Logos: Euripides, 'Suppliants' 163–249," *Ramus* 20 (1991): 16–36. Michelini addresses the speech's place in developmental discourses in depth, and suggests that the speech is purposefully incoherent and "illogically synchronic" (23). It is only "illogically" synchronic if one sees it as a developmental narrative—which I argue it is not.

we are furnished, Theseus implies, with a panoply of skills and capacities that fit us to live in the world.

Theseus' catalog is distinguished from others of the fifth century by its strongly theistic foundation. It is framed by the ascription of these gifts to a god, and Theseus' conclusion reminds Adrastus of humans' good fortune and their intellectual inferiority:

> ἆρ' οὐ τρυφῶμεν, θεοῦ κατασκευὴν βίῳ
> δόντος τοιαύτην, οἷσιν οὐκ ἀρκεῖ τάδε;
> ἀλλ' ἡ φρόνησις τοῦ θεοῦ μεῖζον σθένειν
> ζητεῖ, τὸ γαῦρον δ' ἐν φρεσὶν κεκτημένοι
> δοκοῦμεν εἶναι δαιμόνων σοφώτεροι. (214–18)

> Are we not luxuriant, when the god has given such provision for life, if these things are not sufficient? But thought seeks to be stronger than the god, and having acquired arrogance in our minds, we think that we are wiser than the gods.

The question of human life's portion of good and bad has receded in the catalog, but returns at its close: the gifts enumerated are proof, in Theseus' mind, of humans' sufficient share of good things. The error Theseus diagnoses, that "thought seeks to be stronger than the god," presumably connects Adrastus' rejection of the oracular dictate with the unnamed interlocutor in the argument Theseus recalls.[92] To deny the sufficiency of what humans have been given is to reject the wisdom of the gods. The inferiority of human to divine intellect is a familiar *topos* in Greek thought, but it receives a modern, optimistic spin in Theseus' mouth, emphasizing the good will of the gods rather than their inscrutability.[93] Theseus' speech has often been dismissed as an incoherent combination of an archaic worldview in which the gods determine all human development with a sophistic interest in the history of human culture. This, however, underrates the sophistication of Theseus' theology: his view of a teleological order guaranteed by divinity is actually a novel intellectual development, and a twist on the broader interest in anthropology glimpsed in

---

92. On Theseus' and Adrastus' viewpoints, see Katerina Synodinou, "Wisdom through Experience: Theseus and Adrastus in Euripides' 'Suppliant Women,'" in *Wisdom and Folly in Euripides*, ed. Poulheria Kyriakou and Antonios Rengakos (Berlin: de Gruyter, 2016), 155–76.

93. See Donald J. Mastronarde, "The Optimistic Rationalist in Euripides: Theseus, Jocasta, Teiresias," in *Greek Tragedy and Its Legacy: Essays Presented to D. J. Conacher*, ed. Martin Cropp, Elaine Fantham, and S. E. Scully (Calgary: University of Calgary Press, 1986), 201–11.

the Palamedes and Prometheus catalogs. The combination of these different strands represents a daring intellectual experiment, an attempt to imagine an enlightened anthropo-theology.

The totalizing form and content of the speech place Theseus' optimism in a crucial relationship to his own authority as speaker. He delivers an account that he claims to have rehearsed before, and which is presented as a reasoned argument for a particular worldview. As a form of authoritative speech, the catalog lends weight to his argument that humans have more good than bad fortune. Yet Theseus will reverse the outcome of this speech—the rejection of Adrastus' plea for aid—later in the play when he comes to the aid of the suppliants. Theseus' change of mind is accompanied by quite a different view of human existence. In an exchange after he has resolved to retrieve the bodies, he expresses a view of humanity and divinity that, even if not explicitly contradicting the assertions of the earlier speech, suggests an opposing emphasis:

> ἀλλ', ὦ μάταιοι, γνῶτε τἀνθρώπων κακά·
> παλαίσμαθ' ἡμῶν ὁ βίος· εὐτυχοῦσι δὲ
> οἱ μὲν τάχ', οἱ δ' ἐσαῦθις, οἱ δ' ἤδη βροτῶν·
> τρυφᾷ δ' ὁ δαίμων· (549–52)

Oh, deluded ones, learn the miseries of humans! Our life is a wrestling bout. Some mortals have good fortune just now, some [will] at another time, some [have had it] already, but the god is luxuriant.

The vocabulary of the lines recalls the framing of the catalog speech, especially the verb τρυφάω ("be luxuriant") to describe a state of self-satisfaction—here based on the god's (again singular and unidentified) genuine superiority, in contrast to false human self-confidence. Where before Theseus had advocated an acknowledgment of the good that humans possess, he now calls for a recognition of the "miseries of humans," their subjection to the uncertainties of fortune. Like earlier, he describes a strict division between humans and the gods, but the idea of divine benevolence is replaced here with the god's apparent lack of concern for mortal suffering. The divergence is so extreme that some editors have deleted or reassigned the lines, but this is a desperate remedy.[94] A better approach is to see the divergence between the two passages

---

94. The passage (up to 557) is bracketed by Kovacs for deletion, though all other recent editors have retained it: David Kovacs, *Euripidea altera* (Leiden: Brill, 1996), 85–86. Murray

as an aspect of the play's dialectical thinking.[95] This can be observed throughout the play's first half, as Theseus' initial views on the recovery of the bodies are continuously confronted with challenges and alternative perspectives. Though Theseus is certainly a figure of moral and intellectual authority (and even seems to grow in stature as the play progresses), his viewpoint is nevertheless subject to dialectical pressure.[96]

The anthropology of *Suppliants* has to be understood in relation to the play's politics more generally. The work's reflection on Athenian democracy and empire has often been discussed, but a dialectical understanding of its anthropology contributes an important dimension. The political discourse of *Suppliants* has often been understood to center on the juxtaposition of Theseus and the chorus of lamenting mothers, around which a host of oppositions accrue: male/female, Athenian/Argive, reason/intellect, speech/song, to name a few.[97] Victoria Wohl (drawing on Nicole Loraux) has argued that these oppositions should be viewed as a dialectic of politics and "anti-politics," in which the chorus' lamentations pose a significant challenge to Theseus' affirmations of Athenian ideology.[98] The anthropological discourse of the play seeks to establish continuity across these different relations to the political sphere, and represents a kind of vertical axis in the play's view of culture, in contrast to the horizontal axis of political/anti-political discourse. *Suppliants'*

---

proposed to move the lines into Adrastus' speech of supplication (to follow 179), which would make Theseus' catalog speech a direct response. This emendation, though unwarranted editorially, does show a recognition that the position expressed in the lines is almost opposed to that of Theseus' earlier speech.

95. Michelini also considers the divergence between the different viewpoints, but is inclined to privilege the pessimistic one (and to denigrate the thinking of the catalog speech): Michelini, "The Maze of the Logos." More sympathetic to the optimistic account (though recognizing the opposition as substantive) is Jacqueline Assaël, "ὅς . . . θεῶν: Euripide, 'Suppliantes,' v. 201 sqq.," *Revue des études grecques* 110 (1997): 84–103.

96. Victoria Wohl connects Theseus' "paradoxical person" to the play's structuring oppositions: Wohl, *Euripides and the Politics of Form*, esp. 93–98. See further Sophie Mills, *Theseus, Tragedy, and the Athenian Empire* (Oxford: Clarendon Press, 1997), 104–28.

97. Peter Burian, "Logos and Pathos: The Politics of the 'Suppliant Women,'" in *Directions in Euripidean Criticism*, ed. Peter Burian (Durham: Duke University Press, 1985), 129–55; Helene P. Foley, *Female Acts in Greek Tragedy* (Princeton: Princeton University Press, 2001), 19–55; Mendelsohn, *Gender and the City*, esp. 170–96.

98. Wohl, *Euripides and the Politics of Form*, 98–106; Nicole Loraux, *The Mourning Voice: An Essay on Greek Tragedy*, trans. Elizabeth Trapnell Rawlings (Ithaca: Cornell University Press, 2002), 26–41.

politics is local, focused on tensions within Athenian history and culture, while its anthropology seeks to give a universalizing account of human life. This is consistent with the absence of any mention of political organization in the catalog: Theseus' optimistic view of humanity appears possible only in isolation from the political concerns that dominate the work, and is ultimately brought into stark confrontation with the realities of the situation. *Suppliants'* anthropology, then, is itself in dialectic with the play's political discourse. The catalog's vision of a beneficent god and a grateful humanity does not withstand the challenges posed by Theseus' own changing thought or the play's ideology of Athenian exceptionalism. The authority of Theseus' catalog, of all those discussed in this chapter, is the most profoundly challenged by the developing thinking of the play, but this is no grounds to consider it irrelevant or denigrate its account. Rather, it is the coherence and significance of Theseus' anthropology that renders it a dialectical partner for the play's complex and sophisticated political discourse.

Polar Anthropology: *Antigone*

The first stasimon of Sophocles' *Antigone*, the so-called Ode to Man, presents a strong contrast to Theseus' speech in emphatically ascribing the fundamental skills and capacities for existence to human beings. The stasimon might seem to be out of place when considered in the company of the other texts in this chapter: it is an enumeration of human actions and skills rather than gifts or inventions, the agent is collective *anthrōpos* ("man" or "humanity") rather than an individual god or mortal, and there is no comparison to an early, "animal" state.[99] But these divergences are only significant if one views the other texts primarily as invention catalogs or developmental narratives. If, instead, one sees them primarily as synchronic images of human culture and capacities,

---

99. Many critics have asserted a relation to Protagoras' thought, mainly on the basis of the myth in Plato's dialogue: R.W.B. Burton, *The Chorus in Sophocles' Tragedies* (Oxford: Oxford University Press, 1980), 100–101; Gregory Crane, "Creon and the 'Ode to Man' in Sophocles' 'Antigone,'" *Harvard Studies in Classical Philology* 92 (1989): 108–11; Elizabeth van Nes Ditmars, *Sophocles' "Antigone": Lyric Shape and Meaning* (Pisa: Giardini Editori e Stampatori, 1992), 50–53; Utzinger, *Periphrades Aner*, 134–36. These connections are for the most part quite general, related to the prominence of political life in both texts. Though there is good reason to attribute a developmental narrative something like that of the dialogue to Protagoras, we are far more secure in understanding this as belonging to the same intellectual field (along with the other texts discussed in this chapter), but not necessarily as directly connected to Sophocles.

then the *Antigone* stasimon fits right in—and, indeed, may be in some sense the most thorough manifestation of the cultural catalog form by virtue of *not* being connected to an invention discourse or developmental narrative.

In another respect, the *Antigone* stasimon encapsulates the tradition of the cultural catalog: its most striking quality is the polar image of humanity it provides, making manifest an ambivalence concerning human culture and invention that has been evident, to greater or lesser degree, in all the catalogs. This polarity is present from the very first, famous, phrase, "many are the wonders [*deina*, equally, 'terrors'], but nothing exists more wonderful [or 'terrible'] than man" (332–33: πολλὰ τὰ δεινὰ κοὐδὲν ἀν- / θρώπου δεινότερον πέλει). The key adjective *deinos* is related to a group of words connected to fear, so the most basic meaning of the phrase is probably "there are many fearful things," with "fear" potentially understood as horror or as awe. The lines recall the first stasimon of Aeschylus' *Libation Bearers*, which begins "many are the terrible [*deina*] things earth nourishes" (585–86: πολλὰ μὲν γᾶ τρέφει / δεινά), where the sense of *deina* is unambiguously negative. In both choral odes, these lines open a priamel comparing the many *deina* to aspects of human culture—to *anthrōpos* in the *Antigone*, and to the "overbold thought" (594–95: ὑπέρτολμον ... φρόνημα) of men and the "all-bold desires" (597: παντόλμους ἔρωτας) of women in the *Libation Bearers*.[100] As the *Libation Bearers* song continues, it becomes in effect a catalog of famous female misdeeds, enumerated for comparison with the present situation, which appears to match if not top them.

The sense of *deina* in the *Antigone* stasimon, by contrast, turns out in the most immediate sense to be positive, enumerating the actions that make humanity the most *deinos*: seafaring, agriculture, hunting, and so on. These make man, in the ode's most sweeping formulation, παντοπόρος, "having all resource," and ἄπορος ἐπ' οὐδέν, "without resource toward nothing" (360). The polar linguistic structure is characteristic of the thought of the ode, which even at its most triumphant emphasizes limits of man's *deinotēs*, and points to the range of outcomes for human action.[101] Humans are extraordinarily

---

100. Catalogs and priamels are often found together in Greek poetry (or, perhaps better, priamels have a catalogic tendency): Christopher A. Faraone, "Catalogues, Priamels, and Stanzaic Structure in Early Greek Elegy," *Transactions of the American Philological Association* 135 (2005): 249–65.

101. The ambiguities of the image of man in the stasimon have frequently been explored: Charles Paul Segal, "Sophocles' Praise of Man and the Conflicts of the 'Antigone,'" *Arion* 3 (1964): 46–66; A.P.M.H. Lardinois and Th. C. W. Oudemans, *Tragic Ambiguity: Anthropology, Philosophy and Sophocles' "Antigone"* (Leiden: Brill, 1987), 120–31.

resourceful, but their resource can be directed to good or bad ends, and can make them as terrible as they are wonderful. The ode accordingly ends on a note of disavowal, as the chorus sets itself apart from those who act recklessly to the detriment of the city—lines that in context point to the person who has buried Polyneices (not yet known to them as Antigone) but could, in a broader reading of the play, evoke Creon just as much or more.[102]

Considered within the context of other cultural catalogs, the *Antigone* stasimon appears quite limited in the number of items it enumerates. Moreover, it gives the bulk of its time to describing human *actions* characteristic of *deinotēs*, along the lines of Solon's *Elegy to the Muses*, rather than innate capacities or learned skills. The picture is overwhelmingly synchronic and nondevelopmental, though there are a few interesting suggestions of process. Following the opening priamel, the first strophic pair offers a picture of human actions in the natural world that emphasizes autonomy and mastery:

πολλὰ τὰ δεινὰ κοὐδὲν ἀν-
θρώπου δεινότερον πέλει·
τοῦτο καὶ πολιοῦ πέραν
πόντου χειμερίῳ νότῳ
χωρεῖ, περιβρυχίοισιν
περῶν ὑπ' οἴδμασιν, θεῶν
τε τὰν ὑπερτάταν, Γᾶν
ἄφθιτον, ἀκαμάταν, ἀποτρύεται
ἰλλομένων ἀρότρων ἔτος εἰς ἔτος
ἱππείῳ γένει πολεύων. (332–41)

Many are the wonders, but nothing exists more wonderful than man. It goes over the grey sea by stormy wind, passing beneath engulfing swells. And the highest of the gods, Earth, unwithering, untiring, it wears out as the plows revolve year after year, turning it up with the horselike race.

The descriptions of seafaring and agriculture, both early benefactions in Prometheus' and Theseus' speeches, here suggest danger and even violence. The priority given to seafaring over agriculture (which is reversed in the other speeches) is familiar from Solon's *Elegy to the Muses*, which likewise places the

---

102. On the contextual significance of the ode, see especially Burton, *The Chorus in Sophocles' Tragedies*, 95–104; Crane, "Creon and the 'Ode to Man'"; Utzinger, *Periphrades Aner*, 61–72; Charles Segal, *Tragedy and Civilization: An Interpretation of Sophocles* (Cambridge, MA: Harvard University Press, 1981), 151–206.

two first in its catalog of human pursuits. Solon had emphasized the dangers of seafaring (13 West 43–45), and the *Antigone*'s description of storms and swells shows us this danger in action. Even more striking is the description of agriculture almost as an assault on the goddess Earth (ἀποτρύω, "wear out," is strongly negative in sense): through continual plowing, man is able to wear down the "highest of the gods ... unwithering, untiring." Mastery over the environment has been a concern in all the cultural catalogs discussed, but such mastery here takes on a particularly violent form. Human endeavor appears a danger to itself, its environment, and even to the gods.

The antistrophe moves from control of the environment to control over animals. This is another common catalog *topos*, but in the *Antigone* an intellectualizing tone enters that makes evident the underlying supposition that humans are elevated above animals by their intellect:[103]

κουφονόων τε φῦλον ὀρ-
νίθων ἀμφιβαλὼν ἄγει
καὶ θηρῶν ἀγρίων ἔθνη
πόντου τ' εἰναλίαν φύσιν
σπείραισι δικτυοκλώστοις,
περιφραδὴς ἀνήρ· κρατεῖ
δὲ μηχαναῖς ἀγραύλου
θηρὸς ὀρεσσιβάτα, λασιαύχενά θ'
ἵππον ὀχμάζεται ἀμφὶ λόφον ζυγῷ
οὔρειόν τ' ἀκμῆτα ταῦρον. (342–51)

And the tribe of light-minded birds he carries off, and the races of wild beasts and the water-creatures of the sea, surrounding them with folds woven in mesh, man, clever in all respects. And he rules with contrivances the mountain-dwelling beast of the field and holds fast the shaggy-necked horse with a yoke around its neck and the mountain-dwelling, untiring bull.

In contrast to the violence suggested by the strophe, the antistrophe emphasizes the indirect application of force and qualities of cleverness that enable human mastery. There is a repeated emphasis on humans in contrast to other species, using generic words for animal types ("tribe," φῦλον; "races," ἔθνη; "creature," φύσις; "beast," θήρ), and collective singulars in opposition to "man, clever in all respects." By virtue of this cleverness, man is able to catch those

---

103. A similar idea of humans' intellectual mastery over animals is found in Euripides' *Aiolos* (F 24b) and in the *Protagoras* myth: Egli, *Euripides im Kontext*, 206–7.

animals that can be caught in nets, and to "rule with contrivances" those too large. Humans gain power over animals by their intelligence, which allows them to outwit and subdue even the strongest and fiercest of beasts. While the strophe had emphasized the danger and violence inherent in the human relation to the environment, the antistrophe presents an image of humans in easy control over other living beings. The first strophic pair, though treating relatively few activities (seafaring, agriculture, hunting, domestication), nevertheless suggests a totalizing image of humans as masters over their surroundings, enabled by both force and intellect.

The second strophic pair departs from the extensive and highly elaborated description of human actions to enumerate, in much more condensed form, human intellectual capacities. It introduces the first images of human society the ode has offered, after describing man in relation only to the nonhuman environment. It is also the first moment that any sense of history or process enters, with the suggestion that the *deinotēs* of man has been acquired by a process of learning:

καὶ φθέγμα καὶ ἀνεμόεν φρόνημα καὶ ἀστυνόμους
ὀργὰς ἐδιδάξατο, καὶ δυσαύλων
πάγων ὑπαίθρεια καὶ
δύσομβρα φεύγειν βέλη
παντοπόρος· (353–60)

And voice and windlike thought and city-ruling impulses he taught himself, and to escape the open air of inhospitable frosts and the harsh-raining missiles, all-resourceful.

The middle-voice verb ἐδιδάξατο appears to be used in an unusual reflexive sense, to mean "teach oneself" (rather than the more usual meaning "cause to be taught" or simply "teach"). Here, the unusual usage goes along with a striking thought: that humans collectively acquired language, thought, social qualities, and the means of subsistence amid harsh climate by self-education. Among these capacities, only "city-ruling impulses" have not been encountered in other catalogs, hinting at the political dimension of the song that will become even more apparent in the following antistrophe.[104] Though it is not unique in Greek to encounter *orgai* (usually, "temperaments" or "passions")

---

104. Ditmars, *Sophocles' "Antigone,"* 48–56 emphasizes the political dimensions of the stasimon as a whole.

that are acquired rather than innate, the assertion that man has taught himself these impulses draws attention to the idea of self-education.[105] The basic capacities for subsistence and social existence, according to the chorus, are neither natural characteristics nor gifts of the gods, but endpoints of a process of teaching. Yet there is no sense of a sequence or a continuing development (the aorist tense renders the action completed), and the chorus does not pursue the inquiry into humans' acquisition of their abilities. The lines may not bear further pressure, but they suggest the most strongly anthropic view of cultural origins we have encountered.

After a series of present-tense verbs in the first strophic pair, the finite verbs begin to shift tense: "he taught himself" describes a past action, and is followed by the present-tense "resourceless, he goes toward nothing of what will come" (360–61: ἄπορος ἐπ' οὐδὲν ἔρχεται / τὸ μέλλον), which is closely connected to the previous phrase by the opposites *pantoporos/aporos* (all-resourceful/resourceless). Humans' ability to meet anything the future holds appears to be a result of their self-education. Man's development appears complete, and fits him for anything to come—except, as we learn in the only future-tense verb of the stasimon, "Hades alone he will not gain escape from" (361–62: Ἅιδα μόνον / φεῦξιν οὐκ ἐπάξεται). With striking asyndeton, the chorus sharply qualifies the idea of human resourcefulness by recognizing the limitation of death. This recognition constitutes a kind of upper bound to the abilities enumerated in the foregoing: despite their mastery over the environment and development of social life, humans cannot acquire immortality. The limitation of death significantly tempers the triumphant tone of the song and places humans in the middle of a hierarchy of gods, men, and animals. Even human relation to death, though, is turned into a kind of accomplishment in the following line, as the chorus celebrates that he "has thought out escapes from impossible diseases" (363–64: νόσων δ' ἀμηχάνων φυγὰς / ξυμπέφρασται). The perfect tense here points to the idea of human capacities having reached their point of completion, and this is the last particular ability that the chorus mentions. As in Prometheus' catalog, which described medicine as "the greatest," the knowledge of healing remedies appears to the *Antigone* chorus as the climactic achievement of human thought. Yet, in so strongly emphasizing the idea of escape (359: φεύγειν, 362: φεῦξιν, 363: φυγάς), the strophe as a whole suggests much more

---

105. Mark Griffith, ed., *Sophocles: "Antigone"* (Cambridge: Cambridge University Press, 1999), 188.

of human vulnerability than the previous strophic pair. Human *deinotēs* appears ultimately to be a way of escaping the dangers of earthly existence and dealing with the limitations of human nature.

An element of defamiliarization has been present in all the catalogs discussed in this chapter: pointing to the origin of a practice inevitably makes it appear to some extent as contingent, and isolating individual inventions or capacities brings them under a degree of scrutiny that they do not receive when embedded in daily life. One effect of the catalogs has been to reveal the acquired quality of practices that could be taken as given, as, for example, when Palamedes claims the invention of mealtimes, or when Prometheus and Theseus highlight the practice of divination. The *Antigone* stasimon carries this defamiliarization much further, suggesting an ambiguity to human culture and achievement that effects a double estrangement: not just of the action from its role in life (a property of all cultural catalogs), but of the purpose of the action from its outcome. The opening of the second antistrophe, though not quite a part of the catalog proper, is crucial for the emergent anthropology of the song: "Having some clever thing, the contrivance of skill beyond expectation, he comes sometimes to bad, other times to good" (365–67: σοφόν τι τὸ μηχανόεν / τέχνας ὑπὲρ ἐλπίδ' ἔχων, / τοτὲ μὲν κακόν, ἄλλοτ' ἐπ' ἐσθλὸν ἕρπει). This might be a generalization of the entire catalog: their intellect enables humans to act by means of inventive contrivance beyond their apparent limitations. The unique substantive *to mēchanoen*, which in its very form suggests contrivance or neologism, returns to a group of words that has recurred through the ode: man caught wild animals by *mēchanais* (348) and in the preceding lines devised flight from *amēchanōn* diseases (363)—the point there being, of course, that disease is no longer *amēchanos*. The root has ambiguous connotations, potentially suggesting underhandedness or subterfuge. And we learn that it does not always yield its intended results: "he comes sometimes to bad, other times to good," with the verb *herpō* suggesting slow, even unconscious movement toward an unknown end.[106] Human cleverness has always been a positive through the song, yet here we learn that it can misfire, as was emphatically the case in Solon. Human intellect itself has a polar quality.

The chorus describes one manifestation of this polarity in their famous contrast of the *hupsipolis* with the *apolis*:

---

106. See further Rachel Kitzinger, *The Choruses of Sophokles' "Antigone" and "Philoktetes": A Dance of Words* (Leiden: Brill, 2008), 24–27.

νόμους παρείρων χθονὸς
θεῶν τ' ἔνορκον δίκαν
ὑψίπολις· ἄπολις ὅτῳ τὸ μὴ καλὸν
ξύνεστι τόλμας χάριν.¹⁰⁷ (368–71)

> Interweaving laws of the land and the sworn justice of the gods he is high in the city [or "his city is high"]. He is city-less [or "in a noncity"] with whom the not-noble consorts because of boldness.

In this, the first explicitly moralizing and theological statement of the ode, the chorus turns to the question of the ends of human *deinotēs*. They betray a faith in justice that has both political and religious dimensions: the one whose actions manifest "the laws of the land" and "the sworn justice of the gods" is *hupsipolis*, while "boldness" leads the other to neglect both human and divine law, rendering him *apolis*. Just as clever contrivance can lead either to good or to bad ends, political existence can bring human life to its zenith or to its nadir. Coming at the close of a song praising human achievement, these lines are a stark warning against the pursuit of human ends in the absence of divine sanction. One could see this reminder as reflecting back on the catalog in different ways: either as a validation of the righteousness of human mastery and cultural achievements (since if unjust they would have led to ruin), or, in a more aporetic sense, as raising the question of the ends to which human capacities are put. In either case, the polar moral and political dimension of the second antistrophe returns us to the events of the play, framing the actions of the protagonists in terms of the ode's anthropology.

The stasimon's polar view of human activity will continue to resonate through the rest of the play, and the chorus will return to the themes of the song in a more pessimistic tone. Though the first stasimon has often been extracted from the play as a kind of authoritative statement, the dialectical reading pursued here suggests it has to be read in relation to other utterances of the chorus.¹⁰⁸ Tragic choruses in general offer a stark demonstration of the ways that dramatic authority can expand and contract in different situations: they appear at times as bearers of impersonal, quasidivine wisdom and

---

107. The manuscripts' παρείρων ("inserting") is hard to make sense of, and Reiske's proposed γεραίρων ("honoring") may well be better.

108. My reading of the first stasimon within the *Antigone* is substantially indebted to Ella Haselswerdt's discussion in "Chorality and Lyric Thought in Greek Tragedy" (Ph.D. diss., Princeton University, 2018), esp. 49–51.

knowledge, and at other times as vulnerable individuals caught up in events beyond their control or understanding. The *Antigone* chorus' authority and their trust in human achievement quite notably change over the course of the play: the parodos' patriotic and even jingoistic evocation of Thebes' victory over the Seven undergoes a darkening in the first and second stasima, which are the most explicitly anthropological; the next two odes then focus on the divine and its role in human affairs, and are notable for their disconnection from the actions onstage, while the final stasimon, addressed to Dionysus, has a desperate, beseeching quality that reveals the chorus overwhelmed by the events of the play.[109] The chorus' final lyric utterance in the play calls for Dionysus to "appear" (1149: προφάνηθ') among his attendants, "who, raging, dance for you all night, the controller Iakchos" (1151–52: αἵ σε μαινόμεναι πάννυχοι / χορεύουσι τὸν ταμίαν Ἴακχον), invoking the god's Eleusinian cult-title, and thereby the promise of salvation in the afterlife.[110] The chorus' belief in human abilities appears profoundly shaken, and they appeal to a god for deliverance from the impending catastrophe of the play.

An important shift occurs in the chorus' second stasimon, which returns to the anthropological thought and some of the language of the first, but brings out the potential for human actions to have unforeseen and catastrophic consequences. Having just witnessed Antigone condemned to death, the chorus sing an ode that begins by framing the events of the play within the hereditary misfortunes of the Labdacids.[111] They turn then in the second strophic pair to a series of generalizations about the power of Zeus and the role of *elpis* in human life. Scholars have often puzzled over the application of these lines to one or both of the protagonists, but they are better understood as a generalizing return to the anthropological concerns of the first stasimon than as a

---

109. On the stasimon, see Scott Scullion, "Dionysos and Katharsis in 'Antigone,'" *Classical Antiquity* 17 (1998): 96–122.

110. Albert Henrichs, "Between Country and City: Cultic Dimensions of Dionysus in Athens and Attica," in *Cabinet of the Muses: Essays on Classical and Comparative Literature in Honor of Thomas G. Rosenmeyer*, ed. Mark Griffith and Donald J. Mastronarde (Atlanta: Scholars Press, 1990), 264–69.

111. See Renaud Gagné, *Ancestral Fault in Ancient Greece* (Cambridge: Cambridge University Press, 2013), 362–76. Gagné highlights the importance of Solon's *Elegy to the Muses* for the second stasimon, which is consistent with my observation of continuities between the poem and the first stasimon.

direct commentary on the action.[112] Where divinity had been almost entirely absent from the first stasimon's view of human life, it is now emphatically and ominously present. The chorus begins the second strophe by asking, "your power, Zeus, what transgression of men can constrain it?" (604–5: τεάν, Ζεῦ, δύνασιν τίς ἀν- / δρῶν ὑπερβασία κατάσχοι;), asserting the absolute superiority of divinity over human actions, and proclaiming the eternal law, "great wealth comes to no one of mortals without disaster" (613–14: οὐδὲν' ἕρπει / θνατῶν βίοτος πάμπολυς ἐκτὸς ἄτας).[113] This is a traditional, Solonic notion, but the repetition of the verb from the first stasimon's "he comes [ἕρπει] sometimes to bad, other times to good" presents the statement as the obverse of the earlier focus on human action: now humans appear as passive recipients of good and bad, rather than agents themselves.[114] The polar anthropology, however, is the same: human life is characterized by extremes of achievement and ruin.

The final antistrophe continues to meditate on the polar quality of existence, returning to the first stasimon's discussion of the way that human intentions miscarry:

ἁ γὰρ δὴ πολύπλαγκτος ἐλ-
πὶς πολλοῖς μὲν ὄνησις ἀνδρῶν,
πολλοῖς δ' ἀπάτα κουφονόων ἐρώτων·
εἰδότι δ' οὐδὲν ἕρπει,
πρὶν πυρὶ θερμῷ πόδα τις προσαύσῃ. (615–19)

For much-wandering expectation is to many men a benefit, but to many it is a deception of light-minded desires. It comes to one knowing nothing before he burns his foot in a hot fire.

---

112. On the relation between dramatic character and generalization in the ode, classic is Patricia E. Easterling, "The Second Stasimon of 'Antigone,'" in *Dionysiaca: Nine Studies in Greek Poetry by Former Pupils*, ed. Roger D. Dawe, James Diggle, and Patricia E. Easterling (Cambridge: Cambridge Faculty Library, 1978), 141–58.

113. The text here is highly doubtful; I follow Lloyd-Jones and Wilson's OCT, though Heath's suggestion is even more amenable to my interpretation: οὐδὲν ἕρπει / θνατῶν βιότῳ πάμπολύ γ' ἐκτὸς ἄτας, "nothing enormous comes to the life of mortals without disaster." Human success generally—not just great wealth—would be characterized by the potential for disaster.

114. There is an illuminating discussion of the two stasima and the Solonic intertext in Douglas Cairns, "From Solon to Sophocles: Intertextuality and Interpretation in Sophocles' 'Antigone,'" *Japan Studies in Classical Antiquity* 2 (2014): 3–30.

Earlier, humans had possessed a "contrivance of skill beyond *elpis*," and the excessive quality of this contrivance was loosely but suggestively connected to the way that humans come to bad and good. Here, the focus shifts to *elpis* itself, not as a limit to be surpassed but as itself a quality of presumption or excess, which leads to polar results, success or disappointment.[115] The phrase "deception of light-minded desires" repeats the unusual compound that earlier described "light-minded birds" (342–43), while also looking forward to the next stasimon addressed to *erōs*. In its negative form, as "deception" (*apata*), *elpis* makes human thought bird-like in its insubstantiality, directing it to unattainable objects, and leading to inevitable failure. *Elpis*, the ode suggests, is the reason for the polarity of human outcomes, a hope or expectation that leads humans to their greatest achievements and to their greatest failures. And here, in contrast to the first stasimon, the emphasis is on the possibility of failure, and the consequent suffering and disappointment.

Solon's *Elegy to the Muses* is again an important intertext for its description of humanity's vain expectations of success, which inevitably lead to suffering: "until this point [at which we suffer], gaping we enjoy light expectations" (13 West 35–36: ἄχρι δὲ τούτου / χάσκοντες κούφαις ἐλπίσι τερπόμεθα). Likewise, the *Antigone* chorus describes the moment at which deception "comes to one knowing nothing" (with the verb *herpei* again suggesting a gradual, almost covert process) and quite literally burns the one who was deceived by hope. The final part of the antistrophe explains that such deception comes from the gods, who appear capable of implanting false expectation in humans, and thereby leading them down the path to *atē*, disaster:

> τὸ κακὸν δοκεῖν ποτ' ἐσθλὸν
> τῷδ' ἔμμεν, ὅτῳ φρένας
> θεὸς ἄγει πρὸς ἄταν·
> πράσσει δ' ὀλιγοστὸν χρόνον ἐκτὸς ἄτας.[116] (622–25)

> The bad appears at times to be good to one whose wits the god leads toward disaster. He fares for a little time free from disaster.

The ode closes by pointing to the gods as the agents of deception, who lead humans to ruin by confusing their sense of good and bad. Humans do not

---

115. On the importance of *elpis*, see Lardinois and Oudemans, *Tragic Ambiguity*, 137–38.

116. Reading the manuscripts' ὀλιγοστὸν χρόνον rather than Lloyd-Jones and Wilson's ὀλίγος τὸν χρόνον ("little fares for a time").

just fail to achieve their goals, but their goals are shaped by divinity in ways that lead them, unaware, to catastrophe. The resulting image of human life as only "for a little time free from disaster" presents a stark contrast to the confidence of the first stasimon's celebration of human achievement. While the earlier song recognized limits to human achievement, these were connected to innate qualities rather than divine intervention. Reading the two songs together presents the play's polar anthropology in both optimistic and pessimistic terms, focusing either on the extent of human capacities or the limits set by the gods. The second stasimon brings out the first's latent sense of human ends as radically uncertain, and traces this uncertainty to the powers of the gods. The results is a profound ambivalence concerning human capacities and achievements, which appear as likely to be illusory as real. As the play goes on, one cannot but hear anew the negative polarity of *polla ta deina*.

It is probably not a coincidence that the most explicitly anthropological of the catalogs is also the most ambivalent about human capacities. At the root of this ambivalence, I suggest, is a cultural anxiety concerning human invention and achievement itself, insofar as it threatens to displace divine prerogative. The relation of the catalogs to divine power has been underdetermined in different ways, most visibly in the contradictory impulses of the *Antigone* chorus to celebrate human invention while fearing its results. Likewise, for Palamedes, the claim to be the source for the central inventions of culture implicitly denies the divine provenance of these benefactions, and his almost-superhuman intellect makes him a figure of doubt and suspicion within the play. Both the *Antigone* and the Palamedes dramas as a whole would have explored the ways that human achievement and inventiveness are inadequate in the face of circumstances, and can lead to disaster. The converse relation is displayed in the figure of Prometheus, who, though a god, has an ambiguous relation to divinity in general, and describes his gifts in the terms of human ingenuity. This leaves open an uncertainty surrounding the power of Zeus, which the rest of the work explores by depicting the miseries of Io, an example of humanity's continuing subjection to the gods. Theseus' catalog might seem to avoid such ambiguity by ascribing all human capacities to the gods, but the framing of his catalog as a contribution to a debate concerning divinity opens up the possibility of alternative, pessimistic positions, which the drama's further course explores. While the gods are the sources of human thriving, they are also shown to be the sources of human suffering. Whether attributing the achievements of culture to gods or motals, a dialectical reading of all these catalogs reveals that their apparent confidence belies an anxiety concerning the role of divinity in human existence.

Fictions of Divinity: The Sisyphus Fragment

The thinking of the catalog, this chapter has argued, is crucially a theological inquiry, and as such takes part in a wider questioning of the gods in late fifth-century culture. At its most extreme, this inquiry could issue in atheism or agnosticism, and important thinkers of the late fifth century clearly entertained the idea that divinity is a human fiction, whether created intentionally or not.[117] A particularly apposite comparison to the texts I discuss here is the Sisyphus fragment, which illustrates in dramatic form both an extreme theological skepticism and a developmental account of human culture. Though treating some of the same issues as the cultural catalogs, it develops them in a stepwise theory of culture that is usually taken to be closely related to philosophical speculation.[118] The passage is attributed in ancient sources to both Critias and Euripides, and the speaker named as Sisyphus (though the name of the play is not specified).[119] These questions of provenance can be set aside for now, as can the even more vexed question of how seriously to take the views expressed, which is unanswerable without a fuller knowledge of the text as a whole.[120] What is important for the present context is to see how the fragment reflects an interest in the building-blocks of human culture and the relation to the divine that is familiar from the catalogs, but at the same time departs from them in expounding this image developmentally and genealogically.

---

117. David Sedley, "The Atheist Underground," in *Politeia in Greek and Roman Philosophy*, ed. Verity Harte and Melissa Lane (Cambridge: Cambridge University Press, 2013), 329–48; Mirjam Kotwick, "Interrogating the Gods," in *The Cambridge Companion to the Sophists*, ed. Joshua Billings and Christopher Moore (Cambridge: Cambridge University Press, forthcoming).

118. On the philosophical context, see Charles Kahn, "Greek Religion and Philosophy in the Sisyphus Fragment," *Phronesis* 42 (1997): 247–62. The issue of theological skepticism is discussed more thoroughly in chapter 3.

119. The fragment is edited as Critias F9 in *TrGF*. On the question of attribution, see Albrecht Dihle, "Das Satyrspiel 'Sisyphos,'" *Hermes* 105 (1977): 28–42; Marek Winiarczyk, "Nochmals das Satyrspiel 'Sisyphos,'" *Wiener Studien* 100 (1987): 35–45.

120. See Tim Whitmarsh, "Atheistic Aesthetics: The Sisyphus Fragment, Poetics and the Creativity of Drama," *Cambridge Classical Journal* 60 (2014): 109–26.

Sisyphus begins by describing the bestial state of early humans, employing the comparison of humans to animals that is familiar from the cultural catalogs:

ἦν χρόνος ὅτ' ἦν ἄτακτος ἀνθρώπων βίος
καὶ θηριώδης ἰσχύος θ' ὑπηρέτης,
ὅτ' οὐδὲν ἆθλον οὔτε τοῖς ἐσθλοῖσιν ἦν
οὔτ' αὖ κόλασμα τοῖς κακοῖς ἐγίγνετο. (Critias F 19; B25 DK 1–4)

There was a time when the life of humans was disordered and bestial and subservient to force, when there was no reward for the good or punishment for the wicked.

The comparison of early humans to animals here has the sense less of confusion and lack of organization, which was found in the catalogs, than of moral baseness—more akin to the story told in Plato's *Protagoras*, where Protagoras, a famous agnostic, claims that humans continually wronged one another because they lacked *politikē technē* (321b). Though Sisyphus does not attribute depravity to all humans, he describes wickedness as an inevitable characteristic of some, which is unchecked in their precultural state. Much the same image is found in a fragment of the tragedian Moschion, usually dated to the fourth or third century, in which a character presents an account of early human development from an animal state in which "law was weak, and violence shared a throne with Zeus" (F 6: ὁ μὲν νόμος / ταπεινός, ἡ βία δὲ σύνθρονος Διί).[121] In comparison to the catalogs, the Sisyphus and Moschion fragments present a quite different image of humans' early state: humans lack not the basic skills of subsistence (which do not appear to be at issue), but the social rules that would ensure right conduct. Humanity appears to have a natural tendency toward vice, which keeps it in a state of animal misery.

Sisyphus goes on to describe relief from this bestial state through the enactment of laws, which provide a check on the impunity that previously reigned among humans:

---

121. G. Xanthakis-Karamanos, "Remarks on Moschion's Account of Progress," *Classical Quarterly* 31 (1981): 410–17; Utzinger, *Periphrades Aner*, 186–87. The fragment seems to reflect a much more comprehensive theory of cultural development than we find in any fifth-century text; it furthermore has an interesting catalogic tendency, mainly expressed in the description of all that early humans lacked (thereby suggesting an idea of what makes humans civilized).

κἄπειτά μοι δοκοῦσιν ἄνθρωποι νόμους
θέσθαι κολαστάς, ἵνα δίκη τύραννος ᾖ
<...> τήν θ' ὕβριν δούλην ἔχῃ (Critias F19; B25 DK 5–7)

And then it seems to me that humans set up laws as punishers, so that justice should be tyrant and hold arrogance enslaved.

Sisyphus attributes the invention of laws to humans in general, as they seem to respond to the most basic human need for safety and order. Law has appeared as a human invention in some of the catalogs, though usually as a culminating achievement of civilization rather than a basic constituent of it: Gorgias' Palamedes claimed written laws as one of his inventions, and the *Antigone* chorus had mentioned "city-ruling impulses" as one of the capacities humans taught themselves. Again, however, the closer parallel for the Sisyphus text is in the *Protagoras* myth, in which humans' violent tendencies cause Zeus to send Hermes to distribute shame (αἰδώς) and justice (δίκη) to all, thus allowing them to subsist in communities without continually wronging one another. The image of human life suggested by the Sisyphus fragment and the *Protagoras* myth is notably more social than that of any of the catalogs, emphasizing coexistence over subsistence. This must reflect in part the interest in *nomos* and *phusis* that develops in the sophistic culture of the late fifth century, and investigates the ways that human beings come to live in political collectives.[122]

Sisyphus displays a cynical attitude toward conventional morality, adopting a position similar to that found in a text of Antiphon, which asserts that right and wrong are determined more by law and custom than by nature.[123] The collective invention of laws turns out to be inadequate to ensure social existence, leading a single clever individual to formulate the idea of the gods:

---

122. Guthrie, *The Sophists*, 60–74; Charles H. Kahn, "The Origins of Social Contract Theory," in *The Sophists and Their Legacy*, ed. G. B. Kerferd (Wiesbaden: Steiner, 1981), 92–108; Bett, "Nature and Norms."

123. Antiphon's text, however, sees the conventional quality of laws as reason to disregard them when there is no chance of being caught (B44a DK/D38a LM): Gerard J. Pendrick, *Antiphon the Sophist* (Cambridge: Cambridge University Press, 2002), 59–65; Michael Gagarin, *Antiphon the Athenian: Oratory, Law, and Justice in the Age of the Sophists* (Austin: University of Texas Press, 2002), 65–73. Whether Antiphon actually held such views or expounded them dialectically is uncertain.

ἔπειτ' ἐπειδὴ τἀμφανῆ μὲν οἱ νόμοι
ἀπεῖργον αὐτοὺς ἔργα μὴ πράσσειν βίᾳ,
λάθρᾳ δ' ἔπρασσον, τηνικαῦτά μοι δοκεῖ
<...> πυκνός τις καὶ σοφὸς γνώμην ἀνήρ
<θεῶν> δέος θνητοῖσιν ἐξευρεῖν, ὅπως
εἴη τι δεῖμα τοῖς κακοῖσι, κἂν λάθρᾳ
πράσσωσιν ἢ λέγωσιν ἢ φρονῶσί <τι>. (Critias F19; B25 DK 9–15)

Then, since the laws were holding them back from doing acts with force openly, they started doing them in secret, at which point, it seems to me, some clever man, wise in thought, invented fear of the gods for mortals, so that there would be some fearfulness among the bad, if even in secret they should do or speak or think anything.

Again, the passage emphasizes the immorality of early humans and, maybe surprisingly, their cleverness—first, the cleverness of wrongdoers in evading punishment, and then of the single individual who comes up with the idea of the gods in order to instill fear. Though divinity has been a near-constant concern, the catalogs have shown a range of attitudes toward the gods, ranging from Theseus' extreme theism to the almost complete elision of the divine from the *Antigone*'s first stasimon. Sisyphus here offers an account of the origin of theism that may bear a relation to Democritean and Prodicean thought in ascribing the idea of divinity to humans.[124] But the text goes much further than any other source in describing the invention of the gods as a lie, perpetuated by a single individual—although the cynicism of this view is significantly tempered by the speaker's approval of the positive ethical consequences of belief in the gods.[125]

---

124. The grounds for humans' invention of divinity are very different: Prodicus argued that the idea of the gods emerged from gratitude for beneficial natural occurrences, which caused early humans to worship them, and then this worship came to extend to individuals who had acted beneficially to their society—a significantly less cynical viewpoint (though one that also potentially involves a two-step development): Albert Henrichs, "Two Doxographical Notes: Democritus and Prodicus on Religion," *Harvard Studies in Classical Philology* 79 (1975): 93–123; Robert Mayhew, ed., *Prodicus the Sophist: Texts, Translations, and Commentary* (Oxford: Oxford University Press, 2011), xvii–xviii and commentary on texts 70–78.

125. On the ethical import of the Sisyphus fragment, see Jon Hesk, *Deception and Democracy in Classical Athens* (Cambridge: Cambridge University Press, 2000), 179–88; Patrick O'Sullivan, "Sophistic Ethics, Old Atheism, and 'Critias' on Religion," *Classical World* 105 (2012): 167–85.

Equally important for the present context is that Sisyphus sets the invention of laws and the gods into a stepwise developmental story: the idea of the gods is an attempt to remedy the shortcomings of laws as guarantors of human action. The transition from savagery to civilization takes place as a process over time, requiring multiple steps to bring humans to respect morality. Here, too, the *Protagoras* myth provides a parallel: it tells how Prometheus' gift of fire and technical wisdom ultimately proved inadequate because of humans' antisocial tendencies, leading Zeus to grant them moral capacities. This is quite a different story from that of the Sisyphus fragment, to be sure, but it likewise describes an intermediate stage of development, in which humans have risen out of their bestial state but not attained the morality necessary for social existence. The difference between the myth's theological account of this transition and the Sisyphus' atheistic one is not so stark as it appears: in Plato's dialogue, Protagoras claims to be able to offer a *logos* that would be interchangeable with the mythical account he speaks (320c), presuming the possibility of an alternative, nonmythical, and, given Protagoras' famous agnosticism, likely nontheological account.[126] The Sisyphus fragment, coming from drama, has a more complex relation to doctrine. It should be understood, like the catalog texts, as a dialectical position, which the rest of the drama would reflect back upon in ways that we can only guess at. Yet the very fact that such a speech was possible in a work of the late fifth century points to the theological anxiety that I have argued motivates the catalogs.

The major difference from the catalogs, though, lies in the way of exploring theological questions. The Sisyphus fragment hypothesizes the gods' nonexistence and elaborates a developmental account of belief in the gods (as does Prodicus and the myth of Plato's *Protagoras*). The cultural catalogs, by contrast, ask the prior question of whether human culture is even possible without divinity, and posit an overview of this culture and its relation to the gods. The three-step account of the Sisyphus fragment offers a genealogical explanation for a cultural practice; the binary narrative of the catalogs offers an image of

---

126. Protagoras famously declared, "Concerning the gods, I cannot know either that they exist or do not exist or what they are in form" (B4 DK/D10 LM: περὶ μὲν θεῶν οὐκ ἔχω εἰδέναι, οὔθ' ὡς εἰσὶν οὔθ' ὡς οὐκ εἰσὶν οὔθ' ὁποῖοί τινες ἰδέαν). On Protagoras' agnosticism in relation to the myth, see Carl Werner Müller, "Protagoras über die Götter," *Hermes* 95 (1967): 140–59; Gerd van Riel, "Religion and Morality: Elements of Plato's Anthropology in the Myth of Prometheus ('Protagoras' 320d–322d)," in *Plato and Myth: Studies on the Use and Status of Platonic Myths*, ed. Catherine Collobert, Pierre Destrée, and Francisco J. Gonzalez (Leiden: Brill, 2012), 145–64.

culture as a whole. This difference reflects a meaningfully different idea of the processual nature of human culture. There is no sense of completion at the end of Sisyphus' narrative, nor does any larger, synchronic view of the present emerge. The weight of the account is on the developmental story itself, not the outcome of the development described. The cultural catalogs, by contrast, are not in any meaningful sense processual: they describe a simple transformation, and the weight of their accounts is on the product of this transformation— that is, on the present totality of human culture. All of this together points to two distinct, though parallel, inquiries: one into human civilization as it is constituted in the present (the cultural catalog) and one into the development of early humans into civilized beings (theories of cultural development). The nature of their relationship is impossible to reconstruct, but in the absence of a compelling reason to posit dependence of one tradition on the other, our best assumption is that both emerge independently from a broader cultural questioning of the divine and interest in human culture.

Drama's preference for the anthropological catalog has the effect of foregrounding questions of the ongoing human relation to divinity. The developmental narratives, by contrast, tend to present naturalizing explanations of belief, which diminish the active role of the divine in human culture. The dramatic catalogs assume that divinity is a continual presence, and seek to define the scope for a distinctively human culture. The greatest differences between the catalogs lie not in the specific items they mention, which are relatively constant and often interchangeable, but in the ways they figure human autonomy in relation to the gods. Understanding this relation entails a wider reading of each of the dramas, to see how the image of human culture as presented in the catalog is reflected over the course of the work as a whole. These readings reveal a wide-ranging inquiry that defamiliarizes capacities and skills usually taken for granted, and seeks to understand the sources of human cultural achievement. This inquiry results in significantly different anthropologies, but as a whole it gives us a glimpse into major questions and preoccupations of fifth-century intellectual culture: what is natural to human beings? What are the central achievements of human culture? What role do the gods play in human existence?

The dramatic catalogs are importantly defined by the dialectical nature of their inquiries, through which they not only present a view but subject it to pressure over the course of a drama, questioning human skill and technology just as Thamus interrogates the inventions of Theuth. As a whole, the dramatic catalogs present a counterposition to the progressive narratives of philosophical thinkers: while recognizing and even celebrating humans' distance from brute origins, they depict invention as profoundly ambivalent and autonomy as radically limited. They reflect on the limits of human intellect as much as on its power. Whether by divine gifts or mortal ingenuity, humans survive and flourish, but remain nevertheless in a state of precarity. This appears, on the surface, a more traditional, conservative view than the one informing naturalizing genealogies, but drama's inquiries nevertheless present a form of contemporary, "enlightened" theology insofar as they seek to understand the role of divinity through a generalizing inquiry into human culture. The catalogs present anthropology as theology, defining the respective spheres of humanity and divinity. They thus restage the Promethean division at Mēconē, the moment "when gods and mortal men were reaching a settlement" (*Theogony* 535: ὅτ' ἐκρίνοντο θεοὶ θνητοί τ' ἄνθρωποι), and renegotiate this settlement in light of the intellectual and cultural achievements of the fifth-century *polis*. The cultural catalog describes humanity as at once *pantoporos* and *aporos*, all-resourceful and resourceless—a paradox that, in the intellectual culture of the fifth century, defines what it means to be modern.

2

Intrigue and Ontology

IN THE COURSE of trying to define the sophist in Plato's dialogue of the same name, Theaetetus and the Eleatic Visitor agree that he is an imitator (μιμητής) whose particular skill is "the appearance-making art" (φανταστικὴ τέχνη), an expertise in fashioning "an appearance but not a likeness" (236c: τὴν δὴ φάντασμα ἀλλ᾽ οὐκ εἰκόνα). The sophist's mimetic art is directed not to reproducing reality, but mere appearance, and results in a doubly distorted version of the thing imitated. As often in Plato, sophistry is compared with artistic creation: the sophist and the artist alike are imitators, but their creations do not reproduce things as they are, but things as they appear—and thus, as they are not.[1] With this definition, Theaetetus and the Visitor find themselves in deep ontological waters, and are forced to reckon with the question of nonbeing: how can they even speak of that which is not? Following the trail of the sophist, Theaetetus begins to suspect that "what is not is woven into some kind of weaving with what is" (240c: τινὰ πεπλέχθαι συμπλοκὴν τὸ μὴ ὂν τῷ ὄντι).

---

1. On artistic imitation in Plato, see Alexander Nehamas, "Plato on Imitation and Poetry in 'Republic' 10," in *Plato on Beauty, Wisdom, and the Arts*, ed. Julius Moravcsik and Philip Temko (Totowa: Rowman and Littlefield, 1982), esp. 54–58; Christopher Janaway, *Images of Excellence: Plato's Critique of the Arts* (Oxford: Oxford University Press, 1995), 106–32; Halliwell, *Aesthetics of Mimesis*, 118–47; Jessica Moss, "What Is Imitative Poetry and Why Is It Bad?," in *The Cambridge Companion to Plato's "Republic,"* ed. G.R.F. Ferrari (Cambridge: Cambridge University Press, 2007), esp. 418–21. The crucial passages both in *Sophist* and *Republic* depend on an analogy between sophistry and the visual arts (which in *Republic* is then broadened or shifted to poetry), which is discussed in Noboru Notomi, "Image-Making in 'Republic' X and the 'Sophist': Plato's Criticism of the Poet and the Sophist," in *Plato and the Poets*, ed. Pierre Destrée and Fritz-Gregor Herrmann (Leiden: Brill, 2011), 299–326; Reames, *Seeming and Being in Plato's Rhetorical Theory*, 123–48.

The question of what is not raises the problem of deception. The sophist, as an imitator of what is not, engages in a "deceptive art" (ἀπατητικὴ τέχνη), which causes "our souls to believe falsehoods" (240d: ψευδῆ δοξάζειν τὴν ψυχὴν ἡμῶν). His creations exist somewhere between being and nonbeing; they could be taken for imitations of reality, when in fact they only reproduce appearances. They are thus especially dangerous, since they can engender false belief in a way that imitations of what is real—however imperfect—cannot. The sophist's deceptive creations lead the audience to a broader uncertainty concerning what is real and what is not. The felt etymology of *apatē* ("deception") as "leading astray" (from πάτος, path) suggests a state of disorientation in the listener, and the translation "misleading" may sometimes capture its dynamics best. The problem posed by the sophist is not just that he tells falsehoods, but that he renders the whole issue of truth problematic by confusing basic ontological distinctions of reality and appearance. Understanding the deceptive art of the sophist, for Plato, entails grappling with the problem of nonbeing.

Plato's dialogue forges a connection between sophistry, deception, and ontology that the rest of this chapter will consider in the sophistic era itself.[2] I argue here that concerns of language, truth, and being are profoundly motivating for late fifth-century drama and thought, which explore *apatē* as an ethical and ontological problem. The chapter has as its kernel the similarity of the prologue scenes of Sophocles' *Electra* and *Philoctetes*: two men, unequal in power, plot deception in response to an oracular or prophetic command.[3] These intrigue prologues, I argue, constitute a form in themselves, which can productively be compared across works and authors. To these Sophoclean examples, one can add Aristophanes' *Women at the Thesmophoria*, and, somewhat more loosely, Euripides' *Iphigenia at Aulis*. The prologues establish questions of reality, truth, and language that pervade the works as a whole, and which have a substantial presence in contemporary philosophical discourse. The dramas stage the dilemma of a character who seeks to employ deception

---

2. There is an important account of the dialogue's complex connection between sophistry and ontology in Noboru Notomi, *The Unity of Plato's "Sophist": Between the Sophist and the Philosopher* (Cambridge: Cambridge University Press, 1999).

3. Though their function is similar in the two plays, there is an important difference between an oracle (which forms a part of the *Electra* stories) and a mantic utterance (which motivates the action of the *Philoctetes*). Relevant background is in Hugh Bowden, *Classical Athens and the Delphic Oracle: Divination and Democracy* (Cambridge: Cambridge University Press, 2005); Michael Attyah Flower, *The Seer in Ancient Greece* (Berkeley: University of California Press, 2008).

for his own ends, but finds that the effects of falsehood cannot be fully controlled, and that they harm deceiver and deceived alike. Dramatic stagings, I argue, differ from contemporary philosophical discussions of ontology and epistemology in their ethical and political orientation; in this respect, they look forward to Plato's framing of ontological concerns in relation to questions of justice and political organization. The dramas suggest that intrigue, by rendering it impossible to distinguish reality from appearance, undermines trust within a family or society. While the goal of philosophical inquiries is to dispel *apatē*, the dramas discussed in this chapter reflect on the difficulty of doing so, and the consequences of this difficulty for all involved. They stage ontological questions as problems of ethical action and political community.

Deception and *Dikē*

Drama makes a distinctive contribution to fifth-century thought, I argue, through its ethical and social framing of ontological problems. While this section of the chapter outlines the ethical background to thinking about deception in classical Athens, the next section describes the ontological and epistemological stakes. An ethical dimension is inherent in the concept of *apatē*, which is distinguished from its frequently paired term *pseudos* ("lie" or "falsehood") by the assumption of intentionality. As the Platonic passage quoted above illustrates, *pseudos* describes that which is objectively false, whether spoken deliberately or not, while *apatē* generally refers to an intentional deception, trick, or falsehood. The term seems to relate as much to the effect of deception—the opening up of a gap between reality and appearance, language, or expectation—as to the act of deception itself.[4] *Apatē* describes the totality of a deceptive act, figuring a relationship between agent and victim. This relational quality is important—and distinguishes *apatē* not just from *pseudos* (which characterizes a statement rather than its telling), but also from *dolos*, which can refer simply to a trap without intended victim. *Apatē* implies a close proximity of agent and victim, and, very often, a kind of false trust or intimacy, which gives the concept its ethical charge.

---

4. See Peter Stefan Mazur, "Apatē: Deception in Archaic Greek Culture" (Ph.D. diss., Yale University, 2006). Mazur emphasizes the cause-and-effect quality of *apatē* (12–14) and lists five elements that are frequently, though not inevitably, found together in archaic usages: a gap between appearance and reality, the agent's hiding or secrecy, the agent's intentionality, the victim's unawareness, and harm caused to the victim (18–36).

Apatē was a source of fascination for classical Greek thought, which connected it both to ethical and ontological domains. The next section considers the ontological dimension as it emerges in Eleatic thought of the fifth century, but foremost in the early tradition of *apatē* is its ethical significance. Though *apatē* generally describes a state of harm to the victim, an important strand of thought considers how and when deception can be justified. A fragment of Aeschylus, widely quoted in the ancient scholarly tradition, points to this paradox: "from just deception a god does not stand aloof" (F 301: ἀπάτης δικαίας οὐκ ἀποστατεῖ θεός = *Dissoi Logoi* 3.12).[5] Two readings of the text are possible, both significant for this chapter's argument. One (prevalent in the ancient evidence) emphasizes the end of deception, and reads the passage as claiming divine approval for deception in certain contexts, and thus as a defense of *apatē*.[6] The other possible reading emphasizes the agent of deception, and understands the line as a claim that gods, as well as men, engage in *apatē*. While the first reading raises the question of justice, the second raises the important and related question of authority, of who can and should engage in deception. For humans to do so is inevitably fraught: by introducing a cleft between reality and perception, *apatē* can seem to be a divine or quasidivine action, bringing with it a fearful power. Drama will explore the conjunction of questions of justice and authority in deception, staging both problems, of the agent and the end of deception.

In sophistic sources, *apatē* occurs frequently in relation to the issue of justice (*dikē*), a conjunction that only serves to heighten the paradox that an inherently harmful relation could be considered just. Our earliest citation of the

---

5. F 301 is quoted along with another Aeschylean fragment, "there is a time when the god honors the right occasion for lies" (F 302: ψευδῶν δὲ καιρὸν ἔσθ' ὅπου τιμᾷ θεός = *Dissoi Logoi* 3.12). Both fragments have been plausibly (though not certainly) attributed to Aeschylus' *Philoctetes*: Laura Gianvittorio, "One Deception, Many Lies: Frr. 301/302 Radt and Aeschylus' 'Philoctetes,'" *Wiener Studien* 128 (2015): 19–26.

6. F 301 fragment is quoted, and has an afterlife in the Homeric tradition as asserting that there exists good as well as bad deception: scholion to *Iliad* 2.114, Eustathius 188.42. The commentary tradition appears to connect it most to Agamemnon's claim in *Iliad* 2 that Zeus has engaged in "evil *apatē*" by sending him a dream bidding him to return to Argos. Other readings connect the fragment to Xenophanes' charge that Homer and Hesiod portray the gods "stealing, committing adultery, and deceiving one another" (B11 DK/D8 LM: κλέπτειν μοιχεύειν τε καὶ ἀλλήλους ἀπατεύειν), which would point to reading it as a claim that a god might engage in deception. There is, however, no reason to see the *Dissoi Logoi* or the Homeric commentaries as particularly concerned with the *divine* nature of deception.

Aeschylean line quoted above comes in the *Dissoi Logoi*, a text widely connected to sophistic thought and probably composed around 400.⁷ There, it serves as part of an argument "that it is just to tell lies and deceive" (3.2: ψεύδεσθαι ὡς δίκαιόν ἐστι ... καὶ ἐξαπατᾶν). *Apatē* serves as an example of a paradigmatically unjust action that can nevertheless be used to good ends (as when one deceives friends or family for their own benefit).⁸ One of the constructive uses of *apatē*, mentioned by both the author of the *Dissoi Logoi* and Gorgias in a famous fragment, is poetry, and especially tragedy. A fragment of Gorgias, quoted in Plutarch, presents the relation between tragedian and audience member as characterized by *apate*:

> [ἡ τραγῳδία] παρασχοῦσα τοῖς μύθοις καὶ τοῖς πάθεσιν ἀπάτην, ὡς Γοργίας φησίν, ἥν ὅ τ' ἀπατήσας δικαιότερος τοῦ μὴ ἀπατήσαντος καὶ ὁ ἀπατηθεὶς σοφώτερος τοῦ μὴ ἀπατηθέντος. ὁ μὲν γὰρ ἀπατήσας δικαιότερος ὅτι τοῦθ' ὑποσχόμενος πεποίηκεν, ὁ δ' ἀπατηθεὶς σοφώτερος· εὐάλωτον γὰρ ὑφ' ἡδονῆς λόγων τὸ μὴ ἀναίσθητον. (B 23 DK/D35 LM; Plutarch, *On the Glory of the Athenians* 348c)

> [Tragedy] produc[es] by its stories and sufferings a deception, in which, as Gorgias says, "the one who deceives is more just than the one who does not deceive, and the one is who is deceived is wiser than the one not deceived." For the one who deceives is more just because he has done what he promised, while the one deceived is wiser, since whoever is not insensitive is easily captured by the pleasure of words.

The quotation is, in typically Gorgianic style, based on antitheses: of poets and spectators, and among each group, of successful and unsuccessful entrants into

---

7. The scholarly consensus more or less follows T. M. Robinson, ed., *Contrasting Arguments: An Edition of the "Dissoi Logoi"* (New York: Arno Press, 1979). Robinson dates the text to ca. 400, assuming it to be a sophistic product. Earlier and later datings have also been proposed, though none has found wide acceptance. Extended discussion (with earlier and later datings, respectively) are found in Stefano Maso, ed., *"Dissoi logoi": Edizione criticamente rivista, introduzione, traduzione, commento* (Rome: Edizioni di Storia e Letteratura, 2018), 1–20; Sebastiano Molinelli, ed., *"'Dissoi Logoi': A New Commented Edition"* (Ph.D. diss., Durham University, 2018), 24–48.

8. *Dissoi Logoi* 3.11 also quotes a riddle from the *Cleobulina*, a collection of riddles attributed to the daughter of Cleobulus, one of the Seven Sages: "a man I saw stealing and deceiving violently, and to do this by violence was most just" (2 West: ἄνδρ' εἶδον κλέπτοντα καὶ ἐξαπατῶντα βιαίως / καὶ τὸ βίᾳ ῥέξαι τοῦτο δικαιότατον). The challenge of the riddle comes from making out how theft and deception by violence (almost a paradox itself) could be just.

the deception of tragedy. The qualities of successful deception, the "justice" of the poet and the "wisdom" of the spectator, might seem surprising, but are aspects of the paradox, inherent in the idea of an *apatē* that does no harm.[9] Tragedy is an exceptional case in which deception can be just and being deceived can be wise.[10]

The explanation of the paradox (which could be either Gorgias' or Plutarch's) points strongly to the relational quality of *apatē*: the poet's effort to deceive is based on a kind of contract with the spectator in which the poet promises deception and the spectator agrees to be taken in.[11] Through this contract, the poet is granted the authority to engage, justly, in deception—and even, by the terms of the agreement, obligated to do so.[12] The *Dissoi Logoi*'s description of tragedy as *apatē*, likewise, concentrates on the agent of deception: "In tragedy and painting, whoever deceives the most by creating things like to true

---

9. Plutarch cites Gorgias' description of tragedy along with a story about Simonides in *How a Young Man Should Study Poetry* 15d: when asked why he did not deceive the Thessalians alone, Simonides answered, "Because they are too ignorant to be deceived by me" (ἀμαθέστεροι γάρ εἰσιν ἢ ὡς ὑπ' ἐμοῦ ἐξαπατᾶσθαι). The passage is often suspected as a simple retrojection of the Gorgianic idea, but it may also testify to an earlier discourse of art as *apatē*.

10. Euripides claims in *Frogs* that Aeschylus "deceived" (910: ἐξηπάτα) his audiences with bombast (discussed in chapter 3), but this suggests the more common conception of *apatē* as bad-faith deception. On Aeschylus as a poet of *apatē*, see Thomas G. Rosenmeyer, "Gorgias, Aeschylus, and Apatē," *American Journal of Philology* 76 (1955): 225–60; Cristina Pace, "Tragedia, ἔκπληξις e ἀπάτη nell'anonima 'Vita di Eschilo,'" *Seminari romani di cultura greca* 11 (2008): 229–54.

11. Grethlein offers a thorough and penetrating reading and contextualization of Gorgias' apothegm, arguing that it is foundational for an ancient discourse of deception that combines ethics and aesthetics: Jonas Grethlein, *The Ancient Aesthetics of Deception* (Cambridge: Cambridge University Press, forthcoming). My tendency is to emphasize the ethical and ontological contexts of deception, which emerge more strongly from earlier thought, but Grethlein demonstrates convincingly that an aesthetic dimension becomes central to thinking about *apatē*.

12. On Gorgias' idea of poetry, see Mario Untersteiner, *The Sophists*, trans. Kathleen Freeman (Oxford: Blackwell, 1954), 185–93; Jacqueline de Romilly, "Gorgias et le pouvoir de la poésie," *Journal of Hellenic Studies* 93 (1973): 155–62; W. J. Verdenius, "Gorgias' Doctrine of Deception," in *The Sophists and Their Legacy*, ed. G. B. Kerferd (Wiesbaden: Steiner, 1981), 116–28; Michael Franz, "Fiktionalität und Wahrheit in der Sicht des Gorgias und des Aristoteles," *Philologus* 135 (1991): 240–48; Kurt Sier, "Gorgias über die Fiktionalität der Tragödie," in *Dramatische Wäldchen: Festschrift für Eckard Lefèvre zum 65. Geburtstag*, ed. Ekkehard Stärk and Gregor Vogt-Spira (Hildesheim: Ohms, 2000), 575–618. I see in Gorgias' thought much less of a systematic approach than these authors do, and (as I discuss below) believe Gorgias is more often thinking dialectically.

ones is the best" (3.10: ἐν γὰρ τραγῳδοποιίᾳ καὶ ζωγραφίᾳ ὅστις πλεῖστα ἐξαπατῇ ὅμοια τοῖς ἀληθινοῖς ποιέων, οὗτος ἄριστος). The author relies on the idea of poetry as falsehood given canonical form by Hesiod's Muses, who declare that they can speak "falsehoods like to truths" (*Theogony* 27: ψεύδεα . . . ἐτύμοισιν ὁμοῖα), another claim of deceptive authority.[13] But the *Dissoi Logoi* makes a stronger claim than Hesiod in at least two respects: first, by characterizing this false likeness as *apatē* (rather than the more ambiguous ψεύδεα), and second, in eliding the Muses' following line, in which they tout their ability also "to speak out truth" (28: ἀληθέα γηρύσασθαι). For the *Dissoi Logoi*, false likeness is not just a possibility of the poet's speech or the painter's representation, but its very essence. Poetic (and painterly) authority is closely connected to the ability to deceive, and since this ability is taken as the test of a tragedian, the most deceptive artist is valorized.[14] The paradox of *apatē* in both the *Dissoi Logoi* and Gorgias lies in the way a beneficial result can come from an act that on the surface appears unjust.[15]

Ethical questions surrounding deception inevitably carry social and political implications, which relate both to inter-*polis* relations and internal affairs. As Jon Hesk discusses in detail, Athenian military and civic ideology strongly rejected *apatē*, as associated with their rivals and enemies the Spartans.[16] Deception was widely denigrated, at least rhetorically, as unfair and socially corrosive. This did not, though, prevent Athenians from engaging in deception in war, and even from privileging the quality of *mētis*, "cunning intelligence,"

---

13. On the Muses' claim, see Giovanni Ferrari, "Hesiod's Mimetic Muses and the Strategies of Deconstruction," in *Post-Structuralist Classics*, ed. Andrew Benjamin (London: Routledge, 1988), 45–78; Margalit Finkelberg, *The Birth of Literary Fiction in Ancient Greece* (Oxford: Clarendon Press, 1998), 131–60; Joshua T. Katz and Katharina Volk, "'Mere Bellies'?: A New Look at 'Theogony' 26–8," *Journal of Hellenic Studies* 120 (2000): 122–31; Bruce Heiden, "The Muses' Uncanny Lies: Hesiod, 'Theogony' 27 and Its Translators," *American Journal of Philology* 128 (2007): 153–75.

14. The morality of artistic deception is discussed in Louise H. Pratt, *Lying and Poetry from Homer to Pindar: Falsehood and Deception in Archaic Greek Poetics* (Ann Arbor: University of Michigan Press, 1993).

15. A similar conjunction of artistic deception and justice is present in a difficult passage of the Hippocratic *On Regimen*, which describes acting as deception. The paragraph is framed by the paradox that certain human practices involve "doing injustice justly" (ἀδικεῖν δικαίως): "Acting deceives those who know. They say some things and think others, they enter themselves and exit not themselves" (1.24: ὑποκριτικὴ ἐξαπατᾷ εἰδότας· ἄλλα λέγουσι καὶ ἄλλα φρονέουσιν, οἱ αὐτοὶ ἐσέρπουσι καὶ ἐξέρπουσιν οὐχ οἱ αὐτοί).

16. Hesk, *Deception and Democracy*, esp. 23–40.

as the work of Detienne and Vernant demonstrates.[17] The existence of ritualized training in deception—such as the Spartan *Krupteia* and the Athenian *Apatouria*, both of them rites involving secret, quasimilitary actions—testifies to the perceived value of cunning in both cities. Training in *apatē* formed an important part of a young man's passage into adulthood, and constituted a form of military initiation.[18] At the same time, the containment and segregation of these rituals directed deception outside of the city, in order to preserve civic trust and military order. While strongly disavowed at home, deception could be laudable when directed toward an enemy.

The god Apollo presides over a nexus of issues related to deception in tragedy: as the god of oracular knowledge, he speaks truth that is difficult to extricate from obscurity or falsehood. A fragment of Heraclitus states that "the lord whose oracle is the one in Delphi neither speaks nor hides but signals" (B93 DK; D41 LM: ὁ ἄναξ οὗ τὸ μαντεῖόν ἐστι τὸ ἐν Δελφοῖς οὔτε λέγει οὔτε κρύπτει ἀλλὰ σημαίνει), and such obscure or indirect communication with divinity is a frequent theme of tragedy.[19] Apollo is also the god most closely connected to the ephebic rituals discussed above, which regularly involve deception, and which have important parallels in tragic narratives.[20] Finally, through his

---

17. Marcel Detienne and Jean-Pierre Vernant, *Cunning Intelligence in Greek Culture and Society*, trans. Janet Lloyd (Chicago: University of Chicago Press, 1991).

18. See Pierre Vidal-Naquet, *The Black Hunter: Forms of Thought and Forms of Society in the Greek World*, trans. Andrew Szegedy-Maszak (Baltimore: Johns Hopkins University Press, 1986), 106–28. Many aspects of Vidal-Naquet's analysis are controversial, and receive a more nuanced treatment in Hesk, *Deception and Democracy*, 86–102. On the controversy, see John Ma, "Black Hunter Variations," *Proceedings of the Cambridge Philological Society* 40 (1994): 49–80.

19. On Heraclitus, see the discussion in Shaul Tor, "Heraclitus on Apollo's Signs and His Own: Contemplating Oracles and Philosophical Inquiry," in *Theologies of Ancient Greek Religion*, ed. Esther Eidinow, Julia Kindt, and Robin Osborne (Cambridge: Cambridge University Press, 2016), 89–116. The role of tragic prophecy is discussed below and explored in Mark Griffith, "Apollo, Teiresias, and the Politics of Tragic Prophecy," in *Apolline Politics and Poetics*, ed. Lucia Athanassaki, Richard P. Martin, and John F. Miller (Athens: Hellenic Ministry of Culture, 2009), 473–500.

20. I discuss ephebic narratives in tragedy below; fundamental for this discussion are Jean-Pierre Vernant and Pierre Vidal-Naquet, *Myth and Tragedy in Ancient Greece*, trans. Janet Lloyd (New York: Zone Books, 1990), 161–79; John J. Winkler, "The Ephebes' Song: Tragōidia and Polis," in *Nothing to Do with Dionysos?: Athenian Drama in Its Social Context*, ed. John J. Winkler and Froma I. Zeitlin (Princeton: Princeton University Press, 1990), 20–62. For Apollo as ephebic god, see Jane Ellen Harrison, *Themis: A Study of the Social Origins of Greek Religion*, 2nd ed. (Cambridge: Cambridge University Press, 1927), 439–44; Walter Burkert, "Apellai und

connection to music, Apollo is related to forms of aesthetic illusion, paradigmatically in the song of the Delian maidens in the *Homeric Hymn to Apollo*, who "know how to represent the voices and rhythms of all men. Each one would think that he himself were speaking" (162–64: πάντων δ' ἀνθρώπων φωνὰς καὶ κρεμβαλιαστὺν / μιμεῖσθ' ἴσασιν· φαίη δέ κεν αὐτὸς ἕκαστος / φθέγγεσθ').[21] Tragic *mimēsis*, of course, is most closely connected to Dionysus, but the *Hymn* shows that the confusion between audience and performer, self and other, can be associated with choral celebrations of Apollo as well. Ambiguity, liminality, and confused identity will all be hallmarks of tragic intrigue, which I argue stages truth, falsehood, and deception in a significantly Apollonian context.

The human figure who most focalizes issues of deception is Odysseus.[22] A famously fluid and compelling speaker, Odysseus is often approached with the suspicion that characterizes Athenian attitudes toward political rhetoric generally.[23] As a figure for thinking about speech and deception, Odysseus was broadly important to sophistic culture: Gorgias' Palamedes defends himself by pointing to Odysseus' crimes (B11a DK/D25 LM 27), which he presumes are well known to his Greek audience, while Antisthenes' *Ajax* points to Odysseus' secretive actions as a cause for mistrust (5).[24] Both texts display the sophistic interest in ethical juxtaposition evident also in Plato's *Hippias Minor*, in which the sophist compares Trojan heroes, describing Achilles as "true and simple" (ἀληθής τε καὶ ἁπλοῦς) and Odysseus as "much-turning and false"

Apollon," *Rheinisches Museum* 118 (1975): 1–21; H. S. Versnel, *Inconsistencies in Greek and Roman Religion II: Transition and Reversal in Myth and Ritual* (Leiden: Brill, 1994), 313–19.

21. The majority of manuscripts read κρεμβαλιαστὺν, which appears to be related to the castanetlike instrument *krembala*. Some manuscripts report βαμβαλιαστὺν, a rare word apparently meaning "babble," which has often been adopted by editors. A rich discussion, which I follow in translating as "rhythms", is in Anastasia-Erasmia Peponi, "Choreia and Aesthetics in the 'Homeric Hymn to Apollo': The Performance of the Delian Maidens (Lines 156–64)," *Classical Antiquity* 28 (2009): 39–70.

22. See W. B. Stanford, *The Ulysses Theme: A Study in the Adaptability of a Traditional Hero* (Oxford: Blackwell, 1963); Silvia Montiglio, *From Villain to Hero: Odysseus in Ancient Thought* (Ann Arbor: University of Michigan Press, 2011).

23. Stanford, *Ulysses Theme*, 102–17; Nancy Worman, "Odysseus Panourgos: The Liar's Style in Tragedy and Oratory," *Helios* 26 (1999): 35–68.

24. Despite putting these reproaches in Ajax' mouth, Antisthenes on the whole seems to have a positive view of Odysseus (and the outcome of the Judgment points to Odysseus' speech as the winning one): Susan Prince, *Antisthenes of Athens: Texts, Translations, and Commentary* (Ann Arbor: University of Michigan Press, 2015), 591–622.

(365b: πολύτροπός τε καὶ ψευδής). Hippias associates the *Odyssey*'s opening epithet, πολύτροπος ("much-turning" or "many-wayed"), with deception in support of the contrast between the upright Achilles and the shifty Odysseus.[25] As the dialogue goes on, however, the clear opposition proposed by Hippias breaks down under Socrates' questioning: the liar, they agree, must have knowledge of the truth in order to lie, and therefore is at the same time truthful, rendering Odysseus and Achilles alike both false and true (369b).[26] Expanding on this argument, Socrates arrives at the even more surprising conclusion that the one doing wrong intentionally is better (because he is conscious of the good) than the one doing wrong unintentionally (376b). This scandalous (to both Hippias and Socrates) assertion constitutes a strong—if difficult for a reader to judge—endorsement of Odyssean deception.[27] In the *Hippias Minor* as elsewhere, the figure of Odysseus solicits thought concerning truth and lies, which leads, like the considerations of just *apatē*, to a significantly ambiguous notion of deception and of the deceiver.

Dramatic deception plots stage this ambiguity by bringing out the uncontainable effects of deception, portraying the deceiver caught up in his own falsehoods. The plays treated in this chapter all explore the bind of a figure who takes part in an extended intrigue, in the course of which lies proliferate and come to act on both the target and the perpetrator of deception. This has comic as well as tragic instances, but in all the plays examined here, deceptive stories take on a life of their own and rebound against the deceiver. I will propose ultimately to interpret these problems of deception in political terms, as crystallizing questions of truth and knowledge within a democratic collective. One striking aspect of the works discussed in this chapter is their presentation of deception as something learned and taught, an aspect of

---

25. On the contrast, see Richard Hunter, "The 'Hippias Minor' and the Traditions of Homeric Criticism," *Cambridge Classical Journal* 62 (2016): 85–107. Hippias' view of Odysseus appears opposed to that of Antisthenes: Silvia Venturelli, "L''Ippia Minore' di Platone e il suo rapporto con Antistene: (S.S.R. V A 187)," *Studi classici e orientali* 61 (2015): 77–96. I will have more to say about the tendency to juxtaposition in the next chapter.

26. On Socrates' elenchus of Hippias, see Ruby Blondell, *The Play of Character in Plato's Dialogues* (Cambridge: Cambridge University Press, 2002), 128–64.

27. This seems to be consistent with a generally positive depiction of Odysseus among the Socratics: David Lévystone, "La figure d'Ulysse chez les Socratiques: Socrate polutropos," *Phronesis* 50 (2005): 181–214; Montiglio, *From Villain to Hero*, 20–37; David Corey, "The Sophist Hippias and the Problem of Polytropia," in *Socratic Philosophy and Its Others*, ed. Christopher A. Dustin and Denise Schaeffer (Lanham: Lexington Books, 2013), 91–114.

socialization that allows one to participate fully in collective life. All the plays thus reflect on the extent to which deception is necessary and endemic to the functioning of society. Though this is a question with significant ramifications for the contemporary politics of Athens (which I try to note as they arise), I do not propose to read the plays as direct commentary on the political events of their time or on Athenian ideology, but as more or less hypothetical explorations of the significance of deception in society—that is, as political theory rather than political allegory or critique.[28] Read this way, the intrigue prologue constitutes a form for probing the role of trust and truth within a community.

Apatē and Ontology

For the intellectual culture of the late fifth century, the topic of *apatē* raises questions not just of ethics and politics—which are woven into thinking about deception throughout Greek history—but, just as important, of ontology. The Eleatic exploration of being provides the background for an inquiry into *apatē* that understands deception in a global sense: not simply as a false account, but as a state of basic uncertainty about reality, like that created by Plato's sophist. This section describes an ontological context for thinking about *apatē*, which I argue informs dramatic deception plots in the late fifth century. The importance of setting out the Eleatic background to dramatic investigations of *apatē* is not to demonstrate that Greek dramatists were aware of Parmenides' or Gorgias' arguments—this is nearly impossible to prove (or disprove), and even if proven would tend to limit interpretation rather than expand it. Rather, I hope to show that dramatists are grappling with questions that are related to, but also importantly distinct from, those discussed in fifth-century philosophical thought. In the broadest sense, both philosophical and dramatic writers were grappling with the question of what is real, and how we know (or do not know) this reality.

---

28. Political theorists often read tragedy as bearing on questions of political philosophy, but their approach is by and large to place tragedy in dialogue with modern political questions, rather than its contemporaneous philosophical context. See, for examples, Peter J. Ahrensdorf, *Greek Tragedy and Political Philosophy: Rationalism and Religion in Sophocles' Theban Plays* (Cambridge: Cambridge University Press, 2009); Bonnie Honig, *Antigone, Interrupted* (Cambridge: Cambridge University Press, 2013). Closer to my approach is J. Peter Euben, *The Tragedy of Political Theory* (Princeton: Princeton University Press, 1990).

My elaboration of a late fifth-century or sophistic context for *apatē* is in dialogue with Marcel Detienne's *The Masters of Truth in Archaic Greece*, which sets out a diachronic narrative of regimes of truth in Greek culture. I discuss the specifics of this narrative in the Introduction, but Detienne's work is important here for pointing to the way that concerns of knowledge and truth are understood in relation to individual authority, and questions of who is able to access reality and control appearance.[29] I will have more to say about philosophical authority in the next chapter, but for the present context it is crucial that the ability to distinguish between reality and deception in early Greek philosophical poetry is connected to divinity (as it was in Hesiod): in Parmenides, it is a goddess who instructs; in Empedocles, the speaker is human, but claims religious authority and godlike status. The arguments of both speakers are authorized in some part by their connection to divinity, and introduce a single disciple (the young man in Parmenides, one Pausanias in Empedocles) to an esoteric knowledge. Both poems construct relations of authority and discipleship, and lay out their claims in scenes of instruction or initiation.[30] In neither case is the disciple very fully defined or identified, and there does not seem to have been any meaningful dialogue with the authority figure, but the potential is at least latent in both poems for a form of interchange. Plato's *Sophist*, similarly, is constructed around a relation of instruction, in which the Eleatic Stranger, who is identified at the beginning of the dialogue as a follower of Parmenides and compared to a god (216a–b), leads the young Athenian Theaetetus through a discussion of the nature of the sophist and into the questions of being and nonbeing with which this chapter began. Drama exploits the possibility of exchange even further, constructing relations of authority centered around the knowledge of truth and falsehood.

Early Greek philosophical thought takes deception to be a constant possibility in human perception and cognition, rendering secure knowledge difficult to achieve. One crucial aim of the Eleatic tradition is to delineate the conditions for nondeceptive understanding of reality. In doing so, it casts doubt on the possiblity of secure knowledge in a way that I will suggest is also

---

29. Detienne, *Masters of Truth*, esp. 107–34. There is an important critique of Detienne's tendency to divide strictly "rational" from "mythical" speech in Sassi, *The Beginnings of Philosophy in Greece*, 139–77.

30. For the notion of initiation in Parmenides, see Herbert Granger, "The Proem of Parmenides' Poem," *Ancient Philosophy* 28 (2008): 1–20. On Empedocles: Dirk Obbink, "The Addressees of Empedocles," *Materiali e discussioni per l'analisi dei testi classici* 31 (1993): 51–98.

characteristic of dramatic intrigue. The goddess in Parmenides' poem declares that the young man (conventionally referred to as the *kouros*) must learn "both the unmoved heart of well-rounded reality and the opinions of mortals, in which there is no real trust" (B1 DK/D4 LM 29–30: ἠμὲν ἀληθείης εὐκυκλέος ἀτρεμὲς ἦτορ / ἠδὲ βροτῶν δόξας, ταῖς οὐκ ἔνι πίστις ἀληθής).[31] The relation between the two parts of the poem, known as *Alētheia* (truth or reality) and *Doxa* (opinion), is an enduring scholarly problem. Recent scholarship seems by and large to agree that the *Doxa* represents Parmenides' account of apparent (or "doxastic") entities, in contrast to the prior reality of the *Alētheia*, which is concerned with some more fundamental or necessary sense of being.[32] In turning from one part of the account to the other, the goddess characterizes knowledge of *Doxa* as fundamentally deceptive:

ἐν τῷ σοι παύω πιστὸν λόγον ἠδὲ νόημα
ἀμφὶς ἀληθείης· δόξας δ' ἀπὸ τοῦδε βροτείας
μάνθανε κόσμον ἐμῶν ἐπέων ἀπατηλὸν ἀκούων.
(B8 DK 50–52/D8 LM 55–57)

Here I stop for you the trusty speech and thought concerning reality; from here, learn mortal opinions, hearing the deceptive order of my verses.

The goddess' speech divides into one part that is trustworthy (concerning reality) and one that is deceptive (the content of which is mortal opinion). Both of these must be knowledge in some sense, but of different objects, and with accordingly different means of access.[33] The "deceptive order," we know, lacks "real trust" because its objects cannot be known with the fullest certainty. The one account is trustworthy because connected to fundamental reality,

---

31. I read Simplicius' εὐκυκλέος instead of εὐπειθέος found in other quotations, following the majority of recent commentators (though εὐπειθέος would be even more amenable to the reading I pursue).

32. Different ways of conceiving this relation are found in Patricia Curd, *The Legacy of Parmenides: Eleatic Monism and Later Presocratic Thought* (Princeton: Princeton University Press, 1998), 98–126; John Palmer, *Parmenides and Presocratic Philosophy* (Oxford: Oxford University Press, 2009), 167–80; John E. Sisko and Yale Weiss, "A Fourth Alternative in Interpreting Parmenides," *Phronesis* 60 (2015): 40–59; Shaul Tor, *Mortal and Divine in Early Greek Epistemology: A Study of Hesiod, Xenophanes, and Parmenides* (Cambridge: Cambridge University Press, 2017), 167–221. I am not committed to any particular reading of Parmenides, but I consider it essential that any reading understand the *Doxa* as a valid (in at least some sense) account of physical entities.

33. Tor, *Mortal and Divine*, 196–215.

while the other lacks this trustworthiness by virtue of its reliance on human sense-impression and opinion. If something like this reading is correct, then the "deceptive order" of the *Doxa* is not a false account, but a true (or best possible) account of things that are not, in the fullest sense, real. *Apatē* describes a state of misplaced trust, which threatens to lead the inquirer away from secure knowledge of reality.

For Parmenides, on this interpretation, reality and appearance are not absolutely opposed, but represent two distinct, and hierarchically organized, modes of knowing. The goddess' speech constitutes an instruction in the relation of reality and deception. As has been recognized, this instruction is figured as a kind of initiation: the poem begins by detailing the journey of the *kouros* into a mystical realm "outside of the path [*patos*] of men" (B1 DK/D4 LM 27: ἀπ' ἀνθρώπων ἐκτὸς πάτου).[34] By leaving behind the conventional beliefs and sense-impressions of human beings, he gains access to a more fundamental stratum of reality. The poem's extended account of the *Doxa* constitutes an instruction in how to understand the world he has left as deceptive or misleading, "so that no judgment of mortals will ever outstrip you" (B8 DK 61/D8 LM 66: ὥς οὐ μή ποτέ τίς σε βροτῶν γνώμη παρελάσσῃ). The goddess clearly envisions a return to the mortal world for the *kouros*, and the instruction she offers promises to make him an authority in the deceptive order of appearance. We will observe a similar pattern in the intrigue prologues, in which one figure initiates the other into knowledge of reality and deception.

Parmenides' thought placed in question the relation of fundamental being to physical phenomena, and led the following generation to puzzle over the reality of sensory experience. Empedocles seems to signal this problem with a reference to Parmenides when he introduces his own account of Love (Φιλότης) as a fundamental, though invisible, force by admonishing the listener to "hear the undeceptive course of my account" (B17 26 DK/D73 LM 257: ἄκουε λόγου στόλον οὐκ ἀπατηλόν). Empedocles' claim speaks to the same basic assumption that the phenomenal world is deceptive because it diverts the inquirer from a more basic reality.[35] Asserting that his account of reality is

---

34. On Parmenides and mystery religion, see Walter Burkert, "Das Proömium des Parmenides und die Katabasis des Pythagoras," *Phronesis* 14 (1969): 1–30; David L. Blank, "Faith and Persuasion in Parmenides," *Classical Antiquity* 1 (1982): 167–77.

35. There is a similar use of *apatē* in B23 DK/D60 LM 9, where the speaker warns the hearer not to be deceived by appearances into believing that there are more than four fundamental roots.

not *apatēlos*, Empedocles demands that his listener suspend the impressions of sense in order to access more fundamental truths. His authority as a speaker in turn depends on the ability of the listener to see beyond deceptive appearances and grasp his *logos*. Whether or not this implies a broader rejection of Parmenides, Empedocles' conception of *apatē* tracks the same gap between perceived and fundamental reality, while his conception of an empirical world governed by fundamental, unseen forces moderates the ontological gap that Parmenides had opened.[36]

Others developed Parmenidean thought in directions that widened the gap between *Alētheia* and *Doxa*. Zeno and Melissus, both traditionally associated with Parmenides as members of an Eleatic school, traveled widely and gained fame for their counterintuitive arguments.[37] Our evidence for Zeno is quite sparse, but he seems to have been known particularly for his novel argumentative strategies, most importantly his refutation of arguments for physical change and multiplicity through a series of paradoxes.[38] The arguments of Melissus likewise constitute a sweeping and counterintuitive extension of Parmenidean views. While Parmenides is probably best understood as allowing for a plurality of beings (against the background of a unified, fundamental reality of being), Melissus takes the argument for unity further, and asserts that only one, infinite and unbounded being exists.[39] His treatise, apparently entitled *On Nature* or *On Being*, quickly became notorious for its argument that all things are one and unchanging, and was a particular object of derision for Aristotle.[40] In part because of the scorn heaped on Melissus, we have a fairly clear idea of the consequences of his arguments, which entail a complete denial of change and multiplicity of objects, and consequently, of the evidence

---

36. On Empedocles' relation to Parmenides in this passage, see Palmer, *Parmenides and Presocratic Philosophy*, 273–76.

37. The relation of Zeno's and Melissus' arguments to Parmenides' is controversial; see Patricia Kenig Curd, "Eleatic Monism in Zeno and Melissus," *Ancient Philosophy* 13 (1993): 1–22; Palmer, *Parmenides and Presocratic Philosophy*, 189–224.

38. Curd, *The Legacy of Parmenides*, 171–79.

39. Curd, *The Legacy of Parmenides*, 206–16. Palmer argues for a strong distinction between the views of Parmenides and Melissus, characterizing the latter as an eristic: John Palmer, "Melissus and Parmenides," *Oxford Studies in Ancient Philosophy* 26 (2004): 19–54.

40. Melissus is mentioned derisively in the Hippocratic *On the Nature of Man* 1 (late fifth century) and Isocrates, *Helen* 3 (early fourth century). Aristotle repeatedly refers to Melissus, always negatively, and is reported to have written a treatise refuting his ideas (Diogenes Laertius 5.25).

of the senses:[41] "it follows that we do not see or know the things that are" (B8 DK/D11 LM: συμβαίνει μήτε ὁρᾶν μήτε τὰ ὄντα γινώσκειν). An even more radical view is attributed to one Xeniades of Corinth, who is mentioned repeatedly by Sextus Empiricus as "saying all things are false and all appearance and opinion is false" (D1 LM; *Against the Logicians* 7.53: πάντ' εἰπὼν ψευδῆ καὶ πᾶσαν φαντασίαν καὶ δόξαν ψεύδεσθαι).[42] Xeniades appears to represent an extreme of the questioning of the senses, which does not even retain the idea of fundamental being as true, and so appears to be a form of radical nihilism. His relation to the Eleatic tradition is obscure, but he testifies to a widespread problematization of knowledge and reality in the sophistic era.

Gorgias' treatise *On Nonbeing* (alternately known as *On Nature*) appears to be a direct response to the Eleatic tradition, and became notorious for its argument that nothing is.[43] Gorgias' treatise, according to the account of it in the pseudo-Aristotelian *On Melissus, Xenophanes, and Gorgias* (*MXG*), pursued the radically counterintuitive thesis that nothing is (D26a LM; *MXG* 5.2: οὐκ ἔστι, "it is not" or "there is not").[44] Gorgias supports this claim both by an original argument to the effect that being and nonbeing are the same, and by a systematic refutation of the possible attributes of being countenanced by the Eleatics, turning previous theories against themselves. Then, in a second thesis, which seems more oriented to sophistic (especially Protagorean) epistemology, he grants the existence of beings, but argues that, even if things (πράγματα) existed, they would be unknowable (D26a LM; *MXG* 6.20: ἄγνωστα): we could neither have them in mind nor attain secure knowledge of them.[45] Finally, the third thesis grants the knowability of beings, but denies

---

41. The most complete reconstruction is in Benjamin Harriman, *Melissus and Eleatic Monism* (Cambridge: Cambridge University Press, 2019).

42. Almost nothing is known about Xeniades, and this is the only passage of his in DK (though there are a few more mentions in Sextus, along the same lines). Because of the content of his argument, he is usually grouped among the sophists, but we know nothing about his life or beliefs.

43. Isocrates twice mentions Gorgias (in the company of other theorists of being) as an example of the excesses of sophistic thought: *Helen* 3, *Antidosis* 268; there are, moreover, traces of an attack by Antisthenes on Gorgias (Athenaeus 5.220d). On the influence of Gorgias' text, see (though, I think, overstating the case) Steve Hays, "On the Skeptical Influence of Gorgias's 'On Non-Being,'" *Journal of the History of Philosophy* 28 (1990): 327–37.

44. There is a parallel report of Gorgias' argument in Sextus Empiricus, *Against the Logicians* 7.65–87 (excerpted as B3 DK/D26b LM), but this is now widely considered less reliable.

45. On the second thesis, see Victor Caston, "Gorgias on Thought and Its Objects," in *Presocratic Philosophy: Essays in Honour of Alexander Mourelatos*, ed. Victor Caston and Daniel W.

that what is known (γνωστόν) can be "made clear" (D26a LM; *MXG* 5.1: δηλωτόν) to others by language.[46] In the course of the treatise, then, Gorgias argues against existence, knowledge, and linguistic communication, refuting the strong assertions of Eleatic ontology. The content and target of Gorgias' text remain controversial, but at a minimum the argument renders highly problematic any assertions about being (including possibly its own), and, with them, distinctions between reality and appearance, truth and falsehood.[47]

In its three-step argument, *On Nonbeing* sets out a chain of reasoning that leads from ontology through epistemology to thinking about language and the social world. The last of these is clearly one of Gorgias' central preoccupations, as evidenced by the reflections on language and persuasion in both the *Encomium of Helen* and the *Defense of Palamedes*, and by the range of ancient testimonia to Gorgias' importance as a rhetorician.[48] Scholars have sometimes sought to unify Gorgias' thinking about language into a single, coherent outlook, but I believe it is better understood as bound by a rhetorical strategy of dialectical engagement, exploration, and provocation.[49] Gorgias' statements on language will reappear in this chapter for their parallels to dramatic explorations of the power of speech. I read the dramatic reflections, similarly to the

---

Graham (Burlington: Ashgate, 2002), 205–32. Gorgias' argument against knowledge appears to be diametrically opposed to Protagoras' "man the measure" doctrine, though both could issue (depending on one's reading of Protagoras) in denial of a knowable, fundamental reality: Roberta Ioli, ed., *Gorgia: "Su ciò che non è"* (Hildesheim: Olms, 2010), 50–60.

46. On the third thesis, see Alexander P. D. Mourelatos, "Gorgias on the Function of Language," *Philosophical Topics* 15 (1987): 135–70; Robert N. Gaines, "Knowledge and Discourse in Gorgias's 'On the Non-Existent or On Nature,'" *Philosophy and Rhetoric* 30 (1997): 1–12.

47. Some understand Gorgias' argument to relate primarily to linguistic predication of being: G. B. Kerferd, "Gorgias on Nature or That Which Is Not," *Phronesis* 1 (1955): 3–25; Guido Calogero, *Studi sull'eleatismo* (Florence: La Nuova Italia, 1977), 189–268. Others propose that Gorgias rejects only the fundamental sense of Parmenidean being (and not being *tout court*): Patricia Curd, "Gorgias and the Eleatics," in *La costruzione del discorso filosofico nell'età dei Presocratici*, ed. Maria Michela Sassi (Pisa: Edizioni della Normale, 2006), 183–200; Palmer, *Parmenides and Presocratic Philosophy*, 219–20. Views on Gorgias' point in the text depend inevitably on views of Parmenides' being: Anthony Edward Schiappa, "Interpreting Gorgias's 'Being' in 'On Not-Being or On Nature,'" *Philosophy and Rhetoric* 30 (1997): 13–30.

48. D2–23 LM. It is tempting to imagine that Gorgias' proximity to drama is more than just incidental, given that both of these speeches address important figures of tragedy: Untersteiner, *The Sophists*, 140–75; Sier, "Gorgias über die Fiktionalität der Tragödie."

49. Important attempts at synthesis of Gorgias' views are Charles P. Segal, "Gorgias and the Psychology of the Logos," *Harvard Studies in Classical Philology* 66 (1962): 99–155; Romilly, "Gorgias et le pouvoir de la poésie"; Mourelatos, "Gorgias on the Function of Language."

Gorgianic ones, as positions presented within a dialectic, which the dramas as a whole develop and which consider, like *On Nonbeing*, the relation of language, knowledge, and reality. The deception plots I investigate engage with the philosophical tradition by staging the opaqueness of truth and reality, but with a distinctive focus on the consequences for trust within a community. On the whole, drama reflects a pessimistic viewpoint on the possibility of truthful interaction by portraying circumstances in which intrigue and deceit are pervasive and inescapable. Far from being able to extricate reality from deception—the goal of Parmenides and Empedocles—the masters of truth in drama find themselves caught up in the quasireality their intrigues have established. Drama thus explores questions untouched by the philosophical tradition: how to live, day by day, when deception is inescapable and truth is obscure.

The Ethics of Intrigue: Sophocles' *Electra*

The opaqueness of reality is a central theme of Sophoclean tragedy. Though scholars have most often interpreted Sophocles primarily in terms of a "heroic temper" (Knox's phrase) or heroism more broadly, the fallibility of human belief and knowledge—as much as individual resolve, responsibility, or destiny—is a consistent concern throughout Sophocles' poetic career.[50] Sophocles' dramas frequently revolve around questions of knowledge (especially in both Oedipus plays), are concentrated around oracular utterances, and employ elaborate scenes of deception.[51] I consider the intrigues of the *Electra* and *Philoctetes* in this chapter, but the *Trachiniae* involves an attempted deception of Jocasta by Lichas and Jocasta's own ruse in sending the robe to Heracles (which turns out to be itself a deceptive object), while the *Ajax* has the famous "deception speech" in which Ajax appears to relent, only to kill himself in the

---

50. Classic is Bernard Knox, *The Heroic Temper: Studies in Sophoclean Tragedy* (Berkeley: University of California Press, 1964); more recent studies include Sarah Nooter, *When Heroes Sing: Sophocles and the Shifting Soundscape of Tragedy* (Cambridge: Cambridge University Press, 2012); Thomas Van Nortwick, *Late Sophocles: The Hero's Evolution in "Electra," "Philoctetes," and "Oedipus at Colonus"* (Ann Arbor: University of Michigan Press, 2015).

51. Issues of knowledge are discussed in Marina Coray, *Wissen und Erkennen bei Sophokles* (Basel: Reinhardt, 1993). For Sophoclean deception scenes, see Ursula Parlavantza-Friedrich, *Täuschungsszenen in den Tragödien des Sophokles* (Berlin: de Gruyter, 1969). An overview of Sophoclean oracles and prophetic figures is in Jacques Jouanna, "Oracles et devins chez Sophocle," in *Oracles et prophéties dans l'antiquité*, ed. Jean-Georges Heintz (Paris: Éditions de Boccard, 1997), 283–320.

following scene.[52] Reality in Sophocles' plays is intensely difficult to penetrate, and differential understandings of the truth (between characters onstage and between the audience and characters) offer a major source of dramatic tension.

Despite this wider context for issues related to deception, Sophoclean intrigue plots have often been understood as derivative, and as the assumption of a particularly "Euripidean" form.[53] Euripides, to be sure, frequently stages such intrigue plots (*Electra, Medea, Hecuba, Ion*), often as tragedies of escape (*Iphigenia among the Taurians, Helen, Cyclops, Orestes*), but given the partial state of our evidence and the uncertainties surrounding chronology, we should be wary of assuming the direction of influence goes in one direction or the other.[54] Sophoclean intrigue plots are, moreover, distinctive in their staging of deception as an ethical problem, arising from the use of deception on friends and allies. While the Taurian *Iphigenia* and *Helen* use stories of false belief to delve into epistemological and ontological concerns, these are not particularly concentrated around the plays' intrigues, nor do they raise serious ethical questions, except perhaps insofar as they relate to the gods' treatment of human beings.[55] The most relevant comparison may be the *Ion*, which, like

---

52. On deception in *Trachiniae,* see Stuart E. Lawrence, "The Dramatic Epistemology of Sophocles' 'Trachiniae,'" *Phoenix* 32 (1978): 288–304; D. A. Hester, "Deianeira's 'Deception Speech,'" *Antichthon* 14 (1980): 1–8; Michael R. Halleran, "Lichas' Lies and Sophoclean Innovation," *Greek, Roman, and Byzantine Studies* 27 (1986): 239–47. On *Ajax* (among many others), R. P. Winnington-Ingram, *Sophocles: An Interpretation* (Cambridge: Cambridge University Press, 1980), 47–56; P. T. Stevens, "Ajax in the Trugrede," *Classical Quarterly* 36 (1986): 327–36; André Lardinois, "The Polysemy of Gnomic Expressions and Ajax's Deception Speech," in *Sophocles and the Greek Language: Aspects of Diction, Syntax and Pragmatics*, ed. Irene J. F. de Jong and Albert Rijksbaron (Leiden: Brill, 2006), 213–23.

53. Friedrich Solmsen, "Zur Gestaltung des Intriguenmotivs in den Tragödien des Sophokles und Euripides," *Philologus* 87 (1932): 1–17. Comparison with Euripidean deception is made throughout Reinhardt's influential discussion of the two plays: Karl Reinhardt, *Sophocles*, trans. Hazel Harvey and David Harvey (Oxford: Blackwell, 1979).

54. Sophocles' *Trachiniae*, which is full of deception motifs, is usually dated relatively early in his career, and so probably predates Euripidean deception plots. At the same time, correspondences between the *Electra* and *Philoctetes* (which is securely dated to 409) suggest that both were probably composed later in Sophocles' career, making the Euripidean influence more plausible. On the notoriously difficult dating of Sophocles' plays, see Patrick Finglass, ed., *Sophocles: "Ajax"* (Cambridge: Cambridge University Press, 2011), 1–11.

55. The philosophical dimension of the *Iphigenia among the Taurians* and *Helen* is a focus in Wright, *Euripides' Escape Tragedies*. Important readings of the *Helen* as a philosophical drama are in Charles Segal, "The Two Worlds of Euripides' 'Helen,'" *Transactions of the American*

the Sophoclean examples, involves a deception enacted against (as yet unrecognized) family, and takes place in an oracular context, yet the intrigue plot of the play is quite confined.[56] In the Sophoclean stagings, by contrast, the intrigue plots set out in the prologue condition the entirety of the plays, and are complicated by important realizations and reversals, through which they explore truth and ethical action in tandem.

The intrigue prologue, as I understand the form, consists of two figures engaged in a plot to deceive, with one acting as the instructor of the other, who will undertake the deception. Two sources of tension are latent: the first is the relation between the two figures, particularly the authority of one over the other to compel participation in the plot; the second potential source of tension stems from the target of the deception, a figure whose status is ambiguous between friend and enemy. These tensions are present to different degrees in the different stagings, but constant is an exploration of the way that deception renders trust between individuals difficult or impossible. The social and ethical implications emerge particularly from the two sources of tension mentioned above: between instructor and pupil (raising questions of authority), and between deceivers and deceived (raising questions of morality). As the

---

Philological Association 102 (1971): 553–614; Eric Downing, "Apate, Agon and Literary Self-Reflexivity in Euripides' 'Helen,'" in *Cabinet of the Muses: Essays on Classical and Comparative Literature in Honor of Thomas G. Rosenmeyer*, ed. Mark Griffith and Donald J. Mastronarde (Atlanta: Scholars Press, 1990), 1–16; Victoria Wohl, "Play of the Improbable: Euripides' Unlikely 'Helen,'" in *Probabilities, Hypotheticals, and Counterfactuals in Ancient Greek Thought*, ed. Victoria Wohl (Cambridge: Cambridge University Press, 2014), 142–59. Though the *Iphigenia*'s robbery plot has raised ethical concerns in many of its modern readers and adaptors (including, most famously, Goethe), the play itself seems relatively untroubled by these: see Edith Hall, *Adventures with "Iphigenia in Tauris": A Cultural History of Euripides' Black Sea Tragedy* (Oxford: Oxford University Press, 2013).

56. The fragmentary *Alexander* includes similar elements of intrigue between unrecognized family members: Ioanna Karamanou, ed., *Euripides: "Alexandros"* (Berlin: de Gruyter, 2017), 23–24. On oracles in the *Ion*, see Katerina Zacharia, *Converging Truths: Euripides' "Ion" and the Athenian Quest for Self-Definition* (Leiden: Brill, 2003), 128–39; Julia Kindt, *Revisiting Delphi: Religion and Storytelling in Ancient Greece* (Cambridge: Cambridge University Press, 2016), 55–86. Both *Ion* and *Creusa* are attested as titles of Sophocles. These have often been thought to be the same play, likely a version of the story staged by Euripides, though the evidence is quite scant: Gunther Martin, ed., *Euripides: "Ion"* (Berlin: de Gruyter, 2018), 18–20. Sophocles F 352, attributed to *Creusa*, declares that lying is pardonable when the truth would bring ruin, which would at least fit the context of the deception plot we know from Euripides—and, regardless, evinces Sophocles' wider interest in the ethics of deception.

plays develop, these tensions will come to the fore as deceptive stories escape the control of their authors, and become a kind of reality of their own. The intrigue prologues I discuss establish concerns of truth, justice, and deception that the rest of their dramas will explore, compounding the initial falsehood and complicating the "reality" presented to the audience.

Orestes' return and revenge is the crucial mythological episode for intrigue plots in tragedy. Stagings by the three canonical tragedians survive, which reveal their different interests in the intellectual work of the drama.[57] Sophocles' staging, I argue, is distinguished by the way it shifts the ethical weight of the drama from the matricide—a central concern in Aeschylus' *Libation Bearers* and *Eumenides*, as well as in Euripides' *Electra*—to the act of deception itself. In Aeschylus' and Euripides' stagings, Orestes employs trickery to undertake the murder enjoined by the Delphic oracle, an act that might exemplify the idea of a just *apatē*, even as the morality of the matricide is shown to be questionable. In Sophocles' staging, by contrast, the morality of matricide is almost entirely set aside, and is never explicitly questioned by any of the central characters.[58] At the same time, the act of deception itself bears profound ethical weight, insofar as its victims are not only the intended targets, Clytemnestra and Aegisthus, but Electra and her sister Chrysothemis as well. Their distress proves a kind of collateral damage in the intrigue plot, violating one of the central tenets of Greek ethics: that it is right to help friends and harm enemies.[59] Orestes initially appears indifferent to the effect of his deception on his sisters, but the play will portray the consequences of the falsehood in wrenching detail. Where previous stagings of the Orestes story had concentrated on the grey area between friend and enemy in the figure of Clytemnestra, the ethical world of Sophocles' *Electra* obeys strict lines of

---

57. The relative chronology of the two *Electra* plays is unclear and has been endlessly debated. I see no convincing grounds for either case, so while I employ the Euripidean *Electra* as a comparison, I do not attempt to interpret one as a response to the other (whereas both are clearly responding to Aeschylus' *Libation Bearers*).

58. There is an extensive scholarly discussion of what to make of the ethical world of the play, which is broadly divided between optimistic readings, which vindicate the matricide as a heroic act, and pessimistic or ironic ones, which judge it to be morally bankrupt: Leona MacLeod, *Dolos and Dikē in Sophokles' "Elektra"* (Leiden: Brill, 2001), 4–20. Though my reading tends toward pessimism, I accept that the matricide itself is presented as unproblematic, but see the deception plot as the locus for the play's aporetic moral concerns.

59. Mary Whitlock Blundell, *Helping Friends and Harming Enemies: A Study in Sophocles and Greek Ethics* (Cambridge: Cambridge University Press, 1989), esp. 26–59.

demarcation between friends and enemies, but shows that the harm generated by Orestes' plot crosses these.

Sophocles' deception plot poses questions of reality, truth, and artifice much more centrally than either of the other two stagings. While the plotters in both Aeschylus and Euripides concoct pretenses to gain the trust of Clytemnestra and Aegisthus, these stories receive relatively little emphasis. Sophocles makes this minor detail into a major plot point, introducing an extended narration of Orestes' fall in a chariot race and then a scene in which the plotters bring the "urn" of his ashes onstage, all while depicting Electra's anguished reactions. As he will do in the *Philoctetes*, Sophocles constructs an elaborate, deceptive story that takes in the central character and spans much of the drama. Even though in the *Electra* (unlike the *Philoctetes*) there is no difficulty for the audience in separating truth from fiction, devoting so much of the play to the elaboration of a lie draws significant attention to deception. This has been understood in metatheatrical terms, as a reflection on the fictive character of drama.[60] While I accept that one of the intellectual contexts for Sophocles' staging is an inquiry into dramatic *apatē*, I suggest the ultimate questions are broader: the plays probe not just the deceptive power of drama (Gorgianic *apatē*), but the deceptive power of appearances broadly (Parmenidean *apatē*) and the role of language in forming belief and opinion.

The prologue of Sophocles' *Electra* prologue is distinguished from other treatments of the episode both by its dialogic opening (where both Aeschylus and Euripides begin with monologues), and its emphasis on the here-and-now.[61] The Paidagogos begins the play with an address to Orestes, pointing

---

60. Extended metatheatrical readings are in Charles Segal, "Visual Symbolism and Visual Effects in Sophocles," *Classical World* 74 (1980): 125–42; Segal, *Tragedy and Civilization*, 249–91; Ann G. Batchelder, *The Seal of Orestes: Self-Reference and Authority in Sophocles' "Electra"* (Lanham: Rowman & Littlefield, 1995); Mark Ringer, *Electra and the Empty Urn: Metatheater and Role Playing in Sophocles* (Chapel Hill: University of North Carolina Press, 1998), 127–212.

61. Dialogue prologues seem distinctively Sophoclean: all of Aeschylus' undisputed plays begin with a monologue or choral song, and Euripides' affection for expository monologues was notorious, while all but one of Sophocles' extant works begins with dialogue. On the exception proving the rule, see Irene J. F. de Jong, "Sophocles' 'Trachiniae' 1–48, Euripidean Prologues, and Their Audiences," in *The Language of Literature: Linguistic Approaches to Classical Texts*, ed. Rutger J. Allan and Michel Buijs (Boston: Brill, 2007), 7–28. The construction of the *Electra* prologue is discussed in Francis M. Dunn, "Trope and Setting in Sophocles' 'Electra,'" in *Sophocles and the Greek Language: Aspects of Diction, Syntax and Pragmatics*, ed. Irene J. F. de Jong and Albert Rijksbaron (Leiden: Brill, 2006), 184–200.

out the geography and buildings of Mycenae, and recalling how he saved the child Orestes from the slaughter of Agamemnon, rearing him in order to take revenge on the murderers. There is a subtle negotiation of authority between the two speaking figures of the prologue: Orestes, though of higher status, is (literally) the pupil, and the Paidagogos' opening speech assumes the role of guide, admonishing, "what it is necessary to do must be decided immediately" (16: τί χρὴ δρᾶν ἐν τάχει βουλευτέον). As we learn in his extended response, Orestes has already constructed an elaborate plan, and in the course of the scene he takes over the role of instructor from the Paidagogos, effectively assuming leadership of the expedition. This transfer of authority, though unremarked, is significant in that it depicts Orestes assuming the role of adult and ruler to which he aspires, and doing so by establishing his comprehensive grasp of truth and deception.

The deception plot of the *Electra*, like that of *Libation Bearers*, is presented as a divine command. Orestes describes how the oracle of Apollo prescribed the use of trickery to accomplish his revenge:[62]

ἐγὼ γὰρ ἡνίχ' ἱκόμην τὸ Πυθικὸν
μαντεῖον, ὡς μάθοιμ' ὅτῳ τρόπῳ πατρὶ
δίκας ἀροίμην τῶν φονευσάντων πάρα,
χρῇ μοι τοιαῦθ' ὁ Φοῖβος ὧν πεύσῃ τάχα·
ἄσκευον αὐτὸν ἀσπίδων τε καὶ στρατοῦ
δόλοισι κλέψαι χειρὸς ἐνδίκους σφαγάς. (32–37)

> When I came to the Pythian oracle, in order that I might learn in what way I might gain justice for my father from those who killed him, Phoebus advised me in such a way as you will shortly learn: that alone, unequipped with shields or army, I would accomplish stealthily with tricks the hand's just slaughters.

In emphasizing the justice of the murders and the trickery commanded to achieve them, Orestes attempts to defuse two potential pitfalls: most obviously, the ethical validity of the matricide seems to be taken for granted, and is barely addressed further in the play. The oracle, moreover, approves the use

---

62. The content of the oracle in Aeschylus is uncertain because it was likely explicated in the now-lost prologue speech, after which point the rest of the drama takes it for granted. It probably would have included the use of trickery, since this is implied by 274 and 556–59: Andrew Brown, ed., *Aeschylus: "Libation Bearers"* (Liverpool: Liverpool University Press, 2018), 171–72.

of stealth and trickery, which could well be deemed unheroic (in some earlier versions of the story, Orestes seems to have attacked in full armor).[63] Prominent in Aeschylus, though not explicit in Sophocles, is the idea that Orestes' trickery is warranted by the trickery employed on Agamemnon, in conformity with the *lex talionis* that is frequently invoked in the *Libation Bearers*.[64] The lack of such explicit justification for the *dolos* in Sophocles is significant, and consistent with the absence of a specific oracular command to take revenge (which is emphatic in Aeschylus): the world of the *Electra* presumes divine sanction for the matricide, but does not rely on the gods for support. Though the divine command is largely absent after this initial mention, an Apollonian context is pervasive.[65] Following the Delphic command, Orestes' assumption of power broadly follows an initiatory pattern that would have been associated with Apollo, as the god who presides over ephebes.[66] The murders will constitute Orestes' own initiation by deception, a passage into adulthood by stealthy military action.

Orestes goes on to explain his plan, which sends the Paidagogos into the house for reconnaissance, and to prepare for his own arrival with Pylades. As in Aeschylus, they will gain entry by assuming a false identity and telling the story of Orestes' death, but the trick is far more complex in Sophocles,

---

63. There is visual evidence for a tradition of Orestes armed in the Boston calyx-krater dated to around 470: MFA 63.1246.

64. For *dolos* in response to *dolos*, see *Libation Bearers* 273–74, 556–59, 888; Euripides, *Electra* as well: 276–79, 969–70, 983. Sophocles makes no explicit mention of this as the reason for Orestes' deception, despite the assertion to the contrary in P. J. Finglass, ed., *Sophocles: "Electra"* (Cambridge: Cambridge University Press, 2007), 89–90. Finglass points to passages in which the chorus recall Agamemnon's death by trickery, but which make no connection to revenge by trickery.

65. Apollonian resonances concentrate around the cult of Apollo Lykeios, possibly because the "wolf-killing god" (6) could be associated with revenge or protection: 6–7, 645, 655, 1379. A story in Pausanias (2.9.7) connects the epithet to Apollo's instructions to the Sicyonians to kill the wolves devastating their flocks by setting out poisoned food for them—fittingly, by a *dolos*. See Claire-Françoise de Roguin, "Apollon Lykeios dans la tragédie: Dieu protecteur, dieu tueur, 'dieu de l'initiation,'" *Kernos* 12 (1999): 99–123. On Apollo in the play more broadly: G.H.R. Horsley, "Apollo in Sophokles' 'Elektra,'" *Antichthon* 14 (1980): 18–29; Stefano Jedrkiewicz, "Vengeur? Sauveur? Menteur?: Apollon aux yeux des trois Électres," *Lexis* 30 (2012): 294–307.

66. For Orestes as ephebe, see Anton Bierl, "Apollo in Greek Tragedy: Orestes and the God of Initiation," in *Apollo: Origins and Influences.*, ed. Jon Solomon (Tucson: University of Arizona Press, 1994), 81–96.

involving two stages and an elaborate false narrative. Orestes instructs the Paidagogos,

> ἄγγελλε δ' ὅρκον προστιθείς, ὁθούνεκα
> τέθνηκ' Ὀρέστης ἐξ ἀναγκαίας τύχης,
> ἄθλοισι Πυθικοῖσιν ἐκ τροχηλάτων
> δίφρων κυλισθείς· ὧδ' ὁ μῦθος ἑστάτω. (47–50)
>
> Announce, speaking on oath, that Orestes has died by fated chance, after being tossed from a wheeled chariot-bench in the Pythian Games. Let your story be thus.

The outlines of this story are suggested by Aeschylus, where Orestes relates the news of his own death and requests instructions for burial (674–88). Sophocles transfers the actual narration to the Paidagogos, but portrays Orestes as the effective author of the false report. The placement of Orestes' death in the Pythian Games contributes to the Apollonian resonances of the story, associating the god who speaks truth with deception and falsehood. Confident in the justice of his plot, Orestes appears unconcerned about the falsehoods (even enjoining a false oath) or their effects on his family. After Orestes' preview, we hear a spectacularly expanded version of the lie in the Paidagogos' narration, which takes on the form and much of the function of a tragic messenger speech. It elicits interestingly mixed feelings from Clytemnestra, but utter despair in Electra, who is spurred by the news to concoct a desperate plot of her own. An audience watching the Paidagogos' speech is conscious of its falsehood, but cannot mistake the profound effect it has on its credulous internal audience.[67] The effect is to set the action of the rest of the play on two separate levels of reality: one to which the audience and the plotters are privy, and the other inhabited by the rest of the characters, who believe the false story.[68] This is not, to be sure, a novel device in tragedy, but the *Electra* extends the intrigue and stages its consequences more fully than any other extant tragedy (with the possible exception of the *Philoctetes*).

---

67. On the emotional and imaginative dynamics of the speech, see C. W. Marshall, "How to Write a Messenger Speech (Sophocles, 'Electra' 680–763)," in *Greek Drama III: Essays in Honour of Kevin Lee*, ed. John Davidson, Frances Muecke, and Peter Wilson (London: Institute of Classical Studies, 2006), 203–21.

68. For the speech's implicit reflection on deception, see Grethlein, *The Ancient Aesthetics of Deception*.

The second stage of the plot deepens the story's hold by introducing an urn ostensibly containing Orestes' ashes. Such an urn is mentioned briefly in Aeschylus (686–87), but does not appear onstage; it becomes a crucial stage property in Sophocles' plot, acting as a physical corollary to the story of Orestes' death.[69] After a visit to Agamemnon's grave (another nod to Aeschylus), Orestes and Pylades will approach bearing the urn, "so that cheating with our speech, we may bring them a pleasing report" (56–57: ὅπως λόγῳ κλέπτοντες / ἡδεῖαν φάτιν / φέρωμεν αὐτοῖς). Orestes draws attention again to the fictive power of language: by "cheating with speech" (using the same verb, *kleptō*, that was used for the deception plot earlier) and bringing the "pleasing report" of his death, he will offer Clytemnestra and Aegisthus a false sense of security. The multiple streams of information and forms of proof may be gratuitous— Aeschylus' Orestes did without them entirely—but they give the deceptive story extra dimensions and credibility. Orestes' story of his own death is a particularly apt pretext, since it plays to the fears of Clytemnestra and Aegisthus that he will return, while in the telling accomplishing his return and enabling his revenge.

The pains that Orestes takes to justify his plan demonstrate that narrating one's own death is, at the very least, unsettling:

τί γάρ με λυπεῖ τοῦθ᾽, ὅταν λόγῳ θανὼν
ἔργοισι σωθῶ κἀξενέγκωμαι κλέος;
δοκῶ μὲν, οὐδὲν ῥῆμα σὺν κέρδει κακόν· (59–61)

What does this pain me, when dying in speech, in deeds I am safe and win glory? I think no word with benefit is bad.

This is as close as Orestes comes to considering the possible consequences of his deception. The scruple about "dying in speech" was not in evidence in Aeschylus, and even in denying it, Sophocles' Orestes emphasizes its potential seriousness. The primary concern, though not explicitly stated, seems to be taboo: "to die in speech" (λόγῳ θανεῖν) figures also in the elaborate deception of Euripides' *Helen*, where it is described as a "bad omen" (1050–51: κακὸς ...

---

69. On the role of the urn, see Joshua Billings, "Orestes' Urn in Word and Action," in *The Materialities of Greek Tragedy: Objects and Affect in Aeschylus, Sophocles, and Euripides*, ed. Mario Telò and Melissa Mueller (London: Bloomsbury, 2018), 49–62; Melissa Mueller, *Objects as Actors: Props and the Poetics of Performance in Greek Tragedy* (Chicago: University of Chicago Press, 2016), 111–33; Colleen Chaston, *Tragic Props and Cognitive Function: Aspects of the Function of Images in Thinking* (Leiden: Brill, 2010), 131–79.

ὄρνις).⁷⁰ In both cases, the possibility of benefit (κέρδος) trumps the concern with ill-omened speech, and leads both plotters to employ the story in spite of their unease.⁷¹ Sophocles is much vaguer on the source of concern, leaving open the possibility—which the rest of the play will explore—that Orestes may experience other forms of grief from his deception.

As Orestes explains, the benefit for him consists not just in the advantage he will gain over his enemies, but in the repute that will come from his trickery:

> ἤδη γὰρ εἶδον πολλάκις καὶ τοὺς σοφοὺς
> λόγῳ μάτην θνήσκοντας· εἶθ', ὅταν δόμους
> ἔλθωσιν αὖθις, ἐκτετίμηνται πλέον·
> ὡς κἄμ' ἐπαυχῶ τῆσδε τῆς φήμης ἄπο
> δεδορκότ' ἐχθροῖς ἄστρον ὣς λάμψειν ἔτι. (62–66)

For I know many times wise men have died falsely in speech; and then, when they return again to their homes, they are honored the more. So I am confident that from this report I, living, will yet blaze like a star over my enemies.

There has been much speculation concerning which σοφοί Orestes has in mind here, but more important is the fact—paralleled also in the *Helen*, where Menelaus draws attention to the "antiquity" (1056: παλαιότης, potentially "out-datedness") of the false death story—that such a plot is presented as familiar.⁷² Orestes claims to be adhering to an established pattern of behavior, thereby defusing the anxiety related to taboo. Indeed, he imagines that the false story of his death will add to his glory when he emerges triumphant, suggesting an implicit secondary motivation for the trick: the courting of taboo will ultimately increase Orestes' fame (just as it seems to have done for the σοφοί he

---

70. The correspondence between the scenes has led to speculation about the influence of one on the other, though the direction is disputed.

71. Menelaus agrees to go ahead with the false death story, saying, "If I gain, tell it" (*Helen* 1051: εἰ δὲ κερδανῶ, λέγε). Orestes in the *Iphigenia among the Taurians*, too, encourages Iphigenia to make use of his situation for the purpose of deception "if you gain" (1034: εἰ κερδανεῖς).

72. The fact that such a plot is familiar in tragedy—not only from Aeschylus' *Libation Bearers*, but from Euripides' *Cresphontes* (T iia) as well (in addition to one or the other of the *Helen* and *Electra*)—is adequate to explain its "antiquity." Odysseus' return and revenge on the suitors would also be an important parallel (if not an exact one, because he did not spread the rumor of his death).

mentions). There may be a hint that Orestes' story constitutes a kind of symbolic ritual death, like that experienced in initiation rituals. Returning to society after his feigned death, Orestes will have demonstrated his readiness to take power in Argos.

Orestes' reliance on the power of language, as well as his stark opposition of speech (*logos*) and action (*ergon*), locates him within the fifth-century intellectual context. Gorgias' famous description of *logos* in the *Encomium of Helen* as a "great potentate" that "performs the most divine deeds" (B11 DK/D24 LM 8: δυνάστης μέγας ... θειότατα ἔργα ἀποτελεῖ) is an extreme version of a wider tendency to focus on the power of speech for good or ill.[73] Speech is powerful, according to the *Encomium*, because of the "stumbling and unstable" (B11 DK/D24 LM 11: σφαλερὰ καὶ ἀβέβαιος) quality of opinion (δόξα). Lacking reliable knowledge of past, present, and future, humans rely on opinion as "counselor of the soul" (B11 DK/D24 LM 11: σύμβουλον τῇ ψυχῇ) and are thereby susceptible to persuasion by speech, whether true or false. This power just as often led to suspicion, to a concern that *logos* might manipulate *erga*.[74] Odysseus, as discussed above, is often associated with the deceptive power of speech, in contrast to the truth of actions: Gorgias' Palamedes defends himself against Odysseus' accusations by urging his listeners "not to pay attention more to words than to deeds" (B11a DK/D25 LM 34: μὴ τοῖς λόγοις μᾶλλον ἢ τοῖς ἔργοις προσέχειν τὸν νοῦν), and Antisthenes' *Ajax* likewise cautions the judges, "do not look to words when judging concerning excellence, but rather to deeds" (7: μὴ εἰς τοὺς λόγους σκοπεῖν περὶ ἀρετῆς κρίνοντας, ἀλλ' εἰς τὰ ἔργα μᾶλλον).[75] In both cases, the opposition of *logos* and *ergon* demonstrates a concern—which the myths validate in full—that

---

73. On Gorgias' extreme claims for language, see James I. Porter, "The Seductions of Gorgias," *Classical Antiquity* 12 (1993): 267–99; Jonathan Pratt, "On the Threshold of Rhetoric," *Classical Antiquity* 34 (2015): 163–82. I find both of these views more compelling than the systematizing approaches of earlier scholarship.

74. The contrast between *logos* and *ergon* in the *Electra* is frequently discussed: Thomas M. Woodard, "'Electra' by Sophocles: The Dialectical Design," *Harvard Studies in Classical Philology* 68 (1964): 163–205; Rachel Kitzinger, "Why Mourning Becomes Elektra," *Classical Antiquity* 10 (1991): 298–327; Van Nortwick, *Late Sophocles*, 7–41. For the contrast in fifth-century thought generally, see Adam Parry, *Logos and Ergon in Thucydides* (New York: Arno, 1981), 15–61.

75. See Susan Prince, "Words of Representation and Words of Action in the Speech of Antisthenes' Ajax," in *Antisthenica Cynica Socratica*, ed. Vladislav Suvák (Prague: Oikoumene, 2014), 168–99. The contrast between the speech of Odysseus and the deeds of Ajax is already present in Pindar, *Nemean* 8, 21–33.

the persuasive power of Odysseus' language will win out over the evidence of good actions. Orestes confidently asserts the opposite, that his deeds will render his words insignificant.

Like the other dramatic intriguers, Orestes tries to instrumentalize deception through language for his own ends, but the course of the drama shows that falsehoods are not easily contained, that *logos* cannot be totally divorced from *ergon*. In the prologue, Orestes displays an attitude to the relation of speech and action that both relies on the ability of language to deceive and at the same time minimizes the significance of the deception. The rest of the play, in effect, tests whether these tendencies are compatible by portraying the reactions to the Paidagogos' narration and Orestes' entrance with the urn. As both "enemies" (Clytemnestra and Aegisthus) and "friends" (Electra and Chrysothemis) believe the false story and act accordingly, the play stages the effect of language on belief and action. The audience witnesses the consequences of deception well before and at greater length than Orestes (who is offstage for the central portion of the play) does. Orestes is finally confronted with the effects of his story when he views Electra's lament over the urn he himself has brought.[76] Her speech addresses the urn and then Orestes directly (she thinks, in absence), figuring his death as her own: "dearest, how you have destroyed me, indeed destroyed me" (1663–64: φίλταθ', ὥς μ' ἀπώλεσας. / ἀπώλεσας δῆτ'). Even Orestes' "dying in speech" turns out to be a profoundly destructive act. When Orestes is finally confronted with the effects of his story in watching Electra's grief over the urn, he finds himself bereft of language: "Alas, alas, what will I say? Where among helpless words shall I turn? For I am no longer strong enough to master my tongue" (1174–75: φεῦ φεῦ· τί λέξω; ποῖ λόγων ἀμηχάνων / ἔλθω; κρατεῖν γὰρ οὐκέτι γλώσσης σθένω). This represents a striking reversal: Orestes is left with only "helpless" (ἀμήχανος, also suggesting "without a plan") words, in contrast to his previous control of speech. The power of language to fashion belief appears now significantly double-edged, as Orestes understands that the story of his death has caused his loved ones substantial, and unnecessary, grief.

Orestes' story had introduced a gap between language and reality, which the recognitions of the final scenes gradually bridge. Sophocles' staging of the intrigue is interested primarily in this gap, which appears almost as profound

---

76. On Electra's lament, see the discussions in Foley, *Female Acts*, 145–71; Sarah Hamilton Nooter, "Language, Lamentation, and Power in Sophocles' 'Electra,'" *Classical World* 104 (2011): 399–417.

as Gorgias suggested in *On Nonbeing*: language appears opposed to reality, and this brings with it profound consequences. Once she has recognized Orestes, Electra asks, "Why did you escape my notice, being near, and not greet me fondly, but destroyed me with your words, while having the sweetest deeds for me?" (1359–60: ξυνών μ' ἔληθες οὐδ' ἔσαινες, ἀλλά με / λόγοις ἀπώλλυς, ἔργ' ἔχων ἥδιστ' ἐμοί;). Electra's destruction by *logoi* forms an implicit mirror to Orestes' earlier, false death in speech. Electra asserts that *logos* has real effects, which are not entirely eclipsed by *erga*. Her tone seems to be forgiving, but the question is revealing of the ethical concerns posed by the intrigue: Orestes' words were destructive even as his actions were righteous. This formulation and the course of the play as a whole, I suggest, raise troubling questions about the ethics of intrigue. Orestes' manipulation of truth and falsehood has deleterious effects beyond his control, and demonstrates the power of language to deceive and, through deception, to harm. Mastery over truth and falsehood, the play suggests, is not ethically neutral, and exposes the deceiver to questions of justice. Orestes emerges from the play profoundly compromised by the process of revenge, even as it accomplishes its intended goal. Sophocles stages a skeptical viewpoint on the "just deception" envisioned by Aeschylus and Gorgias: an intrigue in which dubious means call into question the justice of ends.

On Not Being Female: Aristophanes' *Women at the Thesmophoria*

While the *Electra* investigates the ethical implications of deception within a family, Aristophanes' *Women at the Thesmophoria* (here abbreviated *Thesmo*) addresses deception's consequences for life in a political community. *Thesmo* understands intrigue as a pervasive quality of social existence, and brings this conception to bear on religious, aesthetic, and political concerns. It foregrounds the initiatory and philosophical contexts I have suggested surround *apatē* at the close of the fifth century, and connects these to issues of truth and trust within a polity. *Thesmo* thus forms an argumentative bridge between the two Sophoclean intrigue plots: while the *Electra* presents deception within the relatively closed ethical context of the family, the *Philoctetes* will stage intrigue as an ontological and political concern, which significantly complicates notions of truth and falsehood and raises questions about the possibility of trust within a community. *Apatē* in *Thesmo* describes a state of uncertainty that reflects, most directly, on the evidence of the senses and the illusion of drama, but implicates the social world of contemporary Athens as a realm of pervasive deception. Though *Thesmo* plays this state of intrigue for laughs, my reading brings out the darker implications of the work's image of society by pointing to its continuity with tragic deception plots. The reciprocal intrigues of *Thesmo*, I argue, stage an inquiry into the role of truth and trust in Athenian political life.

The situation at the beginning of *Thesmo* is similar to that of the Sophoclean intrigue prologues: two men, one of elevated status and knowledge (in this case Euripides), plot an intrigue, in which the lower-status of the two (the Inlaw) will undertake a mission of deception (impersonating a woman to infiltrate the Thesmophoria). The parallel is not precise—Euripides and the Inlaw first appeal to Agathon to undertake the mission, and are rebuffed—but the structuring of the prologue and the entire play around an intrigue is similar, and distinctive among Aristophanes' extant works. The centrality of deception in the play must reflect the importance of intrigue and escape plots in Euripides (which are parodied in the second part of the play), even as its structure is more like the Sophoclean examples. Although both the plotters in Aristophanes are well beyond ephebic age, the relationship is clearly one of philosophical and then ritual initiation, as Euripides instructs the Inlaw in the origins of sense-perception and then prepares him to take part in the Thesmophoria.

The opening scene of *Thesmo* owes much of its comic effect to the contrast between Euripides' high-flown intellectualism and the Inlaw's obtuseness, which causes a series of linguistic misunderstandings. These are concentrated around the discourse of instruction, the evidence of the senses, and the possibility of negation—all topics with significant Eleatic and post-Eleatic resonances. Euripides takes on the role of philosophical instructor to an intellectual novice, a position occupied by the figure of the goddess in Parmenides, the poetic persona in Empedocles, and the Eleatic Stranger in Plato. The play opens with Euripides and the Inlaw at the end of a long journey toward a destination that Euripides has thus far withheld from his companion. To the Inlaw's impatient demand to know where they are going, Euripides replies with a vatic pronouncement on the senses, "it is not necessary that you hear all that shortly you will see being present" (5–6: ἀλλ' οὐκ ἀκούειν δεῖ σε πάνθ' ὅσ' αὐτίκα / ὄψει παρεστώς). The emphasis on autopsy and Euripides' apparent secrecy concerning their destination suggest a mystical knowledge into which the Inlaw is going to be initiated. Euripides asserts at first that hearing and seeing are in effect redundant: the Inlaw does not need to hear what he will see, and conversely, he need not see what he is about to hear. The Inlaw hears these as prohibitions on sense-experience, that he *should* not see or hear what he will experience by the other sense: "It is necessary that I not hear?" (7: οὐ δεῖ μ' ἀκούειν;), he asks, and his misunderstanding launches the two into a kind of parody of philosophical instruction.

The Inlaw (mis)understands Euripides to be rejecting the evidence of the senses and thus posing an epistemological quandary, while Euripides thinks the conversation is about the relation between hearing and seeing. In a vain attempt to clarify things, Euripides expounds a theory of the nature (*phusis*) of the senses:

ΚΗ. οὐ φὴς σὺ χρῆναί μ' οὔτ' ἀκούειν οὔθ' ὁρᾶν;
ΕΥ. χωρὶς γὰρ αὐτοῖν ἑκατέρου 'στὶν ἡ φύσις.
ΚΗ. τοῦ μήτ' ἀκούειν μήθ' ὁρᾶν; ΕΥ. εὖ ἴσθ' ὅτι.[77] (10–12)

Inlaw. You're saying I should neither hear nor see? *Euripides.* Yes, because the nature of each of the two is distinct. *I.* Of not hearing and not seeing? *E.* Know it well.

Euripides' answer is a non sequitur, not answering the Inlaw's question about what senses he ought (or ought not) to use, but jumping instead to a theory of the distinctness of the senses, which he seems to have in his back pocket. Euripides is so involved in his own speculations that he is oblivious to the Inlaw's increasingly impatient questions concerning not-hearing and not-seeing. The Inlaw has, however, stumbled onto a serious philosophical question: the nature of nonexistence, which had exercised Parmenides and Gorgias.[78] Gorgias had used the distinctness of the senses as evidence that, if anything exists, it could not be known or communicated, arguing that each sense offers completely incommensurate impressions, which cannot be translated into

---

77. Wilson's OCT adopts the deletion of line 12 as a marginal note, though I follow most editors in retaining it.

78. Clements reads the opening lines of the prologue as a highly sophisticated intertextual dialogue with Parmenides' poem: Clements, *Aristophanes' "Thesmophoriazusae,"* 43–158. Though I am in basic agreement with Clements' point that the play is engaged with Eleatic and post-Eleatic thought, I find the specific allusions detected largely unconvincing. The result, moreover, is an Aristophanes whose philosophical interest is validated by his upholding of Parmenidean orthodoxy, a conclusion that I think attributes both too much philosophical engagement and too little independent thought to the comedian.

thought or speech (D26a LM; *MXG* 6.17–19, 21–22).[79] The echo in Aristophanes may be vague, but the scene as a whole shows a general awareness of the problem of nonbeing and the problematization of the senses. Euripides' absentminded affirmation of the distinctness of *not*-seeing and *not*-hearing—a topic he has not even broached—associates him, in buffoonish fashion, with the mind-bending speculations of the philosophical avant garde.

In an effort to explain the distinctness of (not-)hearing and (not-)seeing, Euripides makes a detour into physical theory, seizing the opportunity to enlighten the Inlaw with an eclectic zoogony:

> οὕτω ταῦτα διεκρίθη τότε.
> αἰθὴρ γὰρ ὅτε τὰ πρῶτα διεχωρίζετο
> καὶ ζῷ' ἐν αὑτῷ ξυνετέκνου κινούμενα,
> ᾧ μὲν βλέπειν χρὴ πρῶτ' ἐμηχανήσατο
> ὀφθαλμὸν ἀντίμιμον ἡλίου τροχῷ,
> ἀκοῆς δὲ χοάνην ὦτα διετετρήνατο. (13–18)

They [the senses] were divided in this way once: for when at first *aether* was separating itself and took part in begetting in itself living, moving beings, then first it devised that by which they should see, the eye in imitation of the disc of the sun, and it bore through ears as a funnel for hearing.

A few elements to this theory are recognizably "modern": first, the mention of *aether* as a generative principle of the universe appears to be a Euripidean spin on the tradition of cosmogony going back to Hesiod's Gaia (earth) and Ouranos (sky), which was given new impetus in the later fifth century by identifications of Anaxagoras' *nous* with *aer* or *aether*.[80] The Anaxagorean context is suggested also by the idea of primal division, which was the first act of *nous/*

---

79. The Gorgias passages are difficult, but the basic thought can be filled in with help from Sextus Empiricus, *Against the Logicians* 7.81–86. Some have seen evidence here for Aristophanes' direct knowledge of Gorgias: Hays, "On the Skeptical Influence of Gorgias's 'On Non-Being,'" 333–35. The similarity seems quite approximate to me, and I think a better approach notes the philosophical register, but tries to make sense of it in its immediate context.

80. Euripides' relation to cosmogonic thought is discussed in John Dillon, "Euripides and the Philosophy of His Time," *Classics Ireland* 11 (2004): 47–73; Jacqueline Assaël, *Euripide, philosophe et poète tragique* (Louvain: Peeters, 2001), 45–60; Egli, *Euripides im Kontext*, 79–120. I have more to say about *aether* in the next chapter. On its specific use in Aristophanes and potential Orphic overtones, see Stavros Tsitsiridis, "'Euripideische' Kosmogonie bei Aristophanes ('Thesm.' 14–18)," *Ἑλληνικά* 51 (2001): 43–67.

aer in contemporary theories, and is invoked in other Euripidean cosmogonies.[81] The theory of the development of sense-organs has no obvious Euripidean precedent, but is a topic in physical theories of the fifth century, and especially in Empedocles' extensive zoogony, which describes divine design of human features in great detail.[82] The formulation in Aristophanes, too, implies an idea of divine teleology, like that witnessed in Theseus' speech in *Suppliants* (discussed in the previous chapter): humans are carefully designed by a divine creator.[83] Though critics have tried to pin down specific allusions in these lines, I think it is best to understand all these elements, like the mentions of not-hearing and not-seeing, as invoking contemporary philosophical thought, but without direct reference to a particular theory. More important is what the speech demonstrates about Euripides: that he is given to abstruse, avant-garde speculation, and takes himself extremely seriously.[84]

Euripides' discourse on the senses and the Inlaw's fixation on their negation have significant ritual implications, which include but reach well beyond theater. The Thesmophoria was a mystery festival, which involved rites prohibited

---

81. The idea of primal division is described most clearly in F 484 (*Melanippe the Wise*); F 839 (*Chrysippus*) explains division as the process of change in the world, presided over by earth and *aether*.

82. Some have detected allusions to Empedocles and Gorgias in the passage as a whole, and specifically to Empedocles B84 DK 9/D215 LM in the phrase "bore through a funnel" (χοάνην . . . διετετρήνατο): Patrizia Mureddu, "La 'incomunicabilità' gorgiana in una parodia di Aristofane?: Nota a 'Thesm.' 5–21," *Lexis* 9–10 (1992): 115–20; David Sansone, "Socrates' 'Tragic' Definition of Color (Pl. 'Meno' 76D–E)," *Classical Philology* 91 (1996): 339–45; Marwan Rashed, "The Structure of the Eye and Its Cosmological Function in Empedocles: Reconstruction of Fragment 84 D.-K.," in *Reading Ancient Texts: Essays in Honour of Denis O'Brien 1*, ed. Suzanne Stern-Gillet and Kevin Corrigan (Leiden: Brill, 2007), 21–39. The connection, which relies on a disputed reconstruction of the text of Empedocles, seems rather vague to me, and recognizing it as a specific allusion (rather than general parody) brings very little.

83. Sedley attributes ideas of divine teleology to Anaxagoras and (more emphatically) Empedocles, which may form part of the background for both Euripides' and "Euripides'" texts. It may not be incidental that Aristophanes in Plato's *Symposium* describes divine design in ways that seem reminiscent of Empedocles: David Sedley, *Creationism and Its Critics in Antiquity* (Berkeley: University of California Press, 2007), 55.

84. Some of the diction of the passage suggests quotation: both "in imitation of the disc of the sun" and "funnel for hearing" have been conjectured as Euripidean borrowings or parodies (which does not preclude the Euripidean originals having philosophical backgrounds): Alan H. Sommerstein, ed., *Aristophanes: "Thesmophoriazusae"* (Oxford: Aris & Phillips, 1994), 158–59; Sansone, "Socrates' 'Tragic' Definition of Color."

to men, and probably to noncitizen women as well.[85] As the play continues, the women (and the disguised Inlaw) will invoke prohibitions against others' seeing and hearing their rites (293–94, 628), implicitly recalling the opening dialogue. Our only evidence for the actual rites of the Thesmophoria is quite late, but it suggests that a series of ritual actions commemorated the rape of Persephone and the swineherd who fell into the chasm opened by Hades' abduction. Aristophanes may not have known much more himself, but the secrecy of the rites provides a context for the play's discussions of not-seeing and not-hearing, and the use of deception. Euripides' deception plan (which comically prefigures Pentheus' journey to the mountains in *Bacchae*) will involve the Inlaw seeing and hearing what he should not see or hear.[86]

The atmosphere of secrecy deepens as Euripides and the Inlaw approach their destination. As Euripides points out Agathon's house, the confusion surrounding sense and speech deepens:

ΕΥ. βάδιζε δευρὶ καὶ πρόσεχε τὸν νοῦν. ΚΗ. ἰδού.
ΕΥ. ὁρᾷς τὸ θύριον τοῦτο; ΚΗ. νὴ τὸν Ἡρακλέα
οἶμαί γε. ΕΥ. σίγα νῦν. ΚΗ. σιωπῶ τὸ θύριον.
ΕΥ. ἄκου'. ΚΗ. ἀκούω καὶ σιωπῶ τὸ θύριον. (25–28)

Euripides. Come here and pay attention. *Inlaw.* Here I am [literally: "see"]. *E.* Do you see this door? *I.* By Heracles, I *think* I do. *E.* Be quiet now. *I.* I'm being quiet about the door. *E.* Listen. *I.* I'm listening to and being quiet about the door.

The exchange rapidly recapitulates the prohibitions on seeing and hearing as a prohibition against speaking: the Inlaw is now enjoined to see and hear but not to speak. Again, the Inlaw understands Euripides' commands incorrectly, taking "be quiet" (σίγα) and "listen" (ἄκουε) as commands to be quiet about and listen to the door. Despite the absurdity of these commands, the Inlaw

---

85. On the Thesmophoria, see Robert Parker, *Polytheism and Society at Athens* (Oxford: Oxford University Press, 2005), 270–83; Eva M. Stehle, "Thesmophoria and Eleusinian Mysteries: The Fascination of Women's Secret Ritual," in *Finding Persephone: Women's Rituals in the Ancient Mediterranean*, ed. Maryline Parca and Angeliki Tzanetou (Bloomington: Indiana University Press, 2007), 165–85.

86. For Euripides' appropriation of the cross-dressing motif, see Jendza, *Paracomedy*, 108–18. Pentheus' robing has often been connected to initiatory ritual: Richard Seaford, ed., *Euripides: "Bacchae"* (Oxford: Aris & Phillips, 1996), 222–27. This would support my contention that deception plots in drama importantly evoke initiations.

seems to have given himself over entirely to Euripides' guidance, while Euripides again pays little attention to whether the Inlaw is comprehending him or not. The scene reads as a parody of tragic plotting scenes: Euripides seeks to involve his companion in the intrigue, but the Inlaw proves almost incapable of understanding the plan. He seems unsure who the famous (29: κλεινός, literally, "heard of") Agathon is and claims, emphatically and repeatedly, that he has never seen him (32–34). The Inlaw's ignorance is presented as total, a lack of seeing, hearing, and knowing at once. *Thesmo*'s confused discourse of (not-)seeing, (not-)hearing, and (not-)speaking presents Euripides' instruction of the Inlaw as a failed philosophical and ritual initiation.

The initiatory subtext becomes more explicit with the entrance of a servant, who addresses the apparently empty stage in language that echoes Euripides' command of silence, and suggests the beginning of a ritual act: "Let the entire host be silent, shutting their mouths" (39–40: εὔφημος πᾶς ἔστω λαός, / στόμα συγκλῄσας). The commandment to "be silent" (εὐφημεῖν, literally "speak well") is typical for solemn moments, and a similar formula will introduce the women's proceedings at the Thesmophoria (295, 296).[87] The use of the formula here casts Agathon's appearance as a moment of high ritual seriousness, which the Inlaw's repeated obscene interjections travesty, while also potentially recalling the *aischrologia* preparatory to a mystery initiation.[88] While they await Agathon's arrival, Euripides finally explains to the Inlaw what is going on and what he intends to do about it: the women of Athens "have devised plans" (82: ἐπιβεβουλεύκασι) against him in retaliation for his slandering them, and will decide how to proceed at the Thesmophoria. The language of intrigue is thick in his explanation of his "contrivance" (87: μηχανή). He intends to send Agathon "in secret" (91, 92: λάθρᾳ) to make a case on his behalf, disguising him as a woman—a plot the Inlaw describes as "very much your style" (93: σφόδρ' ἐκ τοῦ σοῦ τρόπου), recalling Euripidean deception plots. Yet this structure of *Thesmo* actually looks much more like the Sophoclean examples examined in this chapter, insofar as the plot is laid out in the prologue and takes place by proxy, than any of the play's Euripidean intertexts. What is most distinctively Euripidean, beyond the generally fantastic design of the intrigue, is the escape plots of the latter part of the play, which would have called to

---

87. On the uses of *euphēmia,* see Susanne Gödde, *Euphēmia: Die gute Rede in Kult und Literature der griechischen Antike* (Heidelberg: Winter, 2011).

88. Laura McClure, *Spoken Like a Woman: Speech and Gender in Athenian Drama* (Princeton: Princeton University Press, 1999), 218–26.

mind the previous year's stagings of the *Helen* and *Andromeda* (both 412, and parodied explicitly), as well as the *Iphigenia among the Taurians* and *Cyclops* (of uncertain date, but from the same period).[89] Especially in the years surrounding *Thesmo*, Euripides had built a reputation for staging wild and implausible deceptions and escapes. "We take the cake," the Inlaw remarks proudly, "for contriving" (94: τοῦ γὰρ τεχνάζειν ἡμέτερος ὁ πυραμοῦς), suggesting that Euripidean *technē* ("art" or "skill") is itself an art of deception.

The ontological concerns deepen with Agathon's entrance and dialogue with Euripides, which constitutes the first major locus of the play's interest in *mimēsis*. The episode and the mimetic discourse of the play as a whole have benefited from a number of valuable readings, which illuminate *Thesmo*'s profound engagement with questions of theatrical representation.[90] More important for my purposes, however, is how the play's ontological concerns bear on the ethical issues raised by deception, which come to a head in the enactment of the intrigue. After Agathon refuses to take part in Euripides' deception-by-proxy, the Inlaw offers himself to play the role that Euripides has scripted. After being shaved, singed, and dressed as a woman, the Inlaw is ready to join the Thesmophoria rites, but not before he extracts a promise from Euripides to save him "with all his skills" (271: πάσαις τέχναις) if anything goes wrong. Euripidean *technē* has been invoked before in the prologue, usually connected to his plotting (94: τεχνάζειν, 198: τεχνάσμασιν, both discussed above), but the word can equally describe Euripides' skill as a dramatist, and here seems general enough to include both. Indeed, as we will come to understand in the second half of the play, Euripides' dramatic artistry and his deceptive machinations are part of the same *technē*.

With the Thesmophoria scenes, the contexts for the play's staging of deception shift, from the sensory and aesthetic discourses of the prologue to ritual and more broadly social concerns.[91] The women's proceedings, as critics and

---

89. On the three tragedies (postulating a thematically connected trilogy), see Wright, *Euripides' Escape Tragedies*.

90. The discussions of the Agathon scene I have found most valuable are Froma I. Zeitlin, "Travesties of Gender and Genre in Aristophanes' 'Thesmophoriazusae,'" in *Playing the Other: Gender and Society in Classical Greek Literature* (Chicago: University of Chicago Press, 1996), 375–416; A. M. Bowie, *Aristophanes: Myth, Ritual, and Comedy* (Cambridge: Cambridge University Press, 1993), 205–27; Platter, *Aristophanes and the Carnival of Genres*, 143–75; Matthew C. Farmer, *Tragedy on the Comic Stage* (Oxford: Oxford University Press, 2017), 155–94.

91. On the play's staging of the ritual, see Anton Bierl, *Ritual and Performativity: The Chorus in Old Comedy*, trans. Alexander Hollmann (Washington, DC: Center for Hellenic Studies,

historians have noticed, suggest an inverted image of the Athenian Assembly, with the women taking over the spaces and functions of the male citizenry.⁹² Though *Thesmo* is often described as a comparatively apolitical work of Aristophanes, the concern with deception would have had profound resonance in the Athens of 411, when oligarchs from Samos were seeking to convince the citizens to dissolve democracy and ally with the Persians.⁹³ In the *Lysistrata*, probably performed two months earlier at the Lenaia festival, the heroine claims that the war is being fought so that Peisander, the most visible member of the delegation from Samos, "would be able to steal" (490: ἔχοι κλέπτειν), associating the oligarchs with deception and underhandedness.⁹⁴ *Thesmo* does not engage directly with the possibility of oligarchy, which may reflect the climate of fear that had set in over the ensuing months, but is notably full-throated in its disparagements of the Persians (335–37, 361–62, 365–66) and tyrants generally (348–49, and very prominently in 1143–44). The prominence of deception as a theme in the women's assembly would have spoken to fears of covert machinations against the democracy.⁹⁵

The assembly of women convenes to take up the matter of Euripides, whom, we learn, the women have already condemned and whose punishment must now be decided.⁹⁶ Euripides' offenses are numerous, but the one that draws the most attention is his exposure of women's secrets. The charge recalls

---

2009); Martha Habash, "The Odd Thesmophoria of Aristophanes' 'Thesmophoriazusae,'" *Greek, Roman, and Byzantine Studies* 38 (1997): 19–40; Angeliki Tzanetou, "Something to Do with Demeter: Ritual and Performance in Aristophanes' 'Women at the Thesmophoria,'" *American Journal of Philology* 123 (2002): 329–67.

92. J. A. Haldane, "A Scene in the 'Thesmophoriazusae' (295–371)," *Philologus* 109 (1965): 39–46; Bierl, *Ritual and Performativity*, 149–71.

93. On the chronology of events in 411, see (with attention to the dating of Aristophanes) Harry C. Avery, "The Chronology of Peisander's Mission to Athens," *Classical Philology* 94 (1999): 127–46.

94. The relative dating of *Thesmo* and *Lysistrata* is discussed in Colin Austin and S. Douglas Olson, eds., *Aristophanes: "Thesmophoriazusae"* (Oxford: Oxford University Press, 2004), xxxiii–xliv.

95. In this scenario, it would seem to be the women, who act in (imperfectly) democratic fashion, who stand in for the Athenian Assembly, and the Inlaw and Euripides who represent subversive foreign elements. Aristophanes makes a joke about Euripides' democratic credentials at *Frogs* 952–53.

96. Faraone suggests that some type of judicial proceeding in which women requested justice for wrongdoing may actually have been a feature of the second day of the Thesmophoria. The comparative evidence suggests that slander and theft would have been typical charges:

the topic of not-speaking from the prologue, and is reinforced by prohibitions against betraying the "unspeakable things" (363: ἀπόρρητα) of the rites. These "unspeakable things" must be understood in domestic, deliberative, and ritual terms simultaneously: the women's secret actions at home, the decisions of their tribunal, and the Thesmophoria rituals alike are prohibited subjects for speech. The assembly goes on to rehearse the charges against Euripides, in which a particular focal point is the women's sexual behavior: the first speaker claims that Euripidean drama slanders women so comprehensively that when the men of the city return from the theater, they immediately look for adulterers hidden in the house (395–97). As the speech goes on, it becomes clear that not all of these suspicions are unfounded, and indeed, the real complaint appears to be that Euripides has told the truth about female deception. It is impossible now, the first speaker complains, for a woman to pass off another's child as her own (407–9), or for a younger woman to marry a (presumably wealthy and docile) older man (410–13). Moreover, the men now take great pains to prevent adultery, locking and keeping watch over the women's quarters, and rearing fierce dogs to scare off potential lovers (414–17). The cumulative effect of these charges is that women's freedom—already severely limited in Athenian society—is even further reduced, and with it, their chances to act in secret.

The Inlaw's response admits these charges against Euripides, but defends him by claiming that the women's behavior is in fact far worse than Euripides portrays. Secrecy is again a major focus of the speech: the Inlaw begins by pointing to the women's ability to speak freely because "we are alone, and there is no one to bring away word" (472: αὐταὶ γάρ ἐσμεν, κοὐδεμί᾽ ἔκφορος λόγου). The Inlaw's speech presents himself and, by extension, the women of Athens as craven, sex-mad, and accomplished in deception of all kinds. The Inlaw claims that Euripides has in fact knowingly suppressed the multitude of their crimes, only revealing a few. He offers examples from his own life, telling a detailed story of adultery on his third day of marriage, and exposing the widespread practices of affairs with servants and chewing on garlic to conceal the evidence of illicit sex. "These things—you see?—he has never mentioned," the Inlaw notes. "And if he reviles Phaedra, what is it to us?" (496–98: ταῦθ᾽—ὁρᾷς,—/ οὐπώποτ᾽ εἶπεν. εἰ δὲ Φαίδραν λοιδορεῖ, / ἡμῖν τί τοῦτ᾽ ἔστ᾽;). Euripides' representations of mythical women like Phaedra, even if they cause men

---

Christopher A. Faraone, "Curses, Crime Detection and Conflict Resolution at the Festival of Demeter Thesmophoros," *Journal of Hellenic Studies* 131 (2011): 25–44.

to suspect their wives, turn out to be mild in comparison to the actual perfidy of Athenian women, which the Inlaw continues to recount. This defense of Euripides obviously indulges Athenian misogyny, but it also paints an image of the city's women as highly resourceful and clever, consistently deceiving the men of Athens—that is, the audience of the performance.

The Inlaw's identity is finally revealed when Cleisthenes, an Athenian politician portrayed as highly effeminate and therefore an ally of the women, enters, in the mode of a tragic messenger. By unspecified means, he has learned that Euripides has sent a relative as a "spy on speeches" (588: λόγων κατάσκοπος), and comes to reveal the plot. The man has "escaped notice" (589: λέληθεν) by dressing as a woman, Cleisthenes goes on to explain, to the surprise and horror of the women. Though the Inlaw seeks to sew doubt about the report, the women turn to the search for "how a man has escaped our notice sitting among us hidden" (599–600: ὅπου / λέληθεν ἡμᾶς κρυπτὸς ἐγκαθήμενος). The women quickly turn to interrogating the Inlaw, and he is revealed by a test of his knowledge of past Thesmophoria rites. The intrigue is undone by what the Inlaw did not see and does not know, and the limits of his initiation into the women's proceedings become evident. Having gained access to the obscure realm of female activity by deception, the Inlaw will be punished for having seen what he should not.

The deception plot launched in the prologue is effectively concluded by this point, and what follows is the sequence in which the Inlaw attempts to escape the women's clutches by enacting various scenes of Euripidean drama. Deception and disguise remain important aspects of the play, but they are not surrounded by the elaborate plotting and preparation of the intrigue of the first half. Ontological and epistemological concerns, to be sure, are prominent in the parodies, and enact a dialogue with Euripidean treatments of related themes in the *Helen*, among other works. Much of the scholarship on *Thesmo* has seen the play's presentation of Euripides largely in terms of a generic contrast between tragedy and comedy. Recognizing the intrigue prologue as a cross-generic form adds another dimension to this contrast, but suggests that more is at stake than competition. Rather, we should understand the discourse of deception in *Thesmo* as a contribution to thinking about *apatē* in ethical and social (as well as aesthetic) terms. *Thesmo* portrays deception as the basic state of Athenian society, with the women operating constantly in stealth and the men machinating to deceive the deceivers. Much of the humor, to be sure, comes from the comparatively small stakes of these reciprocal intrigues, but the play's image of communal relations is noticeably lacking in basic elements of trust and truthfulness on all sides. This places it, I suggest, in an even closer proximity to tragedy than is usually recognized. Its presentation of deception within a political collective is in profound dialogue with tragic stagings of what is not seen, not heard, and not known. *Thesmo* portrays a social world that corresponds to the Eleatic denial of the truth of the senses, in which deception is all-pervasive, and appearance and language do not correspond to reality.

Language and Necessity: Sophocles' *Philoctetes* (I)

Sophocles' *Philoctetes*, first performed in 409 BCE, combines and interweaves the two main strands of thinking about deception traced in this chapter: like the *Electra*, it stages deception as a grave ethical problem, and like *Thesmo*, it represents human knowledge and social relations as characterized by constant falsehood and intrigue. Its prologue is another scene of instruction that figures a plot to deceive as a kind of philosophical initiation. While the ethical problems raised by deception in the *Electra* and *Thesmo* were only hinted at in the prologues and emerged fully as the plays went on, the *Philoctetes* foregrounds these concerns, and makes them into a motive force for the whole drama. Likewise, the staging of truth and falsehood, which in the *Electra* concentrated around the story of Orestes' death and in *Thesmo* around the Inlaw's disguise and the women's deceptions, becomes even more central and complex in the *Philoctetes*, as a series of incomplete and deceptive narratives make it difficult or impossible to grasp the truth behind the various stories. Sophocles stages *apatē* as a state between being and nonbeing, an encompassing quasireality from which there appears to be no escape, and which renders trust between individuals nearly impossible.

The story of Philoctetes on Lemnos had been staged before Sophocles by Aeschylus and Euripides, and we are able to reconstruct some outlines of their respective plots. All three center on the efforts of Odysseus, either alone (in Aeschylus) or aided (in Euripides, by Diomedes), to bring Philoctetes to Troy, in response to a prophecy that the city could not be taken without him.[97] In both earlier versions, Odysseus undertakes elaborate deceptions in order to

---

97. I follow the reconstructions of Aeschylus and Euripides in Carl Werner Müller, ed., *Euripides: "Philoktet," Testimonien und Fragmente* (Berlin: de Gruyter, 2000), 42–71. Aeschylus' play is undated, but we have the secure date of 431 for Euripides', which was performed alongside the extant *Medea* and the lost *Diktys*.

steal Philoctetes' bow—apparently unrecognized in Aeschylus, and disguised by Athena in Euripides. We know relatively little about the course or conclusions of both dramas beyond that Philoctetes yielded, but the prologues can be reconstructed approximately on the basis of summaries in Dio Chrysostom's *Orations* and other fragments that have been preserved. Aeschylus' play likely opened with a monologue by Philoctetes, while Euripides opened with Odysseus alone onstage, apparently in an unusually introspective mode.[98] Sophocles' opening scene in dialogue is again distinct from the prologues of the other tragedians, and sets out the tensions surrounding deception that will come to a head over the course of the play.

The most significant innovation of the Sophoclean *Philoctetes* is to make Neoptolemus the companion of Odysseus, and the one who will actually carry out the deception plot (in earlier versions it was Odysseus himself). The introduction of Neoptolemus as a central figure brings a significantly different ethos and moral outlook into the story, creating a counterweight to the dominant character of Odysseus. Though the framing of the plot establishes Neoptolemus in effect as Odysseus' disciple, he grows into a more ethically authoritative character as the play goes on—a process that has been fruitfully compared to military initiation.[99] Like Orestes, Neoptolemus becomes an heir to his father's heroic reputation over the course of the work, and frequent references to Neoptolemus' paternity and his inborn nature make an Achillean ethos a major factor in the story, which complicates the deception plot.[100] Neoptolemus' presence makes the Sophoclean version of the story into an extended confrontation of Odysseus and (by proxy) Achilles, two Trojan War

---

98. Müller, *Euripides: "Philoktet,"* 42–43. Dio's summary makes probable that Aeschylus' play opened with Philoctetes speaking the prologue (*Orations* 52.9 describes Philoctetes' narration of his troubles to the chorus, which must have come early on, while 52.11 suggests that Euripides' prologue of Odysseus alone onstage was distinctive). A paraphrase of Odysseus' opening speech is contained in *Orations* 59.

99. Vernant and Vidal-Naquet, *Myth and Tragedy*, 161–79; Ismene Lada-Richards, "Staging the Ephebeia: Theatrical Role-Playing and Spiritual Transition in Sophocles' 'Philoctetes,'" *Ramus* 27 (1998): 1–26.

100. There are repeated references to Neoptolemus' father (4, 50, 57, 89), and to his φύσις (79, 88) in the prologue. See Mary Whitlock Blundell, "The 'Phusis' of Neoptolemus in Sophocles' 'Philoctetes,'" *Greece & Rome* 35 (1988): 137–48; Hanna M. Roisman, "The Appropriation of a Son: Sophocles' 'Philoctetes,'" *Greek, Roman, and Byzantine Studies* 38 (1997): 127–71; Seth L. Schein, "Language and Dramatic Action in the Prologue of Sophokles' 'Philoktetes,'" *Dioniso* 1 (2011): 88–91.

heroes with famously opposing ways of living and doing battle.[101] This suggests a parallel with the *Hippias Minor* and other sophistic syncrises of mythological heroes mentioned earlier, as well as Prodicus' moralizing "Choice of Heracles" (B2 DK/D21 LM; Xenophon, *Memorabilia* 2.1). The conflict between Neoptolemus' duty to the Greek forces and his personal loyalty to Philoctetes becomes a choice between lives of expedience and principle. Deception is the primary vector on which the choice plays out, focusing the different ethical views of the play.

The dramaturgy of the *Philoctetes*' opening scene, as has often been recognized, is quite similar to that of the *Electra*, with a dominant character (Orestes, Odysseus) involving a subordinate (the Paidagogos, Neoptolemus—though subordinate in military rank more than social position) in a plot centered around a false story. Both Orestes and Odysseus command their accomplice to tell an elaborate lie concerning themselves, which will gain the trust of a hostile target. It is significant that in both Sophoclean versions, the primary plotters act through intermediaries, rather than (as in other versions) enacting the deceptions themselves. While the *Electra*'s Paidagogos proves a more or less frictionless medium for Orestes' planned deception (and, indeed, a virtuosic fabulist in his own right), much of the tension of Sophocles' *Philoctetes* derives from Neoptolemus' resistance to Odysseus' plan. Neoptolemus' resistance reflects ethical qualms raised by the deception plot, which ultimately issue in his revealing the truth to Philoctetes and endangering his mission. The structure of the play is thus more complex than the *Electra*, in which the intrigue continues through the entirety of the work. Yet, although the second part of the *Philoctetes* is not conditioned by deception to the same extent as the first part, the falsehoods of the intrigue are never fully unraveled, even with the appearance of Heracles *ex machina*. "In this play," Karl Reinhardt writes, "intrigue is not so much an isolated venture as the general state of the world."[102]

Odysseus opens the play with a speech of instruction, which, like the Paidagogos' opening, first establishes the geographical setting and briefly recalls the most important past events before emphasizing the urgency of the present. Both speeches describe the moment as "high time" (ἀκμή: *Electra* 22, *Philoctetes*

---

101. Sophocles had staged the quarrel between Achilles and Odysseus (mentioned in *Odyssey* 8.74–80) in his *Sundeipnoi*: Alan H. Sommerstein, Thomas Talboy, and David Fitzpatrick, eds., *Sophocles: Selected Fragmentary Plays*, Volume I (Oxford: Aris & Phillips, 2006), 90–100.

102. Reinhardt, *Sophocles*, 175.

12), and therefore calling for deeds rather than words. Odysseus introduces what he admits is in some respects a "novel" (52: καινόν) plan, in which Neoptolemus must "assist as a servant" (53: ὑπουργεῖν, ὡς ὑπηρέτης). Odysseus' emphasis on Neoptolemus' subordinate status (also at 15) seems intended to compel submission to a plan that has not been disclosed before, and which Odysseus knows will create ambivalence. He repeats the impersonal construction δεῖ, "it is necessary" (50, 54, 77), to create a sense of external compulsion, on which he relies to convince or compel Neoptolemus to take part in his plan.[103] Odysseus uses a mixture of bullying and persuasion—and possibly (if the "novel" aspects of his plot are ones he has hitherto concealed) even an element of deception. The power dynamics of the opening scene thus foreshadow the interactions of Neoptolemus and Philoctetes, which are characterized by a blend of different tactics to convince Philoctetes to go to Troy, and, in turn, by Philoctetes' convincing Neoptolemus to return to Greece.[104] In fact, in much of what follows it becomes hard to distinguish between trickery, persuasion, and compulsion—a point nicely illustrated in Dio's summary, which describes Philoctetes as yielding, paradoxically, to a kind of "forced persuasion" (*Orations* 52.2: πειθοῖ ἀναγκαίᾳ).

Odysseus' instructions to Neoptolemus form a kind of doublet with Orestes' to the Paidagogos. Odysseus introduces his plan with a series of *klept*-roots, figuring the deception as an act of theft, as Orestes had done in the *Electra* (37): "you must deceive [or steal] the soul of Philoctetes with words by speaking" (54–55: τὴν Φιλοκτήτου σε δεῖ / ψυχὴν ὅπως λόγοισιν ἐκκλέψεις λέγων). The pleonastic "with words by speaking" emphasizes the importance of language as the means to the *erga* at hand. Odysseus goes on to prescribe the story Neoptolemus is to tell in detail, representing his identity honestly— "in this there must be no deception [or stealth]" (57: τόδ' οὐχὶ κλεπτέον)—and explaining that he has left Troy in anger at Odysseus for not surrendering the arms of Achilles to him. This seems, both in the logic of the scene and according to the mythical tradition, to be false, but at no point is the claim ever contradicted, even when Philoctetes recalls it later on, after Neoptolemus has

---

103. Seth L. Schein, "Verbal Adjectives in Sophocles: Necessity and Morality," *Classical Philology* 93 (1998): 296, 301–5. Related to the use of δεῖ are a series of verbal adjectives in the prologue (57, 116), and in Odysseus' attempt to compel Philoctetes to Troy (993, 994).

104. On the multiple persuasions of the work, see R.G.A. Buxton, *Persuasion in Greek Tragedy: A Study of Peithō* (Cambridge: Cambridge University Press, 1982), 118–32.

given up the deception (1362–67).[105] It is characteristic of Sophocles' staging of truth and falsehood in the *Philoctetes* that stories about the past proliferate, some appearing true, some appearing false, without being reliably confirmed or denied.

The story of Odysseus' refusal of the arms has a degree of verisimilitude, relying as it does on Odysseus' general immorality, which the audience and Neoptolemus witness first-hand in the prologue. Odysseus seems to relish this reputation and particularly instructs Neoptolemus to revile him in the telling, remarking, "by this you will not grieve me at all" (66: τούτῳ γὰρ οὐδέν μ' ἀλγυνεῖς). The thought is again similar to Orestes' in the *Electra*, who had asked, "why should this grieve me?" (59: τί γάρ με λυπεῖ τοῦθ᾽) concerning the story of his own death. Both stories aim to gain the trust of the auditors by appealing to their hatred or fear of a third figure. Odysseus clearly recognizes that his plan will encounter ethical resistance, and concludes his initial exposition with a naked justification of subterfuge:

> νῦν δ' εἰς ἀναιδὲς ἡμέρας μέρος βραχὺ
> δός μοι σεαυτόν, κᾆτα τὸν λοιπὸν χρόνον
> κέκλησο πάντων εὐσεβέστατος βροτῶν. (83–85)
>
> Now give yourself to me for a short part of a day without shame, and then for the remaining time be called the most pious of all mortals.

Odysseus effectively admits that he is counseling a shameless act: though trickery was a frequent, and widely accepted, aspect of Greek conduct in war, Philoctetes' status as an ostensible ally renders deception problematic.[106] Odysseus acknowledges the ethical violation involved in treating Philoctetes as an enemy, but offers Neoptolemus the prospect of a long period of renown—either because (taking "then," εἶτα, temporally) he will go on to live a blameless future life in spite of his shameless action now, or (taking εἶτα causally) he will be glorified for undertaking such a shameless action.[107] The ambiguity between the two understandings suits Odysseus' tactic of recognizing the problematic quality of the actions, but downplaying it. In either case,

---

105. Pietro Pucci, ed., *Sofocle: "Filottete"* (Milan: Mondadori, 2003), 165, 313–14.
106. Blundell, *Helping Friends*, 185–87.
107. The same ambiguity about retrospective views of their action is present in Odysseus' δίκαιοι δ' αὖθις ἐκφανούμεθα (82: "we will be revealed to be just at another time"): will they be "revealed to be just" because they will act justly later, or because their present actions will be judged righteous?

he would be rejecting categorical ethical judgments, and insisting that actions must be evaluated in relation to their ends and outcomes.[108] For Odysseus, even shameful actions like deceiving an ally can be undertaken when the end is beneficial.

Odysseus is often described as "sophistic" in a pejorative sense, and his amoral outlook does have affinities with some aspects of contemporary thought, in particular the idea that gain (κέρδος: 111) or what is beneficial (τὰ συμφέροντα: 131) trump ethical considerations. Orestes and Menelaus in the *Helen*, too, had pointed to κέρδος as justification for their deception plots, though there the doubts seemed more superstitious than ethical. Sophocles seems to be particularly interested in ill-gotten gains: a fragment from an unidentified play asserts that "gain is sweet, even if it comes from lies" (F 833: τὸ κέρδος ἡδύ, κἂν ἀπὸ ψευδῶν ἴῃ)—a sentiment that could characterize any of the Sophoclean plotters, but which comes under pressure over the course of the dramas.[109] Questions of just and unjust gains likewise surrounded contemporary conduct in war. A realist political discourse justifying harsh or impious actions for their strategic benefit is found throughout Thucydides, especially in the Melian Dialogue, where the Athenians and Melians explicitly lay aside considerations of the just (τὸ δίκαιον) and argue on the basis of the beneficial (τὸ ξυμφέρον: 5.90).[110] The Peloponnesian War and internal political intrigue in Athens—most importantly, the oligarchic government of 411/10 (which Sophocles probably had a role in setting up)—made urgent the question of what kinds of immoral or dubious actions should be taken for individual and collective

---

108. Nussbaum characterizes Odysseus as a consequentialist in his ethics, aiming at the general welfare: Martha Nussbaum, "Consequences and Character in Sophocles' 'Philoctetes,'" *Philosophy and Literature* 1 (1976): 30–39. Though he certainly claims to be motivated by collective interest, it is difficult to disentangle this from his own self-interest: Mary Whitlock Blundell, "The Moral Character of Odysseus in 'Philoctetes,'" *Greek, Roman, and Byzantine Studies* 28 (1987): 307–29.

109. The excerpt is quoted in Plutarch's *How a Young Man Should Study Poetry* 4.21a, juxtaposed with another, apparently contradictory, Sophoclean statement: "false words do not produce fruit" (F 834: οὐκ ἐξάγουσι καρπὸν οἱ ψευδεῖς λόγοι). Sophocles' interest in the morality of falsehood must have extended well beyond the extant dramas. Further fragments emphasize the pursuit of κέρδος (F 28, 354) or detract from it (807).

110. On realist thought in and beyond Thucydides, see Guthrie, *The Sophists*, 84–101; Gregory Crane, *Thucydides and the Ancient Simplicity: The Limits of Political Realism* (Berkeley: University of California Press, 1998), 61–71.

benefit.¹¹¹ The dramatic figures reflect this questioning, with Odysseus representing an extreme case of amoralism, a nightmare of the loosening of scruples brought on by war.

However, there is nothing necessarily *sophistic* (or even very profoundly philosophical) about Odysseus' reasoning. Despite Plato's and Xenophon's negative depictions, subversive ethical views are not widely attested among the canonical sophists, who on the whole seem to have drawn relatively conventional conclusions surrounding morality.¹¹² An exception is Antiphon, whose fragmentary *On Truth* does recommend that one who would "treat justice most advantageously for himself" (B44a DK/D38a LM: μάλιστα ἑαυτῷ ξυμφερόντως) act in accordance with conventional norms (νόμοι) when in the presence of witnesses, but when alone, act based on the dictates of nature (φύσις).¹¹³ Odysseus seems to suggest a similar view with his emphasis on appearing (82) and being called (85) just and pious, despite having committed what he concedes are unjust actions. But he does not thereby challenge the idea of justice, nor does the distinction between nature and custom that informs Antiphon's immoralism (and also the views of Plato's Callicles and, more obliquely, his Thrasymachus) appear in Odysseus' own thought, which is straightforwardly motivated by self- or collective interest. Unlike Antiphon or the Platonic critics of convention and justice, Odysseus makes no attempt to articulate an ethical framework, and acts simply in the service of expediency.

A much richer strand of contemporary thought, though, is glimpsed in Odysseus' references to the power of language and opinion. I have already suggested some ways that the deception plot of the *Electra* relates to philosophical

---

111. Sophocles is reported to be one of the *probouloi* who voted to suspend rules preventing oligarchy, and thereby contributed to the establishment of the Four Hundred. Aristotle reports that he met a charge that this was wrong with the response, "there was nothing better to do" (*Rhetoric* 1419a: οὐ γὰρ ἦν ἄλλα βελτίω). See Alan H. Sommerstein, "Sophocles and Democracy," *Polis* 34 (2017): 273–87. While it is intriguing to speculate about the connections between this justification of immoral action and the *Philoctetes*, we do not know enough about Sophocles' political views to attempt such a reading.

112. Richard Bett, "Is There a Sophistic Ethics?" *Ancient Philosophy* 22 (2002): 235–62.

113. See David J Furley, "Antiphon's Case against Justice," in *The Sophists and Their Legacy*, ed. G. B. Kerferd (Wiesbaden: Steiner, 1981), 81–91; Fernanda Decleva Caizzi, "Protagoras and Antiphon: Sophistic Debates on Justice," in *The Cambridge Companion to Early Greek Philosophy*, ed. Anthony A. Long (Cambridge: Cambridge University Press, 1999), 311–31; Pendrick, *Antiphon the Sophist*, 59–67.

reflections on language, and the intrigue of the *Philoctetes* similarly relies on the power of language to deceive.[114] Odysseus' initial statement of the plan emphasized the idea of theft, which would take place "with words by speaking" (55: λόγοισιν ... λέγων). To Neoptolemus' qualms concerning the use of deception, Odysseus responds with a generalization about the power of speech that must be closely connected to fifth-century reflections:[115]

> ἐσθλοῦ πατρὸς παῖ, καὐτὸς ὢν νέος ποτὲ
> γλῶσσαν μὲν ἀργόν, χεῖρα δ' εἶχον ἐργάτιν·
> νῦν δ' εἰς ἔλεγχον ἐξιὼν ὁρῶ βροτοῖς
> τὴν γλῶσσαν, οὐχὶ τἄργα, πάνθ' ἡγουμένην. (96–99)

> Child of a noble father, I myself too, when I was young, had an inactive tongue but an active hand. Now, putting it to the test, I see that for mortals the tongue, not deeds, rules all.

The contrast of "inactive tongue" and "active hand" figures in somatic terms the opposition of *logos* and *ergon*, but Odysseus' language unbalances this with its repetition of ἐργ-words (ἀργόν, ἐργάτιν, τἄργα): actions, he suggests, are themselves inactive, a sense reinforced by a near homophony of τἄργα ("deeds," a contraction of τὰ ἔργα) with τἀργά (contracting τὰ ἀργά, "the inactive things"). Odysseus' "test" (*elenchus*, a word connoting examination in speech, and a standard word for Socratic inquiry) has revealed that it is the tongue that "rules." There is an implicit rejoinder to the idea, seen already in Antisthenes' speech of Ajax, that words have no ontological substance, while actions are the true effective forces. Odysseus asserts that, whatever *erga* may accomplish, they are guided by *logos*. To control language *is* to control reality.

Like Ajax in Antisthenes and Achilles in *Hippias Minor*, Neoptolemus takes on the role of foil for Odysseus' status as the paradigmatic representative of the power of *logos*. Initially, he declares himself "ready to take this man by force

---

114. On the role of language in the play, see Anthony J. Podlecki, "The Power of the Word in Sophocles' 'Philoctetes,'" *Greek, Roman, and Byzantine Studies* 7 (1966): 233–50; Segal, *Tragedy and Civilization*, 333–40; Thomas M. Falkner, "Containing Tragedy: Rhetoric and Self-Representation in Sophocles' 'Philoctetes,'" *Classical Antiquity* 17 (1998): 25–58.

115. A scholion to line 99 recognizes the contemporary context, noting that in these words Sophocles "condemns the *rhetors* of his own time for accomplishing all things through speech" (διαβάλλει τοὺς καθ' ἑαυτὸν ῥήτορας ... ὡς διὰ γλώσσης πάντα κατορθοῦντας). I am grateful to Johannes Haubold for discussion of this passage.

and not by tricks" (90–91: ἕτοιμος πρὸς βίαν τὸν ἄνδρ' ἄγειν / καὶ μὴ δόλοισιν), suggesting an Achillean reliance on physical strength (and possibly also reflecting his initial understanding of his mission). As the scene goes on, however, he seems to accept the effectivity of speech, while still disputing its use for purposes of deception:

NE. τί οὖν μ' ἄνωγας ἄλλο πλὴν ψευδῆ λέγειν;
ΟΔ. λέγω σ' ἐγὼ δόλῳ Φιλοκτήτην λαβεῖν.
NE. τί δ' ἐν δόλῳ δεῖ μᾶλλον ἢ πείσαντ' ἄγειν;
ΟΔ. οὐ μὴ πίθηται· πρὸς βίαν δ' οὐκ ἂν λάβοις. (100–103)

Neoptolemus. What then do you order me to do except to speak lies? *Odysseus.* I say that by a trick you should take Philoctetes. *N.* Why is it necessary to bring him with a trick rather than by persuading? *O.* He will not be persuaded. And by force you could not take him.

The juxtaposition of Neoptolemus' description of the intrigue as based on lying (repeated at 108) and Odysseus' characterization of it as a trick (*dolos*) enacts the contrast between their views of Philoctetes: Neoptolemus sees him as a member of the same political community, subject to speech and persuasion, while Odysseus understands him as an enemy, and even an animal (*dolos* is often used of traps) not to be approached directly. Neoptolemus' two preferred methods of bringing Philoctetes—force and persuasion—suggest an effort to define him clearly either as a friend or enemy, and to use methods appropriate to this status.[116] Odysseus' plan of deception targets Philoctetes' place between friend and enemy, creating a false community with a figure who seems both within and outside culture.[117]

The wrangling over the language of the intrigue and the method of bringing Philoctetes to Troy sets out a spectrum of possibilities that the rest of the play will explore. Neoptolemus believes that there are clear distinctions between

---

116. On the polarity of *peithō* and *bia*, see Buxton, *Persuasion in Greek Tragedy*, 58–63. The possibility of persuasion in the play is explored by Akrivi Taousiani, "οὐ μὴ πίθηται: Persuasion versus Deception in the Prologue of Sophocles' 'Philoctetes,'" *Classical Quarterly* 61 (2011): 426–44. Closest to my perspective are the remarks in Falkner, "Containing Tragedy," 40–46.

117. Without subscribing to the entirety of the argument (which maps the action of the play onto sophistic theories of culture), I follow Rose in seeing the encounter between Neoptolemus and Philoctetes as the creation of a political community—though one that is crucially based on bad faith: Peter W. Rose, "Sophocles' 'Philoctetes' and the Teachings of the Sophists," *Harvard Studies in Classical Philology* 80 (1976): 49–105.

deception, persuasion, and force, but the rest of the play will tend to trouble these lines.[118] The language of *peithō* will be used to describe a number of dishonest actions over the course of the play: after the trick has been revealed, Philoctetes recalls how "from noble words I fared badly, persuaded by your words" (1268–69: ἐκ λόγων / καλῶν κακῶς ἔπραξα, σοῖς πεισθεὶς λόγοις), strongly emphasizing λόγος and persuasion as the agent of his deception. Neoptolemus will come to the same conclusion about his persuasion by Odysseus, and will bitterly regret having been "persuaded" (1226: πιθόμενος, and similarly at 1252) to undertake the mission. The suspicion of persuasion evinced by the *Philoctetes* is common in tragedy, which frequently explores the concern that rhetoric and persuasion could be misleading.

Persuasion and deception are closely if not essentially connected for Gorgias: "How many," he remarks in the *Helen*, "have persuaded and persuade how many concerning how many things fashioning a false speech!" (B11 DK/D24 LM 11: ὅσοι δὲ ὅσους περὶ ὅσων καὶ ἔπεισαν καὶ πείθουσι δὲ ψευδῆ λόγον πλάσαντες).[119] Honest persuasion appears the exception rather than the rule, rendering the distinction between true and false speech insignificant. Gorgias goes even further, and suggests that persuasion can act as a kind of compulsion:[120] "Speech that persuades the soul," he claims, "compels the one it has persuaded both to obey the things said and to consent to the things done" (B11 DK/D24 LM 12: λόγος γὰρ ψυχὴν ὁ πείσας, ἣν ἔπεισεν, ἠνάγκασε καὶ πιθέσθαι τοῖς λεγομένοις καὶ συναινέσαι τοῖς ποιουμένοις). The *Philoctetes* reflects an analogous understanding when Odysseus tells Philoctetes "you must be persuaded" (994: πειστέον τάδε, equally, "you must obey"), erasing the distinction between force and persuasion. This slippage is characteristic of the Greek verb *peithō*, which in the middle voice takes on the meaning "obey," and can be used to describe obedience as a result of persuasion and compulsion alike. *Peithō* encompasses a range of relationships, some characterized by

---

118. Garvie reads the play as a progression from deception and force to persuasion: Alexander F. Garvie, "Deceit, Violence, and Persuasion in the 'Philoctetes,'" in *Studi classici in onore di Quintino Cataudella* (Catania: Facoltà di Lettere e Filosofia, 1972), 213–26. This captures something important, but Sophocles' staging tends to blur the edges between them.

119. With different punctuation, the statement could be read as even more categorical: "Whoever has persuaded and persuades anyone about anything does so by fashioning a false speech."

120. Though the text is corrupt, the beginning of *Encomium* 12 suggests some kind of a direct connection between βία (violence, the word used earlier to describe the possibility that Helen was abducted unwillingly) and persuasion.

honest, some by dishonest speech, and some issuing in willing, some in unwilling assent. Despite Neoptolemus' faith in persuasion as a more ethical alternative to deception, one could understand the *Philoctetes* as a study in the dubious ethics and negative effects of *peithō*. The play joins in the period's wider investigation of the power of *logos*, but is distinctive in highlighting the ethical questions surrounding persuasion.

Deception, Myth, and Truth: Sophocles' *Philoctetes* (II)

When Neoptolemus agrees to undertake the intrigue planned by Odysseus, he enters into a complex web of truth and falsehood, which the rest of the play will not fully pull apart. While the prologue was dominated by ethical considerations surrounding deception, the remainder of the first part of the play will deepen the epistemological complications. The *Philoctetes* deploys information about the past almost exclusively through unreliable sources, leaving crucial aspects of its prehistory dubious or uncertain. Questions about truth center on the narratives of Neoptolemus and the False Merchant, which provide much of our information about the past, but in contexts where the deceptive intent of the speakers is apparent to the audience. In both, expected elements jostle with more or less flagrant innovations, and leave the spectator unable to tell what is true and what false, where Sophocles innovates and where he accepts mythical tradition. This has often been remarked, but my suggestion here is that we should understand this uncertainty as a contribution to the philosophical problem of *apatē*.[121] The issues surrounding deception in the *Philoctetes* are most obviously and importantly ethical, but Sophocles' staging places *apatē* in an ontological context as well, using deception scenes to trouble notions of truth and falsehood. The deceptions of the *Philoctetes* contain so much plausibility in them that they demonstrate the difficulty of penetrating beyond opinion to reality.

Aspects of the prologue prefigure the problematic relation to truth of the deception scenes. Odysseus has evidently not divulged crucial information about their mission: his careful introduction of the plan and Neoptolemus' reaction make clear that the intrigue plot comes as a surprise. Neoptolemus is

---

121. Most compelling on the topic is Felix Budelmann, *The Language of Sophocles: Communality, Communication, and Involvement* (Cambridge: Cambridge University Press, 2000), 93–108.

ultimately persuaded by the promise of gain, but seems uncertain how the mission to bring Philoctetes relates to the capture of Troy, and to his own role:

> ΝΕ. κέρδος δ' ἐμοὶ τί τοῦτον ἐς Τροίαν μολεῖν;
> ΟΔ. αἱρεῖ τὰ τόξα ταῦτα τὴν Τροίαν μόνα.
> ΝΕ. οὐκ ἄρ' ὁ πέρσων, ὡς ἐφάσκετ', εἴμ' ἐγώ;
> ΟΔ. οὔτ' ἂν σὺ κείνων χωρὶς οὔτ' ἐκεῖνα σοῦ.
> ΝΕ. θηρατέ' οὖν γίγνοιτ' ἄν, εἴπερ ὧδ' ἔχει. (112–16)

Neoptolemus. What gain is there for me that this man go to Troy? *Odysseus.* This bow alone will take Troy. *N.* Isn't the one who will sack it, as it was said, I myself? *O.* You could not without it [the bow], nor it without you. *N.* It ought to be hunted then, if this is really the case.

Even making allowances for the expository nature of the scene, Neoptolemus seems quite unclear on the reasons that bring them to Lemnos and the role of Philoctetes. He has not fully grasped that his own future and Philoctetes' are crucially connected to one another and to the fall of Troy. Moreover, there is throughout the prologue an ambiguity as to whether it is Philoctetes or his bow that is the actual target: while Odysseus had ordered Neoptolemus specifically to steal the bow (75–76), Neoptolemus seems to understand his task as bringing the man himself (90, 102). Even if Neoptolemus must know something of the prophecy that incited the action, his foggy comprehension makes him entirely subordinate to Odysseus. Odysseus gives and withholds information as it suits his purposes, and the opening scene brings out the different levels of knowledge between the two. Like the audience, Neoptolemus is slowly enlightened as to his real mission, and his understanding of it will undergo important shifts as the play goes on.

Having consented to the deception scheme, Neoptolemus approaches Philoctetes and tells a version of the story that Odysseus laid out, emphasizing his hatred and mistrust of Odysseus. His narration blends familiar details of the mythical tradition with what appear to be novel elements, and effectively creates an atmosphere of trust with Philoctetes. Though Neoptolemus' story includes a number of elements not paralleled in any surviving accounts of the mythical tradition, the anomalies are mostly within the spectrum of plausible innovation that Sophocles (or an earlier author) could have undertaken. It would probably have been impossible for an audience to discern which details are "really" true in the play's backstory and which are Neoptolemus' fabrication. As if to signal the problem, Neoptolemus' telling thematizes uncertainty from its beginning, recalling his recruitment to the Trojan expedition with an emphasis on the doubtful, second-hand nature of his own knowledge:

> ἦλθόν με νηὶ ποικιλοστόλῳ μέτα
> δῖός τ' Ὀδυσσεὺς χὠ τροφεὺς τοὐμοῦ πατρός,
> λέγοντες, εἴτ' ἀληθὲς εἴτ' ἄρ' οὖν μάτην,
> ὡς οὐ θέμις γίγνοιτ', ἐπεὶ κατέφθιτο
> πατὴρ ἐμός, τὰ πέργαμ' ἄλλον ἢ 'μ' ἑλεῖν. (343–47)
>
> They came to me in a ship with a variegated prow, noble Odysseus and the tutor of my father, saying, whether truly or perhaps falsely, that it would not be right, after my father had died, that anyone but me take the citadel [of Troy].

The story is broadly consistent with what we know of the *Little Iliad*, in which Odysseus fetches Neoptolemus after the death of Achilles.[122] But Neoptolemus does not mention the prophecy concerning his participation in the sack of Troy, even though this seems to be presumed by the action. He goes on to recall bitterly that it was a "a noble speech" (352: λόγος καλός) that brought him to Troy, reflecting his disillusionment with the war effort. Neoptolemus' assumption of a general skepticism toward Odysseus' honesty is obviously a helpful tactic for gaining the sympathy of Philoctetes, but it may also reflect a genuine mistrust, for which he has ample reason.

Neoptolemus' telling seems designed to elicit maximum pathos, emphasizing his grief at the loss of his father, and the joy of his reception by the Greek army. Against this background, his disillusionment appears all the more painful. As Neoptolemus relates his demand for the arms of Achilles, the story—at the point when it becomes least plausible to an audience—grows emotional with interjections and shifts into vivid direct speech: the Greek commanders "spoke, alas, a most wretched speech" (363: εἶπον, οἴμοι, τλημονέστατον λόγον), telling him, "another masters [the arms] now, the child of Laertes" (366: ἄλλος κρατύνει νῦν, ὁ Λαέρτου γόνος). The reference to Odysseus' father emphasizes Neoptolemus' own dispossession, and the outrage grows with Odysseus' condescending reply: "Yes, child, they have given these things rightly; for I saved them and that man, being present" (372–73: ναί, παῖ, δεδώκασ' ἐνδίκως οὗτοι τάδε· / ἐγὼ γὰρ αὔτ' ἔσωσα κἀκεῖνον παρών). The implied reproach at

---

122. Proclus' summary does not mention Phoenix' being sent for Neoptolemus, but Apollodorus (*Epitome* 11) does—possibly relying on Sophocles, but possibly on another, lost source.

Neoptolemus' absence seems calibrated for maximum impact, and Odysseus makes the insult even more explicit in response to Neoptolemus' mounting anger: "you were not where we were, but absent from where you should have been" (379: οὐκ ἦσθ' ἵν' ἡμεῖς, ἀλλ' ἀπῆσθ' ἵν' οὔ σ' ἔδει). Even as the audience is conscious that these words almost certainly represent a fabrication, their sting must have a genuine element: the sense of regret and even shame implied is eminently believable. Neoptolemus' story attains greatest vividness and pathos where it departs furthest from the truth.

As the scene goes on, Philoctetes poses a series of questions concerning the Greek forces in Troy, to which Neoptolemus gives answers that broadly conform to the mythical tradition: Ajax is dead, Nestor bereaved, Patroclus dead, while Odysseus and Diomedes live and flourish. Philoctetes' pained reactions create a shared sense of regret with Neoptolemus, and a bitterness at the injustice of fate. The only doubts likely to arise come from Neoptolemus' report concerning Thersites, an exchange that is anomalous in a number of ways:

ΦΙ. ἀναξίου μὲν φωτὸς ἐξερήσομαι,
γλώσσῃ δὲ δεινοῦ καὶ σοφοῦ, τί νῦν κυρεῖ.
ΝΕ. ποίου δὲ τούτου πλήν γ' Ὀδυσσέως ἐρεῖς;
ΦΙ. οὐ τοῦτον εἶπον, ἀλλὰ Θερσίτης τις ἦν,
ὃς οὐκ ἂν εἵλετ' εἰσάπαξ εἰπεῖν, ὅπου
μηδεὶς ἐῴη· τοῦτον οἶσθ' εἰ ζῶν κυρεῖ;
ΝΕ. οὐκ εἶδον αὐτός, ᾐσθόμην δ' ἔτ' ὄντα νιν. (439–45)

Philoctetes. Of an unworthy man I will inquire, formidable and clever in tongue, how he fares now. *Neoptolemus.* Of what sort of person do you ask but of Odysseus? *Ph.* I did not mean him, but there was a certain Thersites, who would not have chosen to speak just once when no one would allow him [to speak at all]. Do you know if this man happens to be living? *N.* I did not see him myself, but I heard that he still was.

It may be surprising that Philoctetes even broaches the question of Thersites, a low-status, relatively minor figure in comparison to the other, more important, aristocratic heroes they discuss. Given Philoctetes' description of Thersites as "formidable and clever in tongue," the confusion with Odysseus (who had earlier extolled the importance of the tongue) is natural. The confusion must also reflect the fixation of both interlocutors on Odysseus, who beats the lame Thersites brutally in *Iliad* 2. The greatest anomaly, though, is that here alone there is an apparent departure from the mythical tradition, which holds that Thersites was killed by Achilles, who then had to be purified from the murder by Odysseus. The story may hit too close to home for Neoptolemus to relate, and though he does not claim certainty (another unusual feature for the exchange), he offers the answer that will most rub salt in Philoctetes' wounds, causing him to despair in the justice of the gods (451–52). For the audience, the effect is significantly to confute expectations concerning mythical tradition. We cannot tell whether Neoptolemus is lying or Sophocles is innovating.

Sophocles' confounding of truth, falsehood, persuasion, and deception reaches its apogee in the False Merchant scene. A member of the Greek forces, disguised as a merchant ship's captain, enters to warn Neoptolemus of the impending arrival of a delegation charged with bringing him back to Troy. As the scene develops, it emerges that another ship, captained by Odysseus and Diomedes, is underway in pursuit of Philoctetes. The report seems intended to increase the sense of urgency to depart, and such a ruse was previewed in the prologue, when Odysseus explained that if Neoptolemus was taking too long, he would send a man "tricked out in form with the ways of a merchant-ship captain, so that ignorance be present" (128–29: ναυκλήρου τρόποις / μορφὴν δολώσας, ὡς ἂν ἀγνοία προσῇ). The idea of the *dolos* recurs in the phrase "tricked out in form," describing a disguise that will ensnare Philoctetes even further in the trap set by Odysseus. The aim of the False Merchant's arrival, Odysseus says, is to create "ignorance" (ἀγνοία, also meaning "lack of recognition")—on the most immediate level, so that the Merchant is not recognized as a member of the Greek crew, but more broadly, so that Philoctetes' (and maybe Neoptolemus' as well) understanding of events is further confused. In drawing attention to the disguise of the Merchant, the play may hint at the fact that it is the same actor who plays both Odysseus and the Merchant (and who will go on to play Heracles). Even when not onstage, Odysseus has a quasipresence in the figure of the Merchant, through which he acts to manipulate the reality of the play.

The Merchant's scene is, like the Paidagogos' narration, strictly gratuitous to the plot. In setting up the scene, Odysseus had enjoined Neoptolemus: "from him speaking craftily, receive what is beneficial of his words from moment to moment" (130–31: ποικίλως αὐδωμένου / δέχου τὰ συμφέροντα τῶν ἀεὶ λόγων), with the benefit presumably lying in the sense of urgency it will impart.[123] Yet despite the emphasis on the artfulness of the Merchant's speech

---

123. The False Merchant also invokes the "benefit" in his ambiguous departing words to Neoptolemus and Philoctetes: "may a god benefit you both in the best way possible" (627: σφῷν

(ποικίλος, "variegated" or "crafty," is frequently used of deceptive rhetoric), its content seems to reflect, more than a careful calculation on Odysseus' part, an effort to confuse matters further, adding to the pervasive "misrecognition" of the intrigue. The narrative, taking on some of the function of a messenger speech, allows Sophocles to fill in the mythological backstory, though in such a way that it is impossible to tell how much should be taken at face value.[124] For a speech intended as a trick, the Merchant's narrative is striking for how much truth—or plausibility—it contains. He reports to Neoptolemus, first, that "there are new plans, and not only plans, but deeds being done, and no longer idle" (554–56: νέα / βουλεύματ' ἐστί, κοὐ μόνον βουλεύματα, / ἀλλ' ἔργα δρῶμεν', οὐκέτ' ἐξαργούμενα). The language recalls Odysseus' repetition of ἐργ-words, which disparaged ἔργα in contrast to γλῶσσα, while the Merchant emphasizes the urgency of acting—though with the irony that his narrative is a prime example of the power of Odyssean speech. The repetition of the word βούλευμα ("plan," again at 560) cannot but suggest the plot that Neoptolemus and the Merchant both participate in, and the mission the Merchant describes turns out to be very much like the one Neoptolemus is engaged in. For the audience, moreover, the delegation of Odysseus and Diomedes would have evoked other versions of the story, since it replicates the plot of Euripides' *Philoctetes*.[125] Even though deceptive, the Merchant's narrative is in a sense trustworthy, conforming to a familiar version of the story. It is a masterful act of misdirection, which is effective for how close it is to the truth.

Though the Merchant's ostensible motivation is to alert Neoptolemus to the force coming for him, the focus of the scene quickly shifts to Philoctetes, as the Merchant narrates, for the first time in the play, the prophecy that has motivated the action.[126] His telling emphasizes the "tricky" (608: δόλιος)

δ' ὅπως ἄριστα συμφέροι θεός). See Seth L. Schein, "The Scene with the False Merchant in Sophokles' 'Philoktetes,'" *Dioniso* 4 (2014): 69–70.

124. On the relation of the Merchant's narrative to myth, see Budelmann, *The Language of Sophocles*, 95–100; Schein, "The Scene with the False Merchant," 71–75.

125. Dio, *Orations* 52.14 reports Diomedes' presence as being "in a Homer manner" (ὁμηρικῶς), though the detail does not figure in Homer. It may appear in the *Little Iliad*: Apollodorus, *Epitome* 5.8 and Hyginus, *Fabulae* 102.3 include both in the mission to bring Philoctetes. It is not clear how significant a role Diomedes played in Euripides' version, in which the figure of Odysseus seems to dominate.

126. Unraveling the details of the prophecy has been a major preoccupation: A. E. Hinds, "The Prophecy of Helenus in Sophocles' 'Philoctetes,'" *Classical Quarterly* 17 (1967): 169–80;

character of Odysseus, who has captured the Trojan seer Helenus, and the degradation inflicted on the captive, who is brought "into the midst of the Achaeans, a noble prey" (609: Ἀχαιοῖς ἐς μέσον, θήραν καλήν). The treatment of Helenus as an animal resonates with Odysseus' approach to Philoctetes through *dolos*, and suggests the unhappy fate that awaits Philoctetes if captured. Helenus' prophecy, in the Merchant's telling, concentrates emphatically on Philoctetes: Troy would not be taken, the Merchant reports, "unless, having persuaded this man with speech, they bring him from this island on which he lives now" (612–13: εἰ μὴ τόνδε πείσαντες λόγῳ / ἄγοιντο νήσου τῆσδ' ἐφ' ἧς ναίει τὰ νῦν). This approximates the expected story, which in Odysseus' allusion earlier in the play (115; confirmed by Neoptolemus at 1326–39) suggests that the prophecy declared both Neoptolemus and Philoctetes necessary to capture Troy.[127] The elision of Neoptolemus from the report of the prophecy is one place where the Merchant's account seems to be fitted to the task at hand. Yet, despite its dubious source, the Merchant's report of the prophecy conforms broadly to audience expectations, and so must somehow stand in for the truth, even as it will be revised later on by Neoptolemus' restatement.[128] The narrative presents a quasireality that perpetuates *apatē*, not just on the characters but on the audience as well.

The other crucial detail of the Merchant's report of the prophecy is that the Greeks are to bring Philoctetes "having persuaded by speech," a point never made before. It recalls the discussion in the prologue, in which Odysseus emphatically rejected the possibility of persuasion. More proximally, it responds, in a displaced manner, to Neoptolemus' question on hearing of the delegation pursuing him, "in order to bring me back by force or with words?" (563: ὡς ἐκ βίας μ' ἄξοντες ἢ λόγοις πάλιν;), and to the Merchant's initial description of the pursuit of Philoctetes: "they [Diomedes and Odysseus] sail, sworn absolutely to bring [him] either having persuaded by speech, or by the

---

Christopher Gill, "Bow, Oracle, and Epiphany in Sophocles' 'Philoctetes,'" *Greece & Rome* 27 (1980): 137–46; Meredith Clarke Hoppin, "What Happens in Sophocles' 'Philoctetes'?" *Traditio* 37 (1981): 1–30.

127. It is not clear whether in the *Little Iliad* Helenus' prophecy extends to Philoctetes alone or to Neoptolemus as well. The summary in Proclus does not make the conjunction explicit. Apollodorus' narration involves two prophecies: one, delivered by Calchas, foretells that Heracles' bow is necessary to the capture of Troy (*Epitome* 8); the other, delivered by Helenus, makes Neoptolemus' arrival one of the conditions of sacking the city (*Epitome* 10).

128. On the Merchant's credibility as messenger, see M. E. Payne, "Three Double Messenger Scenes in Sophocles," *Mnemosyne* 53 (2000): 415–17.

force of strength" (593–94: διώμοτοι πλέουσιν ἦ μὴν ἦ λόγῳ / πείσαντες ἄξειν, ἦ πρὸς ἰσχύος κράτος). In both cases, the presentation of alternatives elides the possibility of deception, while the Merchant's description of the prophecy emphasizes the necessity that Philoctetes come willingly. The detail offers an apparently unambiguous answer to a central question of the play—by what means to bring Philoctetes to Troy—but from a source that casts doubt on the content. The audience must rely on the Merchant for all that they know of the prophecy at this point, but they cannot tell what in his narrative is true and what false.

Discussion of the Merchant scene has often focused on its details, and especially on the issues of force and persuasion. But this misses the most important—and surprising—aspect of the narration, which is that its deceptive story is in fact largely true.[129] Philoctetes *is* being pursued by a Greek delegation in response to a prophecy, and Odysseus *does* intend to bring him to Troy by any means necessary. The details of the delegation, to be sure, are carefully calibrated to mislead Philoctetes, but even these are not wholly fabricated (at least from an audience's perspective), but reflect traditional versions of the myth. The Merchant's story forms a contrasting doublet with Neoptolemus': where Neoptolemus misrepresented the essential facts of his situation (that he was leaving Troy in anger) but was largely reliable on details (including the reports of the Trojan War), the Merchant gives an accurate picture of Philoctetes' situation, but misrepresents decisive details. Both narratives play on the line between truth and falsehood, reflecting obscurely on the truth of the play's history. The narratives place audience and characters alike into a state of uncertainty concerning what is real and what is not.

Knowledge, more than morality, is the hinge on which Neoptolemus' ultimate transformation turns. When Philoctetes has an attack of his disease, he gives his bow to Neoptolemus for safekeeping, making him promise to remain before fainting from the pain. Neoptolemus has the opportunity he has been waiting for, and can simply sneak off with the bow while Philoctetes is unconscious (as he may have done in other versions).[130] But it is at this moment that

---

129. This may be related to what Easterling describes as the play's "lucidity," its impression of clarity even as the "reality" of the story appears uncertain: Patricia E. Easterling, "'Philoctetes' and Modern Criticism," *Illinois Classical Studies* 3 (1978): 29–31.

130. There is no certainty as to how Odysseus obtained the bow in either earlier version, but Philoctetes' incapacity is thought to be the most likely scenario, which seems to be reflected in later visual traditions: Müller, *Euripides: "Philoktet,"* 60–61.

Neoptolemus comes to realize that theft will be inadequate, and that Philoctetes must come himself to Troy. While the chorus encourages him to act, Neoptolemus replies in highly unusual hexameters:

> ἀλλ' ὅδε μὲν κλύει οὐδέν, ἐγὼ δ' ὁρῶ οὕνεκα θήραν
> τήνδ' ἁλίως ἔχομεν τόξων, δίχα τοῦδε πλέοντες·
> τοῦδε γὰρ ὁ στέφανος, τοῦτον θεὸς εἶπε κομίζειν.
> κομπεῖν δ' ἔργ' ἀτελῆ σὺν ψεύδεσιν αἰσχρὸν ὄνειδος. (839–42)

> But this man hears nothing, and I see that we have in vain this prey of the bow if we sail without him. For his is the crown, him the god said to bring. To boast of deeds unaccomplished with falsehoods is a shameful reproach.

The contrast between Philoctetes' not hearing and Neoptolemus' vision marks the speech as a moment of epiphany: he must bring Philoctetes himself to Troy, which will involve an effort at honest persuasion. Dactylic hexameter is almost never heard in tragedy, and its use here is remarkable.[131] It is a primary medium of authoritative (and especially mythical) knowledge, the meter of Homer, Hesiod, and Parmenides, as well as of oracular responses—all of which are relevant to Neoptolemus' sudden intuition concerning the past (what the prophecy meant) and future (how Troy will fall).[132] There is a strong Apolline subtext in this language as well: Neoptolemus' oracular mode of speech, his mention of the command of "the god" and the "crown" (presumably of victory), and his concentration on the bow all point to Apollo as the god of prophecy and archery.[133] His hexameters are delivered, moreover, in the middle of an ode that begins with an address to sleep and calls for Paian (832, usually identified with Apollo, who is widely associated with both disease

---

131. The only other surviving Sophoclean use of dactylic hexameter is at *Trachiniae* 1018–22, and is there connected to—though does not exactly coincide with—a moment of realization of oracular meaning. Parker notes the similarity with Oedipus' revelation of prophecy in *Oedipus at Colonus*: Robert Parker, "Through a Glass Darkly: Sophocles and the Divine," in *Sophocles Revisited: Essays Presented to Sir Hugh Lloyd-Jones* (Oxford: Oxford University Press, 1999), 14.

132. Budelmann, *The Language of Sophocles*, 127–30.

133. Apollo is going to play a role in Neoptolemus' own death too. In the version of the myth staged by Sophocles in his *Hermione*, Neoptolemus goes to Delphi to take revenge on Apollo for his father's death, and is killed there: Sommerstein, Talboy, and Fitzpatrick, *Selected Fragmentary Plays*, Volume I, 1–25. Euripides' *Andromache* presumes the same visit to Delphi, though it places Neoptolemus' death on a second visit, made to atone for the insult of his first.

and healing) to come as a healer for Philoctetes.[134] The chorus intends to take advantage of the respite brought by Paian to rob Philoctetes, invoking Apollo as an accomplice in deception. Neoptolemus' revelation, though, creates a path to the healing that Philoctetes will receive in Troy from the son of Apollo, Asclepius.[135]

Neoptolemus' recognition here is not yet fully a moral awakening—he only rejects the use of lies for "deeds unaccomplished," rather than deception in general. Nevertheless, it marks the beginning of his move away from deception. When Philoctetes wakes, Neoptolemus' anguish increases as they prepare to depart for the ship, ostensibly to return to Greece. The burden of lies appears to grow too much, and like Orestes, Neoptolemus comes to regret his deception and find his speech at an impasse: "I do not know where it is necessary to turn resourceless speech" (897: οὐκ οἶδ' ὅπῃ χρὴ τἄπορον τρέπειν ἔπος). With his newfound clarity on the prophecy, Neoptolemus finds the deception plot a dead end, on grounds of morality and expediency both. The hexameters thus mark an important passage for Neoptolemus, as he emerges from the deception prescribed by Odysseus to the honest dealing that will characterize him in the rest of the play. Crucially, this comes about as a result of a quasidivine insight: his path to maturity, like that of Parmenides' *kouros* and the military ephebe, passes through *apatē* to knowledge and authority.

With the hexameters, Neoptolemus decisively rejects the instructions of Odysseus and his earlier role as disciple. He ceases to rely on the malleability of *logos* to deceive, and appeals to the necessity (922: ἀνάγκη) that Philoctetes go to Troy, a necessity reinforced by his possession of the bow. But it is not enough to convince Philoctetes. After eventually departing and then returning with the bow, Neoptolemus seeks to persuade Philoctetes by recounting the (seemingly actual) prophecy of Helenus, promising that Philoctetes will be healed if he goes to Troy, and that they together will conquer the city (1326–35). This is subtly different from the Merchant's account, which had not mentioned Philoctetes' healing or Neoptolemus as a companion, but even this fuller

---

134. On the tragic paean, see Ian Rutherford, "Apollo in Ivy: The Tragic Paean," *Arion* 3 (1994): esp. 127–29.

135. On the significance of Asclepius in the play, see Robin Mitchell-Boyask, "The Athenian Asklepieion and the End of the 'Philoctetes,'" *Transactions of the American Philological Association* 137 (2007): 85–114. Sophocles was reputed in antiquity to have played a role in the introduction of the Asclepian cult in Athens, though this report, like most ancient biography, should be treated carefully: Jacques Jouanna, *Sophocles: A Study of His Theater in Its Political and Social Context*, trans. Steven Rendall (Princeton: Princeton University Press, 2018), 60–75.

account does not convince Philoctetes. The political implications are significant: once *logos* has been separated from truth, restoring meaningful communication and trust between subjects appears almost insurmountably difficult. Philoctetes has become so alienated from the war effort that he refuses to do anything but return to Greece, leaving the Trojan War unresolved, until the epiphany of Heracles finally restores the story to its mythical course. Though the divine command does convince (or compel—again the difference is slim) Philoctetes to set aside his mistrust and go to Troy, the play has suggested a dim view of the possibility of trust among allies.

The *Philoctetes* demonstrates the initiatory pattern I have argued underlies the three plays examined in this chapter: Neoptolemus is presented as almost completely dependent on Odysseus in the prologue and grows into a figure of authority as the play progresses. His initiation is ethical and intellectual at once, passing through the moral and ontological ambiguities of the prologue through the confusion of the false narratives to the clarity of his hexameters. The play presents truth and moral action as interdependent. This seems a distinctively Sophoclean approach to deception, implicating political life more directly than the intrigues of Aeschylus or Euripides by laying its ethical weight on relations of trust between family and allies. Even when its end is noble, deception within the community appears to be fundamentally unjust, and to create ethical and practical consequences for the intriguer. Truth appears to be the bedrock of political life, and manipulative speech a continual danger to relations within a community. The Sophoclean texts constitute a reflection parallel to those of Parmenides or Gorgias on the relation between reality, perception, and language, which thinks through the consequences of post-Eleatic notions of truth for social and political community. The deceiver's apparent mastery over truth and falsehood appears epistemologically fragile and ethically dubious. The plays present deception—dramatic, ontological, and social—as a state between truth and falsehood, being and nonbeing, from which no one can fully emerge, least of all the audience.

Trust and Community: *Iphigenia at Aulis*

As a coda to this chapter, I turn to Euripides' *Iphigenia at Aulis* (*IA*), which offers an even bleaker view of internal intrigue among the Greeks in the Trojan campaign, and reflects, more directly than any other of Euripides' works, on relations of trust among family and allies. The *IA* creates the most tangled web of intrigue of any surviving Euripidean work, and is populated by an unusually large cast, with widely varying degrees of knowledge, acting in response to hidden and obscure forces. It opens with a scene that, though difficult to reconstruct because of textual problems, has structural similarities to the intrigue prologues of Sophocles and Aristophanes. Its intrigue is, on the whole, even more complex and multilayered than those plays, but also somewhat different in dramaturgy and structure. Accordingly, I will not offer a complete analysis of the play's staging of deception, but will simply signal the elements that suggest a dialogue with the issues I have raised in this chapter. The *IA*, I hope to show, reflects epistemological and ethical quandaries that are familiar from the other deception plots examined here, and likewise reflects on the social consequences of intrigue and the possibility of trust within a polity.

The prologue of the *IA* presents major textual difficulties: the transmitted text seems to combine two different versions of a prologue, one in standard dialogue meter, the other in anapests—parts of both of which have left readers dubious of their authenticity. It seems likely that the work was unfinished at Euripides' death, completed by another hand for its posthumous premiere at the Dionysia in 405, and then at some later point revised for another performance—with our text preserving elements of all these authors, as well as the patently inept attempts of a much later hand to complete the ending of the play, which must have been lost at some point in antiquity.[136] Disentangling the different versions and their histories is probably impossible, but on any reconstruction, the prologue has significant affinities with the plotting scenes I have discussed. The play opens with two men of unequal status, Agamemnon and a servant, the Old Man, secretively discussing a plot to deceive. The *IA*, though, takes place at a point when the deception is somewhat advanced, and the prologue consists of an attempt to retract the plot in progress. Agamemnon, after learning from a prophet that the Greek fleet cannot sail unless he sacrifices his daughter, has sent a false letter to his family requiring them to come to Aulis. The prologue finds Agamemnon having changed his mind, and he dispatches the Old Man to retract his instructions and order the women instead to remain at home—all in an atmosphere of extreme secrecy, lest the other Greeks, and especially his brother Menelaus, find out and press for the sacrifice. Like the Sophoclean deceptions, a great part of the

---

136. The most extensive reconstruction is David Kovacs, "Toward a Reconstruction of 'Iphigenia Aulidensis,'" *Journal of Hellenic Studies* 123 (2003): 77–103. On the textual problems of the play generally, see Sean Alexander Gurd, *Iphigenias at Aulis: Textual Multiplicity, Radical Philology* (Ithaca: Cornell University Press, 2005).

ethical complexity of the plot comes from the fact that the individuals being deceived are family and allies. The play offers a case study in the morality and politics of intrigue, with Agamemnon caught between his allies and his family, and forced to choose between his duties as brother and commander on one hand, and husband and father on the other.

As transmitted, the prologue begins with an unusual anapestic exchange, during which it emerges that Agamemnon has been writing and rewriting a letter with great emotion and apparent indecision. The dynamics of authority in this scene are notable, as Agamemnon appears profoundly reduced by his dilemma while the Old Man draws attention to his distress, and remarks on its unseemliness in a commander. Agamemnon explains his agitation in an expository speech that is often thought to be the beginning of one version of the play. He recounts how, after learning of the prophecy, he changed his mind repeatedly (as he will continue to do over the course of the drama): first he ordered the army to disband, unable to bring himself to the sacrifice (94–96); then Menelaus "persuaded [him] to dare awful things" (98: ἔπεισε τλῆναι δεινά), and he wrote the false letter to Clytemnestra, asking her to send Iphigenia on the pretext that she is to be married to Achilles.[137] This falsehood is another act of *peithō*: "for I applied this persuasion to my wife, fitting together falsehoods concerning the girl's marriage" (104–5: πειθὼ γὰρ εἶχον τήνδε πρὸς δάμαρτ' ἐμήν, / ψευδῆ συνάψας ἀμφὶ παρθένου γάμον). Agamemnon describes an intrigue already in action, fueled by persuasive speech and effected by lies.[138]

The story behind the intrigue turns out to be even more complex: the prophecy appears to be known only to a few of the commanders (106–7, though the lines are widely suspected), creating a further dimension of secrecy.[139] Moreover, Achilles is unaware that marriage to him is being used as a pretense: "his name, no deed [or "nothing real"] Achilles has provided, nor does he

---

137. Torrance reads Agamemnon's two letters and the repeated changes of mind as an engagement with the mythical tradition, posing the question of whether an alternative *muthos* is possible: Torrance, *Metapoetry in Euripides*, 158–65.

138. Caspers argues that the theme of deception and the opposition of word and deed in the prologue offer a continuity with the plot of IA's companion play *Bacchae*: Christiaan L. Caspers, "Diversity and Common Ground: Euripides' 'Iphigenia in Aulis' and 'Bacchae' as Companion Plays," in *Greek Drama IV: Texts, Contexts, Performance*, ed. David Rosenbloom and John Davidson (Oxford: Aris & Phillips, 2012), 127–48.

139. The secret prophecy theme is sometimes thought to be a later addition to the play, inserted haphazardly to increase the complications: Kovacs, "Toward a Reconstruction of 'Iphigenia Aulidensis,'" 78–80.

know of the marriage or what we are doing" (128–29: ὄνομ', οὐκ ἔργον, παρέχων Ἀχιλεὺς / οὐκ οἶδε γάμους, οὐδ' ὅτι πράσσομεν).[140] Agamemnon's contrast of word and deed—familiar from Orestes' and Odysseus' prologues—and his dismissal of the importance of involving Achilles will cause significant difficulty further in the play, as Achilles feels compelled to defend Iphigenia because of his involvement, even though only in name (938–39). Like Orestes and Neoptolemus, Agamemnon will find that the power of deceptive language cannot be contained, as what appeared a mere pretext becomes a major complicating factor. The nominal involvement of Achilles in the plot sets up another contrast, which the latter half of the play will explore, between the machinations of Agamemnon and (later, and only offstage) Odysseus, and the honesty of Achilles. Much about these and the surrounding lines is dubious, but the prologue would have established a background of intra-army intrigue even before Agamemnon's most recent change of mind, and drawn attention to the widely divergent understandings of the reasons for Iphigenia's presence in Aulis. Most important, the prologue would have set out the profound ethical stakes of the play's concerns with knowledge and deception.

The next scene will enact (at least) one more change of Agamemnon's mind, as Menelaus intercepts the Old Man and confronts Agamemnon, leading to an extended debate between the brothers that only hardens their opposition. The confrontation between them hinges, like that of Neoptolemus and Odysseus, around the clash of duty to the Greek army and morality, with Agamemnon reproaching Menelaus' "clever tongue" (333: γλῶσσ' . . . σοφή), and Menelaus in turn condemning Agamemnon's inconstancy toward his allies. Before the brothers can reach any resolution, the women's arrival is announced and Agamemnon, like Neoptolemus and Orestes, despairs at the situation his deception has created:

> ἐς οἷ' ἀνάγκης ζεύγματ' ἐμπεπτώκαμεν.
> ὑπῆλθε δαίμων, ὥστε τῶν σοφισμάτων
> πολλῷ γενέσθαι τῶν ἐμῶν σοφώτερος. (443–45)

> What yokings of necessity I have fallen into! A god has trapped me, and has proven much cleverer than my clever plans.

The "yokings of necessity" (an allusion to the *Agamemnon*'s "yokestrap of necessity," ἀνάγκας . . . λέπαδνον: 218) refer both to Agamemnon's situation in

---

140. Egli, *Euripides im Kontext*, 214–16.

general, caught between his duties as a commander and father, and the particular circumstances of the moment, in which his "clever plans" have proven incapable of preventing the arrival of his family in Aulis. Having committed himself to the deception plot before the play's action, he finds that its progress is ineluctable and he must deal with its consequences.

Moved by his brother's dilemma, Menelaus, surprisingly, has a change of heart and swears to protect Iphigenia. Then, yet another reversal materializes, as Agamemnon recognizes that he has come "into fortunes of compulsion" (511: εἰς ἀναγκαίας τύχας) because he cannot keep the prophecy secret from the army, who will demand Iphigenia's sacrifice. Just as, earlier, Agamemnon could not contain the falsehoods he had told, now he cannot contain the truth of the situation. Though he considers attempting to deceive the army, he fears that Odysseus will unmask the falsehood, and force him to carry out his own plot.[141] There is quite a lot to doubt textually in this entire episode, but its outcome must have been some kind of resolve among the commanders (including both Agamemnon and Menelaus) to go forward with the sacrifice. There would then have been some kind of a second plotting scene as the brothers revert to the original deception plan and prepare for the arrival of the women. Even without the complications probably introduced for a later performance, the play would have involved a sequence of reversal, plots, and counterplots unique in extant tragedy—and, in its baroque complications, almost more akin to comedy.[142] The central ethical conflict of the play is framed by the problem of deception, which appears both too powerful (insofar as it cannot be countermanded) and not powerful enough (insofar as it cannot be practiced on the army as a whole). Agamemnon, like Orestes, the Inlaw, and Neoptolemus, is trapped in the hall of mirrors he has created, caught between truth and falsehood.

The comparison with the *Philoctetes* suggests that the *IA* may have effected an even more extreme version of Sophocles' questioning of mythical truth. The transmitted text gives us conflicting reports as to who is aware of the

---

141. The army (along with Odysseus), though never onstage, make for a major presence in the plot: Brian V. Lush, "Popular Authority in Euripides' 'Iphigenia in Aulis,'" *American Journal of Philology* 136 (2015): 207–42.

142. In fact, one scholar hypothesized that the first episode incorporated substantial pieces of a comedy by another author: Walter Stockert, "Eine 'Komödienszene' in Euripides' Aulischer 'Iphigenie,'" *Wiener Studien* 95 (1982): 71–78. The idea is retracted in Stockert's edition, but the similarity is real.

prophetic utterance, which have often been thought to reflect the conflation of different versions: frequently deleted (and grammatically questionable) lines describe the prophecy as known only to Calchas, Odysseus, and Menelaus beyond Agamemnon (106–7), and the army's ignorance is presumed in a few later passages (425–34, 518). But this seems to conflict with other passages suggesting a public prophecy, and with the army demanding Iphigenia's sacrifice later in the play (1345–48). The army's knowledge could be explained as a result of Calchas' or Odysseus' machinations (as Agamemnon fears will happen at 518, 528–35—lines also deleted by many), and the text as we have it leaves much obscure about what is happening offstage. Instead of seeing the inconsistencies of the transmitted text as problems to be explained away, though, I suggest we interpret them as part of an emphasis on the slipperiness of knowledge and truth. An audience viewing the text as we have it would be confronted with serious difficulty in sorting through the conflicting signals, and might conclude—as I argued the audience of the *Philoctetes* does—that the search for a unified account of the play's prehistory is futile. It is probably not incidental, also, that this slipperiness concentrates around prophecies that motivate the entirety of the action. The authority of prophetic utterances makes them particularly important places for thinking about knowledge, truth, and falsehood, and for interrogating the way that dramatic plot relates to its mythological background. Sophocles presents multiple understandings of what prophecy demands, while the text of the *IA* presents varying signals as to who is aware of the prophetic demands. In both cases, though, prophecy acts as an authoritative, but importantly obscure, discourse, motivating much of the action, but in ways that never become fully clear. The truth of prophecy in the *Philoctetes* and *IA* is enfolded in deception and uncertainty to such an extent that an audience must wonder whether a true account of dramatic reality is possible.

The *IA*, then, is another play in which intrigue is the basic state of the world. Its prologue, like the other prologues examined in this chapter, establishes this state of affairs by introducing a deception plot that will condition much of the rest of the action, and ramify in unexpected ways. Agamemnon repeatedly tries and fails to control information, and finds himself caught up in lies of his own making and in truths he cannot conceal. The play is populated by characters operating with substantially different understandings of reality, the clash of which produces much of the drama. The tangled intrigues of the story demonstrate the power of falsehood to usurp truth, and the dangers of speech untethered from reality. This staging of *apatē* ultimately points back to questions of ethics and politics: whether deception and the deceiver can ever be just, whether trust within a polity is possible. The play's depiction of the Greek commanders engaged in constant, reciprocal machination presents an image of political authority as profoundly compromised by dubious ethics and conflicting loyalties.[143] While the Sophoclean intrigues had concentrated on a relatively closed community, the *IA*, like *Thesmo*, investigates intrigue on the level of an entire polity (and, indeed, one defined by its Panhellenism), presenting the darkest image of society of the works studied in this chapter. The *IA* presents deception as endemic to political life, a constant presence in society that corrodes trust within a family and community. We can, then, recognize in the *IA* Euripides' most sustained engagement with *apatē*, which expands on the intrigue and escape plots of his earlier works, but develops issues surrounding deception in a distinctively ethical and political register.

Dramatic stagings of deception, this chapter has argued, interrogate social, philosophical, and ritual authority. Agamemnon's conflict in the *IA*, his multiple changes of mind, and his plots and counterplots can all be understood as stemming from his power as a commander of the Greeks, able to give and withhold information as he chooses. As in the other examples discussed, this mastery of truth emerges as a fearsome power, an ability to deceive so completely that the deception cannot be undone and entraps the deceiver. Drama's staging of intrigue thus pursues an inquiry parallel to philosophical explorations of *apatē* and the reality of sense-experience. While Parmenides and Empedocles had offered their disciples a truth beyond the evidence of the senses and conflicting mortal opinion, drama considers the possibility, more akin to Gorgias' nihilistic propositions, that such truth is inaccessible or even nonexistent. Yet the plays are on the whole less concerned with the (im)possibility of attaining *alētheia* than with the consequences of its obscurity. For drama, this is primarily a social question, which motivates an inquiry into the way that trust undergirds family and political life, and the danger of falsifying reality through speech. These are pressing issues in any political community, but especially in the Athens of the late fifth century. The contemporary resonances of the intrigue plots would have been interpreted differently by different

---

143. This can be read as commentary on contemporary Athenian political authority: Andreas Markantonatos, "Leadership in Action: Wise Policy and Firm Resolve in Euripides' 'Iphigenia at Aulis,'" in *Crisis on Stage: Tragedy and Comedy in Late Fifth-Century Athens*, ed. Andreas Markantonatos and Bernhard Zimmermann (Berlin: de Gruyter, 2011). Though I have no doubt that an audience member in 405 could have received the play in this way, I do not believe that we today are capable of predicting how they would have responded.

spectators, and seeking to fix these parallels is, I believe, unnecessarily speculative. But we can see that dramatic stagings of intrigue are motivated by both the ontological and political questions of their time, and that they bring these domains of thought to bear on one another in original and provocative ways.

In forging a link between between questions of reality and truth, on one hand, and political life, on the other, the intrigue prologues make a distinctive contribution to fifth-century philosophical thought. This conjunction of concerns anticipates in some ways Plato's explorations of truth and falsehood in political life in the *Republic* and other dialogues.[144] While fifth-century philosophical texts had pointed to the pervasive quality of deception and sought to guide the deceived inquirer toward truth, dramatic texts draw attention to the mechanics of creating deception, and its consequences for the social world. The philosophical goal of extricating truth from falsehood appears impossible in the state of intrigue, rendering trust between deceiver and deceived elusive. This state of pervasive deception evokes the state of *stasis*, the Greek term for factional strife within a city. Thucydides' famous description of the *stasis* at Corcyra records how those involved "changed words' accustomed evaluations of actions according to their idea of justice" (3.82.4: τὴν εἰωθυῖαν ἀξίωσιν τῶν ὀνομάτων ἐς τὰ ἔργα ἀντήλλαξαν τῇ δικαιώσει), a process that the dramatic deceivers enact in employing falsehood and shamelessness in the service of a "just" cause. In *stasis*, plots and counterplots are endemic (3.82.5), family is considered less important than faction (3.82.5), and oaths are broken without a thought (3.82.7). This is the world of intrigue. Drama stages this world within its own, more limited, compass, portraying the way that deception within a community taints social and political life both in everyday relations (comedy) and in mythological situations (tragedy). In the state of intrigue, language becomes unreliable and reality obscure, as deceiver and deceived alike are caught up in *apatē*. The distinctive contribution of the dramatic intrigue plots is to see these philosophical questions as urgent political problems.

---

144. The topic is far too large to discuss here, but the *Republic* likewise considers the ways that falsehood can be just in its notion of the "noble lie": Carl Page, "The Truth about Lies in Plato's 'Republic,'" *Ancient Philosophy* 11 (1991): 1–33; Hesk, *Deception and Democracy*, 143–62; Malcolm Schofield, "The Noble Lie," in *The Cambridge Companion to Plato's "Republic,"* ed. G.R.F. Ferrari (Cambridge: Cambridge University Press, 2007), 138–64; Catherine Rowett, "Why the Philosopher Kings Will Believe the Noble Lie," *Oxford Studies in Ancient Philosophy* 50 (2016): 67–100. A different view of ontological concerns in Sophocles and Plato is explored in Rebecca S. Lubarr-Glasman, "The Finest of Dramas: Knowledge and Deception in Plato's Aesthetics and Sophoclean Tragedy" (Ph.D. diss., Columbia University, 2002).

3
Agōn and Authority

PLATO DID not write a dialogue concerning the definition of *sophia* ("wisdom," "skill," or "expertise"), but the term plays a crucial role throughout his writings, and especially in his portrayal of Socrates' philosophical vocation. In the *Apology*, Socrates recounts how, having learned that the oracle of Delphi has declared no one wiser (21a6: σοφώτερος) than he, he set about interrogating other renowned *sophoi*, who, he thinks, must surely exceed him in wisdom. This search, famously, fails, as Socrates concludes that, unlike those considered *sophoi*, who believe themselves wise when they are not (or when their knowledge is in fact quite limited), he is *sophos* at least in recognizing what he does not know. The paradox of wisdom in ignorance is central to the Platonic portrayal of Socrates, and in the *Apology*, at least, is linked to an idea of wisdom as a possession of the gods alone. Human beings can only aspire to "human *sophia*" (23a7: ἀνθρωπίνη σοφία)—not to the true *sophia* of the gods.[1]

On his way to the conclusion that to be wise is to be conscious of one's ignorance, Socrates visits three groups of *sophoi*: first, "one of the politicians," who is widely believed wise (and has a self-confidence to match), but who, Socrates finds, turns out to know nothing of value (21c). After seeking out other politicians and reaching the same conclusion, he moves on to poets, whom he interrogates as to the meaning of their poetry. They turn out to be utterly unable to furnish answers to his questions, and Socrates hypothesizes that they create "by some nature and while being inspired" (22c: φύσει τινὶ καὶ

---

[1]. Particularly illuminating on Socratic ignorance is Michael N. Forster, "Socrates' Profession of Ignorance," *Oxford Studies in Ancient Philosophy* 32 (2007): 1–35. See further John M. Cooper, *Pursuits of Wisdom: Six Ways of Life in Ancient Philosophy from Socrates to Plotinus* (Princeton: Princeton University Press, 2012), 24–69; Michael C. Legaspi, *Wisdom in Classical and Biblical Tradition* (Oxford: Oxford University Press, 2018), 109–43.

ἐνθουσιάζοντες) rather than by σοφία. Finally, he turns to craftsmen, whom he respects as expert in their craft, but finds, like the poets, unable to explain their work, and consequently no further advanced in σοφία than he (22c–e). To be renowned in the city or skilled in creation, Socrates finds, is no proof of wisdom.

These three groups—politicians, poets, and craftsmen—indicate something of the traditional figure of the *sophos* and the range of meanings of *sophia*.[2] *Sophia* can denote a general wisdom or prudence appropriate to a political leader, a skill or knack found in artists, or a learned expertise found among artisans. In fact, the senses blur into one another and are often impossible to distinguish. Subtending and arguably unifying conceptions of *sophia* is an assumption of religious authority, which guarantees that the activity of the *sophos* is directed to divinely inspired or sanctioned ends.[3] *Sophia* in early Greece seems to encompass religious, political, poetic, and artisanal activity, and the *sophos* is often a figure like Solon whose expertise spans these realms.[4] Poetic and political skill are inseparable from divine authority, and the word in its traditional uses describes a range of people invested with a wide-ranging cultural prestige.

Socrates' rejection of these forms of expertise as inadequate to true *sophia* is a gesture within a much wider contestation of wisdom that this chapter will trace. This contestation has a traditional and a more contemporary aspect: from archaic times in Greece, competitive performance was an important aspect of claims to *sophia*, and an agonistic strand is present in many of the stories surrounding early *sophoi*.[5] Competition took place not only among

2. On early conceptions of *sophia,* see G. B. Kerferd, "The First Greek Sophists," *Classical Review* 64 (1950): 8–10; G. B. Kerferd, "The Image of the Wise Man in Greece in the Period before Plato," in *Images of Man in Ancient and Medieval Thought*, ed. Gerard Verbeke (Leuven: Leuven University Press, 1976), 17–28; Burkhard Gladigow, *Sophia und Kosmos: Untersuchungen zur Frühgeschichte von sophos und sophië* (Hildesheim: Olms, 1965); Kurke, *Aesopic Conversations*, 95–124.

3. The theological aspect is emphasized by both Gladigow, *Sophia und Kosmos* and Kurke, *Aesopic Conversations*.

4. On the traditional Seven Sages, see Richard P. Martin, "The Seven Sages as Performers of Wisdom," in *Cultural Poetics in Archaic Greece: Cult, Performance, Politics*, ed. Carol Dougherty and Leslie Kurke (Oxford: Oxford University Press, 1998), 108–28.

5. On *agōnes*, see Walter Johannes Froleyks, "Der Agōn Logōn in der antiken Literatur" (Ph.D. diss., Rheinischen Friedrich-Wilhelms-Universität zu Bonn, 1973), 40–86; Mark Griffith, "Contest and Contradiction in Early Greek Poetry," in *Cabinet of the Muses: Essays on Classical and Comparative Literature in Honor of Thomas G. Rosenmeyer*, ed. Mark Griffith and Donald J.

practitioners of a single skill (poets against poets, say) but frequently between different forms of excellence, as when Xenophanes famously disparages the value of athletics, claiming that "better than the strength of men and horses is our wisdom" (B2 DK/D61 LM 11–12: ῥώμης γὰρ ἀμείνων / ἀνδρῶν ἠδ' ἵππων ἡμετέρη σοφίη).[6] The *sophiē* that Xenophanes describes here is political, poetic, and philosophical at once, and leads, in contrast to that of the athlete, "the city to be in a state of lawfulness" (B2 DK/D61 LM 19: ἐν εὐνομίῃ πόλις εἴη). How this comes about is not specified, but *sophiē* for Xenophanes describes a skill that is enacted in a community, and is demonstrated in competition.

The fifth century sees significant changes in the idea of *sophia*, which go along with new forms of intellectual authority.[7] There is significant debate about how to understand these shifts, or indeed, whether there was any kind of development. The standard story, which is broadly Aristotelian, sees a gradual broadening of *sophia* from an archaic meaning, roughly, of "technical skill" to a properly philosophical one of "wisdom."[8] This has been disputed—to my mind convincingly—by a rereading of the archaic evidence, which shows that *sophia*, though it can be applied to multiple domains, always signifies a wide-ranging authority defined by a relation to the divine, and is never reducible to simple technical competence.[9] Yet something must have changed, or be changing, for Plato's Socrates to deny the authority of *sophia* to all its traditional exponents. His distinction between divine inspiration and wisdom suggests

---

Mastronarde (Atlanta: Scholars Press, 1990), 185–207; Martin, "The Seven Sages as Performers of Wisdom," 120–22; Derek Collins, *Master of the Game: Competition and Performance in Greek Poetry* (Washington, DC: Center for Hellenic Studies, 2004); Tell, *Plato's Counterfeit Sophists*, 135–50; Kurke, *Aesopic Conversations*, 103–4.

6. The critique of athletes is discussed in John P. Harris, "Revenge of the Nerds: Xenophanes, Euripides, and Socrates vs. Olympic Victors," *American Journal of Philology* 130 (2009): 157–94.

7. Lloyd assesses the degree of innovation in fifth-century intellectual culture: Lloyd, *The Revolutions of Wisdom*, 50–109.

8. The distinction between different senses of *sophia* is sketched in Aristotle, *Nicomachean Ethics* 1141a, and the development described in greater depth in Philoponus, *Commentary on Aristotle's Nicomachean Ethics* 1.1 (=Aristotle, *On Philosophy* F 8 Ross). It forms the basis for most nineteenth- and early twentieth-century accounts (including Gladigow's, cited above) and is followed recently by David Wolfsdorf, "'Sophia' and 'Epistēmē' in the Archaic and Classical Periods," in *The Philosophy of Knowledge: A History,* Volume I: *Knowledge in Ancient Philosophy*, ed. Nicholas D Smith (London: Bloomsbury, 2018), 11–29.

9. The developmental narrative of *sophia* is most importantly disputed in Kerferd, "The Image of the Wise Man."

new demands placed on the *sophos*, which were not made in archaic culture, when the test of a poet's or politician's *sophia* was the excellence of his poetry or the outcome of his leadership, rather than an ability to explain or defend it. Socrates' story suggests an attempt to wrest *sophia* away from the realm of the divine and traditional authority, in order to appropriate it for his own practice of philosophy.

Put differently, Plato's Socrates seeks to replace an idea of intellectual activity defined by heteronomy—governed by existent norms and beliefs—with one defined by autonomy, self-governing and producing its own norms. This autonomy, I should stress, is relative and notional: it is far from clear that any thought could be entirely free from guiding norms (and there is no reason to see Socrates as claiming this), but the idea of intellection that develops at the end of the fifth century stresses that it is more autonomous than previous intellectual regimes. This tendency or ideology seems to have been broadly shared throughout sophistic culture, and Socrates was probably not its most extreme exponent: at least as portrayed by Plato and Xenophon (though not by Aristophanes), he broadly adheres to cultural norms, and seems rather less inclined than some others of his time to pursue radically heterodox thought. Regardless of how to locate the historical Socrates in the development of ideas of *sophia*, the idea that wisdom is defined by autonomous intellection rather than norm-guided thought emerges strongly from the late fifth-century context, with consequences that range well beyond the emerging discipline of philosophy.

The late fifth and early fourth centuries see a widespread contestation of the traditional authority of the *sophos* by those professing novel forms of *sophia*. New kinds of intellectuals, among them Socrates and the sophists, arose and sought to legitimate themselves as *sophoi*, in the process disputing central assumptions concerning wisdom and knowledge. All the traditional domains of *sophia* are active ones; to be *sophos* is not just to possess *sophia*, but to be engaged in using it.[10] Even the earliest Greek philosophical thinkers were no "pure" sages: they were poets, technical experts, religious practitioners, and politicians, and their authority as *sophoi* must have come from these areas as much as from any general claim to wisdom.[11] The new *sophoi*, on the contrary,

---

10. Gladigow, *Sophia und Kosmos*, 128 describes the unity of knowledge [*Wissen*] and action [*Handeln*] inherent in the archaic concept of *sophia*.

11. The contemplative life is discussed in L. B. Carter, *The Quiet Athenian* (Oxford: Oxford University Press, 1986), 131–54. Carter describes the development of the idea of the

did not claim to be practitioners of anything in particular, but rather of *sophia* in general—and this goes as much for those we call "sophists," who seem to have made a profession of practicing wisdom, as it does for Socrates, for whom it was a vocation.[12] Part of Socrates' rejection of the Athenian *sophoi* is a rejection of this idea of *sophia* as inherent in cultural activity of one sort or another: the *sophōtatos* turns out to be the one who thinks the best, not the one whose activity is the best. To debate *sophia* in the late fifth century is to consider the grounds of intellectual authority—whether it is based in divinely guided activity or in human thought, or, put another way, whether it relates to the unseen and unknowable or to the apparent and demonstrable.

Socrates is a partisan within this confrontation, and the way he lays it out is undeniably tendentious, assuming the novel concept of *sophia* and measuring others by it. Plato's depiction of Socrates, moreover, may not reflect the historical Socrates so much as Plato's own idea of *sophia*. But the questions raised by the text—not just who is the more *sophos*, but what *sophia* consists in—are broadly important within late fifth-century Athenian thought. There was an urgent social dimension to this inquiry. A striking development of late fifth-century usage is the simple idea that there are false or deceptive forms of *sophia*—a possibility not countenanced in archaic usages in which the authority connected to the term was basically unquestioned. A suspicion of *sophia* seems to have become virulent in Athens around this time—most visibly, of course, in the condemnation of Socrates himself. Socrates uses the description *sophos* in precisely this pejorative way in the *Apology*, to describe the slanders against him: "there is some Socrates, a *sophos* man, a contemplator of the heavens who has explored all things below the earth, and who makes the weaker argument the stronger" (18b–c: ἔστιν τις Σωκράτης σοφὸς ἀνήρ, τά τε μετέωρα φροντιστὴς καὶ τὰ ὑπὸ γῆς πάντα ἀνεζητηκὼς καὶ τὸν ἥττω λόγον κρείττω ποιῶν).[13] To be *sophos*, it turns out, is a highly equivocal distinction, as the term could denote both the possessors of traditional

---

contemplative life before Plato, suggesting that it comes into its own in Athens around the time of Anaxagoras. David Williams' ongoing dissertation work proposes to see Aristophanes' Socrates as definitive for the Platonic understanding of the *bios theōrētikos*.

12. Most illuminating on the sophists as practitioners of wisdom is Rachel Barney, "Twenty Questions on Protagorean Wisdom" (draft article, 2009: http://individual.utoronto.ca/rbarney/Protagoras.pdf).

13. On the pejorative sense of *sophos*, see Sandra Peterson, *Socrates and Philosophy in the Dialogues of Plato* (Cambridge: Cambridge University Press, 2011), 17–24.

socio-cultural authority, and the practitioners of novel, and suspect, intellectual trends.[14]

Questions of intellectual authority and novelty are at the heart, I will argue, of a dramatic set-piece—a debate between two parties as to what *sophia* is and who possesses it—that seems to be associated particularly with Euripides, and is found in different forms throughout his later works. The chapter moves from more concrete manifestations of the form to looser ones, but suggests that all are determined by the same opposition of traditional and novel understandings of *sophia*. They can thus be read as inquiries into the foundations of intellectual modernity in late fifth-century Athens.[15] Yet though the debates evoke contemporary questions of *sophia*, they do so in ways that render the competing notions exceptionally difficult to pull apart. The effect of this undecidability, I argue, is to move toward a reconciliation of the different ideas of *sophia*, and ultimately to suggest that drama itself can subsume tradition and novelty in its presentation of ideas.

The most distilled example of the *agōn sophias*, and arguably its definitive instance, is found in Euripides' *Antiope*, which was famous in antiquity for its confrontation of different ways of life. Fragments of the *Palamedes*, too, suggest that the question of *sophia* was a major concern, emerging naturally from the confrontation of Odysseus and Palamedes. From these works, the form is picked up by Aristophanes in *Frogs*, in which the juxtaposition of Aeschylus and Euripides can be read as a confrontation between modes of *sophia* that interrogates the possibility of distinguishing and judging between them. Finally, I argue that the question of *sophia* and the form of the *agōn* offer a foundation for Euripides' *Bacchae*, which spans a series of different *agōnes*, all of them hinging on whether Pentheus' secular authority or the Stranger's mystical knowledge constitutes true *sophia*. Reading *Bacchae* as an inquiry into intellectual novelty allows us to understand better the work's puzzling modernity.

---

14. Xenophon's Socrates recognizes this explicitly in *Memorabilia* 4.2.33. See Louis-André Dorion, "The Nature and Status of 'Sophia' in the 'Memorabilia,'" in *Xenophon: Ethical Principles and Historical Enquiry*, ed. Fiona Hobden and Christopher Tuplin (Leiden: Brill, 2012), 455–75.

15. I use the term "modernity," like intellectual historians of the modern period, to designate a category of thought rather than a temporal period; it is defined by a consciousness of rupture and incommensurability between old and new. The shape of this category in late fifth-century Athens is quite different from that of the modern era, but I think that the anachronism is productive.

Debating Wisdom

Debate is arguably the central mode of late fifth-century intellectual culture, whether in philosophical, rhetorical, or dramatic texts, and across prose and poetry. Though an agonistic strand is present throughout archaic and early classical Greek thought, sophistic culture not only emphasizes the practice of disputation in its often-adversarial performances, but begins to elaborate a theory of disputation or antilogy, which holds that any argument can be contradicted, and at the most extreme, that it is possible to make the weaker argument stronger.[16] Much of this disputational culture seems to develop in relation to the public rhetorical contexts of law courts and political assemblies, and many of the most important intellectuals, including Gorgias and Antiphon, were teachers of public speaking or logographers (writers of speeches for others to deliver in public). The period also sees the development of purely epideictic debates: paired speeches such as we find in Antiphon's *Tetralogies* and the *Dissoi Logoi* (which have often been connected to Protagorean antilogy) demonstrate the importance of disputation as a mode of intellectual and rhetorical training.[17] One widespread form, already glimpsed in this book, involves the composition of mock forensic speeches for mythological figures, such as Gorgias' *Defense of Palamedes*, which inspired a pendant *Odysseus against the Treachery of Palamedes* long attributed to Alcidamas (though now sometimes ascribed to a later period), and Antisthenes' paired speeches of Ajax and Odysseus.[18] Whatever philosophical work these speeches do, they

---

16. Classic and still useful on sophistic antilogy is Heinrich Gomperz, *Sophistik und Rhetorik: Das Bildungsideal des εὖ λέγειν in seinem Verhältnis zur Philosophie des 5. Jahrhunderts* (Stuttgart: Teubner, 1912), 130–200. Further: Kerferd, *The Sophistic Movement*, 59–67; Alexander Nehamas, "Eristic, Antilogic, Sophistic, Dialectic: Plato's Demarcation of Philosophy from Sophistry," *History of Philosophy Quarterly* 7 (1990): 3–16.

17. Michael Gagarin, "Did the Sophists Aim to Persuade?" *Rhetorica* 19 (2001): 275–91. On the relation of antithesis to political rhetoric, see Harvey Yunis, "The Constraints of Democracy and the Rise of the Art of Rhetoric," in *Democracy, Empire, and the Arts in Fifth-Century Athens*, ed. Deborah Boedeker and Kurt A. Raaflaub (Cambridge, MA: Harvard University Press, 1998), 223–40.

18. On Alcidamas, see O'Sullivan, "[Alcidamas] 'Odysseus.'" Since I find it hard to be confident that the speech is classical in origin, I do not lay any great weight on it. It is significant that Odysseus is a major player in both disputations. See Nancy Worman, "Odysseus Panourgos: The Liar's Style in Tragedy and Oratory," *Helios* 26 (1999): 35–68; David Lévystone, "La figure d'Ulysse chez les Socratiques: Socrate polutropos," *Phronesis* 50 (2005): 181–214; Silvia Montiglio, *From Villain to Hero: Odysseus in Ancient Thought* (Ann Arbor: University of

seem to appropriate some of the formal possibilities of drama in presenting debate through mythological prosopopoeia.

Related to the agonistic tendency is a syncretic impulse. Even when the forensic or disputational context is absent, sophistic culture is drawn to juxtapositions—of abstractions such as Excellence (Ἀρετή) and Baseness (Κακία) in Prodicus' "Choice of Heracles," or of mythological figures, as in the comparison of Odysseus and Achilles made by the sophist Hippias in Plato's *Hippias Minor*.[19] Taken together, all this suggests the importance to late fifth-century culture of thinking in juxtaposition, contrast, or opposition. Even Socrates, who in Plato and Xenophon consistently sets himself up as an opponent of adversarial displays, shares with sophistic culture the sense that philosophical thought happens in dialogue rather than doctrine, and a whole genre of *Sōkratikoi Logoi* arose to develop the possibilities of such discourse.[20] Distinctions between *agōn*, syncrisis, and dialogue as forms of thought are ultimately difficult if not impossible to draw, but the prevalence of such forms throughout sophistic culture demonstrates a widespread tendency to nonauthoritative presentation of ideas.[21] This emerges especially strongly in comparison to earlier Greek thought, which, like most archaic poetry, relies heavily on the authority of the speaker, variously constructed, in order to make its claims (even as these may also involve argumentative legitimation). For sophistic culture, by contrast, presentation of ideas through dialogue, opposition, or juxtaposition seems to be the dominant mode, and the forms of late fifth-century intellectual culture (Socratic dialogue emphatically included)

Michigan Press, 2011), 20–37; Rachel Ahern Knudsen, "Poetic Speakers, Sophistic Words," *American Journal of Philology* 133 (2012): 31–60.

19. Commentary on Prodicus' speech is in Mayhew, *Prodicus the Sophist: Texts, Translations, and Commentary*, 201–21. The relevant passage of the *Hippias Minor* (discussed in the previous chapter) is 364b–71e.

20. On *Sōkratikoi Logoi*, see Charles H. Kahn, *Plato and the Socratic Dialogue: The Philosophical Use of a Literary Form* (Cambridge: Cambridge University Press, 1996), 1–35; Livio Rossetti, "Le dialogue socratique 'in statu nascendi,'" *Philosophie antique* 1 (2001): 11–35; Andrew L. Ford, "Σωκρατικοὶ λόγοι in Aristotle and Fourth-Century Theories of Genre," *Classical Philology* 105 (2010): 221–35.

21. Whether sophistic thought was in any important sense democratic, as many scholars have suggested, is hard to say, but its discursive forms clearly flourished in democratic Athens: Jacqueline de Romilly, *The Great Sophists in Periclean Athens*, trans. Janet Lloyd (Oxford: Clarendon Press, 1992), 19–24; Reimar Müller, "Sophistique et democratie," in *Positions de la sophistique*, ed. Barbara Cassin (Paris: Vrin, 1986), 179–93; Robinson, "The Sophists and Democracy beyond Athens."

arguably resemble dramatic poetry more than they do the forms of their "philosophical" predecessors or successors.

The relation of dramatic and philosophical modes of writing was reciprocal. Just as nondramatic discourse could appropriate the dialogic form and mythical content of drama, drama also seems to have approached some of the rhetorical self-consciousness of sophistic culture.[22] A more or less formal *agōn* is a frequent feature of Greek comedy from early on, involving a responding sequence of song and speech in which a dispute between two characters is mediated by the chorus.[23] The *agōn* form could be used to simulate philosophical antilogy: Aristophanes' *Clouds* skewers Socrates and fifth-century intellectuals generally by pitting the Weaker against the Stronger Argument, and showing the triumph of the Weaker by various forms of argumentative skullduggery.[24] There is ample evidence from fragmentary comedies to suggest that Aristophanes was not alone in lampooning philosophical figures and philosophical debate, though the state of the evidence makes it hard to connect this specifically to the *agōn* form.[25] Philosophical characters and themes make up only a small portion of comedy's direct engagement with contemporary intellectual culture, but the staging of debate and rhetoric

---

22. There is substantial debate over whether a formal practice of rhetoric existed in the sophistic period, or was a development of the fourth century. I follow the views proposed independently by Edward Schiappa and Thomas Cole that formal rhetoric is primarily a fourth-century development, which codifies practices of earlier periods (though I am agnostic on the precise question of how rhetoric originates, on which Schiappa and Cole differ): Schiappa, *The Beginnings of Rhetorical Theory*; Thomas Cole, *The Origins of Rhetoric in Ancient Greece* (Baltimore: Johns Hopkins University Press, 1991).

23. The standard survey of the comic *agōn* is Thomas Gelzer, *Der epirrhematische Agon bei Aristophanes; Untersuchungen zur Struktur der attischen Alten Komödie* (Munich: Beck, 1960). Based on the relative fixity of Aristophanes' use of the *agōn* in his early works, Gelzer places the development of the form in the generations before Aristophanes.

24. The most direct target is thought to be Protagoras, who is reported to have claimed to be able to make the weaker argument stronger (A21 DK/D28 LM). Protagoras, however, was not the only intellectual suspected for such clever argumentation, or interested in juxtapositions. On the range of possible targets, see Nikolaos Papageorgiou, "Prodicus and the Agon of the Logoi in Aristophanes' 'Clouds,'" *Quaderni urbinati di cultura classica* 78 (2004): 61–69.

25. There is evidence that Socrates appeared in Ameipsias' *Connus* (which won the prize at the Dionysia of 423, beating out *Clouds*), and Protagoras in Eupolis' *Flatterers* (dated to 421). The *Connus* and Plato's *Sophistai* seem to have featured choruses of intellectuals (including, but not limited to philosophers), and there is speculation surrounding Cratinus' *Panoptai* as well. See Christopher Carey, "Old Comedy and the Sophists," in *The Rivals of Aristophanes*, ed. David Harvey and John Wilkins (Swansea: Classical Press of Wales, 2000), 419–36.

frequently betrays a substantial debt to sophistic culture and its self-consciousness concerning speech.[26]

The relation of tragedy and rhetoric, broadly speaking, is still more complex. Persuasion is a major theme of tragedy throughout the fifth century, especially prominent in the *Oresteia*, but the later works of Sophocles and Euripides seem particularly interested in and self-conscious of the possibilities of speech. Aspects of this have already been glimpsed in the previous chapters, largely as a wariness of the deceptive possibilities of language; another, formal, facet is a tendency, especially in Euripides, to highly structured speeches that draw on contemporary forensic practices.[27] Scholars have often noted the relative independence of such rhetorical displays from their context and debated the "relevance" of such speeches to the dramas as a whole. There was evidently substantial cross-fertilization between dramatic language and public rhetorical contexts, especially those connected to political deliberation.[28] Indeed, the premise of Dionysus' decision at the end of *Frogs*, that he will select the poet who offers better advice to the city, suggests that tragedy and comedy could be understood as forms of political speech themselves.

Tragedy most closely approximates Athenian political life in its staging of scenes of debate. This occasionally takes place within an explicitly public, deliberative setting, as in the *Eumenides*, but more often it is form that marks proximity to civic debate, as in the many rhetorical *agōnes* found in later tragedy.[29] Though *agōnes* have been identified from the early works of

---

26. Comedy's appropriation of rhetoric is discussed in Wilfred E. Major, *The Court of Comedy: Aristophanes, Rhetoric, and Democracy in Fifth-Century Athens* (Columbus: Ohio State University Press, 2013). A different view of this engagement is found in Neil O'Sullivan, *Alcidamas, Aristophanes, and the Beginnings of Greek Stylistic Theory* (Stuttgart: Steiner, 1992).

27. On Euripidean debates, see Christopher Collard, "Formal Debates in Euripides' Drama," *Greece & Rome* 22 (1975): 58–71; Ruth Scodel, "Verbal Performance and Euripidean Rhetoric," *Illinois Classical Studies* 24/25 (2000): 129–44; Donald J. Mastronarde, *The Art of Euripides: Dramatic Technique and Social Context* (Cambridge: Cambridge University Press, 2010), 207–22.

28. Different views of this relation are proposed in Josiah Ober and Barry Strauss, "Drama, Political Rhetoric, and the Discourse of Athenian Democracy," in *Nothing to Do with Dionysos?: Athenian Drama in Its Social Context*, ed. John J. Winkler and Froma I. Zeitlin (Princeton: Princeton University Press, 1990), 237–70; Edith Hall, *The Theatrical Cast of Athens: Interactions between Ancient Greek Drama and Society* (Oxford: Oxford University Press, 2006), 353–92.

29. The form of the *agōn* is identified (originally in 1945) by Jacqueline Duchemin, *L'Agon dans la tragédie grecque*, 2nd ed. (Paris: Belles Lettres, 1968). Further major contributions are Michael Lloyd, *The Agon in Euripides* (Oxford: Clarendon Press, 1992); Markus Dubischar, *Die*

Sophocles onward, Euripides seems to have been particularly drawn to such debates, and stages them, with varying formal qualities and degrees of structural closure, throughout his works. The formal consistency of such scenes is looser than that of the comic *agōn*, and there is little agreement on a precise definition or canon of scenes involving an *agōn*. It is therefore preferable to consider the tragic *agōn* less as a fixed form than as a range of possibilities for constructing scenes of disputation. In the broadest sense, an *agōn* involves two (or occasionally, three) characters presenting their positions in more or less balanced speeches, often before an arbiter of some kind. On such a broad construction, *agones* are found in nearly every one of Euripides' extant works, and their prevalence makes evident Euripides' interest in rhetoric as well as the widespread tendency toward thinking in opposition.

The focus of this chapter, which I call the *agōn sophias*, is distinct from, though related to, the form of the Euripidean *agōn* as it is usually defined. I use the term to describe a group of scenes that, despite differences in formal constitution, stage an opposition between two understandings of *sophia* and debate what it is to be *sophos*. These scenes are bound together not so much by their verbal or scenic form (insofar as it can be reconstructed) as by the agonistic setting and the central concern of *sophia*, which both figures seek to define and claim for themselves through debate. There is ample evidence that such debates were a Euripidean specialty, reflecting on novel intellectual currents and interrogating the role of the intellectual in society. All of these *agōnes* pose the question of the value of *sophia* to the wider community, and are thus emphatically political. But the form as a whole, I argue, demonstrates the need for a broader understanding of tragic politics and ideology: at issue are not just the constitution of political communities, their deliberative processes, and their decisions, but the foundations of human politics and thought generally, and in particular, the role of divinity as a basis of human wisdom.[30] The contrasting notions of *sophia* already adumbrated—a traditional conception of

---

Agonszenen bei Euripides: Untersuchungen zu ausgewählten Dramen (Stuttgart: Metzler, 2001). For my purposes, Duchemin's discussion is the most useful because of its wide scope (treating fragmentary as well as transmitted plays) and relatively catholic view of what constitutes an *agōn*.

30. Pucci similarly concentrates on the ambiguous role of *sophia* in Euripides and its connection to the divine: Pietro Pucci, *Euripides's Revolution under Cover* (Ithaca: Cornell University Press, 2016). He argues that there is a criticism of the anthropomorphism of the gods "under cover" in Euripides' works, which is adumbrated especially in relation to concerns of *sophia*. Though I agree that Euripides stages a mix of traditional and novel conceptions of divinity in his works, I reject the thesis of an esoteric message.

community-oriented practice, and a novel one of individual intellection and self-examination—suggest different understandings of the contours of human wisdom. In staging debates concerning *sophia*, drama interrogates the foundations of intellectual, religious, and social authority.

Suspicions of the *Sophos*: *Antiope* (I)

Sophia in late fifth-century Athens could be a dangerous quality, exposing the *sophos* to doubt, suspicion, and persecution. The prominence of figures such as Anaxagoras and Protagoras, whose intelligence was at once demonstrably formidable and removed from any particular domain of socially beneficial activity, led to widespread hostility. It is impossible to do more than speculate as to when and how this hostility developed, but it became concentrated on the circle of Pericles: Damon of Oa, a musician and political advisor, was ostracized in the 440s, and the early 430s saw the trial of Anaxagoras, who was closely identified with Pericles, for impiety.[31] From around this time, the accelerating arrival of foreign intellectuals and the increasing prominence of native-born ones like Socrates contributed to a climate of suspicion toward those who professed *sophia* or were thought to possess it.[32]

Usage of the word *sophia* and its cognates from the mid-fifth century exhibits this suspicion. Though *soph-*roots continued to be used in a more or less unmarked, traditional sense, they could also be used with negative connotations, to describe intelligence that appeared inflated, excessive, or did not conduce to the broader good. The noun σοφιστής, which in its early uses seems unequivocally positive, shows signs of a negative sense as early as the *Prometheus Bound*, where Prometheus is twice called "sophist" by his enemies in a tone of derision (62, 944).[33] Likewise, the words σόφισμα ("invention" or

---

[31]. On Damon, see Robert W. Wallace, *Reconstructing Damon: Music, Wisdom Teaching, and Politics in Perikles' Athens* (Oxford: Oxford University Press, 2015), 51–63. Wallace points to the later 440s as a period of conservative anti-intellectualism in Athens. Anaxagoras' prosecution is investigated in Mansfeld, "The Chronology of Anaxagoras' Athenian Period"; Woodbury, "Anaxagoras and Athens."

[32]. See Jan Dressler, *Wortverdreher, Sonderlinge, Gottlose: Kritik an Philosophie und Rhetorik im klassischen Athen* (Berlin: de Gruyter, 2014).

[33]. The meaning of σοφιστής in the *Prometheus Bound* is discussed in Victoria Mousbahova, "The Meaning of the Terms σοφιστής and σόφισμα in the 'Prometheus Bound,'" *Hyperboreus* 12 (2006): 31–49. Other early pejorative uses are found in *Clouds* 331, 1111, 1309. In none of these usages does the term track the Platonic meaning of "sophist" as a particular profession.

"sly contrivance") and σοφίζομαι ("to act cleverly" or "plot") are frequently used in negative senses in the later fifth century.[34] These semantic possibilities for *soph*-roots may well have been available earlier—we have so little of early Greek usage that it is impossible to draw absolute conclusions—but they clearly become more prominent in the latter part of the fifth century. In Athens, moreover, the word *sophia* and its cognates probably had a somewhat alien sound: the word seems to be Ionic in origin, and is rarely used in Attic prose before the fourth century.[35] In bringing out the pejorative qualities of *soph*-roots, then, Attic writers may be using a foreign-sounding word to characterize suspicious people and practices.

Euripides frequently reflects in his dramas on the quality of *sophia* and the role of the *sophos* in society.[36] A recurrent theme is the burden of *sophia*, which brings little happiness to the possessor and frequently leads to social tensions.[37] A prominent passage comes in the *Medea* (which contains the most *soph*-roots of any play by Euripides besides *Bacchae*), where the title character describes the dilemma of being—or appearing to be—σοφή (which I translate throughout as "wise"):[38]

χρὴ δ' οὔποθ' ὅστις ἀρτίφρων πέφυκ' ἀνήρ
παῖδας περισσῶς ἐκδιδάσκεσθαι σοφούς·
χωρὶς γὰρ ἄλλης ἧς ἔχουσιν ἀργίας

---

34. Negative senses of *soph*-roots are found, for example, in Euripides, *Iphigenia at Aulis* 744, Sophocles, *Philoctetes* 77 (σοφίζομαι to describe deceptive plotting); compare these to the more straightforward uses in Herodotus 2.66, 8.27 (where σοφίζομαι simply describes the making of a plan). For σόφισμα, compare Euripides, *Hecuba* 258 (describing a trap) to Pindar, *Olympian* 13, 17 (where it simply means an invention).

35. Early Attic prose only rarely uses *soph*-roots: there are none in Antiphon or Andocides, one in pseudo-Xenophon's *Constitution of the Athenians*, three in all of Thucydides, and five in Lysias. Herodotus and fourth-century orators and prose writers, by contrast, use them in abundance.

36. The prominence of *soph*-roots in Euripides' works has attracted quite a bit of critical attention: most thorough is Valentina Origa, *Le contraddizioni della sapienza: Sophia e sophos nella tragedia euripidea* (Tübingen: Narr, 2007). There is also substantial material on Euripides in Friedrich Maier, *Der sophos-Begriff: Zur Bedeutung, Wertung und Rolle des Begriffes von Homer bis Euripides* (Augsburg: Blasaditsch, 1970).

37. The burden of *sophia* is suggested by uses in *Orestes* 294–96, *Children of Heracles* 615–17, on which see Burkhard Gladigow, "Zum Makarismos des Weisen," *Hermes* 95 (1967): 430–33. The concern will return strongly in *Bacchae*.

38. *Soph*-roots in the *Medea* are surveyed in Juan Antonio López Férez, "Sophía-sophós dans la 'Médée' d'Euripide," *Pallas* 45 (1996): 139–51.

> φθόνον πρὸς ἀστῶν ἀλφάνουσι δυσμενῆ.
> σκαιοῖσι μὲν γὰρ καινὰ προσφέρων σοφὰ
> δόξεις ἀχρεῖος κοὐ σοφὸς πεφυκέναι·
> τῶν δ' αὖ δοκούντων εἰδέναι τι ποικίλον
> κρείσσων νομισθεὶς ἐν πόλει λυπρὸς φανῇ.
> ἐγὼ δὲ καὐτὴ τῆσδε κοινωνῶ τύχης·
> σοφὴ γὰρ οὖσα, τοῖς μέν εἰμ' ἐπίφθονος,
> τοῖς δ' αὖ προσάντης· εἰμὶ δ' οὐκ ἄγαν σοφή. (294–305)

Whoever was born a sensible man ought never to have his children taught to be exceptionally wise. Since apart from the other [reason], that they take on idleness, they incur hostile envy of the citizens. For in bringing wise novelties to the dim you will appear useless and not to be wise; while if you are thought in the city superior to those who seem to know something intricate you will appear annoying. I myself partake of this very fortune. For I am envied by some for being wise, while to others I am irksome. Yet I am not so very wise.

Medea describes a climate of anti-intellectualism, in which those who are thought to be exceptionally gifted are alternately envied (by those whose claims they threaten) or dismissed (by those who cannot understand their intellect). This climate must have been at least partly recognizable in the Athens of Euripides' time. Envy (φθόνος) was often cited as a cause of the hatred of Socrates and the sophists, and Xenophon's *Memorabilia* discusses the ambiguous good of wisdom, using Palamedes as an example of someone "envied for his wisdom" (4.2.33: διὰ σοφίαν φθονηθείς) and destroyed—an implicit parallel to Socrates' own situation.[39] Though Medea claims, somewhat disingenuously, that she is "not so very wise," she describes her own situation as characteristic of the *sophos* in general. *Sophia*, far from acting only as a political-religious source of authority, could also prove a divisive, suspicion-engendering quality, with severe consequences for those who possessed it.

The two varieties of mistrust mentioned by Medea, envy for wisdom and dismissal for uselessness, are both explored by the Euripidean *agōn sophias*. The most significant figures for these contestations are the *Antiope*'s Amphion and the title character of the *Palamedes*. Amphion and Palamedes are figured

---

39. Envy is often mentioned as a cause in Socrates' condemnation: Plato, *Apology* 18d, 28a (both times paired with διαβολή, "slander"); Xenophon, *Apology* 14, 32. Protagoras expresses the same worry in Plato, *Protagoras* 316d–e.

in terms that encompass varying forms of *sophia*: they are connected both to musical tradition and to intellectual innovation, which gives their *sophia* a paradoxical quality, incorporating both familiar and novel elements. When their claims to *sophia* are contested, the grounds are ultimately political, hinging on whether their intellect is beneficial to the community.[40] Though the dramas ultimately vindicate both—Amphion's talents enable him to build the walls of Thebes, and Palamedes is recognized as innocent (and avenged subsequent to the play's action)—the sharpness of the criticism to which both are subjected is striking, and argues against readings that would make either drama a straightforward apology for the *sophos*. As the chapter will show, Euripides could be thought to embody both novel musical and intellectual currents, so it is striking that his dramas incorporate some of the very criticisms of these new forms of *sophia* that were being lodged against him and others in public. Recognizing the ambiguous quality of the *sophia* of both Amphion and Palamedes, then, demonstrates the way that Euripides' portrayal of these *sophoi* both incorporates and responds to cultural questions concerning intellectual authority and the sources of wisdom.

The *agōn* of the *Antiope* is an encounter between the twin brothers Amphion and Zethus, children of Antiope, daughter of the king of Boeotia, and Zeus. Forced to flee because of her unwedded state, she was eventually captured by her father's successor, and gave birth in captivity on her way back to Boeotia. She left the twins to be raised by a herdsman in Eleutherae, an important Dionysiac site that sits between Boeotia and Attica—and was often disputed between them.[41] While Zethus pursues a life of action (it is not clear precisely in what—he mentions military, political, and agricultural spheres), Amphion is drawn to music, and particularly to the lyre, a recent invention that he is the first human being to possess. The outlines of the confrontation are relatively clear: Zethus reproaches Amphion's absorption in music and absence from public life, which he characterizes as a pursuit of (false) *sophia*, while Amphion defends himself by claiming that his *sophia* is beneficial to the

---

40. The relation of the *sophos* to the community is a major focus of Origa's study, though she does not give substantial treatment to the *Antiope* or *Palamedes*: Origa, *Le contraddizioni della sapienza*, 20–38.

41. Eleutherae is, among other things, the site from which the statue of Dionysus was brought to Athens every year for the Great Dionysia. On the Dionysiac overtones of the drama, see Froma I. Zeitlin, "Staging Dionysus between Thebes and Athens," in *Masks of Dionysus*, ed. Thomas H. Carpenter and Christopher A. Faraone (Ithaca: Cornell University Press, 1993), 171–82.

community. Scholars are divided on the eventual "winner" of the *agōn*, with different reconstructions suggesting different outcomes.[42] There is also significant disagreement on the core qualities of the two brothers and the impressions they would have made.[43] My reading will seek to account for these different scholarly positions by pointing to the way that *sophia* is portrayed in the *agōn* as double-edged. The rest of the drama, moreover, would have vindicated both action (in the form of the intervention that ultimately saves Antiope from captivity) and music (which will build the walls of Thebes). I will argue that this apparent reconciliation of the two ideas of *sophia* on the level of plot is prepared in the play's *agōn*, which can be read as a metadiscourse on musical and philosophical innovation in drama. Understanding the *agōn* in this way allows us to move beyond the question of who "wins" the argument, and see that the far more profound outcome is to envision a constructive civic role for the *sophos*.

Amphion is portrayed as a figure of intellectual innovation from his first appearance. He seems to have entered playing the lyre, and singing a song that marks him as interested in cosmological speculation: "Of Aether and Gaia, progenitor of everything, I sing" (F 182a: Αἰθέρα καὶ Γαῖαν πάντων γενέτειραν ἀείδω). From the single line preserved, it is hard to say much about the cosmogony implied. It recalls the traditional intercourse of Gaia and Ouranos familiar from the *Theogony*, but the invocation of Aether in place of Ouranos marks Amphion's thought as distinct, and evokes contemporary philosophical speculations. *Aer* and *aether* seem to have been hypothesized as the substance of Anaxagoras' *nous*, while the Socrates of Aristophanes' *Clouds* is literally portrayed as airborne, and prays to the gods Air, Aether, and the Clouds while suspended above the stage (264–65).[44] "Aether" was a favorite Euripidean

---

42. Horace, *Epistles* 1.18, 43–44 suggests that Amphion appears to yield at the end (*fraternis cessisse putatur / moribus Amphion*: "Amphion is thought to yield to the will of his brother"), and has led many critics to reconstruct such a conclusion to the *agōn*. It is not clear, however, why he would be "thought" to yield, or what this would have entailed; it is not even certain that the lines refer to Euripides' version rather than the Latin tragedy of Pacuvius.

43. Amphion can appear either a noble artist or a revanchist aristocrat, Zethus a philistine or salt-of-the-earth everyman. On the characters, see Carter, *The Quiet Athenian*, 163–73; Peter Wilson, "Euripides' Tragic Muse," *Illinois Classical Studies* 24/25 (2000): 427–49; John Gibert, "Euripides' 'Antiope' and the Quiet Life," in *The Play of Texts and Fragments: Essays in Honour of Martin Cropp*, ed. J.R.C. Cousland and James R. Hume (Leiden: Brill, 2009), 23–34.

44. See Dillon, "Euripides and the Philosophy of His Time," 51–55. Archelaus A4 DK/D2 LM and Diogenes of Apollonia A5 DK/D8 LM are the main testimonies for the significance of

word, and is frequently discussed in his plays as a fundamental principle (where in the earlier tradition it is simply a physical realm).⁴⁵ Amphion's invocation of an idiosyncratic cosmology in his first appearance suggests that his introduction of a novel instrument was coupled with a modern philosophical outlook.⁴⁶

It is hard to say more about the specifics of Amphion's philosophical interests, but Zethus' criticisms cast Amphion as an intellectual who has abandoned any constructive role in the community. Zethus seems to instigate the dispute by reproaching Amphion for his absorption in music, which makes him inattentive to worldly matters:

κακῶν κατάρχεις τήνδε μοῦσαν εἰσάγων
ἀργόν, φίλοινον, χρημάτων ἀτημελῆ. (F 183)

You make a beginning of evils by introducing this muse, idle, wine-loving, neglectful of affairs.

Both verbal forms (κατάρχεις and εἰσάγων) point to the novel quality of Amphion's pursuits. The word μοῦσα, though suggesting in the first instance Amphion's song, can encompass a wide range of intellectual activity, and so would be directed at the content of Amphion's music as well as its form.⁴⁷ The problem with such pursuits, for Zethus, is that they remove one from labor and communal life. The charges of idleness (ἀργία) and neglect (ἀμέλεια) recur in other fragments, and these qualities make Amphion, Zethus claims, unfit to

---

aether and *aer*. I think there is good reason to see Aristophanes' portrayal of Socrates as based on real meteorological interests, but it is not important for my argument; regardless, the fixation on *aether* is seen to be a marker of dangerous, new learning.

45. On *aether* in Euripides, see Egli, *Euripides im Kontext*, 79–120; Assaël, *Philosophe et poète tragique*, 45–60. A fragment of the *Chrysippus* (F 839) similarly portrays Gaia and Aether as the fundamental principles of life, while F 877 and 941 (the latter sometimes thought to come from the *Antiope*) identify Zeus with Aether. The association of Zeus and *aer* is present in the Derveni Papyrus, Col. 17 and 23. It is not, though, wholly novel: Aeschylus F 70 asserts that "Zeus is *aether*, Zeus is earth, Zeus is sky, Zeus is truly everything and that which is beyond these things" (Ζεύς ἐστιν αἰθήρ, Ζεὺς δὲ γῆ, Ζεὺς δ' οὐρανός, / Ζεύς τοι τά πάντα χὠ τι τῶνδ' ὑπέρτερον). This, however, is not the specific identification we find in the later fifth century.

46. Wilson, "Euripides' Tragic Muse," 440–42 connects Amphion's portrayal to the "New Music" in Athens.

47. Penelope Murray, "The Muses and Their Arts," in *Music and the Muses: The Culture of Mousike in the Classical Athenian City*, ed. Penelope Murray and Peter Wilson (Oxford: Oxford University Press, 2004), 365–79.

contribute to military campaigns or to offer counsel.[48] Zethus returns repeatedly to the way that Amphion is debasing his φύσις (nature, birth, or appearance), deriding Amphion's "womanlike form" (γυναικομίμῳ μορφώματι) as a deviation from his "noble φύσις" (F 185).[49] Zethus fears that Amphion will become "idle in his house and city" (ἀργὸς μὲν οἴκοις καὶ πόλει) and concludes that "one's φύσις is gone, whenever one is overcome by the sweetness of pleasure" (F 187: ἡ φύσις γὰρ οἴχεται / ὅταν γλυκείας ἡδονῆς ἥσσων τις ᾖ). Amphion, it appears, has squandered his possessions and natural gifts in self-indulgent intellectual pursuits. The *agōn* poses the question of whether one should use one's talents for individual or collective ends.[50]

This is a question of the role of the *sophos* in society. One of Zethus' invocations of φύσις comes as a response to (or anticipation of) the claim that Amphion's musical pursuits are somehow *sophos*:

πῶς γὰρ σοφὸν τοῦτ' ἔστιν, ἥτις εὐφυῆ
λαβοῦσα τέχνη φῶτ' ἔθηκε χείρονα; (F 186)

How is this *sophos*, the art which, taking a man of good nature, makes him worse?

Though Amphion's τέχνη of music is traditionally associated with *sophia*, Zethus claims that this pursuit is actually debasing Amphion, presumably by rendering him idle and effeminate. At another point, Zethus appropriates the language of music to describe Amphion's pursuits as pointless "contrivances" (σοφίσματα), contrasted with the "good music" (εὐμουσία) of physical labor (F 188). His call to reject *sophismata* suggests that the *sophia* at issue is not just musical, but intellectual as well. A fragment of the Roman tragedian Pacuvius'

---

48. F 185 5–7: "You would not join in battle with the hollow of a shield or offer any vigorous counsel on behalf of others" (κοὔτ' ἂν ἀσπίδος κύτει / <...> ὁμιλήσειας οὔτ' ἄλλων ὕπερ / νεανικὸν βούλευμα βουλεύσαιό <τι>). The reconstruction of F 185 from Plato's *Gorgias* (485e) is uncertain: Vincenzo Di Benedetto, "Osservazioni su alcuni frammenti dell' 'Antiope' di Euripide," in *Euripide e i papiri*, ed. Guido Bastianini and Angelo Casanova (Florence: Istituto Papirologico G. Vitelli, 2005), 114–20.

49. There is an irony in the repeated invocations of φύσις, since the parentage of both brothers turns out to be much more exalted than the circumstances in which they were raised: Anna Miriam Biga, *L'"Antiope" di Euripide* (Trento: Università degli Studi di Trento, 2015), 283–86.

50. On Amphion's antidemocratic tendencies, see Wilson, "Euripides' Tragic Muse," 442–46. There may be a tension between Amphion's portrayal as a figure at once of novelty and of aristocratic values, but it is hard to determine how the play would have explored this.

Antiope similarly records Zethus' hatred of *philosopha sententia*, speaking to Zethus' anti-intellectual qualities and the portrayal of Amphion as a philosopher-poet.[51]

Within the *agōn*, *sophia* is doubly contested: not just whether Amphion's way of life is *sophos*, but whether *sophia* itself is itself a positive quality. A few fragments preserve evidence that in the play as a whole the *sophos* was a figure of suspicion for the power of his rhetoric.[52] This is most evident in a passage in which the agonistic context is itself thematized, with the speaker (it is unclear who) pointing explicitly, and warily, to the possibility of antilogy:[53]

ἐκ παντὸς ἄν τις πράγματος δισσῶν λόγων
ἀγῶνα θεῖτ' ἄν, εἰ λέγειν εἴη σοφός. (F 189)

From any matter a man might create a contest of double arguments if he were clever in speaking.

The practice of *dissoi logoi* seems to have been associated particularly with Protagoras, who claimed that there were opposing arguments concerning any matter (A1 DK/D26 LM). The dramatic fragment suggests a distance on the practice, noting the possibility of elaborating contradictory arguments on any issue, but not endorsing it—and probably, in context, denigrating it, and the *sophia* that enables such contradiction.[54] Whoever speaks the fragment, it would characterize the *sophia* of one or both of the disputants as a skill of pure argumentation divorced from right or truth. Though this sentiment is not uncommon in the late fifth century, in context it points to the rift opening between traditional and novel conceptions of the *sophos*, with both brothers claiming true *sophia* as their own, against the baseless assertions of the other.

---

51. *Antiope* T viib.5. It is not clear how close to Euripides Pacuvius' drama was, but Amphion's combination of philosophical and poetic interests seems to have been common: C. Collard, M. J. Cropp, and J. Gibert, eds., *Euripides: Selected Fragmentary Plays*, Volume II (Oxford: Aris & Phillips, 2004), 269–70.

52. F 206, usually assigned to later in the play, denigrates the *sophos* who wins an argument by eloquence (εὐγλωσσία), and encourages looking to deeds (πράγματα) rather than words (λόγοι).

53. References to debate or opposition are frequent markers of Euripidean *agōnes*: Lloyd, *The Agon in Euripides*, 4–5.

54. The fragment seems to me to be most likely spoken by Zethus (in which case it would be casting doubt on Amphion's clever response to Zethus' reproaches)—though it has also been attributed to Amphion and the chorus.

Praise of *Sophia*: *Antiope* (II)

Amphion may have been the one to introduce the topic of *sophia* explicitly: Cicero reports that he responds to criticism of music with a *laus sapientiae* (*De inventione* 1.50.94: "praise of wisdom"). Amphion's defense is striking for the way it uses the traditional association of *sophia* with social authority to elaborate a highly individualistic ethos. Amphion offers an apology for the life of the "quiet man" (ἥσυχος) concentrated around two central concepts, pleasure (ἡδονή) and wisdom (σοφία). His defense, like the reproaches leveled against him, sees the community as the final arbiter of the good, but he argues that one can better serve this good by stepping back from daily political life and becoming absorbed in the pursuit of wisdom. The quiet man, he claims, "is a sure friend to his friends and best for the city" (F 194: ὁ δ' ἥσυχος φίλοισί τ' ἀσφαλὴς φίλος / πόλει τ' ἄριστος). The paradox that an individual's retreat from the political could make him a better political agent is familiar from Socrates' defense, but it represents a radical departure from Athenian civic norms and expectations.[55] Amphion's own apology will establish a pattern for portrayals of the *sophos* by seeking to reconcile civic obligation with intellectual inquiry.

Though Amphion has traditionally been understood as a partisan of the contemplative life, he might better be understood as a partisan of the pleasure-seeking life.[56] The danger of pleasure had been a theme in Zethus' reproaches, and was connected to a concern that its pursuit would lead to a loss of self-control and, ultimately, to neglect of civic and household matters.[57] If

---

55. See Carter, *The Quiet Athenian*, 163–73; Simon R. Slings, "The Quiet Life in Euripides' 'Antiope,'" in *Fragmenta dramatica: Beiträge zur Interpretation der griechischen Tragikerfragmente und ihrer Wirkungsgeschichte*, ed. Heinz Hofmann and Annette Harder (Göttingen: Vandenhoeck & Ruprecht, 1991), 137–51.

56. The contemplative life is explored influentially by Bruno Snell, "Vita Activa and Vita Contemplativa in Euripides' 'Antiope,'" in *Scenes from Greek Drama* (Berkeley: University of California Press, 1964), 70–98.

57. F 187, 219. A fuller discussion would lead too far away from the immediate concerns of the chapter, but Amphion's defense of pleasure probably reflects fifth-century philosophical debates around hedonism: both the *Protagoras* (351b–58d) and the *Gorgias* (492d–500d) depict Socrates conversing with sophists concerning pleasure. Xenophon's *Memorabilia* (2.1) also contains an extensive discussion of pleasure between Socrates with Aristippus (who would go on to found the Cyrenaic school, the first philosophical school devoted to hedonism), culminating in Socrates' recounting of Prodicus' *Choice of Heracles*.

Amphion answered this charge directly, his response is not preserved. What we do have records Amphion's argument for pleasure as an aim of life. One fragment, in an apologetic mode, takes the uncertainty of human fortune as a reason to pursue pleasure in the moment.[58] Amphion's defense of pleasure, though, grows far stronger, and entails a celebration of living ἀπράγμων. When one's immediate needs are satisfied, he argues, it is foolish to seek out further activity:

ὅστις δὲ πράσσει πολλὰ μὴ πράσσειν παρόν,
μῶρος, παρὸν ζῆν ἡδέως ἀπράγμονα. (F 193)

Whoever acts in many ways when it is possible not to act is a fool, since it is possible to live pleasurably without acting.

The sense of "acts in many ways" (πολλὰ πράσσειν) is not obvious from the context, but related terms generally describe forms of political or social activity. Often, though not always, they have a negative connotation, indicating excessive action or meddling.[59] But Amphion goes beyond recommending a course of moderation in one's political activity; he suggests, rather, that one should not act at all when action is unnecessary. Though this is not a complete rejection of political participation, it denies political ambition, restricting the scope of engagement to whatever serves as a means to the end of pleasure.

The other aspect of Amphion's defense entails a positive case for the value of individual intellectual achievement as beneficial to the community. Amphion insists that the intellect cultivated in his quiet life is more valuable than the capacities that come from a life of action. He responds to Zethus' charge of physical degeneracy by asserting the importance of intellect over strength: "For if I am able to think well, this is better than a strong arm" (F 199: εἰ γὰρ εὖ φρονεῖν ἔχω, / κρεῖσσον τόδ' ἐστὶ καρτεροῦ βραχίονος).[60] In support of the idea that intellect is the most important quality a man can possess, Amphion invokes the very areas of life that Zethus had claimed he neglected: civic

---

58. F 196 4–5: "Why, when we rest on an uncertain prosperity, do we not live as pleasurably as possible, harming no one?" (τί δῆτ' ἐν ὄλβῳ μὴ σαφεῖ βεβηκότες / οὐ ζῶμεν ὡς ἥδιστα μὴ λυπούμενοι;).

59. See Matthew Leigh, *From Polypragmon to Curiosus: Ancient Concepts of Curious and Meddlesome* (Oxford: Oxford University Press, 2013), 23–45.

60. There are further parallels to fifth-century philosophical syncrises: the opposition of intellect and strength is central to Antisthenes' paired speeches of Ajax and Odysseus, and, in somewhat different form, the *Hippias Minor*'s contrast of Achilles and Odysseus.

deliberation, household management, and warfare. γνώμη (judgment or intellect), Amphion argues, is essential to success in all:

γνώμη γὰρ ἀνδρὸς εὖ μὲν οἰκοῦνται πόλεις,
εὖ δ' οἶκος, εἴς τ' αὖ πόλεμον ἰσχύει μέγα·
σοφὸν γὰρ ἓν βούλευμα τὰς πολλὰς χέρας
νικᾷ, σὺν ὄχλῳ δ' ἀμαθία πλεῖστον κακόν. (F 200)

By the judgment of man cities are well managed, the household well (managed), and it [judgment] is moreover a great strength for war. For one wise counsel defeats many hands, and ignorance together with a mob is the greatest evil.

Where to Zethus, Amphion's absorption in intellectual life renders him unfit for household and public duties, Amphion claims that this is precisely what makes him valuable to the community. In spite of his stated preference for political disengagement, he appears to accept the traditional role of the *sophos* as a political advisor, who would contribute by offering "wise counsel." The value of such advice is juxtaposed with the decisionmaking of a large group, which appears dangerous because of its ignorance. Amphion's elitism is impossible to mistake: even as he contemplates entry into the life of the city, he imagines for himself a role far above that of ordinary citizens because of his intellect. The possession of *sophia*, in his view, sets him apart from the struggles of everyday political life, and makes his retirement from public life, paradoxically, a political act.

In addition to claiming that the *sophos* is able to benefit the city by good judgment, Amphion explains why his choice of a retired life is more beneficial than a life of engagement. Warning against ambitious undertakings, he suggests that the best political act is to cultivate one's own wisdom in isolation:

ἐγὼ μὲν οὖν ᾄδοιμι καὶ λέγοιμί τι
σοφόν, ταράσσων μηδὲν ὧν πόλις νοσεῖ. (F 202)

I, for my part, would sing and speak something wise, stirring none of the things of which the city is sick.

The mention of song and speech associates Amphion with forms of intellectual endeavor beyond music: perhaps the offering of counsel, but more likely referring to philosophical endeavor, whether in the form of conversations or individual researches. Given that Amphion's song assumed a novel cosmogony, to "sing and speak something wise" would suggest both the inquiry into natural principles (mentioned in a fragment that will be discussed below) and the setting of these into music. "Something wise" would refer to the objects of philosophical inquiry, contributing to an image of Amphion as an innovator in intellectual and musical matters both. And this appears a far more salutary pursuit than entering into politics, which threatens to stir up the illness of the city. It is not clear whether Amphion is eschewing all political action or only the meddlesome kind, but the preference for noninvolvement is strongly stated. The idea that the city itself is ill (though the reasons for this are unclear) adds to the sense that political engagement is a perilous endeavor, even for the wise.

It is unclear how the *agōn* ended, though the two brothers must eventually have reconciled and formed a plan of action. A choral passage, generally (though not universally) attributed to the *Antiope*, suggests the possibility of such reconciliation by describing the *sophos* as leading a life retired from civic troubles, which is nevertheless politically beneficial:[61]

> ὄλβιος ὅστις τῆς ἱστορίας
> ἔσχε μάθησιν,
> μήτε πολιτῶν ἐπὶ πημοσύνην
> μήτ' εἰς ἀδίκους πράξεις ὁρμῶν,
> ἀλλ' ἀθανάτου καθορῶν φύσεως
> κόσμον ἀγήρων, πῇ τε συνέστη
> καὶ ὅπῃ καὶ ὅπως. (F 910)

> Happy is the man who has learning from inquiry, setting out neither to troubling of the citizens nor to unjust actions, but contemplating the ageless order of immortal nature, in which way it came to be and where from and how.

A number of elements connect the passage to the portrayal of Amphion: the idea of the quiet life, the assertion of political and moral blamelessness, the idea of the divine, and the inquiry into cosmogony. The particulars of this inquiry have been connected to various philosophical thinkers, but it seems much more a generic description of cosmological speculation, and need not

---

61. The anapestic form of the lines suggests the lead-in to a choral stasimon. Kannicht in *TrGF* leaves the fragment *adespota*, but most other editors have included it as a fragment of the *Antiope*. The most likely placement for the fragment is more or less immediately following the *agōn*, since it responds directly to the question of the value of intellectual endeavor for the city.

refer to any particular theory or method. Most important, the song constitutes a strong endorsement, in civic terms, of cosmological inquiry for its own sake. The quiet life of wisdom, the chorus suggests, is not deleterious to the community, and brings the *sophos* closer to the eternal truths of nature.

The linguistic form of the passage is especially interesting. The formula ὄλβιος ὅστις introduces a *makarismos*, a form of religious speech connected especially to the Eleusinian Mysteries. Such *makarismoi* often contrasted the happy knowledge of the initiate with the miserable ignorance of the uninitiated, so an antithetical framing may be native to the form.[62] Here, it is the inquirer, not the initiate, who is described as divinely blessed. Such blessedness, though, comes not from the knowledge of revelation but from "learning from inquiry" and a life of cosmological speculation. Euripides' formula may recall a line of Empedocles:

ὄλβιος, ὃς θείων πραπίδων ἐκτήσατο πλοῦτον
δειλὸς δ' ᾧ σκοτόεσσα θεῶν πέρι δόξα μέμηλεν. (B132 DK/D8 LM)

Happy is he who has acquired the wealth of divine thoughts, wretched the one who cares for an obscure opinion concerning the gods.

Empedocles' *makarismos* probably emerges from a Pythagorean tradition that viewed scientific inquiry as an element of religious practice, and a key to reincarnation, so the association of knowledge with blessedness is natural.[63] In comparison to the *Antiope* passage, there is a crucial difference in the way initiatory knowledge is figured: for Empedocles, it is a possession of the blessed one, whereas in the Euripides passage, knowledge is the object of inquiry and pursuit. Even as the form of the *Antiope*'s *makarismos* looks back to the traditional grounding of *sophia* in religion, it describes the path to wisdom in the terms of contemporary inquiry, suggesting a reconciliation of the ideas of *sophia* as divine good and scientific pursuit.

The *agōn* of the *Antiope* evidently made a strong impression, both on Euripides' contemporaries (I will discuss Aristophanes in the next section) and on

---

62. Compare the *Homeric Hymn to Demeter* 480–82. See further Gladigow, "Zum Makarismos des Weisen."

63. It is often thought that the subject of the blessing is Pythagoras himself, but the generalizing tendency of the *makarismos* form makes this improbable. On Empedocles' Pythagoreanism, see Charles H. Kahn, "Religion and Natural Philosophy in Empedocles' Doctrine of the Soul," *Archiv für Geschichte der Philosophie* 42 (1960): 3–35; Peter Kingsley, *Ancient Philosophy, Mystery, and Magic: Empedocles and Pythagorean Tradition* (Oxford: Oxford University Press, 1995).

coming generations. Beyond prominent citations in the *Gorgias*, discussed in the Conclusion, the *Antiope* is frequently quoted in Stobaeus' *Anthology*, and crops up in other late antique and Byzantine literature. Most of these later references are to *sententiae*, generalizations that could be extracted from the story and made to serve another context. Though our selection of material from the play (as from ancient tragedy preserved in quotation fragments generally) is clearly biased toward such generalizations, the sheer number of them from the *Antiope* suggests that the play was particularly concerned with such broader statements about human existence. The play seems to be one of the epicenters of Euripides' interest in in the ambiguities of *sophia* and the role of the *sophos*. This interest takes its most substantial and elaborate form in *Bacchae*, which this chapter will return to, but is found throughout fragmentary plays as well, often in what seem to be agonistic contexts. Nothing like the wealth of evidence from the *Antiope* survives from other *agōnes*, but we can discern a similarly contoured confrontation in the *Palamedes*. The context is something like an actual trial, with Palamedes defending himself against the charges of sedition orchestrated (and probably prosecuted) by Odysseus. The verbal confrontation between Odysseus and Palamedes, both famous representatives of *sophia*, seems to have turned, like the *Antiope*'s *agōn*, on the value of intellectual novelty.

Palamedes is a figure of intellectual innovation as Amphion was one of musical novelty: Palamedes' *sophia* was proverbial in the late fifth century, and, as discussed in chapter 1, Euripides' play featured a (likely rather extended) catalog of Palamedes' inventions.[64] It has not been adequately appreciated, however, that Euripides' *Palamedes* was also a musical figure. There may have been a tradition connecting Palamedes to the invention of *mousikē* already in the fifth century (it is mentioned as one of his claimed inventions in Alcidamas' *Odysseus* 22), but Euripides' play is the earliest evidence for it.[65] The association could be seen either as a positive or negative one, depending on the speaker: a fragment, likely from Odysseus' speech against Palamedes, shows a suspicious attitude toward "friends of *mousikē*" (μουσικῆς φίλοι) who,

---

64. At *Frogs* 1451, Dionysus exclaims, in response to Euripides' advice, εὖ γ᾽, ὦ Παλάμηδες, ὦ σοφωτάτη φύσις ("Well done, Palamedes, wisest creature!"). The association with Euripides is consistent with the musical (as well as philosophical) nature of Palamedes discussed below.

65. All the other inventions mentioned in Alcidamas' speech have demonstrable earlier sources, so it seems unlikely that *mousikē* would have been a new addition to the list. Palamedes is described as a poet also in the *Suda*.

just like everyone else, pursue material wealth.⁶⁶ The warning plays to doubts concerning *sophia* generally and seeks to undermine the potential defense that, as a musician (or, more generally, as an intellectual), Palamedes should be considered above reproach. Nevertheless, Palamedes' connection to *mousikē* is also used in diametrically opposed fashion, to memorialize him after his death. A lyric lament describes him as the "all-wise nightingale of the muses, who did no one harm" (F 588: πάνσοφον . . . οὐδέν' ἀλγύνουσαν ἀηδόνα μουσᾶν). The fragment, which was widely quoted in antiquity, emphatically associates Palamedes' *sophia* with *mousikē*.⁶⁷ Like Amphion's self-defense and the choral *makarismos* of the *Antiope*, the fragment draws attention to the harmlessness of Palamedes' life—a riposte to the suspicion of his cleverness that would have informed his condemnation. As we observed also in relation to Amphion, the respect traditionally accorded to the *sophos* is now subject to radical doubt, turning *sophia* into a polar quality.

The relatively exiguous fragments that survive from Euripides' *Palamedes* suggest that *sophia* was a major concern of the play as a whole. On the most likely reconstruction, the accusation and defense of Palamedes would have depicted the speakers seeking to distinguish the truly wise from the powerful and the persuasive. Someone (probably Palamedes) diminishes the importance of military rank in comparison to wisdom:

στρατηλάται τἂν μυρίοι γενοίμεθα,
σοφὸς δ' ἄν εἷς τις ἢ δύ' ἐν μακρῷ χρόνῳ. (F 581)

Countless among us might become generals, but only one or two in a long time becomes wise.

The lines seem to be a warning against undervaluing intellect, suggesting that Palamedes' *sophia* makes him uniquely valuable to the war effort. But such

---

66. F 580: "Both those who are friends of μουσική and as many as live without it, toil for money, and whoever has the most is wisest" (οἵ τε μουσικῆς φίλοι / ὅσοι τε χωρὶς ζῶσι, χρημάτων ὕπερ / μοχθοῦσιν, ὃς δ' ἄν πλεῖστ' ἔχῃ σοφώτατος).

67. The lines are quoted by Diogenes Laertius 2.44, among others, as (impossibly) Euripides' lament for Socrates. The association of Palamedes with Socrates appears to be contemporary (though there is no reason to think it is Euripidean): both Plato and Xenophon record Socrates comparing himself to Palamedes (Plato, *Apology* 41b; Xenophon, *Apology* 26; Xenophon, *Memorabilia* 4.2.33). The lines have inspired ancient and modern scholars to speculate fruitlessly about an "actual" subject of the lament, whether Diagoras, Protagoras, or Anaxagoras: Falcetto, *Il "Palamede" di Euripide,* 146–49.

rhetoric could also be turned against the speaker. A suspicion of well-spokenness, much like that expressed in the *Antiope*, comes out in another fragment:

> ὅστις λέγει μὲν εὖ, τὰ δ' ἔργ' ἐφ' οἷς λέγει
> αἴσχρ' ἐστί, τούτου τὸ σοφὸν οὐκ αἰνῶ ποτέ. (F 583)

> Whoever speaks well, but the deeds about which he speaks are shameful—I never praise the wisdom [or "the wise quality"] of this man.

I discuss the unusual substantive τὸ σοφόν ("the wise") below, but for now it is important to recognize that it is an equivocal quality here, an intellectual power that can be used for ill as well as good. These lines could be spoken about either Odysseus or Palamedes, both of whom would have spoken well while making false or misleading (from the perspective of the speaker) assertions. In any case, the play questions what kind of *sophia* is praiseworthy, and who among its characters possesses it.[68] Palamedes and Odysseus would have appeared as mirror images of one another, debating which of the two uses his intellect for the common benefit, and which for self-interested conspiracy. The play as a whole could be understood as an extended *agōn* between the two versions of *sophia*.

The *Palamedes* must in some sense have vindicated its central character, but it is striking how deeply the play lodges doubts about the *sophos*. As we will see in the next section, similar doubts surrounded Euripides himself, who was suspected both for his apparently amoral intellectualism and his musical innovations. Most of the evidence is quite skewed, because it comes either from Aristophanes or from the unreliable biographical tradition, but the outlines of the criticisms are clear enough, and demonstrate that Euripides was associated with novel philosophical developments as well as musical experimentation.[69] I suggest that we can recognize in the *agōnes* a form of metadiscourse surrounding tragedy's own innovations. In staging these confrontations over the meaning

---

68. The *Alexander*, performed with the *Palamedes* and *Trojan Women* in 415, likewise includes an *agōn* that debates true and apparent wisdom (F 56, 61). See Ioanna Karamanou, "Fragments of Euripidean Rhetoric: The Trial-Debate in Euripides' 'Alexandros,'" in *Connecting Rhetoric and Attic Drama*, ed. Milagros Quijada Sagredo and M. Carmen Encinas Reguero (Bari: Levante, 2017), 161–76. The satyr play of this tetralogy was a *Sisyphus*, and some identify it with the Sisyphus fragment attributed to Critias and Euripides. On the tetralogy as a whole, see Scodel, *The Trojan Trilogy of Euripides*.

69. For a cautious (I think too cautious) view of Euripides' theology, see Mary R. Lefkowitz, *Euripides and the Gods* (Oxford: Oxford University Press, 2016), 24–48.

of *sophia*, Euripides would be staging questions surrounding the role of the poet in society, and perhaps even more, tragedy's role as a traditional source of wisdom and guidance. This is not to imply that the *agōnes* were intended as apologetics or allegories, or that the historical Euripides was even conscious of these resonances; such assertions would presume that dramatic reflections are secondary to a wider, preexisting discourse, on which they comment or reflect. Rather, we should see drama as itself a form of intellectual culture, which is informed by social realities in the same way that philosophical thought is, and constitutes an equally direct—and equally indirect—statement of them. Drama's debates concerning *sophia* are, in an emphatic sense, the debates of fifth-century Athens.

Old and New Learning: *Frogs* (I)

Agonism is at the heart of Old Comedy. Beyond the recurrent form of the epirrhematic *agōn*, comedy constantly reflects on itself in competition with other authors and plays, places itself in opposition to public figures, and stages rivalries and struggles for power. Aristophanes in particular seems to have waged a long-term, mutual *agōn* with Euripides, which runs at least from his earliest extant play, *Acharnians*, performed in 425, to *Frogs*, performed in 405, shortly after Euripides' death.[70] The second half of *Frogs* consists of what the chorus describes as "the great *agōn sophias*" (882: ἀγὼν σοφίας ὁ μέγας), in which Aeschylus and Euripides compete for Hades' chair of poetry and the chance to return to life with Dionysus. This *agōn* of poetic skill clearly evokes the dramatic competitions in which both Aeschylus and Euripides competed, and of which *Frogs* was a part.[71] There may also have existed already a literary tradition of poetic contests, which we know from the *Contest of Homer and Hesiod*, a work of the second century CE, but which is generally thought to have roots in a much earlier tradition.[72] If an early *Contest* tradition was

70. On the mutual nature of the *agōn* of Euripides and Aristophanes, see Farmer, *Tragedy on the Comic Stage*, 155–94.

71. Zachary P. Biles, *Aristophanes and the Poetics of Competition* (Cambridge: Cambridge University Press, 2011), 211–56. On the development of poetic contests, see Andrew Ford, *The Origins of Criticism: Literary Culture and Poetic Theory in Classical Greece* (Princeton: Princeton University Press, 2002), 272–93.

72. The connection between *Frogs* and a *Contest* tradition is most fully pursued by Ralph M. Rosen, "Aristophanes' 'Frogs' and the 'Contest of Homer and Hesiod,'" *Transactions of the American Philological Association* 134 (2004): 295–322.

anything like the extant text, it would provide an even more direct parallel for the *agōn* of *Frogs*, in that the competition proceeds by way of mutual cross-examination and quotation from one's own works, takes place before a single arbiter, and ultimately hinges on who provides the best advice for living.[73] Regardless of the existence or early form of a *Contest* tradition, though, sophistic culture employed many of the same discursive modes in its public performances: question-and-answer, short and long speeches, and advice giving. Whatever the immediate sources for the debate in *Frogs*, Aristophanes had a rich agonistic repertory to draw on.

The *agōn* between Aeschylus and Euripides presents such a range of topics, criteria, and positions that it is impossible to define precisely what is at stake in it. The comic effect relies substantially on this heterogeneity and the lack of seriousness with which the play treats the questions it raises. But at the same time, the questions themselves are substantive and, I argue, consonant with those posed in the Euripidean *agōn*. This must be an aspect of the joke: Aristophanes is placing Euripides into a Euripidean form, and forcing him to do the kind of rhetorical advocacy for his own viewpoint that he has so often staged among his characters—a tactic not so different from that of the *Women at the Thesmophoria*, in which Euripides and the Inlaw are portrayed enacting the plots of Euripidean dramas. My reading shows that the *agōn* puts into play the differing ideas of *sophia* that this chapter has followed: on one hand, a conception connected to divinity and practice in a community, and on the other, a conception of *sophia* as human inquiry and individual pursuit. Aeschylus' and Euripides' respective notions of poetic *sophia* are at the heart of the play's thoroughgoing contrast between old and new, and its perspective on contemporary Athens.[74] Yet rather than offering a decisive choice between tradition and innovation, *Frogs* ultimately envisions a poetry that combines contemporary intellectualism with respect for civic norms and common values. Its reflection on Athenian modernity is thus more complex than is often understood: though clearly informed by a desire to restore the past, the play's vision is ultimately oriented more to the future, and to a vision of modernity that is neither Aeschylean nor Euripidean.

---

73. Rosen, "Aristophanes' 'Frogs,'" 301–2.

74. *Clouds*, likewise, had suggested that the choice between Euripides and Aeschylus was one between traditional civic values and modern intellectualism: Strepsiades recounts asking his son Pheidippides to recite a passage of Aeschylus, and receives instead a condemnation of the older poet and a speech of Euripides (1364–72).

As many critics have noticed, the deck is stacked against Euripides from the beginning of the competition.[75] Though Dionysus conceives of the journey to Hades as an effort to bring Euripides back to life, the language of this effort suggests a wider effort at restoration. Dionysus explains his resolution by saying, "I am in need of a skilled poet, 'for those that are [skilled] no longer live, and those who live are bad'" (71–72: δέομαι ποιητοῦ δεξιοῦ. / οἱ μὲν γὰρ οὐκέτ' εἰσίν, οἱ δ' ὄντες κακοί), quoting a passage from Euripides' *Oeneus* in which the deposed title character is lamenting the current state of affairs to his grandson Diomedes, who will go on to avenge and restore him to the throne.[76] Dionysus takes on Diomedes' part in his own effort to restore poetry to its former glory. The political stakes of this restoration become clear in the choral parabasis, where the chorus leader, speaking in the voice of the poet, compares the city's treatment of its own citizens to its use of "the old coinage and new [or even "newfangled"] gold" (720: τἀρχαῖον νόμισμα καὶ τὸ καινὸν χρυσίον).[77] The Athenians, the chorus leader complains, ignore the older, tested coinage in favor of poorly struck new currency, just like they choose upstarts and

---

75. There is substantial debate over whether to read the *agōn* teleologically, leading to the "right" choice of Aeschylus (which often implies an idea of Dionysus as maturing over the course of the drama), or to see the ultimate choice as arbitrary. For the teleological reading, see Charles Paul Segal, "The Character and Cults of Dionysus and the Unity of the 'Frogs,'" *Harvard Studies in Classical Philology* 65 (1961): 207–42; Ismene Lada-Richards, *Initiating Dionysus: Ritual and Theatre in Aristophanes' "Frogs"* (Oxford: Oxford University Press, 1999); Biles, *Aristophanes and the Poetics of Competition*. The antiteleological reading is found in Rosen, "Aristophanes' 'Frogs'"; Stephen Halliwell, *Between Ecstasy and Truth: Interpretations of Greek Poetics from Homer to Longinus* (Oxford: Oxford University Press, 2011), 93–154. Though I agree with the former that the choice of Aeschylus is overdetermined, I draw on the latter strand in my reading of the play's attempted reconciliation of tradition and modernity.

76. F 565. The quotation relates to a wider discourse of birth and nobility in the scene, as Dionysus seeks a γόνιμος ("fertile," "potent") poet, one able to produce a γενναῖον ("noble," "true to one's birth") phrase (96–97). Dionysus thus aligns himself with the old nobility even while seeking a famously demotic poet. See Pavlos Sfyroeras, "πόθος Εὐριπίδου: Reading Andromeda in Aristophanes' 'Frogs,'" *American Journal of Philology* 129 (2008): 307–12.

77. Aristophanes seems to have abandoned the form of the *parabasis* in his immediately previous works, only to restore it in *Frogs*, which gives the scene an archaizing quality: James Redfield, "Comedy, Tragedy, and Politics in Aristophanes' 'Frogs,'" *Chicago Review* 15 (1962): 107–21; Thomas K. Hubbard, *The Mask of Comedy: Aristophanes and the Intertextual Parabasis* (Ithaca: Cornell University Press, 1991), 205–10.

arrivistes as their leaders ahead of the traditional nobility.⁷⁸ This seems to refer to the way that the oligarchs involved in the coup of 411 have been disenfranchised, while the slaves who participated in the battle of Arginusae have been given rights of citizenship.⁷⁹ The chorus leader urges the spectators, "changing your ways, make use again of the good people" (734–35: μεταβαλόντες τοὺς τρόπους / χρῆσθε τοῖς χρηστοῖσιν αὖθις), and Dionysus seeks the same revival in his poetic quest: to restore the good people of past ages to a degenerate present. That he associates this restoration with the recently dead Euripides is itself slightly comic, and makes the ultimate decision for Aeschylus explicable partly as the fulfillment of his initial intention. Yet my reading will suggest that even though the thrust of the play is to valorize Aeschylus and the Athenian past, the play ultimately endorses a version of poetic *sophia* that reconciles traditional and modern elements.

The contrast between the two poets' respective notions of *sophia* is sketched in the opening prayers that both speak before the contest proper begins. Aeschylus, a native of Eleusis according to the biographical tradition, appropriately prays to Demeter that he be "worthy of your mysteries" (887: τῶν σῶν ἄξιον μυστηρίων), establishing his connection to traditional *polis* religion.⁸⁰ Euripides' prayer, by contrast, sets him entirely outside of the sphere of Athenian ritual, as he prays to gods that are "private ones, a new coinage" (890: ἴδιοί . . . κόμμα καινόν), a description that calls to mind the parabasis' coinage comparison, and so would associate Euripidean religion with the debased new currency:

---

78. The less valuable currency introduced in 407–6 was seen as a source of shame and a reminder of the parlous state of civic finances: Mark Griffith, *Aristophanes' "Frogs"* (Oxford: Oxford University Press, 2013), 46–48.

79. Aristophanes' advice appears to have been received enthusiastically and, according to an ancient tradition (which should be taken with a grain of salt), led to a second performance of the play, probably the next year. On the reperformance, see Alan H. Sommerstein, *Talking about Laughter and Other Studies in Greek Comedy* (Oxford: Oxford University Press, 2009), 258–64; Ralph M. Rosen, "Reconsidering the Reperformance of Aristophanes' 'Frogs,'" *Trends in Classics* 7 (2015): 237–56.

80. A scholion to *Frogs* 886 mentions Eleusis as Aeschylus' birthplace in explaining his prayer to Demeter; this may, though, be a biographical extrapolation from the text. There may be a hint of irony here, as Aeschylus was reported to have inadvertently revealed secrets connected to the Mysteries: Aristotle, *Nicomachean Ethics* 1111a8. A maximalist interpretation of Aeschylus' Eleusinian and Dionysiac connections is found in Lada-Richards, *Initiating Dionysus*, 234–54.

αἰθήρ ἐμὸν βόσκημα, καὶ γλώττης στρόφιγξ
καὶ ξύνεσι καὶ μυκτῆρες ὀσφραντήριοι,
ὀρθῶς μ' ἐλέγχειν ὧν ἂν ἅπτωμαι λόγων. (892–94)

Aether my nourishment, and pivot of tongue, and intellect, and keen-scented nostrils, may I rightly refute whatever arguments I take hold of.

Euripidean aerial theology has already been noted in Amphion's song, and here implies a radically novel pantheon. After *aether*, the divinities he addresses are strictly internal ones—tongue, intellect (*sunesis*, a key word later on), and nose—suggesting a conception of intelligence as lodged in the individual mind. To pray to these divinities marks Euripides, of course, as alien and strange, but also as drawing on a different form of wisdom from Aeschylus, one underpinned by individual intellection rather than divine authority.

The first series of exchanges lays out a relatively clear contrast between Aeschylus as a representative of the poetic tradition and Euripides as the disruptive innovator. Of particular interest is the way that each situates his work within the history of tragedy and poetry in general. In a balanced structure of speech, song, and choral interlude (the epirrhematic *agōn* proper), the poets argue over the value of poetic tradition and the proper role of the poet. Euripides begins with an assault not just on Aeschylus, but on the audiences of his time, whom he characterizes as "fools" (910: μώρους), easily impressed by long silences and bombastic language. Euripides portrays his rival as a "charlatan and cheater" (909: ἀλαζὼν καὶ φέναξ) who used deception (910: ἐξηπάτα) to prey on the crowd's lack of discrimination, awing them with strange and nonsensical phrases.[81] To Euripides, the moment of Aeschylean tragedy was no golden age at all, but a period of benighted spectators and primitive poetry.

Euripides' intervention, he claims, was to give greater sophistication both to the genre and to its audiences. He describes tragedy before him as a bloated body, which he put on a diet and trained with a regimen of exercise. The result was a more nimble, rational form, in which characters spoke clearly and could be drawn from across the social spectrum (949–50)—a "democratic" act (952), he claims. As Dionysus' surprised response suggests, this is a rather

---

81. Aristophanes' self-description in the parabasis of *Clouds* uses language that resonates with Euripides' attack on Aeschylus: he does not seek to deceive (ἐξαπατᾶν) the spectators by introducing (εἰσάγων) the same things, but always "acts cleverly by bringing in new forms" (546–47: καινὰς ἰδέας εἰσφέρων σοφίζομαι). See Hubbard, *The Mask of Comedy*, 92–105. I discuss ἀπάτη in relation to drama at length in chapter 2.

tendentious assertion from a poet who was known to have consorted with the tyrant Archelaus of Macedon (and may have died at the Macedonian court).[82] It is undisputed, however, that Euripides has changed his audience: "I taught these people [the audience] to chatter" (954: τουτουσὶ λαλεῖν ἐδίδαξα), he claims, and, moreover, to reason: "to think, to see, to understand, to turn . . . to scheme, to suspect bad, to consider all things" (957–58: νοεῖν, ὁρᾶν, ξυνιέναι, στρέφειν †ἐρᾶν† τεχνάζειν, / κάχ' ὑποτοπεῖσθαι, περινοεῖν ἅπαντα). The choice of words subtly exposes the negative side of such learning, suggesting that Euripides has made the citizens of the present cleverer, but at the expense of their trust in one another.

Euripides' claim to have taught the audience how to act and think in their own lives suggests a kind of leveling effect to his works, which moves poetry out of the realm of the obscure and mythological to the clear and everyday. Summing up, he sings,

> τοιαῦτα μέντούγὼ φρονεῖν
> τούτοισιν εἰσηγησάμην,
> λογισμὸν ἐνθεὶς τῇ τέχνῃ
> καὶ σκέψιν, ὥστ' ἤδη νοεῖν
> ἅπαντα καὶ διειδέναι
> τά τ' ἄλλα καὶ τὰς οἰκίας
> οἰκεῖν ἄμεινον ἢ πρὸ τοῦ
> κἀνασκοπεῖν, "πῶς τοῦτ' ἔχει;
> ποῦ μοι τοδί; τίς τοῦτ' ἔλαβε;" (971–79)

> In these ways I introduced thinking to these people, implanting reasoning and examination into my art, so that now they understand and comprehend everything, in particular how to manage their houses better than before and to watch out: "How is this doing? Where is that? Who took this?"

Euripides describes himself as an intellectual innovator, using the verb εἰσάγω ("lead in" or "introduce") that had been used of Amphion's music (F 183). The

---

82. On Euripides and democracy in *Frogs*, see Major, *The Court of Comedy*, 162–78. I think Major overstates the case against Euripides and the negative aspects of his portrayal in *Frogs*, but he is right to see this exchange, and the issue of democratic allegiances generally, as crucial for *Frogs*. On the putative journey to Macedon, see Scott Scullion, "Euripides and Macedon, or the Silence of the 'Frogs,'" *Classical Quarterly* 53 (2003): 389–400. Whether or not Euripides ended his life in Macedon (and I think Scullion's doubts should be taken seriously), he definitely staged an *Archelaus* tragedy that glorified the king's ancestry.

"thinking" (φρονεῖν) he has introduced, though, like Amphion's music, is controversial. His description is comically double-edged, employing hyperbolic language ("they understand and comprehend everything") to characterize investigation of the whereabouts of household possessions. Both sides of the *agōn*, however, will agree that his works have affected the intellectual life of the city. Euripides casts himself as a prime architect of Athens' intellectual modernity, suggesting that he acts as a kind of public sophist whose works offer an education grounded in doubt and reason. The question is whether this education and the society it shapes represent a positive development or an unfortunate degeneration.

When Aeschylus' turn comes, he does something unexpected: rather than launching into one of his celebrated tirades, he examines Euripides in quasi-forensic style. This elenchic method, associated with contemporary intellectuals, is one of a number of ways that Aeschylus will adapt characteristically "modern" discourse in the contest, even as his values remain defiantly old-fashioned. Answering Aeschylus' prompt to define poetic excellence, Euripides establishes a rare point of agreement between the poets: "[A poet should be admired for] skill and advice, and because we make people better in their cities" (1009–10: δεξιότητος καὶ νουθεσίας, ὅτι βελτίους γε ποιοῦμεν / τοὺς ἀνθρώπους ἐν ταῖς πόλεσιν). Even as other criteria are brought forward, this formulation goes essentially unchallenged through the rest of the *agōn*, which will ultimately turn on the capacity of each poet to give advice to the city. The question, which was already implicit in Euripides' case for himself, becomes, which poet has made the citizens of Athens better?

Aeschylus' perspective on the present state of affairs in Athens is, unsurprisingly, quite different from Euripides'. Instead of seeing contemporary Athenians as enlightened egalitarians, he describes them as "shirkers" (1014: διαδρασιπολίτας) and "soundrels" (1015: πανούργους), whose intellectual pursuits have made them soft and insubordinate (1070–72). In contrast, Aeschylus emphasizes the martial virtues of the citizens of his own time, and substantially claims credit for having made them "noble" (1019: γενναίους) by instilling these virtues. In combination with Aeschylus' reproaches against modern effeminacy and Euripides' staging of female characters, the gendering of these claims is notable (as it was in the confrontation of Zethus and Amphion).[83] Aeschylus describes his dramatic practice as continuous with the way that poetry has always instructed its audiences since time immemorial, citing the

---

83. On the gendered contrast, see Lada-Richards, *Initiating Dionysus*, 284–93.

teachings that can be gained from Orpheus, Musaeus, Hesiod, and Homer. All of them, he claims, have offered beneficial knowledge to their listeners. This reflects a different sense of improvement from that found in Euripides' speeches, which emphasized rational skills rather than the knowledge gained from poetry. Poets, Aeschylus believes, teach by more or less direct instruction, whereas to Euripides, they do so by improving their audience's intellect. This explains, also, Aeschylus' approach to morals in poetry: unlike Euripides, who portrays lustful women and undignified nobles, he believes "a poet must hide the wicked and not stage it or teach it" (1053–54: ἀποκρύπτειν χρὴ τὸ πονηρὸν τόν γε ποιητήν, / καὶ μὴ παράγειν μηδὲ διδάσκειν), treating the audience as a teacher would his pupils.[84] To Aeschylus, tragedy admonishes the public from an elevated position, while to Euripides, tragedy addresses the public as equals.[85] Their dispute hinges on whether poetic *sophia* is an exalted dispensation or a facet of everyday existence.

Aeschylus and Euripides agree on a historical narrative that sees a radical artistic and intellectual break taking place in the latter part of the fifth century. This break consists of a change in the relation between poetry and society, in which a traditional idea of poetry as exalted wisdom, associated with male nobility, is replaced by an idea of poetry as intellectual exercise, accessible, notionally, to all within society (though the sociology of poetry probably did not change substantially). This shift in the role of poetry and the poet is consistent with the narrative of *sophia* traced earlier in the chapter: what had earlier seemed an exclusive possession of a special, divinely ordained few becomes a more widespread, demonstrable capacity. The skill of the poet is now open to critical examination, where previously it could only be demonstrated.[86] The very form of the *agōn* takes place on the terms and in the language of this

---

84. Aeschylus' sentiment anticipates some of the censures of poetry in Plato: Richard Hunter, *Critical Moments in Classical Literature: Studies in the Ancient View of Literature and Its Uses* (Cambridge: Cambridge University Press, 2009), 27–29. Biles, *Aristophanes and the Poetics of Competition*, 245–49 points out that the view of poetry expressed in the parabasis seems much more akin to that of Aeschylus (despite its contemporary, more "Euripidean" subject matter).

85. Bruce Heiden, "Tragedy and Comedy in the 'Frogs' of Aristophanes," *Ramus* 20 (1991): 101–2.

86. In one of the most interesting recent readings of *Frogs*, Bassi reads the change in tragedy's social presence as closely connected to textualization, and argues that the play as a whole laments the "death" of the genre by sifting through its material remains: Karen Bassi, *Traces of the Past: Classics between History and Archaeology* (Ann Arbor: University of Michigan Press, 2016), 160–75.

new regime, but its content depicts the conflict of traditional and novel ideas of poetic *sophia*.

The chorus have a foot in both worlds. As a group of quasi-Eleusinian initiates, they have a natural sympathy for Aeschylus, and will occasionally comment in a nakedly partisan fashion.[87] At the same time, they also appear as products of the new, Euripidean learning, and their excited engagement in the contest and its subtleties suggests contemporary contexts of disputation.[88] In the choral song following the first part of the contest, they seem to endorse the poets' narrative of a change in the relation of poetry and its audience. This is also the first moment of the *agōn* when *sophia* is substantially thematized: *soph*-roots have been absent from the language of the poets, though they pervade comments on the contest.[89] The chorus admonish the disputants,

ὅ τι περ οὖν ἔχετον ἐρίζειν,
λέγετον, ἔπιτον, ἀνὰ <δὲ> δέρετον
τά τε παλαιὰ καὶ τὰ καινά,
κἀποκινδυνεύετον λεπτόν τι καὶ σοφὸν λέγειν. (1105–8)

So whatever you have to dispute, [go ahead and] argue, attack, expose the old and the new, and take a chance on speaking something subtle and wise.

The chorus' language reveals them as adepts of the new regime of *sophia*: they anticipate more *sophismata* (1104) to come, and encourage the contestants to "take a chance on speaking something subtle and wise," looking forward to ostentatious displays of cleverness from both poets. For the poets to "expose the old and the new" (the violent metaphor imagines flaying tragedy, from δέρω, "to skin") would be to reveal in the other what is outdated (παλαιός can suggest obsolescence) or merely trendy (καινός as "newfangled").[90] Success

---

87. The chorus' preference for Aeschylus appears notably at 1252–59 (which seems to present two versions of the same song), where they praise Aeschylean lyrics and refer to him as "the Bacchic lord" (1259: τὸν Βακχεῖον ἄνακτα), aligning him with Dionysus and the genre generally.

88. Halliwell points out the Euripidean slant to this language: Halliwell, *Between Ecstasy and Truth*, 132–33. On the chorus' identity and their position in relation to the Athens of the present, see Radcliffe G. Edmonds, *Myths of the Underworld Journey: Plato, Aristophanes, and the "Orphic" Gold Tablets* (Cambridge: Cambridge University Press, 2004), 138–47.

89. The only time either Aeschylus or Euripides use a *soph*-root is sarcastic (1154). The contest, though, has been prepared thoroughly using the language of *sophia*: 780, 806 (spoken by the Slave), 872 (Dionysus), 882, 896 (the chorus).

90. On attitudes to novelty, see Armand D'Angour, *The Greeks and the New: Novelty in Ancient Greek Imagination and Experience* (Cambridge: Cambridge University Press, 2011), esp. 184–206.

in the competition will entail reckoning with continuity and change in poetry and poetic *sophia*.

The chorus go on to situate themselves firmly in Aristophanes' present, and to portray themselves as enlightened, in contrast to the less intelligent audiences of the past:

> εἰ δὲ τοῦτο καταφοβεῖσθον, μή τις ἀμαθία προσῇ
> τοῖς θεωμένοισιν, ὡς τὰ λεπτὰ μὴ γνῶναι λεγόντοιν,
> μηδὲν ὀρρωδεῖτε τοῦθ᾽, ὡς οὐκέθ᾽ οὕτω ταῦτ᾽ ἔχει.
> ἐστρατευμένοι γάρ εἰσι,
> βιβλίον τ᾽ ἔχων ἕκαστος μανθάνει τὰ δεξιά·
> αἱ φύσεις τ᾽ ἄλλως κράτισται,
> νῦν δὲ καὶ παρηκόνηνται.
> μηδὲν οὖν δείσητον, ἀλλὰ
> πάντ᾽ ἐπέξιτον, θεατῶν γ᾽ οὕνεχ᾽, ὡς ὄντων σοφῶν. (1109–18)

> If you have any concern that ignorance is present among the spectators, so that they will not understand you two speaking subtleties, don't fear this, since it's no longer that way. For they are veterans, and each has a book and knows the fine points. Their natures, moreover, are very strong, and now they are even sharpened. So do not fear, but attack in all ways, because of the spectators, since they are wise.

The chorus here appear to endorse Euripides' view that the present age is more adept in thought and judgment. They present the content of poetry as highly demanding, requiring an audience that has learned to appreciate "subtleties" and knows "the fine points"—apparently from applying themselves diligently to their books.[91] The chorus claim to have become *sophoi* themselves, implying the democratization (or vulgarization) of *sophia* that both poets have pointed to.[92] As representatives of this new *sophia*, they seem a chorus of

---

91. The mention of a book (and Dionysus' mention of reading in the first scene) has attracted a great deal of attention surrounding issues of literacy; see Leonard Woodbury, "Aristophanes' 'Frogs' and Athenian Literacy: 'Ran.' 52–53, 1114," *Transactions of the American Philological Association* 106 (1975): 349–57; Greg Woolf, "Ancient Illiteracy?" *Bulletin of the Institute of Classical Studies* 58 (2015): 31–42.

92. The chorus seem also to appropriate Aeschylus' military language and conception of virtue for their own intellectual pursuits, describing themselves as "veterans" (1112: ἐστρατευμένοι, literally, "those who have served in the army"), and encouraging the poets to "attack" (1106: ἔπιτον, 1118: ἐπέξιτον).

Euripideans, pointing back to a persistent irony of the *agōn*: that it takes place on the grounds of new learning, and in a distinctively Euripidean form. This would have been even more obvious to the original theatrical audience, who were by and large too young to remember Aeschylus' lifetime (even if his plays may have been reperformed in Athens or the surrounding areas after his death).[93] In making his case for tradition, Aeschylus has to adapt himself to contemporary forms of criticism and argument, and prove that his own *sophia* remains valuable in the changing intellectual culture of the late fifth century.

Sophia and Salvation: *Frogs* (II)

While the first section of the contest had juxtaposed Aeschylus' traditional ethos and morality with Euripides' intellectual and cultural modernism, the second focuses on poetic, and especially musical, innovation. The contest moves on to stylistic discussions, and a series of criticisms and parodies, first of prologues and then of lyrics. Though Aeschylus had been portrayed as an opponent of the intellectual culture of the present, he takes part enthusiastically in one of its characteristic practices: the criticism of poetry on logical and stylistic grounds.[94] This represents a shift from his earlier attacks on Euripides, which had primarily concerned the morality of the transformation brought about by the younger poet's subject matter. The contest, though, quickly degenerates into blunt attacks and more or less clever parodies, in which Aeschylus and Euripides seem increasingly indistinguishable in their mode of argument.[95] At the same time, a contrast emerges relatively clearly, between the

---

93. See Zachary P. Biles, "Aeschylus' Afterlife: Reperformance by Decree in 5th C. Athens?" *Illinois Classical Studies* 31/32 (2007): 206–42; Johanna Hanink and Anna S. Uhlig, "Aeschylus and His Afterlife in the Classical Period: 'My Poetry Did Not Die with Me,'" in *The Reception of Aeschylus' Plays through Shifting Models and Frontiers*, ed. Stratos Constantinidis (Leiden: Brill, 2017), 51–79.

94. The first part of the discussion of prologues concerns "the correctness of the words" (1181: ὀρθότης τῶν ἐπῶν), a critical concern that seems to have been associated with Prodicus: Mayhew, *Prodicus the Sophist: Texts, Translations, and Commentary*, xiv–xvii. Criticism of poetry on logical grounds is central to the *Protagoras* discussion of Simonides, on which see Anne Carson, "How Not to Read a Poem: Unmixing Simonides from Protagoras," *Classical Philology* 87 (1992): 110–30; Glenn W. Most, "Simonides' Ode to Scopas in Contexts," in *Modern Critical Theory and Classical Literature*, ed. Irene J. F. de Jong and J. P. Sullivan (Leiden: Brill, 1994), 127–51.

95. Halliwell, *Between Ecstasy and Truth*, 134–37.

"high" style of Aeschylus, associated with grandeur, elevation, and obscurity, and the "low" style of Euripides, characterized by charm, simplicity, and clarity.[96] These contrasts, which have a long afterlife in literary criticism, broadly track the contrasts already noted between high and low social status, male and female, old and new.

In the contest that follows, Aeschylus is noticeably privileged: he receives the last word in all the major phases of the contest (which typically denotes success in Aristophanic *agōnes*), and shuts Euripides out in the "weighing of verses," the one test with a declared winner (and one that, not incidentally, he had initiated).[97] But when pressed to make a decision, Dionysus is unwilling and unable to do so, and a final series of tests yields no clarity on the logic of his ultimate choice.[98] This is one of the most striking aspects of the contest as a whole: after giving the audience every reason to expect a decision for Aeschylus, Dionysus continually defers this decision, and seems to confuse the opposition between the two poets. The language of *sophia* is at the center of this confusion, which begins with Dionysus' equivocation: "the one I consider wise, the other I enjoy" (1413: τὸν μὲν γὰρ ἡγοῦμαι σοφόν, τῷ δ' ἥδομαι). Who is meant by which phrase is unclear in the text (though it may have been indicated in performance), and has been a subject of controversy since antiquity.[99] The lack of clarity persists through the final test of advice, as Dionysus finds himself again unable to judge, "for one spoke wisely, the other clearly"

---

96. See Hunter, *Critical Moments*, 29–36; James I. Porter, *The Sublime in Antiquity* (Cambridge: Cambridge University Press, 2016), 322–27. Potential negative associations called up by Aeschylus' language are brought out in Elizabeth W. Scharffenberger, "'Deinon Eribremetas': The Sound and Sense of Aeschylus in Aristophanes' 'Frogs,'" *Classical World* 100 (2007): 229–49.

97. Aeschylus declares his intention to examine (1366: ἐξελέγξει) and test (1367: βασανιεῖ) the works of both poets, and the following scene seems to parody his own *Psychostasia*. On weighing and measuring as terms of critical discourse, see James I. Porter, *The Origins of Aesthetic Thought in Ancient Greece: Matter, Sensation, and Experience* (Cambridge: Cambridge University Press, 2010), 262–73.

98. The reasons for not reaching a decision shift: initially he says he does not want to incur the hatred of one (1411–12), but then he claims to be actually unable to decide (1433–44).

99. K. J. Dover, ed., *Aristophanes: "Frogs"* (Oxford: Oxford University Press, 1993), 19. On one hand, since Aeschylus has just won the contest of lines, one might think that he would be accorded the respect of being named *sophos*, while Euripides has been described as the object of enjoyment since Dionysus' desire sent him to Hades. On the other hand, it is Euripides who is most consistently associated with intellect and clarity, while the pleasure of Aeschylus' poetry has seemed to resist rational analysis.

(1434: ὁ μὲν σοφῶς γὰρ εἶπεν, ὁ δ' ἕτερος σαφῶς). Though this appears somewhat less problematic than the earlier statement—Euripides' advice was far more straightforward than Aeschylus'—there is again no verbal index of the distinction between the two, and, in the absence of clarifying stage business, Dionysus' statement might have been difficult to interpret. As discussed above, *soph*-words in the *agōn* have been most prominently used by the chorus, where the tendency was toward a contemporary, "Euripidean" usage. Here, though, this language is used in a way that suggests an ambiguity between Aeschylean and Euripidean *sophia*, if not an endorsement of Aeschylus. The language of *sophia* in the contest as a whole thus seems to be applicable, in different ways, to both poets—Euripides for his clear but trivial reasoning, Aeschylus for his profound obscurity.

The close of the contest, on my reading, does not furnish a clear decision between the two notions of *sophia*. It does, however, suggest a relatively clear criterion for Dionysus' choice (even if its application is somewhat obscure): the poet is to return to life "in order that the city, being saved, might stage choruses" (1419: ἵν' ἡ πόλις σωθεῖσα τοὺς χοροὺς ἄγῃ). As critics have noted, this represents a retrospective reimagining (if not an outright falsification) of what prompted Dionysus' journey in the first place.[100] On my reading, the incongruity is not so jarring given the course of the play: Dionysus' nostalgic desire for poetic restoration, noted earlier, cannot but evoke the parlous political state of Athens in 405, while in the *agōn* itself Aeschylus and Euripides had agreed on the role of the poet as civic advisor and improver and debated who better filled this role. Moreover, the issue of "salvation" (σωτηρία, recurring at 1436) has already been prepared by the presence of the chorus of initiates, who, as observers of the contest, mirror the political collective of the audience.[101] Dionysus' "longing" (53: πόθος) for Euripides was an individual one, but in making a choice between two poets, before the assembled multitude of Hades, his choice inevitably involves the entire community.

---

100. Halliwell, *Between Ecstasy and Truth*, 141–43. See also Heiden, "Tragedy and Comedy," 105–6.

101. See (on Eleusinian themes in the conclusion generally) Donald Sells, "Eleusis and the Public Status of Comedy in Aristophanes' 'Frogs,'" in *No Laughing Matter: Studies in Athenian Comedy*, ed. C. W. Marshall and George Kovacs (London: Bristol Classical Press, 2012), 83–99. The Eleusinian context is probably also significant for the question of Alcibiades, who in 415 had been condemned in absentia for profaning the Mysteries, but who, after returning in 407, had afforded military protection for the Mysteries, allowing them to be held in full for the first time in seven years.

The expectation that the poet should improve his fellow citizens motivates Dionysus to turn, in the final phase of the contest, for direct advice as to what Athens should do: first, in the specific case of Alcibiades, and then, more generally, in order to find salvation at a perilous moment in the Peloponnesian War. This portion of the contest is extremely difficult to parse because of textual difficulties, and there is substantial debate concerning which poet offers which piece of advice—itself an index of the difficulty of distinguishing between the two. What is important for my purposes, however, is that Dionysus never endorses any of the advice offered by either, and declares he will choose "the one whom my soul desires" (1468: ὅνπερ ἡ ψυχὴ θέλει), effectively refusing to claim a wider justification for his decision. There is no reason to think the impasse has been broken by the advice giving, or more broadly, that the political questions raised have been adjudicated. Yet the choice of Aeschylus is not a surprise: beyond the ways that he appears to gain the upper hand in the contest, selecting him is consistent with Dionysus' initial aim to restore poetry to its former glory. Dionysus does not explain the substantive reasons for his decision, but they have been apparent throughout the play. The surprise is how difficult the decision is.

Though it has fallen to Dionysus to adjudicate the contest, it is the chorus who offer the clearest justification for the decision—though one that bears only a vague relation to what Dionysus himself has expressed. Their song suggests, I argue, an attempt to reconcile the different visions of *sophia* expressed in the contest. As Aeschylus is led back to life, the chorus comment on the play's treatment of intellectual and musical innovation. Taking on the language of initiation, they celebrate the value of the intellectual to the community:

μακάριός γ' ἀνὴρ ἔχων
ξύνεσιν ἠκριβωμένην.
πάρα δὲ πολλοῖσιν μαθεῖν.
ὅδε γὰρ εὖ φρονεῖν δοκήσας
πάλιν ἄπεισιν οἴκαδ' αὖ,
ἐπ' ἀγαθῷ μὲν τοῖς πολίταις,
ἐπ' ἀγαθῷ δὲ τοῖς ἑαυτοῦ
ξυγγενέσι τε καὶ φίλοισιν,
διὰ τὸ συνετὸς εἶναι. (1482–90)

Blessed is the man who has intellect that has been made exact. It is possible to learn this in many ways. For this man, since he has been shown to think well, goes back home again, as a good to his fellow citizens, and as a good to his own family and friends, because of his being intelligent.

The lines contain, if not a direct allusion, at the very least a distinct echo of the choral *makarismos* assigned to the *Antiope*.[102] Here, the form of the *makarismos* is particularly appropriate to a chorus of initiates singing about the return to life of one of their own. As in the *Antiope* passage, their blessing is offered for reasons of intellection, and figures knowledge as a kind of initiation.[103] The referent of the blessing is clearly, in the first instance, Aeschylus, but the emphasis on purely intellectual qualities is surprising given his portrayal in the *agōn*. The quality he is praised for, "having precise intellect," has, moreover, been marked as a Euripidean one: he had addressed *sunesis* ("intellect," 891–92) in his opening prayer, and his clear, everyday language seems to be suggested by the phrase "made exact."[104] Even more emphatically than in the *Antiope* passage, where the inquirer was described as politically harmless, the ultimate end of such intelligence in *Frogs* is civic: it is "because of his being intelligent" (διὰ τὸ συνετὸς εἶναι) that he is able to benefit the community. The chorus supply a political logic for the choice of Aeschylus, but do so by attributing to him qualities that have hitherto been associated with Euripides.[105] The ode thus suggests a polar quality to *sunesis* similar to that we have observed operative in the uses of *soph*-roots: employing *sunesis* had earlier marked Euripides as a strange, innovating thinker; *to sunetos* is now used to mark traditional intellectual virtues associated with Aeschylus. The chorus' praise envisions the intellectual as a figure who combines Euripidean insight and Aeschylean values.[106]

---

102. Though on methodological grounds I do not pursue the question of direct influence, I think there is good reason to see the *Antiope* as an important hypotext for *Frogs*.

103. Aristophanes frequently includes *makarismoi*, including in *Clouds* a blessing of Strepsiades as σοφός (1207), which must be taken ironically. Though some irony may be present in the *Frogs* passage as well, the song is not quite so self-undermining.

104. The Euripidean quality of the phrase is noticed by Alan H. Sommerstein, ed., *Aristophanes: "Frogs"* (Oxford: Aris & Phillips, 1996), 294. See further Halliwell, *Between Ecstasy and Truth*, 150–53.

105. Daniela Battisti, "συνετός as Aristocratic Self-Description," *Greek, Roman, and Byzantine Studies* 31 (1990): 5–25.

106. Jedrkiewicz reads the strophe as directed toward an undefined, intelligent citizen spectator (rather than Aeschylus), and this generalizing quality is certainly present—but does not diminish the more obvious reference to Aeschylus: Stefano Jedrkiewicz, "Do Not Sit near Socrates (Aristophanes' 'Frogs,' 1482–1499)," in *Allusion, Authority, and Truth: Critical Perspectives on Greek Poetic and Rhetorical Praxis*, ed. Phillip Mitsis and Christos Tsagalis (Berlin: de Gruyter, 2010), 339–58.

The antistrophe goes on to describe the negative pole of intellectualism, a life of meaningless philosophical chatter:

χαρίεν οὖν μὴ Σωκράτει
παρακαθήμενον λαλεῖν,
ἀποβαλόντα μουσικὴν
τά τε μέγιστα παραλιπόντα
τῆς τραγῳδικῆς τέχνης.
τὸ δ' ἐπὶ σεμνοῖσιν λόγοισι
καὶ σκαριφησμοῖσι λήρων
διατριβὴν ἀργὸν ποιεῖσθαι,
παραφρονοῦντος ἀνδρός. (1491–99)

So it is not charming sitting beside Socrates to chatter, rejecting the arts and neglecting the greatest aspects of the tragic craft. To make an idle pastime with inflated words and the scratchings of nonsense is the act of man who is out of his mind.

The target here is obviously Euripides: the verb λαλεῖν ("to speak," but frequently in classical Greek, "to chatter") has been associated with him from early in the play, and Euripides himself claimed that he taught people how to λαλεῖν (954).[107] He is also, at least in comic contexts, frequently connected with Socrates, with the verb "sit beside" suggesting an intimate gathering of like-minded thinkers, an implicit contrast to the political activities of the inquirer of the strophe.[108] The heart of the chorus' condemnation seems to be that such intellectualism constitutes an abandonment of *mousikē* generally, and of tragedy in particular. This is an extreme position, which seems difficult to square with the relative balance of the *agōn*, but it recalls Dionysus' complaints in the opening scene about the contemporary state of tragedy and his desire to restore poetry—only now with a different poet. Despite the chorus' praise of *sunesis* in the strophe, they seem to reject philosophical activity

---

107. Other associations of Euripides with *lalia* are at 839 (ἀπερίλάλητος, "unable to chatter," as a negative characterization of Aeschylus), 917 (associating the verb with tragic poets in the present), 1069 (λαλιά, "chatter" as the content of Euripides' works).

108. The early version of Aristophanes' *Clouds* associates Euripides and Socrates in their *sophia* and *lalia*: "This is the man [Socrates], the one writing tragedies for Euripides, the talkative, clever ones" (F 392: Εὐριπίδῃ δ' ὁ τὰς τραγῳδίας ποιῶν / τὰς περιλαλούσας οὗτός ἐστι, τὰς σοφάς). Further comic quotations on their connection are reported in Diogenes Laertius 2.18.

in unequivocal terms, associating it with idleness (as Amphion's music was too), pomposity, and even madness. At the same time, their disdain for "inflated words" uses an adjective, *semnos* ("grave" or "pompous"), that has persistently been used in connection with Aeschylus, whose speech was described as lofty and elevated.[109] It is thus hard to align the terms of praise and blame entirely with the two poets—neither of whom, after all, is even mentioned in the song. The chorus praise a composite of the two, rejecting esoteric speculation, but praising a measured, socially embedded intellectualism. Their *makarismos* of the intellectual thus suggests a reconciliation of the *agōn*'s competing claims to *sophia*.

This reconciliation, I suggest, can further be understood as a form of generic self-reflection. In praising the *sunesis* of the tragedian, *Frogs* suggests an ideal of the comedian as well. I have noted how Dionysus' desire for poetic restoration is consistent with the parabasis' recommendation of political reenfranchisement, and this congruence suggests a broader association of Dionysus with the comic voice itself.[110] Another parallel is suggested by the parodos, in which the chorus reject anyone not "initiated in the Bacchic rites of the tongue of bull-eating Cratinus" (357: Κρατίνου τοῦ ταυροφάγου γλώττης Βακχεῖ' ἐτελέσθη), figuring the knowledge of comedy as a Dionysiac initiation. Though the play's extensive metadramatic discourse focuses on tragedy much more than comedy, one can see the tragic poets taking on qualities of the comedian in their parodies of one another's lyrics. Even more striking in this respect is the advice giving of the final scene, which casts tragedy in the political role of comedy, as the tragedians offer direct advice, just as the parabasis had done.[111] The choral *makarismos*, then, would present an ideal of the comic poet as much as the tragic one—and, indeed, this ideal may be closer to reality than the surprising conjunction of traits praised in the tragedian. The blessed comedian would be one whose intellect is as penetrating as Euripides, with an Aeschylean sense of civic obligation. He would offer

---

109. Aeschylus' *semnotēs* is suggested by 833 (ἀποσεμνυνεῖται, "act solemn" or "pompous"), 1004 (Aeschylus as producer of σεμνά, "solemn" words), 1020 (Aeschylus σεμνυνόμενος, "acting pompous"), 1061 (Aechylus claiming that heroes should be dressed in ἱματίοις ... σεμνοτέροισιν, "more solemn clothes").

110. The reflection of the figure Dionysus on comedy is explored differently in Heiden, "Tragedy and Comedy."

111. Something like the parabasis' recommendation is given as advice in the final scene (1441–50), though it is disputed whether it comes from Euripides or Aeschylus. Different reconstructions are found in Sommerstein, "*Frogs*," 286–88; Dover, "*Frogs*," 373–76.

responsible political advice in everyday language, and his wisdom would contribute to saving the city and upholding its dramatic tradition in a devalued present—a description of the *sophos* that unmistakably characterizes Aristophanes' poetic persona.

Reasoning Divinity: *Bacchae* (I)

A few months after *Frogs* was performed at the Lenaea festival of 405, Dionysus appeared onstage again at the City Dionysia in *Bacchae*, as part of Euripides' final trilogy, staged posthumously by his son.[112] And again, a central issue of the drama is the meaning of *sophia*, which is disputed in a series of agonistic scenes. The rest of this chapter will seek to make the case that there is an important connection between Dionysus and the question of *sophia* at the end of the fifth century, for which *Bacchae* is our best evidence. The importance of Dionysus for questions of *sophia* comes, I argue, from the god's polar quality: born to a human mother, he is nevertheless a god; a latecomer to the pantheon, he is nevertheless a figure of veneration; an outsider among the Olympian gods, he creates and solidifies forms of human community. His worship embodies tensions between human and divine, old and new, individual and community—tensions that condition the meanings of *sophia* as well. Within *Bacchae*, the figure of Dionysus complicates the opposition between traditional and novel *sophia* for the simple reason that he is (within the dramatic frame of the play) a strange new appearance who is at the same time (within the ritual framing of the performance) a venerable divinity.[113] The polar quality of the god makes him a focal point for articulating the late fifth century's inquiry into modernity, which is likewise defined by a paradoxical consciousness of continuity and rupture.

---

112. A scholion to *Frogs* 67 relates the posthumous performance of *Bacchae*, along with *Iphigenia at Aulis* and *Alcmaeon in Corinth* at the City Dionysia, and the most likely date for this is 405, since the Dionysia would take place only on a reduced scale in 404, and would have been substantially interrupted in the following two years by the tyranny and restoration of democracy, returning to its earlier form only in 401 with the performance of Sophocles' *Oedipus at Colonus*: Johanna Hanink, "The Great Dionysia and the End of the Peloponnesian War," *Classical Antiquity* 33 (2014): 319–46. Biographical sources report that Euripides had left Athens for Macedon, where he died, on which see Scullion, "Euripides and Macedon."

113. On the paradox, see David Kovacs, "New Religion and Old in Euripides' 'Bacchae,'" in *Looking at Bacchae*, ed. David Stuttard (London: Bloomsbury, 2016), 29–41.

This new-and-old character of Dionysus, I argue, is linked to the central anomaly of *Bacchae*: the copresence of elements suggesting archaism and avant gardism. In its form, *Bacchae* is an archaizing work: its simple plot likely comes directly from Aeschylus' Dionysiac plays (which its language frequently recalls), it involves the chorus and choral song much more fully in the action than most late Euripides does (and includes almost no actor's song), and its language even appears to follow stricter metrical rules than Euripides' other works of the same period.[114] At the same time, *Bacchae* strikingly incorporates elements of its contemporary culture and generic possibilities of the late fifth century: a concern with incorporating new cultic practices, a proximity to comedy, and, most important for this chapter, the prominence and self-consciousness of intellectual themes.[115] *Bacchae* seems to exist in multiple temporalities at once, an effect that I have argued is connected to the dual role of Dionysus as both the subject of the drama and the ritual occasion of its performance.[116] As a drama both about and for Dionysus, *Bacchae* is saturated with the polarities of the god himself.

114. On *Bacchae*'s relation to Aeschylus, see Georgia Xanthaki-Karamanou, "The 'Dionysiac' Plays of Aeschylus and Euripides' 'Bacchae': Reaffirming Traditional Cult in Late Fifth Century," in *Crisis on Stage: Tragedy and Comedy in Late Fifth-Century Athens*, ed. Andreas Markantonatos and Bernhard Zimmermann (Berlin: de Gruyter, 2012), 323–42; Alan H. Sommerstein, "'Bacchae' and Earlier Tragedy," in *Looking at "Bacchae,"* ed. David Stuttard (London: Bloomsbury, 2016), 29–41. On the musical design: Eric Csapo, "Later Euripidean Music," *Illinois Classical Studies* 24/25 (2000): 405–15; Naomi A. Weiss, *The Music of Tragedy: Performance and Imagination in Euripidean Theater* (Berkeley: University of California Press, 2018), 241–46. On metrical criteria: A. M. Devine and Laurence D. Stephens, "A New Aspect of the Evolution of the Trimeter in Euripides," *Transactions of the American Philological Association* 111 (1981): 43–64.

115. On new cult practices, see H. S. Versnel, *Inconsistencies in Greek and Roman Religion, Volume I: Ter Unus. Isis, Dionysos, Hermes. Three Studies in Henotheism* (Leiden: Brill, 1990); Rubel, *Stadt in Angst*, 233–61. On the proximity to comedy: Helene P. Foley, "Generic Boundaries in Late Fifth-Century Athens," in *Performance, Iconography, Reception: Studies in Honour of Oliver Taplin*, ed. Martin Revermann and Peter Wilson (Oxford: Oxford University Press, 2008), 15–36; Craig Jendza, *Paracomedy*, esp. 108–18.

116. Joshua Billings, "'Bacchae,'" in *Brill's Companion to Euripides*, ed. Andreas Markantonatos (Leiden: Brill, forthcoming). See further Barbara Kowalzig, "'And Now All the World Shall Dance!' Dionysus' Choroi between Drama and Ritual," in *The Origins of Theater in Ancient Greece and Beyond*, ed. Eric Csapo and Margaret C. Miller (Cambridge: Cambridge University Press, 2007), 221–51; Anton Bierl, "Maenadism as Self-Referential Chorality in Euripides' 'Bacchae,'" in *Choral Mediations in Greek Tragedy*, ed. Renaud Gagné and Marianne Govers Hopman (Cambridge: Cambridge University Press, 2013), 211–26.

Like *Frogs*, *Bacchae* takes the basic form of the *agōn* and expands its scope massively, turning it from a discrete scene type into a structuring principle for much of the work. The *agōn* of *Bacchae*, for the purposes of this chapter, is understood not as a single scene, but as a series of confrontations between the Stranger and Pentheus, which begin as highly disputatious, but gradually (and ominously) shift toward cooperation. At the center of the play are three successive episodes featuring these two characters (with the brief appearance of an attendant and a longer interruption by a messenger), a construction that is unique within Euripides' corpus for its economy, and which allows the confrontation of the two figures to play out as an extended *agōn*. Though not *agōnes* in the tradition sense, each scene presents a relatively matched (at least in terms of spoken lines) juxtaposition of the two protagonists. What they lack, which is often characteristic of agonistic scenes in Euripides generally, are substantial *rheseis* and rhetorical self-consciousness, such as one finds in the formal *agōn* of Teiresias, Cadmus, and Pentheus, which draws flagrantly on contemporary philosophical thought.[117] But this is not to say that the confrontations between Dionysus and Pentheus lack such self-consciousness: rather, I suggest, this is concentrated most of all around the language of *sophia*, which pervades not only their three agonistic scenes, but the play as a whole. It is this self-consciousness that most links *Bacchae* to the *agōnes sophias* of *Antiope*, *Palamedes*, and *Frogs*: different understandings of *sophia* are opposed, and through their opposition, the play explores the place of intellectual activity in a time of radical change.

The language of *sophia* is employed liberally throughout *Bacchae*, in contexts agonistic and otherwise. As in *Frogs*, reflection on intellectual activity is concentrated especially in the role of the chorus, whose utterances offer both direct commentary on the action and general reflection on the meaning of *sophia*. My discussion will proceed in three stages: first, it will consider the way the discourse of *sophia* is established in the first episode, when Teiresias, Cadmus, and Pentheus debate the new god and his worship. Then it will move on to the central confrontations between Dionysus and Pentheus, which span the third, fourth, and fifth episodes, to consider the agonistic uses of *soph*-words. Finally, it will turn to the choral songs and their famously difficult language of τὸ σοφόν, which I argue must be understood in relation to the polar quality of *soph*-roots in the play as a whole. By situating the chorus' discourse of *sophia*

---

117. The scene is categorized as a formal *agōn* by Duchemin, *L'Agon dans la tragédie grecque*, 73–74; Dubischar, *Die Agonszenen bei Euripides*, 72.

within the play's representation of intellectual activity more generally, we are able to understand better *Bacchae*'s puzzling modernity.

The seer Teiresias is as traditional a representative of the *sophos* as it is possible to imagine: venerated in Thebes for his mantic gifts, he is a familiar figure on the tragic stage, who often comes into conflict with the ruling powers because of his prophetic knowledge.[118] He is characterized as σοφός three times by his interlocutor Cadmus (another venerable figure, though less known for *sophia*) in the first lines of their exchange.[119] But there is an incongruity to the portrayal of both old men: appearing in the dress of Bacchants, ready to set out for the mountains, they are, in the words of Pentheus, "very laughable" (250: πολὺν γέλων).[120] The incongruities are heightened in a controversial passage in which Teiresias, prompted by Cadmus' avowal of his respect for the gods, appears to disavow σοφίζεσθαι ("acting wise") and τὸ σοφόν (literally, "the wise") in divine matters:

ΚΑ. οὐ καταφρονῶ 'γὼ τῶν θεῶν θνητὸς γεγώς.
ΤΕ. οὐδὲν σοφιζόμεσθα τοῖσι δαίμοσιν.
πατρίους παραδοχάς, ἅς θ' ὁμήλικας χρόνῳ
κεκτήμεθ', οὐδεὶς αὐτὰ καταβαλεῖ λόγος,
οὐδ' εἰ δι' ἄκρων τὸ σοφὸν ηὕρηται φρενῶν.[121] (199–203)

Cadmus. I do not disdain the gods, being a mortal. *Teiresias.* We do not act wise in relation to the gods. The paternal traditions, as old as time, which we have acquired, no word will strike down, not even if the wise were found by the heights of intellect.

The passage presents a number of linguistic difficulties, and is bracketed in its entirety in Diggle's Oxford Classical Text, an extreme and unprecedented

---

118. The recurrent conflict between Teiresias and a city's ruler is treated in Gherardo Ugolini, *Untersuchungen zur Figur des Sehers Teiresias* (Tübingen: Narr, 1995), 117–50.

119. 178–79: "Listening I perceived your voice, wise, from a wise man" (σὴν γῆρυν ᾐσθόμην / κλυὼν / σοφὴν σοφοῦ παρ' ἀνδρός); 186: "for you are wise" (σὺ γὰρ σοφός).

120. On the comic dimension (which would have relied in part on the staging), see Bernd Seidensticker, "Comic Elements in Euripides' 'Bacchae,'" *American Journal of Philology* 99 (1978): 303–20. See further Bernd Seidensticker, "The Figure of Teiresias in Euripides' 'Bacchae,'" in *Wisdom and Folly in Euripides*, ed. Poulheria Kyriakou and Antonios Rengakos (Berlin: de Gruyter, 2016), 275–83.

121. The division of lines between Cadmus and Teiresias is difficult; Kovacs prints lines 199–200 as Cadmus', and assumes that a line is lost from the beginning of Teiresias' speech answering.

editorial decision.[122] The lines have been thought to present problems of interpretation, on two grounds: first, Teiresias appears to be defending "paternal traditions" while celebrating a new god; and second, his rejection of clever reasoning may be contradicted by his "sophistic" explanation of stories concerning Dionysus' birth later on in the scene. These incongruities, I suggest, are real, but can best be understood as emergent from the complexities of *sophia* in the play as a whole: it is characteristic, we will see, of Dionysiac *sophia* that it appears to be both new and old at once.

The paradox of a new "paternal tradition" is of a piece with the incongruity of Teiresias' and Cadmus' attire noted above: because of the novelty of Dionysiac worship, the authorities of old take on new customs. The transformation is surprising, but it is not necessarily contradictory, especially if one understands "paternal traditions" to relate to an attitude of respect toward the gods, rather than the specifics of worship—as is suggested by the affirmation "I do not disdain the gods." The opposite relation to divinity is characterized by the verb σοφίζεσθαι, "to act wise," which would be to seek to explain away what is strange and mysterious in divinity with rationalizing stories of the gods.[123] The verb used for this threat, καταβάλλω, evokes contemporary thought: a work with the name Καταβάλλοντες ("overthrowings": B1 DK/D10 LM) was attributed to Protagoras, which seems to have used a doctrine of relativism to "overthrow" common beliefs (and would have been informed by his agnosticism concerning divinity).[124] καταβάλλειν may not be quite technical terminology, but in the late fifth-century context it clearly suggests the skeptical results of intellectual speculation. Such investigation, according to

---

122. The most problematic feature of the text as transmitted is its asyndeton (between 199 and 200, and between 200 and 201). A number of emendations have been proposed, the most convincing (and modest) of which is Musgrave's οὐδ᾽ ἐνσοφιζόμεσθα, which involves a different word division and resolves the first asyndeton without substantially altering the text or the sense. The difficulty is that the verb ἐνσοφίζεσθαι, while plausible, is nowhere attested (though it has the advantage of explaining the dative, which is otherwise difficult with σοφίζεσθαι). Even if the lines require mending, there is no good reason to see them as an interpolation. For a defense of the transmitted text, see Albert Rijksbaron, *Grammatical Observations on Euripides' "Bacchae"* (Amsterdam: J. C. Gieben, 1991), 34–36.

123. A similar usage of σοφίζεσθαι is found in Plato's *Phaedrus* (229c), where Socrates describes it as an activity characteristic of those who disbelieve traditional stores.

124. Sextus Empiricus, *Against the Mathematicians* 7.60 suggests the book began with the famous "man is the measure" statement, though the text containing this passage is also known as *Truth*. Most likely, multiple titles circulated in antiquity, but the terminology is likely to be Protagorean regardless of which title (if either) he used.

Teiresias, seeks to discover τὸ σοφόν, an unusual substantive that will recur in three choral passages, where its meaning is the subject of significant critical dispute. I will have much more to say about it later in the chapter, but my suggestion is to take it quite straightforwardly: as a substantive derived from the adjective σοφός, τὸ σοφόν would mean something like "the wise" or "wisdom" in the abstract. Such wisdom is the goal of high-flown intellect, Teiresias claims, but even if this height of inquiry were reached, it would be in conformity with paternal traditions—a nuance lost on many critics, who understand τὸ σοφόν here as necessarily hostile to religion. On the contrary, Teiresias asserts that intellect and traditional religion are ultimately congruent.[125]

In the denial that he "acts *sophos* in relation to the gods," Teiresias does not thereby reject all speculation or heightened intellectual activity; as the scene goes on to show, he is himself quite adept at reasoning concerning divinity—though, crucially, not with the aim of "overthrowing" established beliefs. In response to Pentheus' tirade, he offers a eulogy of Dionysus and Demeter (275–85) as grain and wine, respectively, identifying the gods with their most important natural manifestations. This passage has often been thought to evoke the ideas of Prodicus, who suggested that belief in gods, and specifically Dionysus and Demeter, arose from the attribution of divinity to beneficial natural occurrences.[126] For Prodicus, this reasoning offered a naturalistic explanation of religion in general, and may have led to an atheistic outlook.[127] Teiresias, however, does not address the origin of belief in the gods in any way, so a better way of understanding his relation to contemporary thought might be as a parallel development of a naturalizing view of divinity, already apparent in the identification of Zeus and *aether*, and which is pursued at length in the

---

125. On the figure of Teiresias as a figure of both intellect and traditional religion, see Paul Roth, "Teiresias as Mantis and Intellectual in Euripides' 'Bacchae,'" *Transactions of the American Philological Association* 114 (1984): 56–69; Mastronarde, "Optimistic Rationalist."

126. Mayhew, *Prodicus the Sophist: Texts, Translations, and Commentary*, xvii–xviii. Texts 70–78 collect the evidence (compare B5 DK/D15–18 LM). There is some question as to exactly how Prodicus imagined this process, but it is not material to this discussion. There is a suggestion in Philodemus, *On Piety* 1 that Prodicus' explanation of divinity may have relied not just on naturalizing divinity, but on etymology as well—which would make Teiresias' etymologizing doubly interesting.

127. Prodicus was often cited as destroying belief in divinity: the earliest known instance is Philodemus, *On Piety* 1. There is, though, a minority strand (represented by Themistius, *Oration* 30.349a–b) that seems to see Prodicus' views as consistent with belief in divinity. Teiresias, to the extent he is a Prodicean, clearly belongs to this latter strand.

Derveni Papyrus.[128] Teiresias takes the identification of divinity with natural phenomena for granted (which is precisely what Prodicus did not do) and sees Dionysus and Demeter as the sources of agriculture and all the goods that flow from it. The thrust of his identification of divinity with nature is thus supportive of traditional piety.[129] Indeed, if we imagine that naturalizing viewpoints like those of Prodicus were circulating at the time, Teiresias' intervention would be to use them in a theologically constructive, rather than skeptical, way: he accepts the close identification of divinity with natural occurrences, but rejects the historical speculation that posits this as the origin of belief in the gods.

In an even more ostentatious intellectual display, Teiresias addresses Pentheus' ridicule (243–45) of the idea that Dionysus was sewn into Zeus' thigh by offering a correction to the story.[130] He explains that Dionysus was not in fact sewn into Zeus' thigh (μηρός), but that the story arose because a portion (μέρος) of *aether* was given to Hera in place of the baby Dionysus as a hostage (ὅμηρος), leading humans to invent the story of the thigh-birth (286–97). The explanation is certainly strange, and may be comical, but myth-correction was a common enough intellectual activity, with deep roots in Greek culture.[131] Like many such corrections, Teiresias' serves pious goals, defending the anomalous divine birth of Dionysus, while at the same time removing the bizarre (and potentially effeminizing) image of birth from Zeus' thigh. The explanation presents a strong contrast to the rationalizing activity Teiresias had rejected, in that it does not in any way "overthrow" the tradition of Dionysus' divinity, but seeks on the contrary to secure it from attacks like the one Pentheus has just launched. It is much more Pentheus' scorn toward the traditional story that constitutes "acting wise in relation to the gods" by subjecting an accepted story to skeptical

---

128. See Gábor Betegh, *The Derveni Papyrus: Cosmology, Theology and Interpretation* (Cambridge: Cambridge University Press, 2004), 182–223.

129. There is a parallel in the Derveni Papyrus Col. 22, where the commentator explains that Demeter and Gē/Gaia are the same by etymology. Teiresias asserts their identity (275–76) by naturalizing Demeter as earth itself: Seaford, *Euripides: "Bacchae,"* 175–76.

130. The passage has occasionally been deleted on the grounds that it seems to contradict the chorus' narrative of Dionysus' birth at 94–99 and 521–27, both of which describe Dionysus sewn into Zeus' thigh. On the various stories, see David D. Leitao, *The Pregnant Male as Myth and Metaphor in Classical Greek Literature* (Cambridge: Cambridge University Press, 2012), 81–99.

131. Myth correction was a well-established feature of Greek thought, and there is no reason to see it as especially sophistic: Pindar, *Olympian* 1 famously offers a correction to the story of Pelops. See the essays in Martin Vöhler and Bernd Seidensticker, eds., *Mythenkorrekturen: Zu einer paradoxalen Form der Mythenrezeption* (Berlin: de Gruyter, 2005).

critique. Teiresias clearly reasons in ways that evoke contemporary intellectuals, but he places his speculations in the service of traditional divine authority.[132] His "sophistic" reasoning, then, is consistent with his rejection of "acting wise in relation to the gods": intellectual sophistication is not itself the danger, but rather, the misuse of intellect to overthrow traditional piety.

In the confrontations of the Stranger and Pentheus, we see shifting uses of *soph*-roots to denote both the traditional wisdom of divine authority (in the Stranger's uses) and the cleverness of human intellect (in Pentheus'), which is strongly associated with novelty.[133] This presents significant difficulties of translation: rendering σοφός as "clever" when used pejoratively and "wise" when used positively (as many translators do) confuses the essential continuity between the uses: what appears to Pentheus as dangerously novel *sophia* is precisely what the Stranger describes as established wisdom. It is significant that both uses are only ever predicated of the Stranger and Dionysiac worship (Pentheus is never described with a *soph*-root), so they track the protagonists' opposing views of the new religious practice.[134]

The different ideas of *sophia* are evident from the first confrontation of Pentheus and the Stranger. Both in this scene and in the previous one, with Cadmus and Teiresias, Pentheus has repeatedly drawn attention to the newness of the god: he is a "new divinity" (256: νέος δαίμων) bringing a "new disease" (353–54: νόσον / καινήν).[135] And his follower, Pentheus recognizes, possesses the same newfangled intellect in evading questions about Dionysus and his cult:

---

132. Segal reads Teiresias' rationalizing language as patently inadequate to the realities of Dionysiac worship: Charles Segal, *Dionysiac Poetics and Euripides' "Bacchae,"* expanded ed. (Princeton: Princeton University Press, 1997), 297–305.Though I have emphasized the incongruities in Teiresias' portrayal, I see this in more constructive terms, as representing a plausible defense of Dionysus in the language of contemporary thought. Teiresias' "rationalism" is not necessarily opposed to the mystery of divinity, as Segal argues.

133. The different usages have been noted many times before. See Valdis Leinieks, *The City of Dionysus: A Study of Euripides' "Bakchai"* (Stuttgart: Teubner, 1996), 257–76; Origa, *Le contraddizioni della sapienza*, 89–91.

134. Hutchinson points out that an interest in the *sophia* of the gods (as opposed to human) is distinctively Euripidean: G. O. Hutchinson, "Gods Wise and Foolish: Euripides and Greek Literature from Homer to Plutarch," in *Wisdom and Folly in Euripides*, ed. Poulheria Kyriakou and Antonios Rengakos (Berlin: de Gruyter, 2016), 37–44.

135. Compare 216–19: there are "new evils" (νεοχμὰ . . . κακά) in the city, brought by a "new divinity" (νεωστὶ δαίμονα); and 467: does Zeus bear "new gods" (νέους . . . θεούς)? See D'Angour, *The Greeks and the New*, 157–61.

ΠΕ. ὁ θεός, ὁρᾶν γὰρ φὴς σαφῶς, ποῖός τις ἦν;
ΔΙ. ὁποῖος ἤθελ'· οὐκ ἐγὼ 'τασσον τόδε.
ΠΕ. τοῦτ' αὖ παρωχέτευσας, εὖ γ' οὐδὲν λέγων.
ΔΙ. δόξει τις ἀμαθεῖ σοφὰ λέγων οὐκ εὖ φρονεῖν. (477–80)

Pentheus. The god, you say you saw him clearly, what was he like? *Dionysus*. As he wished to be. I did not command him in this way. *P*. You diverted this again, saying nothing well. *D*. Someone speaking wise things appears to an ignorant person not to think well.

The accusation that the Stranger has "diverted" (παρωχέτευσας, usually used of bodies of water) Pentheus speaks to a conception of his intellect as powerful and unnatural. In response, the Stranger asserts that there are more "wise things" (σοφά) in what he says than Pentheus has recognized. In the Stranger's mouth, this evokes the norms of ritual speech, which to the uninitiated appear as nonsense—or as mere sophistry. As in the *Antiope*, the word for such vacuous intellectualisms is *sophismata*, and Pentheus a few lines later threatens, "You must pay the penalty for your evil *sophismata*" (489: δίκην σε δοῦναι δεῖ σοφισμάτων κακῶν).[136] The Stranger's response retains the theme of intellect, but turns it, as before, against Pentheus' ἀμαθία ("ignorance," with the connotation of not being initiated): "And you [must pay] for your ignorance and for dishonoring the god" (490: σὲ δ' ἀμαθίας γε κἀσεβοῦντ' ἐς τὸν θεόν). Pentheus recognizes the *sophia* of the Stranger but understands it as facile cleverness, while the Stranger insists on the divine foundation of his wisdom.

The next encounter, elevating the tension of the first, takes place after the Palace Miracles have freed the Stranger from captivity. It makes particularly plain the opposed usages of the language of *sophia*. Seeing Pentheus entering angrily, the Stranger emphasizes his own *sophia*, which is connected to levelheadedness: "It is the part of a wise man to practice sound good temper" (641: πρὸς σοφοῦ γὰρ ἀνδρὸς ἀσκεῖν σώφρον' εὐοργησίαν). The Stranger's calm in the face of high emotion and danger is repeatedly emphasized throughout the scenes of confrontation, and finds a particularly stark contrast in Pentheus' high dudgeon. Repeatedly tripped up in his attempt to interrogate the Stranger, Pentheus sputters, "You are *sophos, sophos*, except in that in which you ought to be *sophos*" (653: σοφὸς σοφὸς σύ, πλὴν ἃ δεῖ σ' εἶναι σοφόν). Pentheus sees

---

136. Dionysus in the prologue reports that daughters of Cadmus claimed that it was due to the *sophismata* of Cadmus (30) that Zeus was named as the person who impregnated Semele, as a means of shielding her from shame—again implying underhanded cleverness.

the Stranger's intellect as removed from any constructive uses, a form of partial or superficial *sophia*, characterized especially by novelty: a few lines earlier he had accused the Stranger of "always introducing newfangled stories" (650: τοὺς λόγους γὰρ ἐσφέρεις καινοὺς ἀεί).[137] These stories, of course, relate to the divinity of Dionysus, which Pentheus regards as a strange and dangerous falsehood. To Pentheus, the Stranger's *sophia* consists in the verbal skill that enables him to cloak his new practices in the mantle of divine authority and tradition. In response, the Stranger seeks to impress the traditional, established character of Dionysiac worship on Pentheus. To the charge of overcleverness, he responds, "In those things that are most important, I was born *sophos*" (654: ἃ δεῖ μάλιστα, ταῦτ' ἔγωγ' ἔφυν σοφός). The Stranger's claim for the natural quality of his wisdom—an ironic understatement given his real identity— serves as a reproach to the idea that it is something novel. His *sophia*, as the audience knows, comes from his divine birth, and is connected to the most fundamental sources of authority.

When Pentheus comes under the Stranger's spell, he finally recognizes, in an ironic and eerie reversal, the Stranger's *sophia*. With a surprising readiness, Pentheus assents to the suggestion that he go to Cithaeron in female dress:

ΠΕ. εὖ γ' εἶπας αὖ τόδ'· ὥς τις εἶ πάλαι σοφός.
ΔΙ. Διόνυσος ἡμᾶς ἐξεμούσωσεν τάδε. (824–25)

Pentheus. You spoke these things again well. How wise a man you have been all along. *Dionysus.* Dionysus trained me in these things.

The recognition that the Stranger is *sophos* carries with it an acceptance of the established quality of his wisdom. As the Stranger contends, his knowledge is directly connected to worship: the verb ἐκμουσόω, related to *mousikē*, in the Stranger's reply suggests a connection to ritual celebration (and possibly even initiation specifically). Of course, this is precisely what the Stranger has claimed and Pentheus has strenuously denied up until this point. Only here, when it is too late, does Pentheus recognize the intellectual and religious authority of his antagonist. A few lines later, he accepts the Stranger's reasoning that "it is wiser [to go as a spy] than to hunt evils with evils" (839: σοφώτερον γοῦν ἢ κακοῖς θηρᾶν κακά), again attributing to the Stranger the *sophia* that is

---

137. Compare 353–54: the Stranger "introduces [literally: brings in] a new disease" (ἐσφέρει νόσον / καινήν), using the same verb. Similarly, in the *Antiope*, Amphion had been accused of introducing (F 183: εἰσάγων) his novel muse, and Euripides in *Frogs* claimed that he introduced (972: εἰσηγησάμην) capacities for thought to the Athenians.

about to destroy him. This is echoed in the play's final use of the adjective, when Agaue claims exultantly that "the wise Bacchic hunter wisely urged the maenads against this beast" (1189–91: ὁ Βάκχιος κυναγέτας / σοφὸς σοφῶς ἀνέπηλ' ἐπὶ θῆρα / τόνδε μαινάδας). σοφός here carries the same troubling truth to it: Dionysus' *sophia* is demonstrated to humans in the act of destruction. As if to ratify this emergent understanding, the messenger who reports Pentheus' awful death closes his speech by saying,

τὸ σωφρονεῖν δὲ καὶ σέβειν τὰ τῶν θεῶν
κάλλιστον· οἶμαι δ' αὐτὸ καὶ σοφώτατον
θνητοῖσιν εἶναι κτῆμα τοῖσι χρωμένοις. (1150–52)

Moderation and respect for divine matters is the noblest; I think that this is also the wisest possessions for mortals to make use of.

Faced with the terrifying power of the gods, human *sophia* consists in recognizing its own limits. The sentiment, though conventional in substance, gains piquancy from its context, in which the wisdom of traditional piety had been demonstrated in terrifying fashion.[138]

"What Is the Wise?": *Bacchae* (II)

The question of what *sophia* consists in and its relation to ritual worship is central to the choral songs of the play. Much of the chorus' reflection on *sophia* is concentrated around τὸ σοφόν, an unusual substantive usage that appears with exceptional frequency in *Bacchae* (though in practically no other Euripidean text).[139] Its lexical meaning is clear enough: just as τὸ καλόν means "the beautiful," τὸ σοφόν means "the wise."[140] As we would expect from the discourse of *sophia* in the play more generally, this quality can be instantiated for

---

138. On the messenger as a figure for the audience, see James Barrett, *Staged Narrative: Poetics and the Messenger in Greek Tragedy* (Berkeley: University of California Press, 2002), 102–31.

139. The most substantial concentration of usages before *Bacchae* is found in Heraclitus, where it seems to be a clear positive quality, associated with divinity: B32 DK/D45 LM and B41 DK/D44 LM both use τὸ σοφόν prominently; see also B108 DK/D43 LM (without the article, but apparently a similar usage). On the uses, see Shirley Darcus Sullivan, "τὸ σοφόν as an Aspect of the Divine in Heraclitus," in *Greek Poetry and Philosophy: Studies in Honour of Leonard Woodbury*, ed. Douglas E. Gerber (Chico: Scholars Press, 1984), 285–301. The change in valence is consistent with the broader changes in thinking about *sophia* traced in this chapter.

140. Such substantives may show up with increasing frequency in later Euripides: τὸ καλόν, for example, appears only in the *Helen* (952), the *Orestes* (819), and three times in the *Iphigenia at Aulis* (20, 21, 387)—and never in Aeschylus or Sophocles.

good or bad ends. τὸ σοφόν, I suggest, is best understood as a heightened, autonomous form of *sophia*, a mode of intellection that does not take norms for granted, and so represents a potential challenge to (especially religious) tradition. The unusual formation τὸ σοφόν is appropriate to the relatively unfamiliar idea expressed in it—something like "the wise" in the abstract or in opposition to its individual instances. It is understood, I argue, as a distinctively modern intellectual category, and its uses in the play show an attempt to come to grips with the philosophical abstraction it implies. In Teiresias' speech discussed earlier, τὸ σοφόν was the goal of subtle reasoning (σοφίζεσθαι) concerning divinity, and suggested a height of intellect that went beyond the normal human sphere—even though, properly understood, it would support piety. τὸ σοφόν, then, points to extremes of human intellect, and raises the question of what ends this intellect is put to. Euripides' only other usage in the *Palamedes* was discussed earlier in the chapter, and conforms to this outline, suggesting that τὸ σοφόν is ambiguous in a strong sense, an intellectual capacity abstracted from traditional norms, which is potentially threatening.[141]

Much of the critical discourse surrounding τὸ σοφόν (and there has been quite a lot of it) has sought to determine whether it is a positive or a negative quality, roughly "wisdom" or "cleverness." There are substantial factions on both sides, and the debate is complicated by textual and linguistic difficulties surrounding the passages in which τὸ σοφόν appears.[142] I suggest that the aim to unify τὸ σοφόν as either consistently positive or negative is an error. In fact, as has been argued throughout this chapter, the meaning of *soph*-roots is substantially determined by use and context. There is no evidence that an audience hearing τὸ σοφόν would have had fixed associations for the term

---

141. F 583: "Whoever speaks well, but the deeds about which he speaks are shameful—I never praise *to sophon* of this man" (ὅστις λέγει μὲν εὖ, τὰ δ' ἔργ' ἐφ' οἷς λέγει / αἴσχρ' ἐστί, τούτου τὸ σοφὸν οὐκ αἰνῶ ποτέ). τὸ σοφόν here must potentially an object of praise (and so cannot have a basically negative meaning)—even though the speaker is wary of its misuse.

142. Most see τὸ σοφόν as universally disparaged, and would translate as "cleverness": R. P. Winnington-Ingram, "Euripides, 'Bacchae' 877–881 = 897–901," *Bulletin of the Institute of Classical Studies* 13 (1966): 34–37; Rijksbaron, *Grammatical Observations*, 109–13; David Kovacs, *Euripidea tertia* (Leiden: Brill, 2002), 131. But there are others who see it as universally praised or neutral: Marylin Arthur, "The Choral Odes of the 'Bacchae' of Euripides," in *Studies in Fifth-Century Thought and Literature*, ed. Adam Parry (Cambridge: Cambridge University Press, 1972), 145–79; Martin Cropp, "τί τὸ σοφόν;" *Bulletin of the Institute of Classical Studies* 28 (1981): 39–42; Patricia Reynolds-Warnhoff, "The Role of τὸ σοφόν in Euripides' 'Bacchae,'" *Quaderni urbinati di cultura classica* 57 (1997): 77–103. The most illuminating discussion is Origa, *Le contraddizioni della sapienza*, 120–25. Origa notes the abstraction implied in the term, though draws different conclusions from my own.

(beyond the general ones surrounding σοφός), so whatever valence the term has in *Bacchae* must be developed in the play. In fact, I argue that the value of τὸ σοφόν is substantially open, and that its uses show the chorus seeking to grasp the relation of autonomous intellection and traditional religious thought.

The chorus' first usage of τὸ σοφόν, coming in the first stasimon, illustrates the polar quality of *soph*-roots in the play as a whole. The ode begins with an address to Ὁσία (holiness or purity) and concentrates in its first half on the contrast between the impious anger of Pentheus, which will bring bad fortune, and the pleasures of Dionysiac worship, which will bring rewards. After asserting the continual watchfulness of the gods over human actions, the chorus makes a gnomic utterance contrasting τὸ σοφόν with σοφία:

> τὸ σοφὸν δ' οὐ σοφία,
> τό τε μὴ θνατὰ φρονεῖν.
> βραχὺς αἰών· ἐπὶ τούτῳ
> δέ τις ἂν μεγάλα διώκων
> τὰ παρόντ' οὐχὶ φέροι. μαι-
> νομένων οἵδε τρόποι καὶ
> κακοβούλων παρ' ἔμοιγε φωτῶν. (395–401)[143]

The wise is not wisdom, nor is thinking nonmortal thoughts. Life is short. Given this, someone pursuing great things would not carry off what is present. These are the ways of raving and ill-advised men, in my opinion.

σοφία, on most readings, is contrasted with two things: τὸ σοφόν and "thinking nonmortal thoughts."[144] The two are not quite the same, but they do seem to be importantly related: τὸ σοφόν could potentially lead to "thinking nonmortal thoughts" (as it threatened to do in Teiresias' speech), suggesting a norm-free intellection. These pretensions to intellect are contrasted with σοφία, a familiar

---

143. I have altered Diggle's punctuation of the first five lines, which would read "the wise is not wisdom, and thinking nonmortal thoughts leads to a short life. Given this, who pursuing great things would not carry off what is present?" Though this is actually more useful for my reading, I think the more widely accepted punctuation I print here is decidedly preferable: the assertion "thinking mortal thoughts leads to a short life" provides only a very loose premise for the *carpe diem* sentiment expressed just after (whether punctuated as a question or not), while "life is short" makes the logic quite clear. The text signals the logical connection emphatically with ἐπὶ τούτῳ, and I see no reason to ignore it.

144. Some have sought to align σοφία (rather than τὸ σοφόν) with τό . . . μὴ θνατὰ φρονεῖν in order to argue that the rejected value is σοφία, but this requires an implausible stretching of the Greek, which is most naturally heard as "the wise is not wisdom, nor [is] thinking nonmortal thoughts [wisdom]."

word used in a familiar sense (roughly "wisdom") to describe traditional, norm-guided thought.[145] The opposition between σοφία and τὸ σοφόν is elaborated in the following lines, contrasting a due recognition of one's human status with seeking after "great things," which leads one to neglect the here and now. σοφία, then, is associated with an acceptance of divine superiority, while τὸ σοφόν points to a form of thought that seeks to rise above the everyday sphere of human activity.

The contrast I have outlined between norm-guided σοφία and norm-independent τὸ σοφόν fits the context of an ode decrying impiety. To strive for τὸ σοφόν would be to consider tradition and religion as subject to human reason. Despite textual problems, this seems to be the sense of the final lines of the ode, which assert that Dionysus hates those who do not "hold a wise heart and mind away from excessive men" (428–29: σοφὰν δ' ἀπέχειν πραπίδα φρένα τε / περισσῶν παρὰ φωτῶν) and counsels acceptance of "what the more common multitude believe and practice" (430–31: τὸ πλῆθος ὅτι τὸ φαυλότερον ἐνόμισε χρῆ- / ταί τε). The chorus, like Teiresias, associates worship of Dionysus with accepted custom, which accords with a more or less traditional notion of *sophia* as human wisdom guided by divinity. In the contrast of τὸ σοφόν and σοφία, τὸ σοφόν is the rejected value, but it is not rejected as in itself a bad thing, but rather for the way it is associated with thinking "nonmortal thoughts." The chorus, then, is pointing to a genuine paradox: to pursue the heights of wisdom is unwise, since it threatens to lead one away from custom and religion.[146]

Another use of τὸ σοφόν, in the fourth stasimon, is explicable in the terms just developed (while the third stasimon's refrain requires the most involved discussion, so is left for last). The ode hopefully anticipates Pentheus' violent destruction by the raging maenads, and so shows continuity with the theme of piety developed in the first stasimon. The chorus again expresses confidence in the justice of the gods and celebrates the value of a life lived in acknowledgment

---

145. Origa points out that σοφία in choral passages is universally positive in Euripides and associated with divinity, which fits this usage well: Origa, *Le contraddizioni della sapienza*, 104–15.

146. A similar contrast seems to be present in the *Orestes*: "The noble is not noble, to cut the flesh of parents with fire-wrought palm" (819–21: τὸ καλὸν οὐ καλόν, τοκέων / πυριγενεῖ τεμεῖν παλάμᾳ / χρόα). What is demanded by nobility in the abstract (revenge) is at odds with what is characteristic of a noble person (not to kill one's parents). The paradox expresses Orestes' dilemma effectively.

of one's human status, declaring that "to act mortally [brings] an untroubled life" (1004: βροτείως τ' ἔχειν ἄλυπος βίος).¹⁴⁷ They continue,

> τὸ σοφὸν οὐ φθονῶ · χαίρω θηρεύου-
> σα τὰ δ' ἕτερα μεγάλα φανερὰ †τῶν ἀεὶ
> ἐπὶ τὰ καλὰ βίον,†
> ἦμαρ ἐς νύκτα τ' εὐ-
> αγοῦντ' εὐσεβεῖν, τὰ δ' ἔξω νόμιμα
> δίκας ἐκβαλόντα τιμᾶν θεούς.¹⁴⁸ (1005–10)

> I do not grudge the wise; I rejoice hunting after the other, great, apparent things . . . to act reverently being pure by day and into the night, and to honor the gods, rejecting customs that are beyond justice.

To "grudge the wise" is to refuse it to (unspecified) others, suggesting that the chorus do not reject it absolutely, but, as they say, choose to pursue other things.¹⁴⁹ This is consistent with my suggestion that τὸ σοφόν is not itself bad—it is one of the "great, apparent things"—but that its pursuit is not salutary for a human. The stasimon, like the first discussed above, is built around a basic opposition of piety and impiety: in contrast to the chorus' life lived in conformity with religious tradition, "hunting after" τὸ σοφόν is aligned with "customs that are beyond justice." The phrase makes explicit the chorus' (and Teiresias') concern that the view of divinity associated with τὸ σοφόν could entail a rejection of established custom. They will remain within the bounds of traditional piety and count on the gods for protection. Bacchus' avenging epiphany, which they call for at the end of the ode, will validate their choice to act in conformity with custom rather than pursuing τὸ σοφόν.

---

147. The passage is very difficult, and obelized in its entirety by Diggle, but the correction (Murray's, now widely accepted) needed to secure this line is relatively slight: the manuscripts have βροτείῳ.

148. Diggle's brackets extend from 1002 to 1007, and there is good reason to suspect wider corruption. But the crucial text for my purposes is at least legible by reading φθονῶ for φθόνῳ and inserting a stop in the first line. The emendation preferred by Diggle in the apparatus is even more congenial to my perspective: τὸ σοφὸν οὐ φθονῶ καιρῷ θηρεύουσι ("I do not grudge those pursuing the wise in due measure"). To pursue "the wise" in moderation would be to pursue it within the limits of human capacity (if this is not an oxymoron).

149. The bare accusative with φθονέω is rare (when construed with a noun, it generally requires a genitive object), but found also at *Oedipus the King* 310 and *Iphigenia among the Taurians* 503; it must mean grudge a thing (to an unspecified someone). See Rijksbaron, *Grammatical Observations*, 129–30.

This brings us to the most difficult and controversial use of τὸ σοφόν, in a refrain of the third stasimon. Aspects of the context of the first and fourth stasima are shared: in the strophe, the chorus imagine themselves as a fawn escaping a hunter, a projection that reflects the hope for divine liberation from Pentheus (and so looks back to the desire for escape expressed in the first stasimon).[150] After the first refrain, the chorus in the antistrophe express faith in the power of divinity to punish impiety and repeatedly recommend adherence to νόμος (891, 893, 895, looking forward to the theme of punishment and rejection of overstepping custom). On my reading, τὸ σοφόν in the refrain again points to the limits of human intellection, and is implicitly rejected or set aside in favor of adherence to conventional worship:

τί τὸ σοφόν, ἢ τί τὸ κάλλιον
παρὰ θεῶν γέρας ἐν βροτοῖς
ἢ χεῖρ' ὑπὲρ κορυφᾶς
τῶν ἐχθρῶν κρείσσω κατέχειν;
ὅτι καλὸν φίλον αἰεί.[151] (877–81 = 897–901)

What is the wise, or what is the nobler privilege from the gods among mortals than to hold one's hand above the heads of enemies? What is noble is dear always.

The chorus pose two questions as alternatives: what is "the wise," and what is "the nobler privilege from the gods" than superiority over one's enemies, to which "what is noble is dear always" furnishes some kind of answer. The form of the lines suggests a kind of priamel in which "the wise" and "to hold one's

---

150. Compare 402–16, another projection of escape in direct proximity to discussion of τὸ σοφόν. On the importance of hunting imagery in the play, see Segal, *Dionysiac Poetics*, 27–54; Chiara Thumiger, *Hidden Paths: Self and Characterization in Greek Tragedy: Euripides' "Bacchae"* (London: Institute of Classical Studies, 2007), 128–38.

151. Diggle obelizes the first line, but this is unnecessary: even if the text requires emendation (which is itself disputed), there are relatively minor ones that will restore it adequately. I follow Kovacs' second thoughts in reading the manuscript text (revising his Loeb, which prints the emendation ἤ τι for ἢ τί τὸ): David Kovacs, *Euripidea* (Leiden: Brill, 1994), 130–32. This entails accepting the awkward sequence τί τὸ κάλλιον . . . ἢ, but the sense is clear enough: Cropp, "τί τὸ σοφόν;" 40. One popular alternative is to read ἢ for ἤ in 879, and punctuate with a question mark at the end of 878: Valdis Leinieks, "Euripides, 'Bakchai' 877–81 = 897–901," *Journal of Hellenic Studies* 104 (1984): 178–79. He reads σοφόν as an adjective looking ahead to γέρας (as Seaford does as well): this seems implausible to me, given the marked uses of τὸ σοφόν through the rest of the play.

hand above the heads of enemies" are implicitly compared.¹⁵² The basic contrast is between intellectual endeavor and success in the here and now, with the chorus preferring the latter. Particularly important in this comparison is that the latter is described as a "privilege from the gods among mortals," associating victory with divinity. The status of τὸ σοφόν is left open, and the chorus' question, "what is the wise?" seems genuine: it probes the ends of autonomous intellectual inquiry in comparison with the certainty of divine favor represented by successful action. The conclusion "what is noble is dear always" serves as an explanation of their preference: that which is granted by the gods—in this case, victory over enemies—is always desirable. The chorus, again, would not be rejecting τὸ σοφόν absolutely, but asserting their choice of the more modest aim of immediate happiness in conformity with divine dictates.

A related idea is expressed in the epode, a *makarismos* in priamel form that compares various εὐδαίμων ("happy" or "blessed") states. The first items mentioned, escape from danger and completion of toils, speak directly to the chorus' immediate situation.¹⁵³ The chorus go on to contemplate the varieties of human pursuit of wealth and power and the uncertainty such pursuits bring, reserving their ultimate praise for the one who eschews great ambition and "to whom day by day the living is happy" (911–12: τὸ δὲ κατ' ἦμαρ ὅτῳ βίοτος / εὐδαίμων). The sentiment recalls the first stasimon's rejection of seeking after great things, and looks forward to the fourth stasimon's recommendation of a life lived in conformity with custom. In both these cases, τὸ σοφόν was dismissed in favor of pious activity in the present. All these contexts guide my suggestion of how to read the third stasimon's refrain: as an acceptance of what is granted by the gods and rejection of intellectual pursuits in the absence of divine sanction. The *makarismos* with which the stasimon closes offers a summation of this strand of thought: the chorus "consider blessed" (911: μακαρίζω) a life lived in recognition of one's human limits and in conformity with custom concerning the gods. In contrast to the *makarismoi* of *Antiope* and *Frogs*, which countenanced a reconciliation of philosophical thought with religious and

---

152. Willink's emendation ἤ τι for ἤ τί τὸ (with a question mark after τί τὸ σοφόν, as printed by Kovacs' Loeb) is attractive, since it makes the comparative structure clearer—though this is not necessary to make sense of the manuscript in the way I suggest. The emendation is proposed in C. W. Willink, "Some Problems of Text and Interpretation in the 'Bacchae' II," *Classical Quarterly* 16 (1966): 230–31; it is retracted in C. W. Willink, ed., *Euripides: "Orestes"* (Oxford: Oxford University Press, 1986), 222.

153. The key words of the epode repeat directly some of the language of the strophe: ἔφυγε (903, looking back to 868, φύγῃ), μόχθων (904, looking back to 873, μόχθοις).

civic norms, *Bacchae*—or at least its chorus—appears quite negative concerning the value of intellectual inquiry for its own sake.[154]

Bacchae's concern with novel intellectual inquiry is especially notable given that it seems entirely extraneous to the mythical outline. Pentheus' resistance to Dionysus might be portrayed simply as a story of human *hubris* and divine punishment, and substantial parts of *Bacchae* can be read along these lines.[155] Pentheus is no Prodicean skeptic, and nothing in his portrayal suggests that his objection to Dionysiac religion is philosophically grounded or broadly atheistic in outlook. Yet the chorus and Teiresias clearly envision the threat to their practice as much broader and more consequential than a single opponent. The challenge to Dionysiac practice, at least as envisioned by its adherents, consists in an attitude that rejects traditional piety and ritual in the name of τὸ σοφόν. It is not hard to see where this concern would come from: as discussed above, the existence of the gods was a major topic of sophistic discussions, which at their most extreme could countenance outright statements of atheism like that of the Sisyphus fragment.[156] It was not an idle concern that τὸ σοφόν would seek to overthrow paternal traditions, and, as demonstrated by *Frogs*, related charges were being made against Euripides. Regardless of whether Euripides was actually a religious skeptic or the atheism of the Sisyphus fragment reflects an "earnest" philosophical position, questioning of theological norms was an urgent concern in the late fifth century. *Bacchae*'s presentation of the story of Dionysus' arrival in Thebes in terms of a conflict between religious custom and novel intellectualism has to be understood as one form of this concern.

My reading of *Bacchae*'s discourse of religious tradition and intellectual innovation has revealed relatively conservative tendencies. Again, these may or may not have been Euripides' own, and should not be mistaken for an assertion of fidelity to Dionysiac religion (as some past critics have read them).[157] The choral odes, which concentrate the play's conservative tendencies, are not

---

154. Another *makarismos* from the parodos offers the converse, praising the one who "knowing rites of the gods makes his life holy" (74–75: τελετὰς θεῶν εἰ- / δὼς βιοτὰν ἁγιστεύει); it is knowledge in connection to custom that leads to happiness, not knowledge in the abstract.

155. This is roughly the approach adopted in Gyburg Radke, *Tragik und Metatragik: Euripides' "Bakchen" und die moderne Literaturwissenschaft* (Berlin: de Gruyter, 2003).

156. On the wider context of theological skepticism, see Sedley, "The Atheist Underground"; Kotwick, "Interrogating the Gods."

157. See Joshua Billings, "'Bacchae' as Palinode," *International Journal of the Classical Tradition* 25 (2018): 57–71.

authorial statements and have to be understood as expressions of the chorus' dramatic role. In fact, one could well find, as some critics have (Winnington-Ingram most eloquently), that the drama casts traditional devotion in a poor light, and ultimately portrays Dionysiac worship as dangerous.[158] Though I have suggested that the play offers a kind of referendum on traditional and novel *sophia*, I see no reason to think that the Athenian audience would have reacted uniformly. In fact, as the play's agonistic context emphasizes, these questions remain urgent and open. Even though the play's action clearly assumes the divinity and overwhelming power of Dionysus, it does not furnish a final judgment on this power. *Bacchae* is not a declaration of theism or atheism, but a staging of the place of religious practice in a moment of intellectual upheaval.

I believe that we can say more, though, about the quality of this staging, without speculating on authorial intent or privileging a single strand of the play as its "position." The imbrication of concerns surrounding novel intellection and those related to Dionysus, drama, and representation as such (usually grouped under the category of metatheater) enables a reading of the agonistic contexts of *sophia* that speaks to the question of drama's role in society.[159] The ultimate context for *Bacchae*'s metatheatrical tendencies and its self-consciousness concerning intellectual novelty would be, on this reading, the question of drama's value in an age of philosophical skepticism. This would represent a continuity with the *Antiope* and *Frogs*, in which a Dionysiac and metadramatic (or metamusical, in the case of the *Antiope*) context encouraged speculation on the value of intellectual and artistic novelty to the community. *Bacchae* can be understood as a similar inquiry into the place of innovation itself, which explores the value of traditional, ritual knowledge in its own intellectual modernity.

The most distinctive characteristic of *Bacchae*'s staging of tradition and innovation is the way that it confutes the very categories of opposition, staging the arrival of a new religious practice, while at the same time insisting on its traditional quality. The Dionysiac religion of *Bacchae* is both new and old, and

---

158. In an approach obviously influenced by the threat of fascism, Winnington-Ingram reads the play as effecting a progressive alienation from the Dionysiac, concentrating particularly on the choral odes: R. P. Winnington-Ingram, *Euripides and Dionysus: An Interpretation of the "Bacchae"* (Cambridge: Cambridge University Press, 1948).

159. Studies of metatheater in *Bacchae* have largely ignored the play's reflections on intellectualism, and have seen the discourse of *sophia* in terms of ritual or theatrical knowledge: e.g., Anton Bierl, *Dionysos und die griechische Tragödie: Politische und "metatheatralische" Aspekte im Text* (Tübingen: Gunter Narr, 1991), 199–201; Segal, *Dionysiac Poetics*, 307.

its depiction at once conservative and strikingly of the moment. This suggests a final, speculative conclusion: that the confrontation of traditional and novel *sophia* in *Bacchae* stages the relation of drama itself to the emerging discourse of philosophy, of the *sophos poiētēs* to the *sophistēs*. The interweaving of tradition and innovation in *Bacchae*'s religious and intellectual discourse would demonstrate the capacity of drama to encompass the *sophia* of philosophy within the frame of religion and poetry. *Bacchae*'s *sophia* is traditional and novel at once; it integrates new modes of thinking about divinity, constructive and critical, into the frame of established ritual. As such, it furnishes an implicit answer to the Socratic demand for an account of one's own *sophia*, but in the form of *muthos* rather than *logos*: *Bacchae* offers an account of drama as grounded in the wisdom of Dionysiac religion, which is both established and continually new.

I propose, then, that *Bacchae*'s self-consciousness concerning innovation speaks to the place of drama in an age when the sources and modes of intellectual authority were changing. The play's discourse surrounding intellectualism would constitute an implicit claim that dramatic representation is a form of thought that subsumes old and new. *Antiope* and *Frogs*, too, had demonstrated a striking consciousness of their own intellectual context, and my readings emphasized the way that they sought to reconcile traditional and novel conceptions of *sophia* by figuring innovative inquiry in the terms of established ritual. *Bacchae*'s major concern is ritual tradition as such, and its most striking feature the way it depicts this tradition as venerable even at the moment of its inception. Dionysiac ritual reconciles old and new modes of intellection and can claim to be more *sophos* than *philosophia*. *Bacchae* can thus be read as an encapsulation of the project of this book as a whole, insofar as it asserts the priority of dramatic over philosophical thinking. Though we have come to see drama as less authoritative intellectually than philosophy, in 405 in Athens the situation would have been the reverse: drama was the incumbent form of *sophia*, philosophy the challenger for intellectual authority. *Bacchae* demonstrates that dramatic *sophia* still matters despite—and even because of—the intellectual revolutions of its time.

CONCLUSION

The Stages of Early Greek Thought

PLATO'S DIALOGUES represent both a rupture and a *telos* in the history described by this study: a rupture in that they mark philosophy's increasing differentiation of itself from poetry, and from some of the dramatic aspects of earlier philosophical forms; a *telos* in that they epitomize the elevation of one dramatic form, the dialogue, into a self-conscious philosophical method. Though a harsh critic of tragedy's outlook and claim to authority, Plato is also one of the greatest practitioners of philosophical drama—a paradox that I hope emerges in heightened form from this study.[1] There is a temptation to see Plato's dialogue form as a Hegelian *Aufhebung*, a negation and elevation at the same time, which preserves drama's mimetic mode while shedding its ambiguities and mythological entanglements to become a dedicated form for thought. Conversely, this study offers material for an anti-Platonic narrative, which would see the institutionalization of philosophy as a catastrophe for intellectual culture, the end of the fifth century's productive coexistence of discursive forms and genuinely dialectical mode of inquiry. The challenge for intellectual history is to do justice to continuity while resisting teleology.

Nietzsche narrates a compelling version of this history in *The Birth of Tragedy*. Following Socrates' critique of tragic unreason, Plato's challenge, Nietzsche writes, was "to create a form of art that was inwardly related to the existing

---

1. For almost diametrically opposed reasons, Karl Popper and Martin Heidegger both see Platonic philosophy as a decline from earlier Greek thought and culture, Popper because of its idealistic and totalitarian impulses, Heidegger because of its dialectical ones: Karl R. Popper, *The Open Society and Its Enemies*, Volume I: *The Spell of Plato* (Princeton: Princeton University Press, 1945); Martin Heidegger, "Plato's Doctrine of Truth," in *Pathmarks*, ed. William McNeil (Cambridge: Cambridge University Press, 1998), 155–82.

forms of art he had rejected."[2] Crucial here is the description of the dialogue as an "art form" (rather than a method or a discipline) in continuity with earlier forms, chief among them drama.[3] The Platonic dialogue became "the barge on which the older forms of poetry, together with all her children, sought refuge after their shipwreck."[4] It is thus profoundly heterogeneous, incorporating and subsuming a range of discourses into its poetics. Though the shipwreck of poetry is a consequence of philosophical critique, Plato's rescue, according to Nietzsche, is undertaken in earnest. In *Birth*, Nietzsche sees Socrates and Euripides as the agents of rupture and Plato as a belated acolyte, though elsewhere he would offer a narrative more like that of this and more recent studies, which point to Plato and the early fourth-century context of disciplinary definition as the significant break.[5] Nevertheless, Nietzsche offers a way of understanding Greek literary and intellectual history across the political and social upheavals of the late fifth century and the deaths of Sophocles, Euripides, and Socrates. Plato's dialogues represent neither a cataclysmic rupture nor a heroic beginning, but a tortured continuity.

The story told here could be understood either as a prehistory to the Platonic dialogue or, conversely, as an elegy for the dramatic modes of thinking that the philosophical dialogue both appropriated and obscured. I hope this study supports and challenges both narratives. When approaching the intellectual culture of the fifth century, Plato cannot be ignored, given how much of the evidence he provides, but neither should he be trusted uncritically or his perspective normalized. Plato's role in this book is as a kind of limit. The brief discussions of Platonic texts that open each chapter orient the discussion of philosophical questions, and serve to demonstrate the persistence of the chapter's concerns beyond the fifth century, and into the disciplinary context of philosophy. Plato's dialogues crystallize, in exceptionally lucid form, conceptual elements of the fifth-century philosophical context in which they are set, and so provide invaluable witness to

2. §14; Nietzsche, *The Birth of Tragedy*, 68.

3. Martin Puchner approaches the dramatic and philosophical qualities of the Platonic dialogue against the backdrop of modern drama: Puchner, *The Drama of Ideas*, esp. 9–35.

4. §14; Nietzsche, *The Birth of Tragedy*, 69.

5. Both Nietzsche's notes to the lecture course *The Pre-Platonic Philosophers* and the unfinished manuscript for a book entitled *Philosophy in the Tragic Age of the Greeks* see Socrates as still belonging to the older style of philosopher, and Plato as the point of rupture: Friedrich Nietzsche, *The Pre-Platonic Philosophers*, trans. Greg Whitlock (Urbana: University of Illinois Press, 2001); Nietzsche, *Philosophy in the Tragic Age of the Greeks*.

the important questions of the period. At the same time, by placing the Platonic material at the beginning of each chapter, I have sought to undermine teleology and allow the richness of the earlier material to develop on its own terms.

I seek now, in closing, to outline some of the possibilities of my approach to scenic thought for the Platonic dialogue. This has a dual goal: it demonstrates how attention to drama as a philosophical form allows us better to grasp continuity and rupture in classical Greek intellectual history, and it suggests ways that the study of Platonic dialogue might investigate scenic form as a mode of thought. While sensitive readers of Plato dialogue have always been attentive to its formal heterogeneity, there has been a tendency to see the forms and genres it incorporates as in some kind of tension with content—rather than, as I propose, an organic element of the dialogue's method. The thinking of the dialogue, on this understanding, is not distinct from the forms it incorporates, but is essentially composed of them—and these forms are much wider-ranging than is often recognized, composed not just of set pieces and allusions, but of the myriad ways in which Plato stages thought in his dialogues. Formal and generic heterogeneity is the rule (as it is for earlier philosophical writing), not the exception.[6] By attending to the scenic grammar of the Platonic dialogue, we see how form shapes thinking in the emergent disciplinary context of philosophy.

The *Gorgias* offers an obvious place to begin, since the confrontation between Socrates and Callicles in the third part of the dialogue openly declares its debt to the *Antiope*'s *agōn* of Amphion and Zethus. Andrea Nightingale has influentially read the presence of the *Antiope* in the *Gorgias* as Platonic parody, intended to mark out the domain of philosophy from that of poetry.[7] Though such an effort is both implicit and explicit in the dialogue, much of the substance of the *Gorgias*' engagement with dramatic thought goes lost in reading

---

6. We know too little about Socratic dialogue as a genre to determine whether Plato is exceptional in this respect, but there is strong evidence for affinities between Socratic dialogue and contemporary prose forms: Andrew Ford, "The Beginnings of Dialogue: Socratic Discourses and Fourth-Century Prose," in *The End of Dialogue in Antiquity*, ed. Simon Goldhill (Cambridge: Cambridge University Press, 2008), 29–44.

7. Andrea Wilson Nightingale, "Plato's 'Gorgias' and Euripides' 'Antiope': A Study in Generic Transformation," *Classical Antiquity* 11 (1992): 121–41; Nightingale, *Genres in Dialogue*, 60–92. I have learned greatly from Nightingale's work, but it is paradigmatic of the approach to literary form in Plato that sees generic hybridity as something that requires explanation—rather than understanding it, as I do, as a fundamental quality of early philosophical writing.

the dialogue as a polemic. Such a reading assumes that there is a tension between dramatic form and philosophical content that needs to be accounted for, rather than viewing the form as a meaningful element of the thinking of the dialogue. I suggest that understanding the scene as a part of the *agōn sophias* tradition—rather than a parody of it—offers a much richer reading than one that sees the dialogue primarily in terms of textual appropriation or generic competition.[8] On this reading, the citations of the *Antiope* function not primarily as allusions to the specifics of the work or to tragedy as genre, but rather, as substantive engagements with the drama's philosophical discourse. Approaching the confrontation between Callicles and Socrates as an *agōn sophias* helps us to see not only that it is engaging with central questions and positions of fifth-century thought, but also how it is refiguring these positions to suit its own intellectual context and aims.

The *Gorgias* is constructed as three relatively discrete dialogues between Socrates and a single interlocutor, increasing in substance and contentiousness.[9] By far the most serious challenge is the final one, posed by Callicles, a figure about whom we know nothing except what we glean from the dialogue, which suggests that he is young, wealthy, and politically inclined—just the sort of person for whom Gorgias' training in rhetoric would be valuable. He breaks into the discussion after the second interlocutor, Polus, has shown himself unable to counter Socrates' wildly counterintuitive argument that one should hope for one's enemies to avoid consequences for wrongdoing while one should vigorously prosecute the crimes of friends, so that they can gain the benefits of punishment and live better (480b–81b). Callicles' intervention

---

8. Nightingale's case for reading the dialogue as parody is argued mainly on the basis of Plato's hostility to tragedy elsewhere—not on the way the allusions are staged: Nightingale, *Genres in Dialogue*, 87–92. Franco Trivigno offers an effective response, arguing that the dialogue is instead "paratragedy" and takes its Euripidean intertext quite seriously: Franco V. Trivigno, "Paratragedy in Plato's 'Gorgias,'" *Oxford Studies in Ancient Philosophy* 36 (2009): 73–105. On the dialogue's (highly critical) discussion of tragedy as a genre, see Fritz-Gregor Herrmann, "Poetry in Plato's 'Gorgias,'" in *Plato and the Poets*, ed. Pierre Destrée and Fritz-Gregor Herrmann (Leiden: Brill, 2011), 21–40. My interest here is not in the dialogue's specific relation to the *Antiope* or tragedy as genre, but in the way it carries forward the substantive concerns of the *agōn sophias*.

9. Charles Kahn reads the three refutations as examinations of the three interlocutors' characters, and thus as part of a larger staging of ways of living and human desire: Charles H. Kahn, "Drama and Dialectic in Plato's 'Gorgias,'" *Oxford Studies in Ancient Philosophy* 1 (1983): 75–121. On the agonistic character of the dialogue as a whole, see Robert D. Metcalf, *Philosophy as Agōn: A Study of Plato's "Gorgias" and Related Texts* (Evanston: Northwestern University Press, 2018).

points back to a moment in the discussion when Polus had agreed with Socrates' claim that doing injustice is more shameful than suffering it—an admission obtained only, Callicles claims, because Polus was ashamed to state the opposite (482d–e). Callicles, though, is not ashamed to state his belief to the contrary, and bolsters it with an argument that redefines justice as what is dictated by nature (*phusis*) rather than by the custom (*nomos*) that has compelled the sense of shame in Socrates' previous interlocutors.[10] As we have seen, this opposition is a familiar sophistic topic, and Callicles' theory is comparable to Antiphon's in using a theory of *phusis* to recommend actions conventionally considered immoral.[11] *Phusis*, according to Callicles, dictates that strength rule in human affairs, and that actions are only good or bad insofar as they serve the interests of the stronger. Under this code, to suffer injury of any kind is the worst thing one can experience, while injuring another is simply an expression of natural superiority (483c–84a). Though Callicles admits that this ethic is not widely accepted, he claims emphatically that those who follow it act "truly, by Zeus, according to the custom [or "law"] of nature" (483e: ναὶ μὰ Δία κατὰ νόμον γε τὸν τῆς φύσεως). Callicles counters Socrates' counterintuitive argument with a novel position of his own, pointing to a kind of symmetry between the two interlocutors, both of whom propose surprising and unconventional views of justice.

Socrates, Callicles continues, would recognize the correctness of this view of justice if he would only "set aside philosophy and go on to greater things" (484c: ἐπὶ τὰ μείζω ἔλθῃς ἐάσας ἤδη φιλοσοφίαν). This reproach, that the practice of philosophy has blinded Socrates to more important realities, introduces a broader contrast between the two figures and their respective ways of life. Callicles will invoke the *Antiope* to exhort Socrates to give up philosophy and seek political power, while Socrates will adhere tenaciously to his own reasoning, and in the process draw attention to the inconsistency of Callicles' views (e.g., 482a–c, 499c, 509a–b). Much of the scholarship on the dialogue has focused on locating Callicles' inconsistency, but it is nevertheless striking that Callicles presents such a serious challenge to Socrates'

---

10. Shame is a major issue in the dialogue as a whole and will color even Callicles' apparent free-spokenness: Christina H. Tarnopolsky, *Prudes, Perverts, and Tyrants: Plato's "Gorgias" and the Politics of Shame* (Princeton: Princeton University Press, 2010).

11. Decleva Caizzi, "Protagoras and Antiphon"; Furley, "The Origins of Social Contract Theory."

ideas and way of life.¹² Socrates treats Callicles' ideas with respect, and claims (no doubt with a touch of irony) to be delighted to find an interlocutor intelligent and frank enough to act as a touchstone for his own views (486e). The dialogue thus encourages a reading of their confrontation as a juxtaposition of two consequential viewpoints, and Callicles proves to be one of the most compelling antagonists in the entire Platonic corpus. His dismissive view of philosophical reasoning, in comparison to the more fundamental dictates of *phusis*, strikes at the heart of the Socratic attempt to articulate a consistent, rational view of moral conduct. Callicles claims that the authority of his view is founded on the most basic facts of existence, which would preempt Socrates' conclusions from questioning and argumentation. Though Socrates is clearly vindicated in the dialogue as a whole, we should not dismiss Callicles' challenge, which could easily have been lodged against the historical Socrates, and a version of which was very definitely being lodged at the time of composition against Plato.¹³

Quotations from the *Antiope* signal a broadening of the dialogue's concerns, from questions surrounding rhetoric and justice to how best to live. Like Zethus, Callicles instigates the debate, reproaching Socrates for taking philosophy too seriously. Though philosophy is a pleasant diversion for the young, it threatens "ruin" (484c: διαφθορά) if practiced too long by leaving those who pursue it "in every way inexperienced of customs" (484d: τῶν ἠθῶν παντάπασιν ἄπειροι). With his first citation of Euripides, Callicles makes the point that people tend to give their time to pursuits they excel in and to disparage those in which they are less able—implying that Socrates' devotion to philosophy is a result of his lack of other skills (484e). Philosophy, for Callicles, has a place in

---

12. Discussions of Callicles' views are found in Raphael Woolf, "Callicles and Socrates: Psychic (Dis)Harmony in the 'Gorgias,'" *Oxford Studies in Ancient Philosophy* 18 (2000): 1–40; Rachana Kamtekar, "The Profession of Friendship: Callicles, Democratic Politics, and Rhetorical Education in Plato's 'Gorgias,'" *Ancient Philosophy* 25 (2005): 319–39; Tushar Irani, *Plato on the Value of Philosophy: The Art of Argument in the "Gorgias" and "Phaedrus"* (Cambridge: Cambridge University Press, 2017), 67–87. Barney convincingly describes Callicles' intervention as a sequence of polemics rather than a single, coherent argument: Rachel Barney, "Callicles and Thrasymachus," The Stanford Encyclopedia of Philosophy, 2017, https://plato.stanford.edu/archives/fall2017/entries/callicles-thrasymachus/.

13. Isocrates was highly critical of the impracticality of Platonic philosophy in ways that seem to parallel Callicles: compare *Antidosis* 261–69. See Harold Tarrant, "The Dramatic Background of the Arguments with Callicles, Euripides' 'Antiope,' and an Athenian Anti-Intellectual Argument," *Antichthon* 42 (2008): 20–39.

life, but a restricted one. It is appropriate for the purposes of education, and for practice when young, but if pursued into adulthood threatens to remove one from more important realms of activity, and cause one "never to utter anything free and great and suitable" (485e: ἐλεύθερον δὲ καὶ μέγα καὶ ἱκανὸν μηδέποτε φθέγξασθαι). Callicles' case against Socratic intellectualism, though, is not the absolute one made by Zethus or Aristophanes' Aeschylus, but a more nuanced one, which assumes the value of intellectual inquiry, but sees it as a danger when divorced from more practical pursuits. This is not surprising given the context of the dialogue, a debate between members of the same broad intellectual culture, in which the value of abstract pursuits is to a degree accepted. Callicles, though, prompts the question of what philosophy is for: cultivation of the individual in isolation from society, or preparation to enter society.

Callicles insists, perhaps somewhat disingenuously, that his advice is given in a friendly manner, out of a brotherly concern for Socrates, like that of Zethus for Amphion. Adapting Zethus' words, he reproves,

ἀμελεῖς, ὦ Σώκρατες, ὧν δεῖ σε ἐπιμελεῖσθαι, καὶ φύσιν ψυχῆς ὧδε γενναίαν μειρακιώδει τινὶ διατρέπεις μορφώματι, οὔτ' ἂν δίκης βουλαῖσι προσθεῖ' ἂν ὀρθῶς λόγον, οὔτ' εἰκὸς ἂν καὶ πιθανὸν ἂν λάκοις, οὔθ' ὑπὲρ ἄλλου νεανικὸν βούλευμα βουλεύσαιο. (485e–86a)

You take no care, Socrates, for the things you should care for, and you pervert such a noble nature of spirit with some childish form, and you could not rightly contribute any speech in councils of justice, nor utter anything likely or believable, nor counsel any vigorous plan for another.

Much of this is borrowed from the *Antiope* (the precise amount is disputed), but Callicles adapts the quotation to emphasize Socrates' inability to participate in public forums centering on speech and persuasion.[14] He names three activities Socrates is incapable of taking part in, from the official (courtroom matters) to the semi-official (persuasive speech, presumably in public contexts) to the private (offering individual counsel). Socrates' refusal to engage in rhetorical training, despite his philosophical pursuits, appears to Callicles

---

14. Kannicht takes up the entirety of the passage (with modifications) in F 185 *TrGF*, but this is far from certain: Di Benedetto, "Osservazioni su alcuni frammenti dell' 'Antiope' di Euripide," 114–20. It seems clear that the original mentioned at least military matters and council as the activities Amphion was incapable of joining.

to neglect the ultimate good such pursuits might bring. Whereas the *Antiope*'s *agōn* broadly contrasted physical and mental activities, the debate in the *Gorgias* concerns the proper use of intellectual cultivation. But this makes Socrates' rejection of politics all the starker, since the ability to offer civic advice had been one of Amphion's claims on behalf of his own learning (F 199, 200). Socrates will eventually offer a fuller defense of himself in political terms, but he willingly accepts Callicles' basic contention that he is incapable of engaging in rhetoric and persuasion.

The most powerful claim Callicles makes, which recurs multiple times in the dialogue, is that Socrates would be unable to defend himself in a court action against him. The charge, obviously, has teeth, and Socrates' challenge in the dialogue (and Plato's too) will consist in showing that it is better to be condemned unjustly than to do what would be necessary for acquittal. After drawing attention to Socrates' rhetorical inability, Callicles imagines the consequences: if Socrates were accused of some crime, "you would not be able to be of use to yourself, but you would become dizzy and gape, not having anything to say" (486a–b: οὐκ ἂν ἔχοις ὅτι χρήσαιο σαυτῷ, ἀλλ' ἰλιγγιῴης ἂν καὶ χασμῷο οὐκ ἔχων ὅτι εἴποις). Such defenselessness, for Callicles, constitutes the greatest reproach against Socrates' way of life and conception of wisdom. He asks, quoting the *Antiope* again, "and yet how can this be wise, Socrates, such an art that, taking a well-born man, makes him worse?" (486b: καίτοι πῶς σοφὸν τοῦτό ἐστιν, ὦ Σώκρατες, ἥτις εὐφυῆ λαβοῦσα τέχνη φῶτα ἔθηκε χείρονα;). The question of what makes an individual better or worse has been and remains a major point of contention in the dialogue, and will turn out to constitute one of the greatest differences between Socrates and Callicles. For Callicles, it is obvious that being unjustly condemned makes a man worse, while for Socrates, the real danger will turn out to lie in being acquitted by unworthy means.

Callicles' notions of better and worse will be shown to be confused in various ways, but it is clear that for him the value of a pursuit is judged in relation to individual ends. Socrates' inability to gain his way through rhetoric appears, then, a dangerous weakness. This differentiates Callicles from Zethus (and from Aristophanes' Aeschylus and Euripides' Pentheus), who claim to be acting for the good of the city. Callicles makes no such claim, and his philosophy of *phusis* would seem to deny the value of any end beyond personal advancement. This constitutes a reversal of the dichotomy of tradition and novelty seen in the fifth-century *agōnes*. Callicles' position, though he quotes both Pindar and Euripides and demonstrates a respect for political authority and conventional success, is motivated by an egoistic conception that is at odds with the traditional figure of the *sophos*, and is expressed in the contemporary language of *nomos* and *phusis*. By contrast, Socrates' *sophia*—which in *Frogs* had been aligned with Euripidean novelty and individuality—emphasizes the common good, and ultimately casts itself in the religious language of eschatological myth. Both speakers claim the mantle of tradition, though both outline profoundly untraditional views concerning justice and the best life. The strategy is familiar from the dramatic *agōnes*, all of which present novel forms of *sophia* under the guise of tradition, and thus point to the ultimate reconciliation of old and new in a single figure.

Socrates recognizes Callicles' challenge as addressing the value of *sophia*, but understands this in a somewhat restricted sense, as a question of whether one should practice philosophy. He recalls hearing a conversation between Callicles and his friends concerning "up to what point wisdom should be practiced" (μέχρι ὅποι τὴν σοφίαν ἀσκητέον), with the opinion prevailing "not to be eager to philosophize to the point of exactness" (487c: μὴ προθυμεῖσθαι εἰς τὴν ἀκρίβειαν φιλοσοφεῖν). Callicles and his friends feared that "having become wiser than was necessary they would unwittingly be destroyed" (487d: ὅπως μὴ πέρα τοῦ δέοντος σοφώτεροι γενόμενοι λήσετε διαφθαρέντες). The basic concern, that being too *sophos* could lead one astray, is familiar from fifth-century texts, but it is striking that here *sophia* is directly equated with the practice of *philosophia*. The text may well be overstating the extent to which *philosophia* was recognized as an established practice in the fifth century, but it demonstrates the way that, for Plato at least, *sophia* was not a general quality of the sage but was tied directly to a specific form of investigation. Even as the concerns of the dramatic *agōnes* recur, Plato translates them into the disciplinary context of his own time, turning Zethus' reproaches against Amphion's musical and intellectual *sophia* into attacks on the practice of *philosophia*.

Socrates recognizes that Callicles' reproaches address "the most noble inquiry of all," concerning "what kind of person a man should be and what he should practice and until when, both when he is older and younger" (487e–88a: πάντων δὲ καλλίστη ἐστὶν ἡ σκέψις . . . ποῖόν τινα χρὴ εἶναι τὸν ἄνδρα καὶ τί ἐπιτηδεύειν καὶ μέχρι τοῦ, καὶ πρεσβύτερον καὶ νεώτερον ὄντα). These questions should be understood both in relation to the topics discussed (chiefly, how to live in accordance with justice) and in terms of the lives of the discussants, whether one should pursue philosophy on the margins of public life or practice rhetoric as a politician. Ultimately, the two aspects of the question will emerge as linked: for Callicles, the theory of *phusis* preempts detailed philosophical inquiry and calls for a life of ambition and the pursuit of personal gain, while for Socrates, living in accordance with philosophy necessitates a life of justice and reticence in civic affairs.[15] In what follows, Callicles will prove an exceptionally contentious discussion partner, at least in part because he does not accept Socrates' basic premise that dialectic and careful argumentation lead to the best conclusions.

The contrast between the two approaches comes out particularly strongly in the greatest concession Callicles makes, after Socrates has argued at length that effective political rhetoric amounts to nothing more than conformity to the audience's beliefs and habits. Callicles admits that Socrates has made a compelling argument, but nevertheless finds that he is not persuaded: "I do not know in what way you seem to me to speak well, Socrates, but I have the feeling that most people have: I am not wholly persuaded by you" (513c: οὐκ οἶδ' ὅντινά μοι τρόπον δοκεῖς εὖ λέγειν, ὦ Σώκρατες, πέπονθα δὲ τὸ τῶν πολλῶν πάθος· οὐ πάνυ σοι πείθομαι). His reservation points to the way that he conceives of intellectual authority differently from Socrates: not as what emerges from philosophical argumentation, but as what "feels" right. Callicles' ethic of *phusis* causes him to believe argumentation less than his own intuitions, making him an exemplary practitioner (and audience) of rhetoric, which similarly addresses itself to its listeners' feelings rather than to any greater truth. Callicles' resistance to dialectic is fundamentally related to his resistance to Socrates' ethic of justice and understanding of political life.

Socrates' response to Callicles' challenge is worked out over the rest of the encounter. The discussion of the political life culminates in Socrates' claim that a politician should make his fellow citizens better, even if this involves not satisfying their desires as the rhetorician does. Coming back to the concern that he might be condemned unjustly, Socrates offers a statement of how he views his own political art (*technē*):

οἶμαι μετ' ὀλίγων Ἀθηναίων, ἵνα μὴ εἴπω μόνος, ἐπιχειρεῖν τῇ ὡς ἀληθῶς πολιτικῇ τέχνῃ καὶ πράττειν τὰ πολιτικὰ μόνος τῶν νῦν· ἅτε οὖν οὐ πρὸς χάριν λέγων τοὺς λόγους οὓς λέγω ἑκάστοτε, ἀλλὰ πρὸς τὸ βέλτιστον, οὐ πρὸς τὸ ἥδιστον, καὶ οὐκ ἐθέλων ποιεῖν ἃ σὺ παραινεῖς, τὰ κομψὰ ταῦτα, οὐχ ἕξω ὅτι λέγω ἐν τῷ δικαστηρίῳ. (521d–e)

---

15. See the discussion in James Doyle, "The Fundamental Conflict in Plato's 'Gorgias,'" *Oxford Studies in Ancient Philosophy* 30 (2006): esp. 91–93.

I think that with a few Athenians, so as not to say I am the only one, I truly undertake the political art and I practice politics alone of those today. So because I do not speak the words I speak at any time in order to please, but with a view to what is best, and not to what is most enjoyable, and because I do not wish to do the things you advise, these "subtleties," I will not have anything to say in court.

Socrates had earlier averred, "I am not one of the politicians" (473e: οὐκ εἰμὶ τῶν πολιτικῶν), and his claim here represents a paradox: that, unlike the many who are politicians, he "practices *ta politika* ["political things" or "politics"] alone among those now." What Socrates means by this must be implicit in the claim that he strives to make his fellow citizens (*politai*) better, which the dialogue has shown that none of the recognized politicians are capable of doing (513c–17c). The argumentative strategy is familiar from Amphion's claim that he can benefit his fellow citizens by his intellectual activity (F 200). Socrates drives the point home by turning back Callicles' earlier dismissal of philosophical "subtleties" (486c: τὰ κομψά), itself drawn from Zethus' tirade (F 188), to reject rhetorical persuasion. Assuming both tragic characters' agonistic roles, Socrates presents his strongest claim on his own behalf, insisting that his practice of politics and the "political art" are the only true ones.[16] In doing so, he takes Callicles' earlier position as the one haranguing and urging the other to practice politics. The long dialogue between Socrates and Callicles is thus structured by a kind of symmetry, in which Callicles' attack on Socrates' retirement from political life is answered by Socrates' claim that he himself—and not Callicles—is actually practicing politics.

Socrates admits that his political art will render him liable to being judged harshly in a court of law, and in doing so returns to the theme of justice and injustice, and to his belief that the sole meaningful threat to an individual is acting unjustly (522d–e). Though he has argued this throughout the dialogue and successfully refuted his interlocutors' claims, he still has not persuaded Callicles. Callicles' rejection of dialectic causes Socrates to attempt a more traditional form of persuasion, telling an eschatological myth concerning the importance of justice that brings the dialogue to a close.[17] Earlier in the

---

16. On Socrates' understanding of political *technē* as a scientific knowledge, see Anders Dahl Sorensen, *Plato on Democracy and Political Technē* (Leiden: Brill, 2016), 35–62.

17. On Plato's three major eschatological myths (in the *Gorgias*, *Phaedo*, and *Republic*), see Julia Annas, "Plato's Myths of Judgement," *Phronesis* 27 (1982): 119–43; Kathryn A. Morgan,

dialogue, Socrates had employed an allegorical myth in his attempt to convince Callicles of the value of temperance, though to little effect.[18] Here, he returns to myth (*muthos*; equally "story") as a means of persuasion, but presents his telling as a *logos* ("account" or even "argument"): "Listen then, as they say, to a very noble account [*logos*], which you will consider a story [*muthos*], I think, but I consider an account [*logos*], since what I am about to say I will tell you as being true" (523a: ἄκουε δή, φασί, μάλα καλοῦ λόγου, ὃν σὺ μὲν ἡγήσῃ μῦθον, ὡς ἐγὼ οἶμαι, ἐγὼ δὲ λόγον· ὡς ἀληθῆ γὰρ ὄντα σοι λέξω ἃ μέλλω λέγειν). Socrates had been rather dismissive of the validity of his previous foray into myth, so it is significant that he makes such a strong claim for the truth of what he is about to say.[19] The story he tells is a mix of familiar and novel story elements, describing judgment in the afterlife and the punishments for living an unjust life.[20] Though he repeatedly cites Homer as a witness (523a, 525d, 526d), Socrates delivers a myth that is in many respects utterly untraditional. The conclusion he draws, however, is a familiar one, "that one must beware of doing injustice more than suffering injustice, and that a man should practice most of all not seeming good but being good, both in private and public" (527b: ὡς εὐλαβητέον ἐστὶν τὸ ἀδικεῖν μᾶλλον ἢ τὸ ἀδικεῖσθαι, καὶ παντὸς μᾶλλον ἀνδρὶ μελετητέον οὐ τὸ δοκεῖν εἶναι ἀγαθὸν ἀλλὰ τὸ εἶναι, καὶ ἰδίᾳ καὶ δημοσίᾳ). Whether understood as *logos* or *muthos*, the story leads to the same conclusion as the dialectical portion of the dialogue, turning the tables on Callicles by exhorting him to change his way of life and follow philosophy.

Though the myth contributes directly to the development of the themes of justice and politics that have dominated the dialogue, my concern here is more

---

Myth and Philosophy from the Presocratics to Plato (Cambridge: Cambridge University Press, 2000), 185–210.

18. Socrates had earlier reported an allegorical myth that figures human desires as a jar, *pithos*, playing on the concept of persuasion, *peithō* (493a–94a): Brooks Sommerville, "The Image of the Jars in Plato's 'Gorgias,'" *Ancient Philosophy* 34 (2014): 235–54.

19. Socrates described the story of the jars as "on the whole rather strange" (493c: ἐπιεικῶς μέν ἐστιν ὑπό τι ἄτοπα). On the "truth" of the myth, see Christopher Rowe, "The Status of the Myth of the 'Gorgias,' Or: Taking Plato Seriously," in *Plato and Myth: Studies on the Use and Status of Platonic Myths*, ed. Catherine Collobert, Pierre Destrée, and Francisco J. Gonzalez (Leiden: Brill, 2012), 187–98.

20. The backgrounds of the myth are laid out in E. R. Dodds, ed., *Plato: "Gorgias,"* 2nd ed. (Oxford: Clarendon Press, 1959), 373–76.

with its form and role in the dialogue's *agōn* of Socrates and Callicles.[21] The myth can be understood formally as Socrates' final response to the harangue of Callicles that had opened their confrontation, completing the symmetry of their exchange. It further represents a kind of argumentative last resort after Socrates' dialectical attempts at persuasion have failed. As a reply to Callicles' initial challenge, the shift to eschatological myth represents a different strategy from the dialectic that Socrates had initially attempted. If, as Socrates expects, Callicles understands the narrative as *muthos*, it might preempt his oft-repeated objections to philosophical argument. Still more, it might address Callicles at the level of feeling and persuasion that he evidently prizes, and, by invoking divinity as a fundamental reality, supersede Callicles' dismissive view toward human custom. Whether this has any effect at all on Callicles is left open by the dialogue, which ends with the admonition that Callicles follow the way of life outlined by Socrates. If Callicles was a real person, Plato's initial readers may have had a notion of his future career that would have colored their understanding of the dialogue's conclusion (much as the fact of Socrates' trial hangs over the text), but lacking any evidence for a historical Callicles, we can do little more than speculate. As in the dramatic *agōn*, though, having the last word implies a degree of vindication (and in this case, not a very subtle one).

The myth suggests some conclusions about the dialogue's exploration of different notions of intellectual authority and its contribution to the *agōn sophias* tradition. I have suggested that a central reason for the extreme contentiousness of the discussion between Socrates and Callicles is that they hold opposed notions of what constitutes an authoritative claim: while Socrates understands authority as a result of argumentation (and therefore as being within the domain of philosophy), Callicles sees authority simply as a function of effective power over another, whether defensible rationally or not. Both of these conceptions claim the mantle of tradition—Callicles by invoking poets and politicians of the past, Socrates by employing the language of myth—in order to legitimate what are actually quite radical ideas. The myth represents

21. For the significance of the myth as a response to the questions of the dialogue, see David Sedley, "Myth, Punishment and Politics in the 'Gorgias,'" in *Plato's Myths*, ed. Catalin Partenie (Cambridge: Cambridge University Press, 2009), 51–76. Nightingale reads the myth as an allusion to the deus ex machina of the *Antiope*, and is followed (with a different interpretation of the relation) by Trivigno: Nightingale, *Genres in Dialogue*, 86–87; Trivigno, "Paratragedy in Plato's 'Gorgias,'" 85–87. I think this is overly literal (as well as highly speculative), and suggest instead that we understand the myth as part of a pattern of reconciliatory conclusions to the *agōnes*.

a final claim to traditional authority on Socrates' behalf, presenting the conclusions of his philosophical *logos* in a religious *muthos*. The story, Socrates claims, can be viewed in both lights, and thus seems to collapse tradition and novelty. In this sense, the myth resembles the final chorus of Aristophanes' *Frogs*, in which the *makarismos* casts the older tragedian in the language of the new learning. Socrates does the reverse, presenting a novel argument in the form of a familiar myth, but similarly claiming blessedness for the one who adheres to his ethic. The effect is to present Socrates as a figure transcending the dichotomy of tradition and innovation, whose *sophia* is guaranteed both by established belief and by autonomous intellection.

All of the *agōnes*, I have argued, ultimately offer a reconciliatory vision of tradition and novelty, of religious-poetic with intellectual authority. The *Gorgias*' reconciliation takes place in the figure more identified with intellectual innovation, casting Socrates as Amphion or Palamedes (who, as noted before, is often compared to Socrates). Like the dramatic texts, the *Gorgias* presents its negotiation in ways that evoke mystical initiation: its description of rewards and punishments in the afterlife seems to be eclectic, but would at a minimum have evoked an Eleusinian context.[22] The connection Socrates proposes between philosophical *logos* and salvation, moreover, offers a parallel to the dramatic staging of knowledge as initiation.[23] All these texts use agonistic forms to think through changing ideas of intellectual authority, and though they resolve their confrontations in different ways, there is a commonality in the way that the resolutions merge traditional religious and novel philosophical language. This reading suggests that we should understand the second half of the *Gorgias* as being in quite close dialogue with the *Antiope*, but not so much with the particularities of the drama—rather, with the substantive issues raised by its *agōn sophias*. This represents a weaker reading of the *Gorgias*' relation to tragedy than Nightingale's, which attributes less intentionality to Plato's choice of the *Antiope* as an intertext, and to his invocation of tragedy as a genre. But it enables us to see a more interesting and multifaceted dialogue, which the *Gorgias* enters not as polemic or parody, but as a consequential engagement with opposing claims

---

22. Dodds notes that the doctrine of judgment was taught at Eleusis, and that Socrates in the *Apology* (41a) names Triptolemus, who was strongly associated with Eleusis as one of the judges of the dead: Dodds, *Plato: "Gorgias,"* 373–74.

23. The myth of the jars, earlier, had equated knowledge and initiation, and described the ignorant/uninitiated as the most miserable in the afterlife (493a–c). See David Blank, "The Fate of the Ignorant in Plato's 'Gorgias,'" *Hermes* 119 (1991): 22–36.

to intellectual authority. It demonstrates that continuity between Platonic and dramatic dialogue is not just formal, but substantive as well.

The *Gorgias* is probably Plato's most dramalike dialogue, in that it presents a relatively structured story in multiple parts, with a small cast of sharply drawn characters engaged in conflictual interactions. But even if it is an extreme case within the Platonic corpus, it demonstrates the extent of the Socratic dialogue's potential formal and thematic continuities with drama. My reading has emphasized these continuities, since the differences are probably too many and too apparent to require enumeration. The Platonic dialogue is, on the whole, far more flexible formally than drama, able to encompass a vast range of scenes, characters, and discursive modes. Understanding the scenic grammar of the Platonic dialogue would be a massively complex project, though it would have some obvious starting places: narrating voices and frames, entrances and exits, monologue and dialogue, and recurrent elements like allegories and myths (which have been the subject of extensive research already).[24] The wider formal possibilities of the Socratic dialogue probably demand a stronger notion of intentional form than drama does, though it would be crucial to develop this intentionality from the Platonic texts themselves.[25] Attention to the grammar of staging across the dialogues and across discourses would be a valuable project, and would develop the rich vein of scholarship that seeks to bridge literary and philosophical readings of Plato.

The gap between literary and philosophical approaches to Plato, as to early Greek thought in general, is in large part a difference of historical perspective, whether one approaches from the messy past of earlier writing and thinking or from the rigorous future of philosophical method. Though approaching disciplinary philosophy from its chronological origins has an obvious explanatory priority over interpretations that assume later philosophy as a normative model, it is also the more speculative course. This is due, certainly, to evidentiary limitations, but even more, to the basic difficulty of imagining the past otherwise. This is the necessity we are always confronted with in the investigation of history, but the history of philosophy offers the further difficulty that

---

24. Recent volumes on Plato's use of myth are Catalin Partenie, ed., *Plato's Myths* (Cambridge: Cambridge University Press, 2009); Catherine Collobert, Pierre Destrée, and Francisco J. Gonzalez, eds., *Plato and Myth: Studies on the Use and Status of Platonic Myths* (Leiden: Brill, 2012).

25. See the remarks in Mary Margaret McCabe, *Platonic Conversations* (Oxford: Oxford University Press, 2015), 4–7.

so many of the individuals it studies present their own, inevitably partial, versions of this history—and no one does so more brilliantly than Plato. This study has sought to imagine a story that might have been told at the end of the fifth century, when debates concerning the form of philosophical thought had not yet been won by the followers of Socrates, and a more public, performative, and mythological discourse—like that of Gorgias or, indeed, of Euripides—was still a viable contender for intellectual authority. The development of philosophy has made such a story exceptionally difficult to imagine, but it has also furnished us with powerful tools to do so, especially in the form of the Platonic dialogues. If we attend closely to their voices, we catch an echo of the philosophical age of the Greeks.

WORKS CITED

Ahrensdorf, Peter J. *Greek Tragedy and Political Philosophy: Rationalism and Religion in Sophocles' Theban Plays.* Cambridge: Cambridge University Press, 2009.
Annas, Julia. "Plato's Myths of Judgement." *Phronesis* 27 (1982): 119–43.
Arp, Meggan Jennell. "Pre-Socratic Thought in Sophoclean Tragedy." Ph.D. diss., University of Pennsylvania, 2006.
Arthur, Marylin. "The Choral Odes of the 'Bacchae' of Euripides." In *Studies in Fifth-Century Thought and Literature,* edited by Adam Parry, 145–79. Cambridge: Cambridge University Press, 1972.
Assaël, Jacqueline. *Euripide, philosophe et poète tragique.* Louvain: Peeters, 2001.
———. "ὅς . . . θεῶν: Euripide, 'Suppliantes,' v. 201 sqq." *Revue des études grecques* 110 (1997): 84–103.
Austin, Colin, and S. Douglas Olson, eds. *Aristophanes: "Thesmophoriazusae."* Oxford: Oxford University Press, 2004.
Avery, Harry C. "The Chronology of Peisander's Mission to Athens." *Classical Philology* 94 (1999): 127–46.
Bakola, Emmanuela, Lucia Prauscello, and Mario Telò, eds. *Greek Comedy and the Discourse of Genres.* Cambridge: Cambridge University Press, 2013.
Balaudé, Jean-François. "Hippias le passeur." In *La costruzione del discorso filosofico nell'età dei Presocratici,* edited by Maria Michela Sassi, 287–304. Pisa: Edizioni della Normale, 2006.
Barney, Rachel. "Callicles and Thrasymachus." The Stanford Encyclopedia of Philosophy, 2017. https://plato.stanford.edu/archives/fall2017/entries/callicles-thrasymachus/.
———. "Twenty Questions about Protagorean Wisdom." 2009. http://individual.utoronto.ca/rbarney/Protagoras.pdf.
Barrett, James. *Staged Narrative: Poetics and the Messenger in Greek Tragedy.* Berkeley: University of California Press, 2002.
Bassi, Karen. *Traces of the Past: Classics between History and Archaeology.* Ann Arbor: University of Michigan Press, 2016.
Batchelder, Ann G. *The Seal of Orestes: Self-Reference and Authority in Sophocles' "Electra."* Lanham: Rowman & Littlefield, 1995.
Battisti, Daniela. "συνετός as Aristocratic Self-Description." *Greek, Roman, and Byzantine Studies* 31 (1990): 5–25.
Behler, Ernst. "A. W. Schlegel and the Nineteenth-Century *Damnatio* of Euripides." *Greek, Roman, and Byzantine Studies* 27 (1986): 335–67.

Belknap, Robert. "The Literary List: A Survey of Its Uses and Deployments." *Literary Imagination* 2 (2000): 35–54.
Benardete, Seth. "The Crimes and Arts of Prometheus." *Rheinisches Museum* 107 (1964): 126–39.
Benjamin, Walter. *Origin of the German Trauerspiel*. Translated by Howard Eiland. Cambridge, MA: Harvard University Press, 2019.
Betegh, Gábor. "Archelaus on Cosmogony and the Origins of Social Institutions." *Oxford Studies in Ancient Philosophy* 51 (2016): 1–40.
———. *The Derveni Papyrus: Cosmology, Theology and Interpretation*. Cambridge: Cambridge University Press, 2004.
———. "Socrate et Archélaos dans les 'Nuées': Philosophie naturelle et éthique." In *Comédie et philosophie: Socrate et les "Présocratiques" dans les "Nuées" d'Aristophane*, edited by André Laks and Rosella Saetta Cottone, 87–106. Paris: Rue d'Ulm, 2013.
Bett, Richard. "Is There a Sophistic Ethics?" *Ancient Philosophy* 22 (2002): 235–62.
———. "Nature and Norms." In *The Cambridge Companion to the Sophists*, edited by Joshua Billings and Christopher Moore. Cambridge: Cambridge University Press, forthcoming.
Bierl, Anton. "Apollo in Greek Tragedy: Orestes and the God of Initiation." In *Apollo: Origins and Influences*, edited by Jon Solomon, 81–96. Tucson: University of Arizona Press, 1994.
———. *Dionysos und die griechische Tragödie: Politische und "metatheatralische" Aspekte im Text*. Tübingen: Gunter Narr, 1991.
———. "Maenadism as Self-Referential Chorality in Euripides' 'Bacchae.'" In *Choral Mediations in Greek Tragedy*, edited by Renaud Gagné and Marianne Govers Hopman, 211–26. Cambridge: Cambridge University Press, 2013.
———. *Ritual and Performativity: The Chorus in Old Comedy*. Translated by Alexander Hollmann. Washington, DC: Center for Hellenic Studies, 2009.
Biga, Anna Miriam, ed. *L' "Antiope" di Euripide*. Trento: Università degli studi di Trento, 2015.
Biles, Zachary P. "Aeschylus' Afterlife: Reperformance by Decree in 5th C. Athens?" *Illinois Classical Studies* 31/32 (2007): 206–42.
———. *Aristophanes and the Poetics of Competition*. Cambridge: Cambridge University Press, 2011.
Billings, Joshua. "Bacchae." In *Brill's Companion to Euripides*, edited by Andreas Markantonatos, 376–94. Leiden: Brill, 2020.
———. "'Bacchae' as Palinode." *International Journal of the Classical Tradition* 25 (2018): 57–71.
———. *Genealogy of the Tragic: Greek Tragedy and German Philosophy*. Princeton: Princeton University Press, 2014.
———. "Orestes' Urn in Word and Action." In *The Materialities of Greek Tragedy: Objects and Affect in Aeschylus, Sophocles, and Euripides*, edited by Mario Telò and Melissa Mueller, 49–62. London: Bloomsbury, 2018.
Billings, Joshua, and Miriam Leonard, eds. *Tragedy and the Idea of Modernity*. Oxford: Oxford University Press, 2015.
Blank, David. "The Fate of the Ignorant in Plato's 'Gorgias.'" *Hermes* 119 (1991): 22–36.
———. "Faith and Persuasion in Parmenides." *Classical Antiquity* 1 (1982): 167–77.
Blondell, Ruby. *The Play of Character in Plato's Dialogues*. Cambridge: Cambridge University Press, 2002.

Blundell, Mary Whitlock. *Helping Friends and Harming Enemies: A Study in Sophocles and Greek Ethics*. Cambridge: Cambridge University Press, 1989.

———. "The Moral Character of Odysseus in 'Philoctetes.'" *Greek, Roman, and Byzantine Studies* 28 (1987): 307–29.

———. "The 'Phusis' of Neoptolemus in Sophocles' 'Philoctetes.'" *Greece & Rome* 35 (1988): 137–48.

Bowden, Hugh. *Classical Athens and the Delphic Oracle: Divination and Democracy*. Cambridge: Cambridge University Press, 2005.

Bowie, A. M. *Aristophanes: Myth, Ritual, and Comedy*. Cambridge: Cambridge University Press, 1993.

Brisson, Luc. "L'Égypte de Platon." *Études philosophiques* 2–3 (1987): 153–68.

Brown, Andrew, ed. *Aeschylus: "Libation Bearers."* Liverpool: Liverpool University Press, 2018.

Budelmann, Felix. *The Language of Sophocles: Communality, Communication, and Involvement*. Cambridge: Cambridge University Press, 2000.

Burger, Ronna. *Plato's "Phaedrus": A Defense of a Philosophic Art of Writing*. Tuscaloosa: University of Alabama Press, 1980.

Burian, Peter. "Logos and Pathos: The Politics of the 'Suppliant Women.'" In *Directions in Euripidean Criticism*, edited by Peter Burian, 129–55. Durham: Duke University Press, 1985.

Burkert, Walter. "Apellai und Apollon." *Rheinisches Museum* 118 (1975): 1–21.

———. "Das Proömium des Parmenides und die Katabasis des Pythagoras." *Phronesis* 14 (1969): 1–30.

Burton, R.W.B. *The Chorus in Sophocles' Tragedies*. Oxford: Oxford University Press, 1980.

Burzacchini, Gabriele. "Remarques sur quelques fragments élégiaques de Critias." In *La muse au long couteau: Critias, de la création littéraire au terrorisme d'état*, edited by Jean Yvonneau, 35–59. Bordeaux: Ausonius, 2018.

Buxton, R.G.A. *Persuasion in Greek Tragedy: A Study of Peitho*. Cambridge: Cambridge University Press, 1982.

Cairns, Douglas. "From Solon to Sophocles: Intertextuality and Interpretation in Sophocles' 'Antigone.'" *Japan Studies in Classical Antiquity* 2 (2014): 3–30.

Cairns, Douglas, ed. *Tragedy and Archaic Greek Thought*. Swansea: Classical Press of Wales, 2013.

Calogero, Guido. *Studi sull'eleatismo*. Florence: La nuova Italia, 1977.

Carey, Christopher. "Old Comedy and the Sophists." In *The Rivals of Aristophanes*, edited by David Harvey and John Wilkins, 419–36. Swansea: Classical Press of Wales, 2000.

Carson, Anne. "How Not to Read a Poem: Unmixing Simonides from Protagoras." *Classical Philology* 87 (1992): 110–30.

Carter, L. B. *The Quiet Athenian*. Oxford: Oxford University Press, 1986.

Caspers, Christiaan L. "Diversity and Common Ground: Euripides' 'Iphigenia in Aulis' and 'Bacchae' as Companion Plays." In *Greek Drama IV: Texts, Contexts, Performance*, edited by David Rosenbloom and John Davidson, 127–48. Oxford: Aris & Phillips, 2012.

Caston, Victor. "Gorgias on Thought and Its Objects." In *Presocratic Philosophy: Essays in Honour of Alexander Mourelatos*, edited by Victor Caston and Daniel W. Graham, 205–32. Burlington: Ashgate, 2002.

Ceccarelli, Paola. *Ancient Greek Letter Writing: A Cultural History (600 BC–150 BC)*. Oxford: Oxford University Press, 2013.

Chaston, Colleen. *Tragic Props and Cognitive Function: Aspects of the Function of Images in Thinking.* Leiden: Brill, 2010.
Christesen, Paul. "Imagining Olympia: Hippias of Elis and the First Olympian Victor List." In *A Tall Order: Writing the Social History of the Ancient World*, edited by Jean-Jacques Aubert and Zsuzsanna Várhelyi, 319–56. Munich: Saur, 2005.
Clements, Ashley. *Aristophanes' "Thesmophoriazusae": Philosophizing Theatre and the Politics of Perception in Late Fifth-Century Athens.* Cambridge: Cambridge University Press, 2014.
Cole, Thomas. *Democritus and the Sources of Greek Anthropology.* Cleveland: Western Reserve University Press, 1967.
———. *The Origins of Rhetoric in Ancient Greece.* Baltimore: Johns Hopkins University Press, 1991.
Collard, Christopher. "Formal Debates in Euripides' Drama." *Greece & Rome* 22 (1975): 58–71.
Collard, Christopher, ed. *Euripides: "Supplices."* Groningen: Bouma, 1975.
Collard, Christopher, and James Morwood, eds. *Euripides: "Iphigenia at Aulis."* Liverpool: Liverpool University Press, 2017.
Collard, C., M. J. Cropp, and J. Gibert, eds. *Euripides: Selected Fragmentary Plays,* Volume II. Oxford: Aris & Phillips, 2004.
Collins, Derek. *Master of the Game: Competition and Performance in Greek Poetry.* Washington, DC: Center for Hellenic Studies, 2004.
Collobert, Catherine, Pierre Destrée, and Francisco J. Gonzalez, eds. *Plato and Myth: Studies on the Use and Status of Platonic Myths.* Leiden: Brill, 2012.
Conacher, Desmond J. *Euripides and the Sophists: Some Dramatic Treatments of Philosophical Ideas.* London: Duckworth, 1998.
———. "Prometheus as Founder of the Arts." *Greek, Roman, and Byzantine Studies* 18 (1977): 189–206.
———. "Rhetoric and Relevance in Euripidean Drama." *American Journal of Philology* 102 (1981): 3–25.
Cooper, John M. *Pursuits of Wisdom: Six Ways of Life in Ancient Philosophy from Socrates to Plotinus.* Princeton: Princeton University Press, 2012.
Coray, Marina. *Wissen und Erkennen bei Sophokles.* Basel: Reinhardt, 1993.
Corey, David. "The Sophist Hippias and the Problem of Polytropia." In *Socratic Philosophy and Its Others*, edited by Christopher A. Dustin and Denise Schaeffer, 91–114. Lanham: Lexington Books, 2013.
Crane, Gregory. "Creon and the 'Ode to Man' in Sophocles' 'Antigone.'" *Harvard Studies in Classical Philology* 92 (1989): 103–16.
———. *Thucydides and the Ancient Simplicity: The Limits of Political Realism.* Berkeley: University of California Press, 1998.
Cropp, Martin. "τί τὸ σοφόν;" *Bulletin of the Institute of Classical Studies* 28 (1981): 39–42.
Csapo, Eric. "Later Euripidean Music." *Illinois Classical Studies* 24/25 (2000): 399–426.
Curd, Patricia. "Eleatic Monism in Zeno and Melissus." *Ancient Philosophy* 13 (1993): 1–22.
———. "Gorgias and the Eleatics." In *La costruzione del discorso filosofico nell'età dei Presocratici*, edited by Maria Michela Sassi, 183–200. Pisa: Edizioni della Normale, 2006.
———. *The Legacy of Parmenides: Eleatic Monism and Later Presocratic Thought.* Princeton: Princeton University Press, 1998.

D'Angour, Armand. *The Greeks and the New: Novelty in Ancient Greek Imagination and Experience*. Cambridge: Cambridge University Press, 2011.
Decleva Caizzi, Fernanda. "Protagoras and Antiphon: Sophistic Debates on Justice." In *The Cambridge Companion to Early Greek Philosophy*, edited by Anthony A. Long, 311–31. Cambridge: Cambridge University Press, 1999.
Derrida, Jacques. "Plato's Pharmacy." In *Dissemination*, translated by Barbara Johnson, 61–171. Chicago: University of Chicago Press, 1981.
Detienne, Marcel. *The Masters of Truth in Archaic Greece*. Translated by Janet Lloyd. New York: Zone Books, 1996.
Detienne, Marcel, and Jean-Pierre Vernant. *Cunning Intelligence in Greek Culture and Society*. Translated by Janet Lloyd. Chicago: University of Chicago Press, 1991.
Devine, A. M., and Laurence D. Stephens. "A New Aspect of the Evolution of the Trimeter in Euripides." *Transactions of the American Philological Association* 111 (1981): 43–64.
Di Benedetto, Vincenzo. "Osservazioni su alcuni frammenti dell' 'Antiope' di Euripide." In *Euripide e i papiri*, edited by Guido Bastianini and Angelo Casanova, 97–122. Florence: Istituto Papirologico G. Vitelli, 2005.
Dihle, Albrecht. "Das Satyrspiel 'Sisyphos.'" *Hermes* 105 (1977): 28–42.
Dillon, John. "Euripides and the Philosophy of His Time." *Classics Ireland* 11 (2004): 47–73.
Ditmars, Elizabeth van Nes. *Sophocles' "Antigone": Lyric Shape and Meaning*. Pisa: Giardini, 1992.
Dodds, E. R. "The Ancient Concept of Progress." In *The Ancient Concept of Progress and Other Essays on Greek Literature and Belief*, 1–25. Oxford: Clarendon Press, 1973.
———. *The Greeks and the Irrational*. Berkeley: University of California Press, 1951.
Dodds, E. R., ed. *Euripides: "Bacchae."* 2nd ed. Oxford: Clarendon Press, 1960.
———. *Plato: "Gorgias."* 2nd ed. Oxford: Clarendon Press, 1959.
Dorion, Louis-André. "The Nature and Status of 'Sophia' in the 'Memorabilia.'" In *Xenophon: Ethical Principles and Historical Enquiry*, edited by Fiona Hobden and Christopher Tuplin, 455–75. Leiden: Brill, 2012.
Dover, K. J. "The Freedom of the Intellectual in Greek Society." *Talanta* 7 (1975): 24–54.
Dover, K. J., ed. *Aristophanes: "Frogs."* Oxford: Oxford University Press, 1993.
Downing, Eric. "Apate, Agon and Literary Self-Reflexivity in Euripides' 'Helen.'" In *Cabinet of the Muses: Essays on Classical and Comparative Literature in Honor of Thomas G. Rosenmeyer*, edited by Mark Griffith and Donald J. Mastronarde, 1–16. Atlanta: Scholars Press, 1990.
Doyle, James. "The Fundamental Conflict in Plato's 'Gorgias.'" *Oxford Studies in Ancient Philosophy* 30 (2006): 87–100.
Dressler, Jan. *Wortverdreher, Sonderlinge, Gottlose: Kritik an Philosophie und Rhetorik im klassischen Athen*. Berlin: de Gruyter, 2014.
Dubischar, Markus. *Die Agonszenen bei Euripides: Untersuchungen zu ausgewählten Dramen*. Stuttgart: Metzler, 2001.
Duchemin, Jacqueline. *L'Agon dans la tragédie grecque*. 2nd ed. Paris: Belles Lettres, 1968.
Dunn, Francis. "'On Ancient Medicine' and Its Intellectual Context." In *Hippocrates in Context*, edited by Philip J. van der Eijk, 49–67. Leiden: Brill, 2005.
———. "Trope and Setting in Sophocles' 'Electra.'" In *Sophocles and the Greek Language: Aspects of Diction, Syntax and Pragmatics*, edited by Irene J. F. de Jong and Albert Rijksbaron, 184–200. Leiden: Brill, 2006.

Eagleton, Terry. *Sweet Violence: The Idea of the Tragic.* Oxford: Blackwell, 2003.
Easterling, Patricia E. "'Philoctetes' and Modern Criticism." *Illinois Classical Studies* 3 (1978): 27–39.
———. "The Second Stasimon of 'Antigone.'" In *Dionysiaca: Nine Studies in Greek Poetry by Former Pupils,* edited by Roger D. Dawe, James Diggle, and Patricia E. Easterling, 141–58. Cambridge: Cambridge Faculty Library, 1978.
Ebbott, Mary. "The List of the War Dead in Aeschylus' 'Persians.'" *Harvard Studies in Classical Philology* 100 (2000): 83–96.
Eco, Umberto. *The Infinity of Lists.* Translated by Alastair McEwen. New York: Rizzoli, 2009.
Edelstein, Ludwig. *The Idea of Progress in Classical Antiquity.* Baltimore: Johns Hopkins University Press, 1967.
Edmonds, Radcliffe G. *Myths of the Underworld Journey: Plato, Aristophanes, and the "Orphic" Gold Tablets.* Cambridge: Cambridge University Press, 2004.
Edwards, Mark W. "The Structure of Homeric Catalogs." *Transactions of the American Philological Association* 110 (1980): 81–105.
Egli, Franziska. *Euripides im Kontext zeitgenössischer intellektueller Strömungen: Analyse der Funktion philosophischer Themen in den Tragödien und Fragmenten.* Munich: Saur, 2003.
Euben, J. Peter. *The Tragedy of Political Theory.* Princeton: Princeton University Press, 1990.
Falcetto, Raffaella, ed. *Il "Palamede" di Euripide: Edizione e commento dei frammenti.* Alessandria: Edizioni dell'Orso, 2002.
Falkner, Thomas M. "Containing Tragedy: Rhetoric and Self-Representation in Sophocles' 'Philoctetes.'" *Classical Antiquity* 17 (1998): 25–58.
Faraone, Christopher A. "Catalogues, Priamels, and Stanzaic Structure in Early Greek Elegy." *Transactions of the American Philological Association* 135 (2005): 249–65.
———. "Curses, Crime Detection and Conflict Resolution at the Festival of Demeter Thesmophoros." *Journal of Hellenic Studies* 131 (2011): 25–44.
———. "The Poetics of the Catalogue in the Hesiodic 'Theogony.'" *Transactions of the American Philological Association* 143 (2013): 293–323.
———. *The Stanzaic Architecture of Early Greek Elegy.* Oxford: Oxford University Press, 2008.
Farmer, Matthew C. *Tragedy on the Comic Stage.* Oxford: Oxford University Press, 2017.
Ferrari, G.R.F. "Hesiod's Mimetic Muses and the Strategies of Deconstruction." In *Post-Structuralist Classics,* edited by Andrew Benjamin, 45–78. London: Routledge, 1988.
———. *Listening to the Cicadas: A Study of Plato's "Phaedrus."* Cambridge: Cambridge University Press, 1987.
Finglass, P. J., ed. *Sophocles: "Ajax."* Cambridge: Cambridge University Press, 2011.
———. *Sophocles: "Electra."* Cambridge: Cambridge University Press, 2007.
Finkelberg, Margalit. *The Birth of Literary Fiction in Ancient Greece.* Oxford: Clarendon Press, 1998.
Flower, Michael Attyah. *The Seer in Ancient Greece.* Berkeley: University of California Press, 2008.
Foley, Helene P. *Female Acts in Greek Tragedy.* Princeton: Princeton University Press, 2001.
———. "Generic Boundaries in Late Fifth-Century Athens." In *Performance, Iconography, Reception: Studies in Honour of Oliver Taplin,* edited by Martin Revermann and Peter Wilson, 15–36. Oxford: Oxford University Press, 2008.

Ford, Andrew. "The Beginnings of Dialogue: Socratic Discourses and Fourth-Century Prose." In *The End of Dialogue in Antiquity*, edited by Simon Goldhill, 29–44. Cambridge: Cambridge University Press, 2008.

———. *The Origins of Criticism: Literary Culture and Poetic Theory in Classical Greece*. Princeton: Princeton University Press, 2002.

———. "Σωκρατικοὶ λόγοι in Aristotle and Fourth-Century Theories of Genre." *Classical Philology* 105 (2010): 221–35.

Forster, Michael N. "Socrates' Profession of Ignorance." *Oxford Studies in Ancient Philosophy* 32 (2007): 1–35.

Franz, Michael. "Fiktionalität und Wahrheit in der Sicht des Gorgias und des Aristoteles." *Philologus* 135 (1991): 240–48.

Fraser, Lilah-Grace. "A Woman of Consequence: Pandora in Hesiod's 'Works and Days.'" *Cambridge Classical Journal* 57 (2011): 9–28.

Froleyks, Walter Johannes. "Der Agōn Logōn in der antiken Literatur." Ph.D. diss., Rheinischen Friedrich-Wilhelms-Universität zu Bonn, 1973.

Furley, David J. "Antiphon's Case against Justice." In *The Sophists and Their Legacy*, edited by G. B. Kerferd, 81–91. Wiesbaden: Steiner, 1981.

Gagarin, Michael. *Antiphon the Athenian: Oratory, Law, and Justice in the Age of the Sophists*. Austin: University of Texas Press, 2002.

———. "Did the Sophists Aim to Persuade?" *Rhetorica* 19 (2001): 275–91.

Gagné, Renaud. *Ancestral Fault in Ancient Greece*. Cambridge: Cambridge University Press, 2013.

———. "What Is the Pride of Halicarnassus?" *Classical Antiquity* 25 (2006): 1–33.

Gaines, Robert N. "Knowledge and Discourse in Gorgias's 'On the Non-Existent or On Nature.'" *Philosophy & Rhetoric* 30 (1997): 1–12.

Garvie, Alexander F. "Deceit, Violence, and Persuasion in the 'Philoctetes.'" In *Studi classici in onore di Quintino Cataudella*, 213–26. Catania: Facoltà di Lettere e Filosofia, 1972.

Garvie, Alexander F., ed. *Aeschylus: "Persae."* Oxford: Oxford University Press, 2009.

Gelzer, Thomas. *Der epirrhematische Agon bei Aristophanes: Untersuchungen zur Struktur der attischen Alten Komödie*. Munich: Beck, 1960.

Gera, Deborah Levine. *Ancient Greek Ideas on Speech, Language, and Civilization*. Oxford: Oxford University Press, 2003.

Gianvittorio, Laura. "One Deception, Many Lies: Frr. 301/302 Radt and Aeschylus' 'Philoctetes.'" *Wiener Studien* 128 (2015): 19–26.

Gibert, John. "Euripides' 'Antiope' and the Quiet Life." In *The Play of Texts and Fragments: Essays in Honour of Martin Cropp*, edited by J.R.C. Cousland and James R. Hume, 23–34. Leiden: Brill, 2009.

Gill, Christopher. "Bow, Oracle, and Epiphany in Sophocles' 'Philoctetes.'" *Greece & Rome* 27 (1980): 137–46.

Gladigow, Burkhard. *Sophia und Kosmos: Untersuchungen zur Frühgeschichte von sophos und sophiē*. Hildesheim: Olms, 1965.

———. "Zum Makarismos des Weisen." *Hermes* 95 (1967): 404–33.

Glauthier, Patrick. "Playing the Volcano: 'Prometheus Bound' and Fifth-Century Volcanic Theory." *Classical Philology* 113 (2018): 255–78.

Gödde, Susanne. *Euphêmia: Die gute Rede in Kult und Literatur der griechischen Antike*. Heidelberg: Winter, 2011.
Goldhill, Simon. "Battle Narrative and Politics in Aeschylus' 'Persae.'" *Journal of Hellenic Studies* 108 (1988): 189–93.
Gomperz, Heinrich. *Sophistik und Rhetorik: Das Bildungsideal des εὖ λέγειν in seinem Verhältnis zur Philosophie des 5. Jahrhunderts*. Stuttgart: Teubner, 1912.
Goody, Jack. *The Domestication of the Savage Mind*. Cambridge: Cambridge University Press, 1977.
Gordon, Richard. "'What's in a List?' Listing in Greek and Graeco-Roman Malign Magical Texts." In *The World of Ancient Magic: Papers from the First International Samson Eitrem Seminar at the Norwegian Institute at Athens, 4–8 May 1997*, edited by David R. Jordan, Hugo Montgomery, and Einar Thomassen, 239–77. Bergen: Norwegian Institute at Athens, 1999.
Granger, Herbert. "The Proem of Parmenides' Poem." *Ancient Philosophy* 28 (2008): 1–20.
Grethlein, Jonas. *The Ancient Aesthetics of Deception*. Cambridge: Cambridge University Press, forthcoming.
Griffith, Mark. "Apollo, Teiresias, and the Politics of Tragic Prophecy." In *Apolline Politics and Poetics*, edited by Lucia Athanassaki, Richard P. Martin, and John F. Miller, 473–500. Athens: Hellenic Ministry of Culture, 2009.
———. *Aristophanes' "Frogs."* Oxford: Oxford University Press, 2013.
———. "Contest and Contradiction in Early Greek Poetry." In *Cabinet of the Muses: Essays on Classical and Comparative Literature in Honor of Thomas G. Rosenmeyer*, edited by Mark Griffith and Donald J. Mastronarde, 185–207. Atlanta: Scholars Press, 1990.
Griffith, Mark, ed. *Aeschylus: "Prometheus Bound."* Cambridge: Cambridge University Press, 1983.
———. *Sophocles: "Antigone."* Cambridge: Cambridge University Press, 1999.
Gurd, Sean Alexander. *Iphigenias at Aulis: Textual Multiplicity, Radical Philology*. Ithaca: Cornell University Press, 2005.
Guthrie, W.K.C. *The Sophists*. Cambridge: Cambridge University Press, 1971.
Habash, Martha. "The Odd Thesmophoria of Aristophanes' 'Thesmophoriazusae.'" *Greek, Roman, and Byzantine Studies* 38 (1997): 19–40.
Haldane, J. A. "A Scene in the 'Thesmophoriazusae' (295–371)." *Philologus* 109 (1965): 39–46.
Hall, Edith. *Adventures with "Iphigenia in Tauris": A Cultural History of Euripides' Black Sea Tragedy*. Oxford: Oxford University Press, 2013.
———. *The Theatrical Cast of Athens: Interactions between Ancient Greek Drama and Society*. Oxford: Oxford University Press, 2006.
Halleran, Michael R. "Lichas' Lies and Sophoclean Innovation." *Greek, Roman, and Byzantine Studies* 27 (1986): 239–47.
Halliwell, Stephen. *The Aesthetics of Mimesis: Ancient Texts and Modern Problems*. Princeton: Princeton University Press, 2002.
———. *Between Ecstasy and Truth: Interpretations of Greek Poetics from Homer to Longinus*. Oxford: Oxford University Press, 2011.
Hanink, Johanna. "The Great Dionysia and the End of the Peloponnesian War." *Classical Antiquity* 33 (2014): 319–46.

Hanink, Johanna, and Anna S. Uhlig. "Aeschylus and His Afterlife in the Classical Period: 'My Poetry Did Not Die with Me.'" In *The Reception of Aeschylus' Plays through Shifting Models and Frontiers*, edited by Stratos Constantinidis, 51–79. Leiden: Brill, 2017.

Harriman, Benjamin. *Melissus and Eleatic Monism*. Cambridge: Cambridge University Press, 2019.

Harris, John P. "Revenge of the Nerds: Xenophanes, Euripides, and Socrates vs. Olympic Victors." *American Journal of Philology* 130 (2009): 157–94.

Harrison, Jane Ellen. *Themis: A Study of the Social Origins of Greek Religion*. 2nd ed. Cambridge: Cambridge University Press, 1927.

Haselswerdt, Ella. "Chorality and Lyric Thought in Greek Tragedy." Ph.D. diss., Princeton University, 2018.

Havelock, Eric A. *The Liberal Temper in Greek Politics*. New Haven: Yale University Press, 1957.

Hays, Steve. "On the Skeptical Influence of Gorgias's 'On Non-Being.'" *Journal of the History of Philosophy* 28 (1990): 327–37.

Heath, John. *The Talking Greeks: Speech, Animals, and the Other in Homer, Aeschylus, and Plato*. Cambridge: Cambridge University Press, 2005.

Heidegger, Martin. "Plato's Doctrine of Truth." In *Pathmarks*, edited by William McNeil, 155–82. Cambridge: Cambridge University Press, 1998.

Heiden, Bruce. "The Muses' Uncanny Lies: Hesiod, 'Theogony' 27 and Its Translators." *American Journal of Philology* 128 (2007): 153–75.

———. "Tragedy and Comedy in the 'Frogs' of Aristophanes." *Ramus* 20 (1991): 95–111.

Heinimann, Felix. *Nomos und Physis: Herkunft und Bedeutung einer Antithese im griechischen Denken des 5. Jahrhunderts*. Basel: Reinhardt, 1965.

Henrich, Dieter. *Konstellationen: Probleme und Debatten am Ursprung der idealistischen Philosophie (1789–1795)*. Stuttgart: Klett-Cotta, 1991.

Henrichs, Albert. "Between Country and City: Cultic Dimensions of Dionysus in Athens and Attica." In *Cabinet of the Muses: Essays on Classical and Comparative Literature in Honor of Thomas G. Rosenmeyer*, edited by Mark Griffith and Donald J. Mastronarde, 257–77. Atlanta: Scholars Press, 1990.

———. "The Last of the Detractors: Friedrich Nietzsche's Condemnation of Euripides." *Greek, Roman, and Byzantine Studies* 27 (1986): 369–97.

———. "The Sophists and Hellenistic Religion: Prodicus as the Spiritual Father of the Isis Aretalogies." *Harvard Studies in Classical Philology* 88 (1984): 139–58.

———. "Two Doxographical Notes: Democritus and Prodicus on Religion." *Harvard Studies in Classical Philology* 79 (1975): 93–123.

Herrmann, Fritz-Gregor. "Poetry in Plato's' 'Gorgias.'" In *Plato and the Poets*, edited by Pierre Destrée and Fritz-Gregor Herrmann, 21–40. Leiden: Brill, 2011.

Hesk, Jon. *Deception and Democracy in Classical Athens*. Cambridge: Cambridge University Press, 2000.

Hester, D. A. "Deianeira's 'Deception Speech.'" *Antichthon* 14 (1980): 1–8.

Hinds, A. E. "The Prophecy of Helenus in Sophocles' 'Philoctetes.'" *Classical Quarterly* 17 (1967): 169–80.

Honig, Bonnie. *Antigone, Interrupted*. Cambridge: Cambridge University Press, 2013.

Hoppin, Meredith Clarke. "What Happens in Sophocles' 'Philoctetes'?" *Traditio* 37 (1981): 1–30.

Horky, Phillip Sidney. *Plato and Pythagoreanism*. Oxford: Oxford University Press, 2013.

Horsley, G.H.R. "Apollo in Sophokles' 'Elektra.'" *Antichthon* 14 (1980): 18–29.

Hose, Martin. *Euripides als Anthropologe*. Munich: Bayerische Akademie der Wissenschaften, 2009.

Hubbard, Thomas K. *The Mask of Comedy: Aristophanes and the Intertextual Parabasis*. Ithaca: Cornell University Press, 1991.

Humar, Marcel. "Catalogs and Ring Compositions in Hesiod's 'Theogony.'" *Hermes* 144 (2016): 384–400.

Hunter, Richard. *Critical Moments in Classical Literature: Studies in the Ancient View of Literature and Its Uses*. Cambridge: Cambridge University Press, 2009.

———. "The 'Hippias Minor' and the Traditions of Homeric Criticism." *Cambridge Classical Journal* 62 (2016): 85–107.

Hutchinson, G. O. "Gods Wise and Foolish: Euripides and Greek Literature from Homer to Plutarch." In *Wisdom and Folly in Euripides*, edited by Poulheria Kyriakou and Antonios Rengakos, 37–44. Berlin: de Gruyter, 2016.

Iannucci, Alessandro. *La parola e l'azione: I frammenti simposiali di Crizia*. Bologna: Nautilus, 2002.

Ioli, Roberta, ed. *Gorgia: "Su ciò che non è."* Hildesheim: Olms, 2010.

Irani, Tushar. *Plato on the Value of Philosophy: The Art of Argument in the "Gorgias" and "Phaedrus."* Cambridge: Cambridge University Press, 2017.

Irby-Massie, Georgia L. "'Prometheus Bound' and Contemporary Trends in Greek Natural Philosophy." *Greek, Roman, and Byzantine Studies* 48 (2008): 133–57.

Iversen, Erik. *The Myth of Egypt and Its Hieroglyphs in European Tradition*. Princeton: Princeton University Press, 1993.

Jameson, Fredric. *Marxism and Form: Twentieth-Century Dialectical Theories of Literature*. Princeton: Princeton University Press, 1971.

———. *The Political Unconscious: Narrative as a Socially Symbolic Act*. Ithaca: Cornell University Press, 1981.

Janaway, Christopher. *Images of Excellence: Plato's Critique of the Arts*. Oxford: Oxford University Press, 1995.

Jay, Martin. *Reason after Its Eclipse: On Late Critical Theory*. Madison: University of Wisconsin Press, 2016.

Jedrkiewicz, Stefano. "Do Not Sit near Socrates (Aristophanes' 'Frogs,' 1482–1499)." In *Allusion, Authority, and Truth: Critical Perspectives on Greek Poetic and Rhetorical Praxis*, edited by Phillip Mitsis and Christos Tsagalis, 339–58. Berlin: de Gruyter, 2010.

———. "Vengeur? Sauveur? Menteur?: Apollon aux yeux des trois Électres." *Lexis* 30 (2012): 294–307.

Jendza, Craig. *Paracomedy: Appropriations of Comedy in Greek Tragedy*. Oxford: Oxford University Press, 2020.

Jong, Irene J. F. de. "Sophocles 'Trachiniae' 1–48, Euripidean Prologues, and Their Audiences." In *The Language of Literature: Linguistic Approaches to Classical Texts*, edited by Rutger J. Allan and Michel Buijs, 7–28. Boston: Brill, 2007.

Jouanna, Jacques. *Hippocrates*. Baltimore: Johns Hopkins University Press, 1999.

———. "Oracles et devins chez Sophocle." In *Oracles et prophéties dans l'antiquité*, edited by Jean-Georges Heintz, 283–320. Paris: Éditions de Boccard, 1997.

———. *Sophocles: A Study of His Theater in Its Political and Social Context*. Translated by Steven Rendall. Princeton: Princeton University Press, 2018.
Judet de la Combe, Pierre. *Les tragédies grecques sont-elles tragiques? Théâtre et théorie*. Montrouge: Bayard, 2010.
Kahn, Charles. "Greek Religion and Philosophy in the Sisyphus Fragment." *Phronesis* 42 (1997): 247–62.
Kahn, Charles H. "Drama and Dialectic in Plato's 'Gorgias.'" *Oxford Studies in Ancient Philosophy* 1 (1983): 75–121.
———. "The Origins of Social Contract Theory." In *The Sophists and Their Legacy*, edited by G. B. Kerferd, 92–108. Wiesbaden: Steiner, 1981.
———. *Plato and the Socratic Dialogue: The Philosophical Use of a Literary Form*. Cambridge: Cambridge University Press, 1996.
———. "Religion and Natural Philosophy in Empedocles' Doctrine of the Soul." *Archiv für Geschichte der Philosophie* 42 (1960): 3–35.
Kamtekar, Rachana. "The Profession of Friendship: Callicles, Democratic Politics, and Rhetorical Education in Plato's 'Gorgias.'" *Ancient Philosophy* 25 (2005): 319–39.
Kant, Immanuel. *Critique of Pure Reason*. Translated by Paul Guyer and Allen W. Wood. Cambridge: Cambridge University Press, 1998.
Karamanou, Ioanna. "Fragments of Euripidean Rhetoric: The Trial-Debate in Euripides' 'Alexandros.'" In *Connecting Rhetoric and Attic Drama*, edited by Milagros Quijada Sagredo and M. Carmen Encinas Reguero, 161–76. Bari: Levante, 2017.
Karamanou, Ioanna, ed. *Euripides: "Alexandros."* Berlin: de Gruyter, 2017.
Katz, Joshua T., and Katharina Volk. "'Mere Bellies'?: A New Look at 'Theogony' 26–8." *Journal of Hellenic Studies* 120 (2000): 122–31.
Kerferd, G. B. "The First Greek Sophists." *Classical Review* 64 (1950): 8–10.
———. "Gorgias on Nature or That Which Is Not." *Phronesis* 1 (1955): 3–25.
———. "The Image of the Wise Man in Greece in the Period before Plato." In *Images of Man in Ancient and Medieval Thought*, edited by Gerard Verbeke, 17–28. Leuven: Leuven University Press, 1976.
———. *The Sophistic Movement*. Cambridge: Cambridge University Press, 1981.
Kindt, Julia. *Revisiting Delphi: Religion and Storytelling in Ancient Greece*. Cambridge: Cambridge University Press, 2016.
Kingsley, Peter. *Ancient Philosophy, Mystery, and Magic: Empedocles and Pythagorean Tradition*. Oxford: Oxford University Press, 1995.
Kirk, Athena. *The Tally of Text: Catalogues and Inventories in Ancient Greece*. Forthcoming.
Kitzinger, Rachel. *The Choruses of Sophokles' "Antigone" and "Philoktetes": A Dance of Words*. Leiden: Brill, 2008.
———. "Why Mourning Becomes Elektra." *Classical Antiquity* 10 (1991): 298–327.
Kleingünther, Adolf. πρῶτος εὑρετής: *Untersuchungen zur Geschichte einer Fragestellung*. Leipzig: Dieterich, 1933.
Knox, Bernard. *The Heroic Temper: Studies in Sophoclean Tragedy*. Berkeley: University of California Press, 1964.
Knudsen, Rachel Ahern. "Poetic Speakers, Sophistic Words." *American Journal of Philology* 133 (2012): 31–60.

Kotwick, Mirjam. "Interrogating the Gods." In *The Cambridge Companion to the Sophists*, edited by Joshua Billings and Christopher Moore. Cambridge: Cambridge University Press, forthcoming.

Kovacs, David. *Euripidea*. Leiden: Brill, 1994.

———. *Euripidea altera*. Leiden: Brill, 1996.

———. *Euripidea tertia*. Leiden: Brill, 2002.

———. "New Religion and Old in Euripides' 'Bacchae.'" In *Looking at "Bacchae,"* edited by David Stuttard, 29–41. London: Bloomsbury, 2016.

———. "Toward a Reconstruction of 'Iphigenia Aulidensis.'" *Journal of Hellenic Studies* 123 (2003): 77–103.

Kowalzig, Barbara. "'And Now All the World Shall Dance!' Dionysus' Choroi between Drama and Ritual." In *The Origins of Theater in Ancient Greece and Beyond*, edited by Eric Csapo and Margaret C. Miller, 221–51. Cambridge: Cambridge University Press, 2007.

Kremmer, Martin. *De catalogis heurematum*. Leipzig, 1890.

Kurke, Leslie. *Aesopic Conversations: Popular Tradition, Cultural Dialogue, and the Invention of Greek Prose*. Princeton: Princeton University Press, 2011.

———. *Coins, Bodies, Games, and Gold: The Politics of Meaning in Archaic Greece*. Princeton: Princeton University Press, 1999.

Lada-Richards, Ismene. *Initiating Dionysus: Ritual and Theatre in Aristophanes' "Frogs."* Oxford: Oxford University Press, 1999.

———. "Staging the Ephebeia: Theatrical Role-Playing and Spiritual Transition in Sophocles' 'Philoctetes.'" *Ramus* 27 (1998): 1–26.

Laks, André. *The Concept of Presocratic Philosophy: Its Origin, Development, and Significance*. Translated by Glenn Most. Princeton: Princeton University Press, 2018.

Laks, André, and Glenn W. Most. *Early Greek Philosophy*. 9 vols. Cambridge, MA: Harvard University Press, 2016.

Lamari, Anna A. "Aeschylus' 'Seven against Thebes' vs. Euripides' 'Phoenissae': Male vs. Female Power." *Wiener Studien* 120 (2007): 5–24.

Lambropoulos, Vassilis. *The Tragic Idea*. London: Duckworth, 2006.

Lardinois, André. "The Polysemy of Gnomic Expressions and Ajax's Deception Speech." In *Sophocles and the Greek Language: Aspects of Diction, Syntax and Pragmatics*, edited by Irene J. F. de Jong and Albert Rijksbaron, 213–23. Leiden: Brill, 2006.

Lardinois, A.P.M.H., and Th. C. W. Oudemans. *Tragic Ambiguity: Anthropology, Philosophy and Sophocles' "Antigone."* Leiden: Brill, 1987.

Lawrence, Stuart E. "The Dramatic Epistemology of Sophocles' 'Trachiniae.'" *Phoenix* 32 (1978): 288–304.

Lefèvre, Eckard. *Studien zu den Quellen und zum Verständnis des "Prometheus Desmotes."* Göttingen: Vandenhoeck & Ruprecht, 2003.

Lefkowitz, Mary R. *Euripides and the Gods*. Oxford: Oxford University Press, 2016.

Legaspi, Michael C. *Wisdom in Classical and Biblical Tradition*. Oxford: Oxford University Press, 2018.

Leigh, Matthew. *From Polypragmon to Curiosus: Ancient Concepts of Curious and Meddlesome*. Oxford: Oxford University Press, 2013.

Leinieks, Valdis. *The City of Dionysus: A Study of Euripides' "Bakchai."* Stuttgart: Teubner, 1996.

———. "Euripides, 'Bakchai' 877–81 = 897–901." *Journal of Hellenic Studies* 104 (1984): 178–79.
Leitao, David D. *The Pregnant Male as Myth and Metaphor in Classical Greek Literature.* Cambridge: Cambridge University Press, 2012.
Leonard, Miriam. *Tragic Modernities.* Cambridge, MA: Harvard University Press, 2015.
Lesher, J. H. "Xenophanes on Inquiry and Discovery: An Alternative to the 'Hymn to Progress' Reading of Fr. 18." *Ancient Philosophy* 11 (1991): 229–48.
Levine, Caroline. *Forms: Whole, Rhythm, Hierarchy, Network.* Princeton: Princeton University Press, 2015.
Lévystone, David. "La figure d'Ulysse chez les Socratiques: Socrate polutropos." *Phronesis* 50 (2005): 181–214.
Lincoln, Bruce. *Authority: Construction and Corrosion.* Chicago: University of Chicago Press, 1994.
Lipka, Michael. "Aretalogical Poetry: A Forgotten Genre of Greek Literature." *Philologus* 162 (2018): 208–31.
Lloyd, G.E.R. *The Revolutions of Wisdom: Studies in the Claims and Practice of Ancient Greek Science.* Berkeley: University of California Press, 1987.
Lloyd, Michael. *The Agon in Euripides.* Oxford: Clarendon Press, 1992.
Loraux, Nicole. *The Mourning Voice: An Essay on Greek Tragedy.* Translated by Elizabeth Trapnell Rawlings. Ithaca: Cornell University Press, 2002.
Lubarr-Glasman, Rebecca S. "The Finest of Dramas: Knowledge and Deception in Plato's Aesthetics and Sophoclean Tragedy." Ph.D. diss., Columbia University, 2002.
Lush, Brian V. "Popular Authority in Euripides' 'Iphigenia in Aulis.'" *American Journal of Philology* 136 (2015): 207–42.
Ma, John. "Black Hunter Variations." *Proceedings of the Cambridge Philological Society* 40 (1994): 49–80.
MacLeod, Leona. *Dolos and Dikē in Sophokles' "Elektra."* Leiden: Brill, 2001.
Maier, Friedrich. *Der sophos-Begriff: Zur Bedeutung, Wertung und Rolle des Begriffes von Homer bis Euripides.* Augsburg: Blasaditsch, 1970.
Mainberger, Sabine. *Die Kunst des Aufzählens: Elemente zu einer Poetik des Enumerativen.* Berlin: de Gruyter, 2003.
Major, Wilfred E. *The Court of Comedy: Aristophanes, Rhetoric, and Democracy in Fifth-Century Athens.* Columbus: Ohio State University Press, 2013.
Mansfeld, Jaap. "Aristotle, Plato, and the Preplatonic Doxography and Chronology." In *Studies in the Historiography of Greek Philosophy,* 22–83. Assen: Van Gorcum, 1990.
———. "The Chronology of Anaxagoras' Athenian Period and the Date of His Trial. Part II. The Plot against Pericles and His Associates." *Mnemosyne* 33 (1980): 17–95.
Markantonatos, Andreas. "Leadership in Action: Wise Policy and Firm Resolve in Euripides' 'Iphigenia at Aulis.'" In *Crisis on Stage: Tragedy and Comedy in Late Fifth-Century Athens,* edited by Andreas Markantonatos and Bernhard Zimmermann. Berlin: de Gruyter, 2011.
Marshall, C. W. "How to Write a Messenger Speech (Sophocles, 'Electra' 680–763)." In *Greek Drama III: Essays in Honour of Kevin Lee,* edited by John Davidson, Frances Muecke, and Peter Wilson, 203–21. London: Institute of Classical Studies, 2006.
Martin, Gunther, ed. *Euripides: "Ion."* Berlin: de Gruyter, 2018.

Martin, Richard P. "The Seven Sages as Performers of Wisdom." In *Cultural Poetics in Archaic Greece: Cult, Performance, Politics*, edited by Carol Dougherty and Leslie Kurke, 108–28. Oxford: Oxford University Press, 1998.

Martzavou, Paraskevi. "Isis Aretalogies, Initiations, and Emotions: The Isis Aretalogies as a Source for the Study of Emotions." In *Unveiling Emotions: Sources and Methods for the Study of Emotions in the Greek World*, edited by Angelos Chaniotis, 267–91. Stuttgart: Steiner, 2012.

Maso, Stefano, ed. *"Dissoi logoi": Edizione criticamente rivista, introduzione, traduzione, commento.* Rome: Edizioni di Storia e Letteratura, 2018.

Mastronarde, Donald J. *The Art of Euripides: Dramatic Technique and Social Context*. Cambridge: Cambridge University Press, 2010.

———. "The Optimistic Rationalist in Euripides: Theseus, Jocasta, Teiresias." In *Greek Tragedy and Its Legacy: Essays Presented to D. J. Conacher*, edited by Martin Cropp, Elaine Fantham, and S. E. Scully, 201–11. Calgary: University of Calgary Press, 1986.

Mastronarde, Donald J., ed. *Euripides: "Phoenissae."* Cambridge: Cambridge University Press, 1994.

Mayhew, Robert. *Prodicus the Sophist: Texts, Translations, and Commentary*. Oxford: Oxford University Press, 2011.

Mazur, Peter Stefan. "Apatē: Deception in Archaic Greek Culture." Ph.D. diss., Yale University, 2006.

McCabe, Mary Margaret. *Platonic Conversations*. Oxford: Oxford University Press, 2015.

McClure, Laura. *Spoken Like a Woman: Speech and Gender in Athenian Drama*. Princeton: Princeton University Press, 1999.

McCoy, Marina. *Plato on the Rhetoric of Philosophers and Sophists*. Cambridge: Cambridge University Press, 2007.

Meier, Christian. "Ein antikes Äquivalent des Fortschrittsgedankens: Das 'Könnens-Bewusstsein' des 5. Jahrhunderts v. Chr." *Historische Zeitschrift* 226 (1978): 265–316.

Mendelsohn, Daniel. *Gender and the City in Euripides' Political Plays*. Oxford: Oxford University Press, 2002.

Metcalf, Robert D. *Philosophy as Agôn: A Study of Plato's "Gorgias" and Related Texts*. Evanston: Northwestern University Press, 2018.

Michelini, Ann. "The Maze of the Logos: Euripides, 'Suppliants' 163–249." *Ramus* 20 (1991): 16–36.

Mills, Sophie. *Theseus, Tragedy, and the Athenian Empire*. Oxford: Clarendon Press, 1997.

Minchin, Elizabeth. "The Performance of Lists and Catalogs in the Homeric Epics." In *Voice into Text: Orality and Literacy in Ancient Greece*, edited by Ian Worthington, 3–20. Leiden: Brill, 1996.

Mitchell-Boyask, Robin. "The Athenian Asklepieion and the End of the 'Philoctetes.'" *Transactions of the American Philological Association* 137 (2007): 85–114.

Molinelli, Sebastiano, ed. "'Dissoi Logoi': A New Commented Edition." Ph.D. diss., Durham University, 2018.

Montiglio, Silvia. *From Villain to Hero: Odysseus in Ancient Thought*. Ann Arbor: University of Michigan Press, 2011.

Moore, Christopher. *Calling Philosophers Names: On the Origin of a Discipline*. Princeton: Princeton University Press, 2020.

———. "The Myth of Theuth in the 'Phaedrus.'" In *Plato and Myth: Studies on the Use and Status of Platonic Myths*, edited by Catherine Collobert, Pierre Destrée, and Francisco J. Gonzalez, 279–303. Leiden: Brill, 2012.

———. "Promētheia ('Forethought') until Plato." *American Journal of Philology* 136 (2015): 381–420.

Morgan, Kathryn A. *Myth and Philosophy from the Presocratics to Plato*. Cambridge: Cambridge University Press, 2000.

Moss, Jessica. "What Is Imitative Poetry and Why Is It Bad?" In *The Cambridge Companion to Plato's "Republic,"* edited by G.R.F. Ferrari, 415–44. Cambridge: Cambridge University Press, 2007.

Most, Glenn W. "Simonides' Ode to Scopas in Contexts." In *Modern Critical Theory and Classical Literature*, edited by Irene J. F. de Jong and J. P. Sullivan, 127–51. Leiden: Brill, 1994.

Mourelatos, Alexander P. D. "Gorgias on the Function of Language." *Philosophical Topics* 15 (1987): 135–70.

Mousbahova, Victoria. "The Meaning of the Terms σοφιστής and σόφισμα in the 'Prometheus Bound.'" *Hyperboreus* 12 (2006): 31–49.

Mueller, Melissa. *Objects as Actors: Props and the Poetics of Performance in Greek Tragedy*. Chicago: University of Chicago Press, 2016.

Müller, Carl Werner. "Protagoras über die Götter." *Hermes* 95 (1967): 140–59.

Müller, Carl Werner, ed. *Euripides: "Philoktet," Testimonien und Fragmente*. Berlin: de Gruyter, 2000.

Müller, Reimar. "Sophistique et democratie." In *Positions de la sophistique*, edited by Barbara Cassin, 179–93. Paris: Vrin, 1986.

Mureddu, Patrizia. "La 'incomunicabilità' gorgiana in una parodia di Aristofane?: Nota a 'Thesm.' 5–21." *Lexis* 9–10 (1992): 115–20.

Murray, Penelope. "The Muses and Their Arts." In *Music and the Muses: The Culture of Mousike in the Classical Athenian City*, edited by Penelope Murray and Peter Wilson, 365–79. Oxford: Oxford University Press, 2004.

Nehamas, Alexander. "Eristic, Antilogic, Sophistic, Dialectic: Plato's Demarcation of Philosophy from Sophistry." *History of Philosophy Quarterly* 7 (1990): 3–16.

———. "Plato on Imitation and Poetry in 'Republic' 10." In *Plato on Beauty, Wisdom, and the Arts*, edited by Julius Moravcsik and Philip Temko, 47–78. Totowa: Rowman and Littlefield, 1982.

Nestle, Wilhelm. *Vom Mythos zum Logos: Die Selbstentfaltung des griechischen Denkens von Homer bis auf die Sophistik und Sokrates*. Stuttgart: Kröner, 1940.

Netz, Reviel. "Counter Culture: Towards a History of Greek Numeracy." *History of Science* 40 (2002): 321–52.

Nietzsche, Friedrich. *The Birth of Tragedy and Other Writings*. Translated by Ronald Speirs. Cambridge: Cambridge University Press, 1999.

———. *Philosophy in the Tragic Age of the Greeks*. Translated by Marianne Cowan. Chicago: Regnery, 1962.

———. *The Pre-Platonic Philosophers*. Translated by Greg Whitlock. Urbana: University of Illinois Press, 2001.

Nightingale, Andrea Wilson. *Genres in Dialogue: Plato and the Construct of Philosophy*. Cambridge: Cambridge University Press, 1995.

Nightingale, Andrea Wilson. "Plato's 'Gorgias' and Euripides' 'Antiope': A Study in Generic Transformation." *Classical Antiquity* 11 (1992): 121–41.
Nooter, Sarah. "Language, Lamentation, and Power in Sophocles' 'Electra.'" *Classical World* 104 (2011): 399–417.
———. *When Heroes Sing: Sophocles and the Shifting Soundscape of Tragedy*. Cambridge: Cambridge University Press, 2012.
Notomi, Noburu. "Image-Making in 'Republic' X and the 'Sophist': Plato's Criticism of the Poet and the Sophist." In *Plato and the Poets*, edited by Pierre Destrée and Fritz-Gregor Herrmann, 299–326. Leiden: Brill, 2011.
———. *The Unity of Plato's "Sophist": Between the Sophist and the Philosopher*. Cambridge: Cambridge University Press, 1999.
Noussia Fantuzzi, Maria, ed. *Solon the Athenian: The Poetic Fragments*. Leiden: Brill, 2010.
Nussbaum, Martha C. "Consequences and Character in Sophocles' 'Philoctetes.'" *Philosophy and Literature* 1 (1976): 25–53.
———. *The Fragility of Goodness: Luck and Ethics in Greek Tragedy and Philosophy*. 2nd ed. Cambridge: Cambridge University Press, 2001.
Obbink, Dirk. "The Addressees of Empedocles." *Materiali e discussioni per l'analisi dei testi classici* 31 (1993): 51–98.
Ober, Josiah, and Barry Strauss. "Drama, Political Rhetoric, and the Discourse of Athenian Democracy." In *Nothing to Do with Dionysos?: Athenian Drama in Its Social Context*, edited by John J. Winkler and Froma I. Zeitlin, 237–70. Princeton: Princeton University Press, 1990.
O'Brien, Michael J. "Xenophanes, Aeschylus, and the Doctrine of Primeval Brutishness." *Classical Quarterly* 35 (1985): 264–77.
Origa, Valentina. *Le contraddizioni della sapienza: Sophia e sophos nella tragedia euripidea*. Tübingen: Narr, 2007.
Osborne, Catherine. *Dumb Beasts and Dead Philosophers: Humanity and the Humane in Ancient Philosophy and Literature*. Oxford: Clarendon Press, 2007.
O'Sullivan, Neil. *Alcidamas, Aristophanes, and the Beginnings of Greek Stylistic Theory*. Stuttgart: Steiner, 1992.
———. "The Authenticity of [Alcidamas'] 'Odysseus': Two New Linguistic Considerations." *Classical Quarterly* 58 (2008): 638–47.
O'Sullivan, Patrick. "Sophistic Ethics, Old Atheism, and 'Critias' on Religion." *Classical World* 105 (2012): 167–85.
Pace, Cristina. "Tragedia, ἔκπληξις e ἀπάτη nell'anonima 'Vita di Eschilo.'" *Seminari romani di cultura greca* 11 (2008): 229–54.
Page, Carl. "The Truth about Lies in Plato's 'Republic.'" *Ancient Philosophy* 11 (1991): 1–33.
Palmer, John. "Melissus and Parmenides." *Oxford Studies in Ancient Philosophy* 26 (2004): 19–54.
———. *Parmenides and Presocratic Philosophy*. Oxford: Oxford University Press, 2009.
Papageorgiou, Nikolaos. "Prodicus and the Agon of the Logoi in Aristophanes' 'Clouds.'" *Quaderni urbinati di cultura classica* 78 (2004): 61–69.
Parker, Robert. *Polytheism and Society at Athens*. Oxford: Oxford University Press, 2005.
———. "Through a Glass Darkly: Sophocles and the Divine." In *Sophocles Revisited: Essays Presented to Sir Hugh Lloyd-Jones*, 11–30. Oxford: Oxford University Press, 1999.

Parlavantza-Friedrich, Ursula. *Täuschungsszenen in den Tragödien des Sophokles*. Berlin: de Gruyter, 1969.
Parry, Adam. *Logos and Ergon in Thucydides*. New York: Arno Press, 1981.
Partenie, Catalin, ed. *Plato's Myths*. Cambridge: Cambridge University Press, 2009.
Patzer, Andreas. *Der Sophist Hippias als Philosophiehistoriker*. Freiburg: K. Alber, 1986.
Payne, M. E. "Three Double Messenger Scenes in Sophocles." *Mnemosyne* 53 (2000): 403–18.
Pendrick, Gerard J, ed. *Antiphon the Sophist*. Cambridge: Cambridge University Press, 2002.
Peponi, Anastasia-Erasmia. "Choreia and Aesthetics in the 'Homeric Hymn to Apollo': The Performance of the Delian Maidens (Lines 156–64)." *Classical Antiquity* 28 (2009): 39–70.
Peterson, Sandra. *Socrates and Philosophy in the Dialogues of Plato*. Cambridge: Cambridge University Press, 2011.
Pirrotta, Serena, ed. *Plato Comicus: Die fragmentarischen Komödien*. Berlin: Verlag Antike, 2009.
Platter, Charles. *Aristophanes and the Carnival of Genres*. Baltimore: Johns Hopkins University Press, 2007.
Podlecki, Anthony J. "The Power of the Word in Sophocles' 'Philoctetes.'" *Greek, Roman, and Byzantine Studies* 7 (1966): 233–50.
Popper, Karl R. *The Open Society and Its Enemies*. Volume I: *The Spell of Plato*. Princeton: Princeton University Press, 1945.
Porter, James I. *The Origins of Aesthetic Thought in Ancient Greece: Matter, Sensation, and Experience*. Cambridge: Cambridge University Press, 2010.
———. "The Seductions of Gorgias." *Classical Antiquity* 12 (1993): 267–99.
———. *The Sublime in Antiquity*. Cambridge: Cambridge University Press, 2016.
Pownall, Frances. "Critias' Commemoration of Athens." *Mouseion* 8 (2008): 333–54.
Pratt, Jonathan. "On the Threshold of Rhetoric." *Classical Antiquity* 34 (2015): 163–82.
Pratt, Louise H. *Lying and Poetry from Homer to Pindar: Falsehood and Deception in Archaic Greek Poetics*. Ann Arbor: University of Michigan Press, 1993.
Prince, Susan. "Words of Representation and Words of Action in the Speech of Antisthenes' Ajax." In *Antisthenica Cynica Socratica*, edited by Vladislav Suvák, 168–99. Prague: Oikoumene, 2014.
Prince, Susan, ed. *Antisthenes of Athens: Texts, Translations, and Commentary*. Ann Arbor: University of Michigan Press, 2015.
Pucci, Pietro. "Between Narrative and Catalog: Life and Death of the Poem." *Métis* 11 (1996): 5–24.
———. *Euripides's Revolution under Cover*. Ithaca: Cornell University Press, 2016.
Pucci, Pietro, ed. *Sofocle: "Filottete."* Milan: Mondadori, 2003.
Puchner, Martin. *The Drama of Ideas: Platonic Provocations in Theater and Philosophy*. Oxford: Oxford University Press, 2014.
Rader, Richard. "The Radical Theology of 'Prometheus Bound'; or, on Prometheus' God Problem." *Ramus* 42 (2013): 162–82.
Radke, Gyburg. *Tragik und Metatragik: Euripides' "Bakchen" und die moderne Literaturwissenschaft*. Berlin: de Gruyter, 2003.
Rashed, Marwan. "The Structure of the Eye and Its Cosmological Function in Empedocles: Reconstruction of Fragment 84 D.-K." In *Reading Ancient Texts: Essays in Honour of Denis O'Brien 1*, edited by Suzanne Stern-Gillet and Kevin Corrigan, 21–39. Leiden: Brill, 2007.

Reames, Robin. *Seeming and Being in Plato's Rhetorical Theory*. Chicago: University of Chicago Press, 2018.

Redfield, James. "Comedy, Tragedy, and Politics in Aristophanes' 'Frogs.'" *Chicago Review* 15 (1962): 107–21.

Reinhardt, Karl. *Sophocles*. Translated by Hazel Harvey and David Harvey. Oxford: Blackwell, 1979.

Reynolds-Warnhoff, Patricia. "The Role of τὸ σοφόν in Euripides' 'Bacchae.'" *Quaderni urbinati di cultura classica* 57 (1997): 77–103.

Riel, Gerd van. "Religion and Morality: Elements of Plato's Anthropology in the Myth of Prometheus ('Protagoras' 320d–322d)." In *Plato and Myth: Studies on the Use and Status of Platonic Myths*, edited by Catherine Collobert, Pierre Destrée, and Francisco J. Gonzalez, 145–64. Leiden: Brill, 2012.

Rijksbaron, Albert. *Grammatical Observations on Euripides' "Bacchae."* Amsterdam: J. C. Gieben, 1991.

Ringer, Mark. *Electra and the Empty Urn: Metatheater and Role Playing in Sophocles*. Chapel Hill: University of North Carolina Press, 1998.

Robinson, Eric W. "The Sophists and Democracy beyond Athens." *Rhetorica* 25 (2007): 109–22.

Robinson, T. M., ed. *Contrasting Arguments: An Edition of the "Dissoi Logoi."* New York: Arno Press, 1979.

Roguin, Claire-Françoise de. "Apollon Lykeios dans la tragédie: Dieu protecteur, dieu tueur, 'dieu de l'initiation.'" *Kernos* 12 (1999): 99–123.

Roisman, Hanna M. "The Appropriation of a Son: Sophocles' 'Philoctetes.'" *Greek, Roman, and Byzantine Studies* 38 (1997): 127–71.

Rokem, Freddie. *Philosophers and Thespians: Thinking Performance*. Stanford: Stanford University Press, 2009.

Romilly, Jacqueline de. "Gorgias et le pouvoir de la poésie." *Journal of Hellenic Studies* 93 (1973): 155–62.

———. *The Great Sophists in Periclean Athens*. Translated by Janet Lloyd. Oxford: Clarendon Press, 1992.

Rose, Peter W. "Sophocles' 'Philoctetes' and the Teachings of the Sophists." *Harvard Studies in Classical Philology* 80 (1976): 49–105.

Rosen, Ralph M. "Aristophanes' 'Frogs' and the 'Contest of Homer and Hesiod.'" *Transactions of the American Philological Association* 134 (2004): 295–322.

———. "Reconsidering the Reperformance of Aristophanes' 'Frogs.'" *Trends in Classics* 7 (2015): 237–56.

Rosenmeyer, Thomas G. *The Art of Aeschylus*. Berkeley: University of California Press, 1982.

———. "Gorgias, Aeschylus, and Apate." *American Journal of Philology* 76 (1955): 225–60.

Rösler, Wolfgang. *Reflexe vorsokratischen Denkens bei Aischylos*. Meisenheim am Glan: Hain, 1970.

Rossetti, Livio. "Le dialogue socratique 'in statu nascendi.'" *Philosophie antique* 1 (2001): 11–35.

Roth, Paul. "Teiresias as Mantis and Intellectual in Euripides' 'Bacchae.'" *Transactions of the American Philological Association* 114 (1984): 56–69.

Rowe, Christopher J. "The Status of the Myth of the 'Gorgias,' or: Taking Plato Seriously." In *Plato and Myth: Studies on the Use and Status of Platonic Myths*, edited by Catherine Collobert, Pierre Destrée, and Francisco J. Gonzalez, 187–98. Leiden: Brill, 2012.

Rowe, Christopher J., ed. *Plato: "Phaedrus."* Oxford: Aris & Phillips, 1986.

Rowett, Catherine. "Why the Philosopher Kings Will Believe the Noble Lie." *Oxford Studies in Ancient Philosophy* 50 (2016): 67–100.

Rubel, Alexander. *Stadt in Angst: Religion und Politik in Athen während des Peloponnesischen Krieges.* Darmstadt: Wissenschaftliche Buchgesellschaft, 2000.

Rutherford, Ian. "Apollo in Ivy: The Tragic Paean." *Arion* 3 (1994): 112–35.

Rutherford, Ian, ed. *Greco-Egyptian Interactions: Literature, Translation, and Culture, 500 BC–AD 300.* Oxford: Oxford University Press, 2016.

Saïd, Suzanne. *Sophiste et tyran: ou Le problème du "Prométhée enchaîné."* Paris: Klincksieck, 1985.

———. "Tragedy and Reversal: The Example of the 'Persians.'" In *Oxford Readings in Classical Studies: Aeschylus*, edited by Michael Lloyd, 71–92. Oxford: Oxford University Press, 2007.

Sammons, Benjamin. *The Art and Rhetoric of the Homeric Catalog.* Oxford: Oxford University Press, 2010.

Sansone, David. "Socrates' 'Tragic' Definition of Color (Pl. 'Meno' 76D–E)." *Classical Philology* 91 (1996): 339–45.

Sassi, Maria Michela. *The Beginnings of Philosophy in Greece.* Princeton: Princeton University Press, 2018.

Scapin, Nuria. *The Flower of Suffering: Theology, Justice, and the Cosmos in Aeschylus' "Oresteia" and Presocratic Thought.* Berlin: de Gruyter, 2020.

Scharffenberger, Elizabeth W. "'Deinon Eribremetas': The Sound and Sense of Aeschylus in Aristophanes' 'Frogs.'" *Classical World* 100 (2007): 229–49.

Schein, Seth L. "Language and Dramatic Action in the Prologue of Sophokles' 'Philoktetes.'" *Dioniso* 1 (2011): 78–97.

———. "The Scene with the False Merchant in Sophokles' 'Philoktetes.'" *Dioniso* 4 (2014): 65–81.

———. "Verbal Adjectives in Sophocles: Necessity and Morality." *Classical Philology* 93 (1998): 293–307.

Schiappa, Edward. *The Beginnings of Rhetorical Theory in Classical Greece.* New Haven: Yale University Press, 1999.

———. "Interpreting Gorgias's 'Being' in 'On Not-Being or On Nature.'" *Philosophy and Rhetoric* 30 (1997): 13–30.

———. "'Rhêtorikê': What's in a Name? Toward a Revised History of Early Greek Rhetorical Theory." *Quarterly Journal of Speech* 78 (1992): 1–15.

Schiefsky, Mark J., ed. *Hippocrates: "On Ancient Medicine."* Leiden: Brill, 2005.

Schofield, Malcolm. "The Noble Lie." In *The Cambridge Companion to Plato's "Republic,"* edited by G.R.F. Ferrari, 138–64. Cambridge: Cambridge University Press, 2007.

Scodel, Ruth. *The Trojan Trilogy of Euripides.* Göttingen: Vandenhoeck & Ruprecht, 1980.

———. "Verbal Performance and Euripidean Rhetoric." *Illinois Classical Studies* 24/25 (2000): 129–44.

Scullion, Scott. "Dionysos and Katharsis in 'Antigone.'" *Classical Antiquity* 17 (1998): 96–122.

———. "Euripides and Macedon, or the Silence of the 'Frogs.'" *Classical Quarterly* 53 (2003): 389–400.

Seaford, Richard. *Cosmology and the Polis: The Social Construction of Space and Time in the Tragedies of Aeschylus*. Cambridge: Cambridge University Press, 2012.
Seaford, Richard, ed. *Euripides: "Bacchae."* Oxford: Aris and Phillips, 1996.
Sedley, David. "The Atheist Underground." In *Politeia in Greek and Roman Philosophy*, edited by Verity Harte and Melissa Lane, 329–48. Cambridge: Cambridge University Press, 2013.
———. *Creationism and Its Critics in Antiquity*. Berkeley: University of California Press, 2007.
———. "Myth, Punishment and Politics in the 'Gorgias.'" In *Plato's Myths*, edited by Catalin Partenie, 51–76. Cambridge: Cambridge University Press, 2009.
Segal, Charles P. "The Character and Cults of Dionysus and the Unity of the 'Frogs.'" *Harvard Studies in Classical Philology* 65 (1961): 207–42.
———. *Dionysiac Poetics and Euripides' "Bacchae."* Expanded ed. Princeton: Princeton University Press, 1997.
———. "Gorgias and the Psychology of the Logos." *Harvard Studies in Classical Philology* 66 (1962): 99–155.
———. "Sophocles' Praise of Man and the Conflicts of the 'Antigone.'" *Arion* 3 (1964): 46–66.
———. *Tragedy and Civilization: An Interpretation of Sophocles*. Cambridge, MA: Harvard University Press, 1981.
———. "The Two Worlds of Euripides' 'Helen.'" *Transactions of the American Philological Association* 102 (1971): 553–614.
———. "Visual Symbolism and Visual Effects in Sophocles." *Classical World* 74 (1980): 125–42.
Seidensticker, Bernd. "Comic Elements in Euripides' 'Bacchae.'" *American Journal of Philology* 99 (1978): 303–20.
———. "The Figure of Teiresias in Euripides' 'Bacchae.'" In *Wisdom and Folly in Euripides*, edited by Poulheria Kyriakou and Antonios Rengakos, 275–83. Berlin: de Gruyter, 2016.
Sells, Donald. "Eleusis and the Public Status of Comedy in Aristophanes' 'Frogs.'" In *No Laughing Matter: Studies in Athenian Comedy*, edited by C. W. Marshall and George Kovacs, 83–99. London: Bristol Classical Press, 2012.
Sfyroeras, Pavlos. "πόθος Εὐριπίδου: Reading Andromeda in Aristophanes' 'Frogs.'" *American Journal of Philology* 129 (2008): 299–317.
Sier, Kurt. "Gorgias über die Fiktionalität der Tragödie." In *Dramatische Wäldchen: Festschrift für Eckard Lefèvre zum 65. Geburtstag*, edited by Ekkehard Stärk and Gregor Vogt-Spira, 575–618. Hildesheim: Ohms, 2000.
Silk, M. S. *Aristophanes and the Definition of Comedy*. Oxford: Oxford University Press, 2002.
Sisko, John E., and Yale Weiss. "A Fourth Alternative in Interpreting Parmenides." *Phronesis* 60 (2015): 40–59.
Slings, Simon R. "The Quiet Life in Euripides' 'Antiope.'" In *Fragmenta dramatica: Beiträge zur Interpretation der griechischen Tragikerfragmente und ihrer Wirkungsgeschichte*, edited by Heinz Hofmann and Annette Harder, 137–51. Göttingen: Vandenhoeck & Ruprecht, 1991.
Snell, Bruno. "Vita Activa and Vita Contemplativa in Euripides' 'Antiope.'" In *Scenes from Greek Drama*, 70–98. Berkeley: University of California Press, 1964.
Solmsen, Friedrich. *Hesiod and Aeschylus*. Ithaca: Cornell University Press, 1949.
———. "Zur Gestaltung des Intriguenmotivs in den Tragödien des Sophokles und Euripides." *Philologus* 87 (1932): 1–17.

Sommerstein, Alan H. "'Bacchae' and Earlier Tragedy." In *Looking at "Bacchae,"* edited by David Stuttard, 29–41. London: Bloomsbury, 2016.

———. "The Prologue of Aeschylus' 'Palamedes.'" *Rheinisches Museum* 143 (2000): 118–27.

———. "Sophocles and Democracy." *Polis* 34 (2017): 273–87.

———. "Sophocles' Palamedes and Nauplius Plays: No Trilogy Here." In *The Tangled Ways of Zeus and Other Studies in and around Greek Tragedy*, 250–58. Oxford: Oxford University Press, 2010.

———. *Talking about Laughter and Other Studies in Greek Comedy.* Oxford: Oxford University Press, 2009.

Sommerstein, Alan H., ed. *Aeschylus: Fragments.* Cambridge, MA: Harvard University Press, 2009.

———. *Aristophanes: "Frogs."* Oxford: Aris & Phillips, 1996.

———. *Aristophanes: "Thesmophoriazusae."* Oxford: Aris & Phillips, 1994.

Sommerstein, Alan H., and Thomas H. Talboy, eds. *Sophocles: Selected Fragmentary Plays*, Volume II. Oxford: Aris & Phillips, 2011.

Sommerstein, Alan H., Thomas Talboy, and David Fitzpatrick, eds. *Sophocles: Selected Fragmentary Plays*, Volume I. Oxford: Aris and Phillips, 2006.

Sommerville, Brooks. "The Image of the Jars in Plato's 'Gorgias.'" *Ancient Philosophy* 34 (2014): 235–54.

Sorensen, Anders Dahl. *Plato on Democracy and Political Technē.* Leiden: Brill, 2016.

Spyropoulos, Elias S. *L'accumulation verbale chez Aristophane: Recherches sur le style d'Aristophane.* Thessaloniki: Aristotelian University Thessaloniki, 1974.

Stamatopoulou, Zoe. *Hesiod and Classical Greek Poetry: Reception and Transformation in the Fifth Century BCE.* Cambridge: Cambridge University Press, 2017.

Stanford, W. B. *The Ulysses Theme: A Study in the Adaptability of a Traditional Hero.* Oxford: Blackwell, 1963.

Stehle, Eva M. "Thesmophoria and Eleusinian Mysteries: The Fascination of Women's Secret Ritual." In *Finding Persephone: Women's Rituals in the Ancient Mediterranean*, edited by Maryline Parca and Angeliki Tzanetou, 165–85. Bloomington: Indiana University Press, 2007.

Steiner, Deborah Tarn. *The Tyrant's Writ: Myths and Images of Writing in Ancient Greece.* Princeton: Princeton University Press, 1994.

Stevens, P. T. "Ajax in the Trugrede." *Classical Quarterly* 36 (1986): 327–36.

Stockert, Walter. "Eine 'Komödienszene' in Euripides' Aulischer 'Iphigenie.'" *Wiener Studien* 95 (1982): 71–78.

Struck, Peter T. *Divination and Human Nature: A Cognitive History of Intuition in Classical Antiquity.* Princeton: Princeton University Press, 2016.

Sullivan, Shirley Darcus. "το σοφόν as an Aspect of the Divine in Heraclitus." In *Greek Poetry and Philosophy: Studies in Honour of Leonard Woodbury*, edited by Douglas E. Gerber, 285–301. Chico: Scholars Press, 1984.

Synodinou, Katerina. "Wisdom through Experience: Theseus and Adrastus in Euripides' 'Suppliant Women.'" In *Wisdom and Folly in Euripides*, edited by Poulheria Kyriakou and Antonios Rengakos, 155–76. Berlin: de Gruyter, 2016.

Taousiani, Akrivi. "οὐ μὴ πίθηται: Persuasion versus Deception in the Prologue of Sophocles' 'Philoctetes.'" *Classical Quarterly* 61 (2011): 426–44.

Taplin, Oliver. "Fifth-Century Tragedy and Comedy: A Synkrisis." *Journal of Hellenic Studies* 106 (1986): 163–74.

Tarnopolsky, Christina H. *Prudes, Perverts, and Tyrants: Plato's "Gorgias" and the Politics of Shame*. Princeton: Princeton University Press, 2010.

Tarrant, Harold. "The Dramatic Background of the Arguments with Callicles, Euripides' 'Antiope,' and an Athenian Anti-Intellectual Argument." *Antichthon* 42 (2008): 20–39.

Tell, Håkan. *Plato's Counterfeit Sophists*. Washington, DC: Center for Hellenic Studies, 2011.

Thalmann, William G. *Conventions of Form and Thought in Early Greek Epic Poetry*. Baltimore: Johns Hopkins University Press, 1984.

Thomas, Rosalind. *Herodotus in Context: Ethnography, Science and the Art of Persuasion*. Cambridge: Cambridge University Press, 2002.

Thraede, Klaus. "Das Lob des Erfinders: Bemerkungen zur Analyse der Heuremata-Kataloge." *Rheinisches Museum* 105 (1962): 158–86.

Thumiger, Chiara. *Hidden Paths: Self and Characterization in Greek Tragedy: Euripides' "Bacchae."* London: Institute of Classical Studies, 2007.

Tor, Shaul. "Heraclitus on Apollo's Signs and His Own: Contemplating Oracles and Philosophical Inquiry." In *Theologies of Ancient Greek Religion*, edited by Esther Eidinow, Julia Kindt, and Robin Osborne, 89–116. Cambridge: Cambridge University Press, 2016.

———. *Mortal and Divine in Early Greek Epistemology: A Study of Hesiod, Xenophanes, and Parmenides*. Cambridge: Cambridge University Press, 2017.

Torrance, Isabelle. *Metapoetry in Euripides*. Oxford: Oxford University Press, 2013.

Trivigno, Franco V. "Paratragedy in Plato's 'Gorgias.'" *Oxford Studies in Ancient Philosophy* 36 (2009): 73–105.

Tsagalis, Christos. "The Dynamic Hypertext: Lists and Catalogs in the Homeric Epics." *Trends in Classics* 2 (2010): 323–47.

———. "Poetry and Poetics in the Hesiodic Corpus." In *Brill's Companion to Hesiod*, edited by Franco Montanari, Antonios Rengakos, and Christos Tsagalis, 131–77. Leiden: Brill, 2009.

Tsitsiridis, Stavros. "'Euripideische' Kosmogonie bei Aristophanes ('Thesm.' 14–18)." Ελληνικά 51 (2001): 43–67.

Tulin, Alexander. "Xenophanes Fr. 18 D.-K. and the Origins of the Idea of Progress." *Hermes* 121 (1993): 129–38.

Tzanetou, Angeliki. "Something to Do with Demeter: Ritual and Performance in Aristophanes' 'Women at the Thesmophoria.'" *American Journal of Philology* 123 (2002): 329–67.

Ugolini, Gherardo. *Untersuchungen zur Figur des Sehers Teiresias*. Tübingen: Narr, 1995.

Uhlig, Anna. *Theatrical Reenactment in Pindar and Aeschylus*. Cambridge: Cambridge University Press, 2019.

Untersteiner, Mario. *The Sophists*. Translated by Kathleen Freeman. Oxford: Blackwell, 1954.

Utzinger, Christian. *Periphrades Aner: Untersuchungen zum ersten Stasimon der Sophokleischen "Antigone" und zu den antiken Kulturentstehungstheorien*. Göttingen: Vandenhoeck & Ruprecht, 2003.

Uxkull-Gyllenband, Woldemar. *Griechische Kultur-Entstehungslehren*. Berlin: Simion, 1924.

Van Nortwick, Thomas. *Late Sophocles: The Hero's Evolution in "Electra," "Philoctetes," and "Oedipus at Colonus."* Ann Arbor: University of Michigan Press, 2015.

Venturelli, Silvia. "L' 'Ippia Minore' di Platone e il suo rapporto con Antistene: (S.S.R. V A 187)." *Studi classici e orientali* 61 (2015): 77–96.
Verdenius, W. J. "Gorgias' Doctrine of Deception." In *The Sophists and Their Legacy*, edited by G. B. Kerferd, 116–28. Wiesbaden: Steiner, 1981.
Vernant, Jean-Pierre. "At Man's Table: Hesiod's Foundation Myth of Sacrifice." In *The Cuisine of Sacrifice among the Greeks*, edited by Marcel Detienne and Jean-Pierre Vernant, translated by Paula Wissing, 21–86. Chicago: University of Chicago Press, 1989.
———. "The Myth of Prometheus in Hesiod." In *Myth and Society in Ancient Greece*, translated by Janet Lloyd, 183–201. New York: Zone Books, 1990.
Vernant, Jean-Pierre, and Pierre Vidal-Naquet. *Myth and Tragedy in Ancient Greece*. Translated by Janet Lloyd. New York: Zone Books, 1990.
Versnel, H. S. *Inconsistencies in Greek and Roman Religion*. Volume I: *Ter Unus. Isis, Dionysos, Hermes. Three Studies in Henotheism*. Leiden: Brill, 1990.
———. *Inconsistencies in Greek and Roman Religion*. Volume II: *Transition and Reversal in Myth and Ritual*. Leiden: Brill, 1994.
Vidal-Naquet, Pierre. *The Black Hunter: Forms of Thought and Forms of Society in the Greek World*. Translated by Andrew Szegedy-Maszak. Baltimore: Johns Hopkins University Press, 1986.
Vöhler, Martin, and Bernd Seidensticker, eds. *Mythenkorrekturen: Zu einer paradoxalen Form der Mythenrezeption*. Berlin: de Gruyter, 2005.
Wallace, Robert W. *Reconstructing Damon: Music, Wisdom Teaching, and Politics in Perikles' Athens*. Oxford: Oxford University Press, 2015.
Weiss, Naomi A. *The Music of Tragedy: Performance and Imagination in Euripidean Theater*. Berkeley: University of California Press, 2018.
Werner, Daniel S. *Myth and Philosophy in Plato's "Phaedrus."* Cambridge: Cambridge University Press, 2012.
West, M. L. "The Orphics of Olbia." *Zeitschrift für Papyrologie und Epigraphik* 45 (1982): 17–29.
West, Stephanie. "Prometheus Orientalized." *Museum Helveticum* 51 (1994): 129–49.
White, Stephen. "Io's World: Intimations of Theodicy in 'Prometheus Bound.'" *Journal of Hellenic Studies* 121 (2001): 107–40.
Whitmarsh, Tim. "Atheistic Aesthetics: The Sisyphus Fragment, Poetics and the Creativity of Drama." *Cambridge Classical Journal* 60 (2014): 109–26.
Wildberg, Christian. *Hyperesie und Epiphanie: Versuch über die Bedeutung der Götter in den Dramen des Euripides*. Munich: Beck, 2002.
Willink, C. W. "Some Problems of Text and Interpretation in the 'Bacchae' II." *Classical Quarterly* 16 (1966): 220–42.
Willink, C. W., ed. *Euripides: "Orestes."* Oxford: Oxford University Press, 1986.
Wilson, Peter. "Euripides' Tragic Muse." *Illinois Classical Studies* 24/25 (2000): 427–49.
Winiarczyk, Marek. *Diagoras of Melos: A Contribution to the History of Ancient Atheism*. Berlin: de Gruyter, 2016.
———. "Nochmals das Satyrspiel 'Sisyphos.'" *Wiener Studien* 100 (1987): 35–45.
Winkler, John J. "The Ephebes' Song: Tragōidia and Polis." In *Nothing to Do with Dionysos?: Athenian Drama in Its Social Context*, edited by John J. Winkler and Froma I. Zeitlin, 20–62. Princeton: Princeton University Press, 1990.

Winnington-Ingram, R. P. "Euripides, 'Bacchae' 877–881 = 897–901." *Bulletin of the Institute of Classical Studies* 13 (1966): 34–37.

———. *Euripides and Dionysus: An Interpretation of the "Bacchae."* Cambridge: Cambridge University Press, 1948.

———. *Sophocles: An Interpretation.* Cambridge: Cambridge University Press, 1980.

Wohl, Victoria. *Euripides and the Politics of Form.* Princeton: Princeton University Press, 2015.

———. "Play of the Improbable: Euripides' Unlikely 'Helen.'" In *Probabilities, Hypotheticals, and Counterfactuals in Ancient Greek Thought*, edited by Victoria Wohl, 142–59. Cambridge: Cambridge University Press, 2014.

Wolfsdorf, David. "'Sophia' and 'Epistēmē' in the Archaic and Classical Periods." In *The Philosophy of Knowledge: A History. Volume I: Knowledge in Ancient Philosophy*, edited by Nicholas D. Smith, 11–29. London: Bloomsbury, 2018.

Woodard, Thomas M. "'Electra' by Sophocles: The Dialectical Design." *Harvard Studies in Classical Philology* 68 (1964): 163–205.

Woodbury, Leonard. "Anaxagoras and Athens." *Phoenix* 35 (1981): 295–315.

———. "Aristophanes' 'Frogs' and Athenian Literacy: 'Ran.' 52–53, 1114." *Transactions of the American Philological Association* 106 (1975): 349–57.

Woolf, Greg. "Ancient Illiteracy?" *Bulletin of the Institute of Classical Studies* 58 (2015): 31–42.

Woolf, Raphael. "Callicles and Socrates: Psychic (Dis)Harmony in the 'Gorgias.'" *Oxford Studies in Ancient Philosophy* 18 (2000): 1–40.

Worman, Nancy. "Odysseus Panourgos: The Liar's Style in Tragedy and Oratory." *Helios* 26 (1999): 35–68.

Wright, Matthew. *Euripides' Escape Tragedies: A Study of "Helen," "Andromeda," and "Iphigenia among the Taurians."* Oxford: Oxford University Press, 2005.

Xanthaki-Karamanou, Georgia. "The 'Dionysiac' Plays of Aeschylus and Euripides' 'Bacchae': Reaffirming Traditional Cult in Late Fifth Century." In *Crisis on Stage: Tragedy and Comedy in Late Fifth-Century Athens*, edited by Andreas Markantonatos and Bernhard Zimmermann, 323–42. Berlin: de Gruyter, 2012.

———. "Remarks on Moschion's Account of Progress." *Classical Quarterly* 31 (1981): 410–17.

Yoon, Florence. "Against a Prometheia: Rethinking the Connected Trilogy." *Transactions of the American Philological Association* 146 (2016): 257–80.

Yunis, Harvey. "The Constraints of Democracy and the Rise of the Art of Rhetoric." In *Democracy, Empire, and the Arts in Fifth-Century Athens*, edited by Deborah Boedeker and Kurt A. Raaflaub, 223–40. Cambridge, MA: Harvard University Press, 1998.

———. "Dialectic and the Purpose of Rhetoric in Plato's 'Phaedrus.'" *Proceedings of the Boston Area Colloquium in Ancient Philosophy* 24 (2009): 229–59.

Zacharia, Katerina. *Converging Truths: Euripides' "Ion" and the Athenian Quest for Self-Definition.* Leiden: Brill, 2003.

Zeitlin, Froma I. "Staging Dionysus between Thebes and Athens." In *Masks of Dionysus*, edited by Thomas H. Carpenter and Christopher A. Faraone, 147–82. Ithaca: Cornell University Press, 1993.

———. "Travesties of Gender and Genre in Aristophanes' 'Thesmophoriazusae.'" In *Playing the Other: Gender and Society in Classical Greek Literature*, 375–416. Chicago: University of Chicago Press, 1996.

Zeller, Eduard. *Die Philosophie der Griechen in ihrer geschichtlichen Entwicklung*. 2nd ed. Tübingen: Fues, 1856.

Zhmud, Leonid. *The Origin of the History of Science in Classical Antiquity*. Translated by Alexander Chernoglazov. Berlin: de Gruyter, 2006.

Ziolkowski, Theodore. *The Sin of Knowledge: Ancient Themes and Modern Variations*. Princeton: Princeton University Press, 2000.

INDEX

Achilles, 99, 132–33, 138–39, 143, 145, 153–4, 166, 179n60
Achilles Tatius, 43
Aeschylus, 3–4: *Agamemnon*, 154; in Aristophanes' *Clouds*, 187n74; in Aristophanes' *Frogs*, 22, 164, 186–203; catalogs in, 21, 31–32, 38–41, 50–52; *Eumenides*, 111, 168; fragments and fragmentary plays, 51–52, 94–95, 175n45, 197n97, 204; *Libation Bearers*, 52n63, 73, 111–16, 117n72, 120; *Palamedes*, 26n10, 38–41, 46, 48, 50, 54, 78; *Persians*, 31; *Philoctetes*, 94n5, 131–33; *Prometheus Bound*, 25n6, 32, 38–40, 50–64, 66, 68, 70, 77–78, 83, 170
aether, 123–24, 174–75, 190, 208–9
Agathon, 2, 121, 125–27
agōn (formal debate): in comedy (epirrhematic *agōn*), 167–69, 186–7, 190; in tragedy (tragic *agōn*), 168–69, 205. *See also* rhetoric; syncrisis
agōn sophias (debate concerning wisdom). *See* wisdom (sophia)
agnosticism. *See* atheism
agriculture, 55–56, 67, 73–75
Ajax, 17, 99, 108–9, 118–19, 138, 144, 165, 179n60
Alcibiades, 198n101, 199
Alcidamas, 44n51, 47n56, 165, 183n65
Anaxagoras, 3, 4, 26n10, 40n41, 49, 123–23, 170, 174
Andocides, 171n35
animals (nonhuman), 26–27, 35, 39–40, 54–56, 58, 63, 66–67, 72
anti-intellectualism, 49–50, 163–64, 170–73, 185–86

antilogy, 16–18, 165, 177. *See also* rhetoric; syncrisis
Antiphon, 16, 17, 86, 137, 165, 171n35, 227
Antisthenes, 17, 99, 106n43, 118–19, 138, 165, 179n60
apatē. *See* deception
Apollo, 98–99, 113–15, 149–50
Apollodorus, 143n, 146n125, 147n127
Archelaus (philosopher), 3n4, 26n10, 40n41, 174n44
Archelaus of Macedon. *See* Macedon
Arginusae, 189
Aristophanes, 2, 20–21; *Acharnians*, 186; *Clouds*, 16–17, 162, 167, 174, 190n, 200n103, 201n108; *Frogs*, 2, 22, 66n87, 128n95, 164, 168, 183n64, 186–203, 205, 212n, 219–22, 229–30, 236; *Lysistrata*, 128; *Women at the Thesmophoria*, 92, 120–31, 155, 157, 187
Aristotle, 12, 49n60, 105–7, 137n111, 161, 189n80
Asclepius, 150
astronomy, 38–39, 43–44, 51, 55–56
atheism, 20, 49, 84–89, 170, 208–210, 215–18, 220–21
Athens: philosophical developments in, 1–5, 15–16, 162–64, 170; politics in, 15–16, 21, 97–98, 101, 128, 136–37, 157–58, 168

Benjamin, Walter, 10n17

catalogs, 27–32, 36; as "cultural catalog," 8, 21–22, 25–27, 32–84, 88–90; in drama, 30–32; in epic, 28–30, 31, 36n32; in ritual, 37
Cleobulina, 95n8
Cicero, 178

265

comedy, in contrast to tragedy, 20–21, 130–31, 202–3, 206
constellation, 10–11, 22
Contest of Homer and Hesiod, 186–87
cosmogony, 123–24; 174–75, 180–82
Cratinus, 202
Critias, 34, 45n54, 84. *See also* Sisyphus fragment

Daedalus, 49
Damon, 170
deception, 8, 18, 21, 81–83, 92–108, 158, 190; in Aristophanes' *Women at the Thesmophoria*, 92, 120–31, 157; in Euripides' *Iphigenia in Aulis*, 92, 151–58; in Sophocles' *Electra*, 92–93, 108–20, 133–35; in Sophocles' *Philoctetes*, 92–93, 112, 115, 120, 131–51, 155–56
Delphi. *See* Apollo; oracles
Demeter, 189, 208–9. *See also* Eleusinian Mysteries (and Eleusis)
Democritus, 33, 34n26, 40n41, 54n67, 59n76, 67n88, 68, 87
Derrida, Jacques, 24n1, 45n54
Derveni Papyrus, 175n45, 209
Detienne, Marcel, 18–19, 21, 98, 102
Diogenes of Apollonia, 174n44
Diogenes Laertius, 16n, 17n, 49n59, 105n40, 184n67, 201n108
Diagoras of Melos, 49n59
dialogue, as philosophical form, 8–9, 17, 18n28, 19, 223–25, 236–38
Diggle, James, 206–7, 215n143, 217n147, 217n148, 218n151
Dio Chrysostom, 132, 134, 146n125
Diomedes, 131, 144–47, 188
Dionysus, 80, 99, 173; in Aristophanes' *Frogs*, 168, 186–203; in Euripides' *Bacchae*, 203–22
Diopeithes' decree, 49
divination, 58–59, 67–68, 78. *See also* oracles; prophets (and prophecy)
Dissoi Logoi, 16, 94–97, 165, 177
draughts, 23, 25, 42–43, 47–48

Early Greek Philosophy (Loeb edition), 2, 6, 35
Egypt, 23–25
Eleusinian Mysteries (and Eleusis), 67, 80, 182, 189, 194, 198n101, 236. *See also* initiation; makarismos
Eleutherae, 173
elpis (hope or expectation), 61–62, 80–82
Empedocles, 21, 102, 104–5, 108, 121, 124, 157, 182
Epicharmus, 61n
Euripides, 1–4, 22, 31–32, 84, 168–70, 173, 185–87, 220, 230, 238; *Aiolos*, 75n; *Alexander*, 110n56, 185n68; *Andromache*, 149n13;3 *Andromeda*, 127; *Antiope*, 164, 172–86, 190–92, 200, 202, 205, 211, 212n11, 219, 221–22, 225–33, 236–37; in Aristophanes' *Clouds*, 187n74; in Aristophanes' *Frogs*, 2, 22, 164, 186–203; in Aristophanes' *Women at the Thesmophoria*, 121–30, 187; *Bacchae*, 125, 164, 171, 183, 203–22, 230; *Children of Heracles*, 171n37; *Chrysippus*, 124n81, 175n45; *Cresphontes*, 117n72; *Cyclops*, 109, 127; *Electra*, 109, 111–12, 114n64, 117n72; *Hecuba*, 109, 171n34; *Helen*, 109, 116–17, 127, 130, 136, 213n140; *Ion*, 66n85, 109–10; *Iphigenia in Aulis*, 31n21, 92, 151–57, 171n34, 213n140; *Iphigenia among the Taurians*, 109, 117n71, 127, 217n149; *Medea*, 109, 171–72; *Melanippe the Wise*, 124n81; *Oeneus*, 188; *Orestes*, 40n41, 171n37, 213n140, 216n146; *Palamedes*, 41, 44–46, 164, 172–73, 183–86, 205, 214, 236; *Philoctetes*, 131–33, 146, 148; *Phoenician Women*, 31n21, 44n52; *Sisyphus*, 185n68; *Trojan Women*, 185n68; *Suppliants*, 27, 31n21, 39, 64–72, 78, 83, 87, 124

fire, 50–51, 53–54, 57, 59, 61–63

German Idealism, 9, 10n17
Gorgias, 165, 226, 238; on deception, 95–96, 112, 120; *Defense of Palamedes*, 17, 44n51, 47–48, 86, 99, 107, 118–19, 165; *Encomium of Helen*, 17, 107, 118, 140; *On Nonbeing*, 101, 106–8, 120, 122–23, 124n82, 151, 157. *See also* Plato: *Gorgias*

Hegel, G.W.F., 12, 223
Heraclitus, 3n4, 55n, 98, 213n139
Herodotus, 171n34, 171n35
Hesiod, 97, 102, 149, 193; catalogs in, 28–29; cosmogony in, 123, 174; Prometheus myth in, 50–51, 53n66, 54, 59, 61–62, 90
Hesk, Jon, 97–98
Hippias, 32; in Plato's *Hippias Minor*, 99–100, 133, 166, 179n60
Hippocrates/Hippocratic Corpus: *On Ancient Medicine*, 33–34, 58; *On the Nature of Man*, 105n40; *On Regimen*, 97n15
Homer, 30n17, 31n21, 94n6, 149, 193, 234; catalogs in, 28–29; 36n32; Odysseus in, 100, 133n101, 144, 146n125
Homeric Hymn to Apollo, 99
Homeric Hymn to Demeter, 182n62
Homeric Hymn to Hephaestus, 55
Horace, 174n42
Hyginus, 146n125

impiety. *See* atheism
initiation, 98, 182; in Aristophanes' *Frogs*, 194, 197–200, 202; in Aristophanes' *Women at the Thesmophoria*, 121, 124–26, 130; in early Greek philosophical texts, 102, 104, 182; in Euripides' *Bacchae*, 211–12; in Plato's *Gorgias*, 236; in Sophocles' *Electra*, 114, 118; in Sophocles' *Philoctetes*, 131–32, 150–51. *See also* Eleusinian Mysteries (and Eleusis); *makarismos*
inventors (*prōtoi heuretai*), 25–27, 32, 34–37. *See also* Palamedes; Prometheus
Io, 63, 83
Isocrates, 105n40, 106n43, 228n13

Jameson, Fredric, 13n19, 13n20

Kant, Immanuel, 12, 35n31

Little Iliad (Cyclical Epic), 143, 146n125, 147n127
logos: in contrast to *muthos*, 18–20, 222, 234–36; as "speech," 118–20, 138–41, 146, 150–51, 153–54. *See also* Gorgias; rhetoric

Loraux, Nicole, 71
Lysias, 171n35

Macedon, 191
makarismos, 182, 184, 200–202, 219–20, 236. *See also* Eleusinian Mysteries (and Eleusis); initiation
Marx, Karl, 12–13
medicine, 8, 33–34, 57–59, 77. *See also* Hippocrates/Hippocratic corpus
Melissus, 105–6
metatheater, 112, 221
mimesis, 91–92, 99, 127, 223
Moore, Christopher, 6–7
Moschion, 85
Musaeus, 193
music, 5, 15, 98–99; in Aristophanes' *Frogs*, 196, 199–202; in Euripides' *Antiope*, 173–76, 178, 180–81, 191–92; in Euripides' *Bacchae*, 204, 212; in Euripides' *Palamedes*, 183–86. *See also* Damon; Diagoras of Melos
muthos. *See logos*

Nietzsche, Friedrich, 3–4, 223–24
Nightingale, Andrea, 25n7, 225–26, 235n, 236
nomos. *See phusis*
number, 23, 25, 38–41, 43–44, 47–48, 51, 55–56
Nussbaum, Martha, 9, 136n108

Odysseus, 17, 117n72; in Euripides' *Iphigenia in Aulis*, 154–56; in the Palamedes story, 37, 42–43, 164, 183–85; in philosophical thought, 99–100, 165–66, 179n60; in Sophocles' *Philoctetes*, 131–51
oligarchy, 21, 128, 136–37, 189. *See also* Athens
oracles, 92, 149; Delphic oracle, 1, 98, 111, 113–14, 159; in Sophocles, 108, 113–14. *See also* divination; prophets (and prophecy)
Orpheus, 49, 193

Pacuvius, 174n43, 176–77
Palamedes: and anti-intellectualism, 49–50, 172–73, 183–86; in contrast to Odysseus, 37, 42–43, 99, 118, 164–65, 183–85; as inventor, 25, 27, 36–50, 53, 55–57, 60, 64, 66, 70, 78, 83, 86, 183
Parmenides, 21, 101–6, 107n47, 108, 112, 121–22, 131, 149, 151, 157
Pericles, 170
Peloponnesian War, 128, 136–37, 158, 198–99
persuasion (*peithō*), 15, 168, 234n18; in Euripides' *Iphigenia in Aulis*, 153; philosophical thought concerning, 107, 118–19, 234n18; in Sophocles' *Philoctetes*, 134, 139–41, 147–49. See also *logos*; rhetoric
philosophy, as discipline, 1–2, 5–8, 14, 162, 222, 223–25, 227–34, 237–38
phusis, 7n, 122, 132n100, 176, 181, 229; in contrast to *nomos*, 32–33, 86, 137, 227, 231–32
Pindar, 118n75, 171n34, 230
Plato (comic playwright), 53
Plato, 3, 17, 223–25, 228, 236–38; *Apology*, 25n7, 159–64, 172n, 184n67, 236n22; *Gorgias*, 62n80, 137, 178n57, 183, 225–37; *Hippias Minor*, 99–100, 133, 138, 166, 179n60; *Phaedo*, 7n, 233n17; *Phaedrus*, 23–27, 31–32, 36–37, 45, 49, 89, 203n123; *Protagoras*, 33, 53, 55–57, 62n80, 68, 75n, 85–86, 88, 172, 178n57, 196n94; *Republic*, 25n6, 91n, 137, 158, 233n17; *Sophist*, 16n, 91–93, 102, 121; *Statesman*, 62n80; *Symposium*, 2, 124n83
Plutarch, 51–52, 95, 136n109
Proclus, 143n, 147n127
Prodicus, 3; *Choice of Heracles*, 17, 133, 166, 167n24, 178n57; on the gods, 49, 87–88, 208–9, 220; on language, 196n94
progress, theory of, 27, 32–35, 48, 56, 68, 72–73, 89–90. See also catalogs
prologues, 8, 21, 92–93, 104, 110–12, 121, 126; Aristophanes' *Women at the Thesmophoria*, 121–27; in Euripides' *Iphigenia in Aulis*, 152–54, 156; in Sophocles' *Electra*, 112–19, 133–36; in Sophocles' *Philoctetes*, 131, 133–39, 141–42, 145, 151

Prometheus: in Aeschylus' *Prometheus Bound*, 25n6, 27, 32, 36–39, 50–64, 66–68, 70, 74, 77–78, 83, 90, 170; in Hesiod, 50–51, 54, 59, 61–62, 90; in Plato's *Protagoras*, 33, 53, 55, 57, 62n80, 68, 88
prophets (and prophecy), 49n58, 63, 92, 98; in Euripides' *Iphigenia in Aulis*, 152–56; in Sophocles' *Philoctetes*, 146–51. See also divination; oracles
prosopopoeia, 17–18, 165–66
Protagoras, 3, 72n, 167n25, 170; antilogy in, 16, 17n, 165, 167n24, 177, 184n67; on the gods, 49, 85, 88, 207; epistemology of, 106, 207. See also Plato: *Protagoras*
prōtos heuretēs. See inventors (*prōtoi heuretai*)
Pythagoras, 25n5, 182

Reinhardt, Karl, 109n53, 133
rhetoric, 5n11, 15–17, 24, 165, 167–69, 205; attitudes toward, 99, 138n115, 140, 146, 168, 177; in Plato's *Gorgias*, 226, 228–32. See also antilogy; *logos*

Sassi, Maria Michela, 14–15, 19n32, 102n29
Schelling, F.W.J., 9
Sextus Empiricus, 106
Sisyphus fragment, 20, 27, 33, 68, 84–89, 220. See also Critias
Socrates, 1, 3–4, 5, 14, 49, 66, 166, 170, 223–24; in Aristophanes' *Clouds*, 162, 167, 174; in Aristophanes' *Frogs*, 201; in Plato's *Apology*, 159–64, 178, 184n67, 222; in Plato's *Gorgias*, 225–37; in Plato's *Hippias Minor*, 100; in Plato's *Phaedrus*, 23–27; in Plato's *Symposium*, 2; in Xenophon, 25n7, 66n86, 133, 162, 164n14, 172, 184n67
Sōkratikoi Logoi, 17, 166, 225n6. See also Plato; Xenophon
Solon, 160, *Elegy to the Muses* (13 West), 29–30, 32, 58, 74–75, 78, 80n111, 81–82
sophists (and sophistic thought), 4–5, 14, 32, 69, 86, 136–37, 162–63, 170, 172, 222; on deception, 94–97; ethics of, 136–37; in Plato's writings, 91–91, 137. See also

Antiphon; *Dissoi Logoi*; Gorgias; Hippias; Prodicus; Protagoras; Thrasymachus

sophia. *See* wisdom (*sophia*)

Sophocles, 1, 3–4, 31, 136–37, 168–69; *Ajax*, 108–9; *Antigone*, 27, 32, 58, 64, 71–84, 86–87; *Electra*, 92, 108, 109n54, 111–20, 131, 133–37, 145, 150, 154–55; fragments of lost plays, 110n56, 133n101, 136, 149n131; *Oedipus at Colonus*, 108, 149n131, 203n112; *Oedipus the King*, 9, 108, 217n149; Palamedes plays (*Palamedes, Nauplius Katapleōn, Nauplius Pyrkaeus*), 41–46, 48, 59n76; *Philoctetes*, 92, 108, 109n54, 115, 131–51, 154–56, 171n34; prologues in, 21, 112, 121, 132; *Trachiniae*, 108–9, 112n61, 149n131

Sparta, 97–98

Stobaeus, 38–39, 50, 183

syncrisis, 17, 99–100, 132–33, 138, 154, 165–67, 179n60. *See also* antilogy; rhetoric

Thersites, 144–45

Thesmophoria, 124–31

Thebes, 173–74

Thrasymachus, 16, 137

Thucydides, 136, 158, 171n35

Titanomachy (Cyclical epic), 61

Vernant, Jean-Pierre, 54, 98

Winnington-Ingram, R. P. 221

wisdom (*sophia*), 1–2, 5, 8, 95–96, 160–64, 169–73, 184–86, 193–96; in Aristophanes' *Frogs*, 186–203; in Euripides' *Antiope*, 172–83; in Euripides' *Bacchae*, 171, 183, 203–22; in Euripides' *Medea*, 171–72; in Euripides' *Palamedes*, 172–73, 183–86; in Plato's *Apology*, 159–64; in Plato's *Gorgias*, 230–31, 235–36; in Xenophanes, 160–61

Wohl, Victoria, 13n19, 57n72, 71

writing, 23–26, 28, 39n39, 40n43, 41n45, 44–48, 51, 55–56

Xeniades, 106

Xenophanes, 26n10, 94n6, 160–61

Xenophon, 17, 137, 162, 166, 171n35; *Apology*, 1n, 25n7, 172n, 172n39, 184n67; *Memorabilia*, 25n7, 66n86, 133, 164n14, 172, 178n57, 184n67

Zeno, 105

Zeus, 80–81, 83, 85, 94n6, 173, 175n45, 208–9, 210n135, 211n, 227; in the Prometheus myth, 37, 50, 57, 61–63, 86, 88

A NOTE ON THE TYPE

This book has been composed in Arno, an Old-style serif typeface in the classic Venetian tradition, designed by Robert Slimbach at Adobe.

GPSR Authorized Representative: Easy Access System Europe - Mustamäe tee
50, 10621 Tallinn, Estonia, gpsr.requests@easproject.com

www.ingramcontent.com/pod-product-compliance
Lightning Source LLC
Chambersburg PA
CBHW021852230426
43671CB00006B/353